STORY AND ART BY

suu Morishita

Story Thus Far

# SHORTCAKE CAKE

NEKOCHIYA HIGH SCHOOL

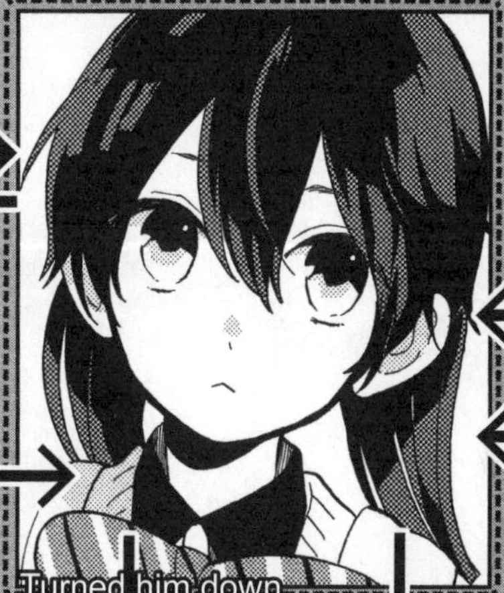
Turned him down.

## TEN

First-year. She moved into the boardinghouse about a month after the new school year started. She has pluck.

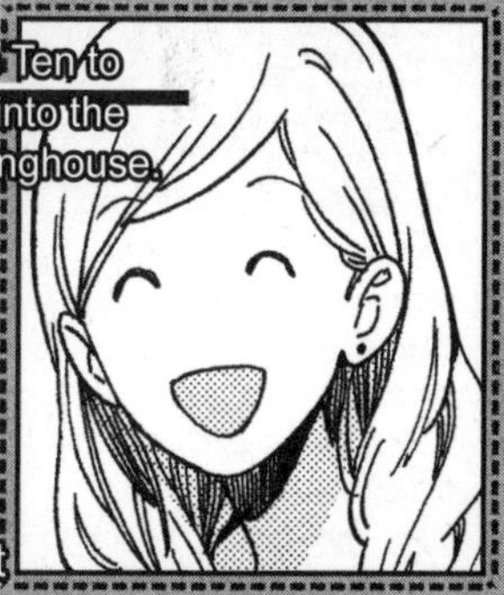
Invites Ten to move into the boardinghouse.
Enjoys talking to him.
"Ten, I want to do what I can for you."

## AGEHA

First-year. She attended the same junior high school as Ten.

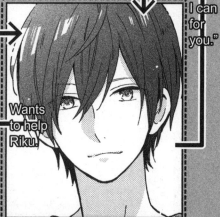

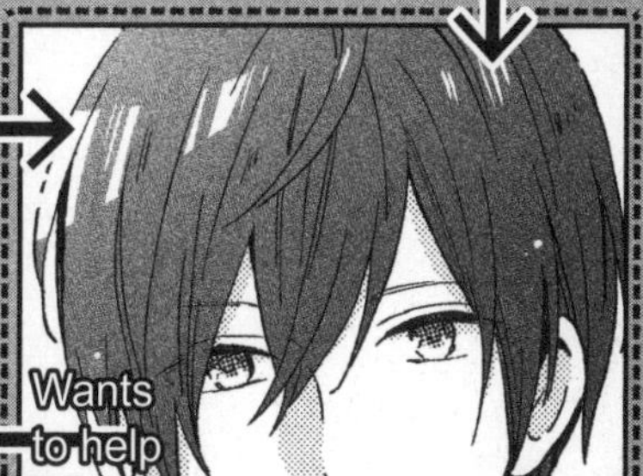
Wants to help Riku.

## CHIAKI

First-year. A gorgeous guy who loves reading books.

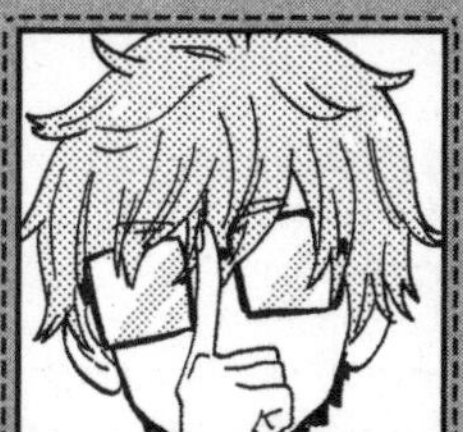

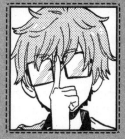

## YUTO

Second-year. He tutors Ten and the other first-years.

## REI

**Age 16. A mysterious boy who is referred to as "Young Master."**

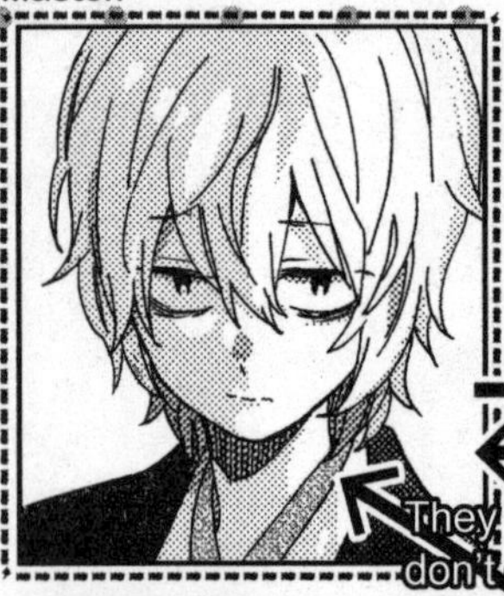

## SHIRAOKA

**Rei's driver. What's his connection to Ran?**

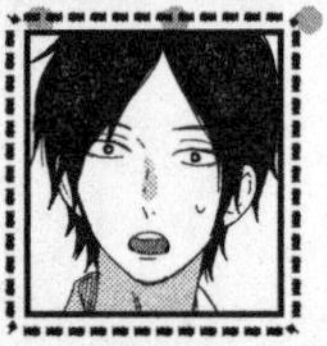

Hoshino Boardinghouse

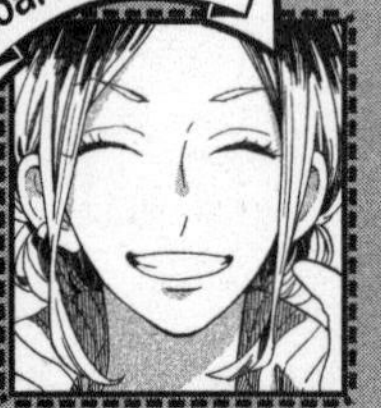

## RAN

**House mom. She likes cooking and cars.**

"Be my girlfriend."

She thinks he's weird.

They don't get along.

NEKOCHIYA SHOGYO HIGH SCHOOL

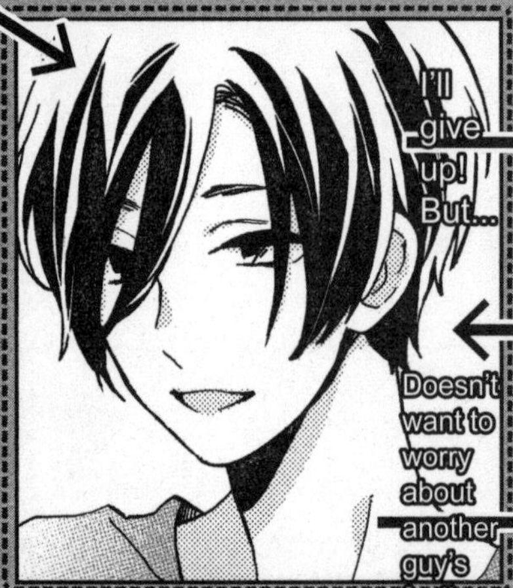

I'll give up! But...

Doesn't want to worry about another guy's feelings.

## RIKU

**First-year. Lives in the boardinghouse though he grew up nearby. Very friendly with girls.**

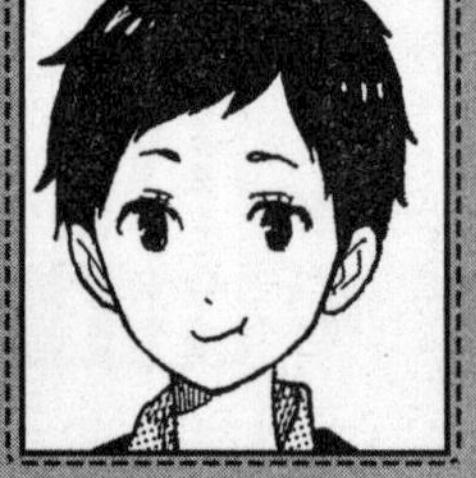

## AOI

**Third-year. She's the oldest in the boarding-house. Likes talking about relationships.**

### Story Thus Far

Ten is a first-year in high school who lives in a boardinghouse with boys. When the house-mates head into town, they encounter Rei, who suddenly refers to Ten as "ugly." Riku stands up for her and the two boys end up arguing, seeming to know each other. On the bus ride home, Riku admits to Ten that he likes her, but Ten can't imagine going out with him and turns him down.

Rei intercepts Ten on her way home from school and says he wants her to be his girlfriend. Ten refuses and returns home to find the boardinghouse filled with flowers sent by Rei. Riku discovers that Rei is trying to get at him through Ten and storms off to settle things, but Ten and Chiaki hold him back.

When the persistent Rei shows up at the boardinghouse, Chiaki tells him, "Ten is mine." Ten and Chiaki pretend they're dating, leaving Riku in an uncomfort-able position...

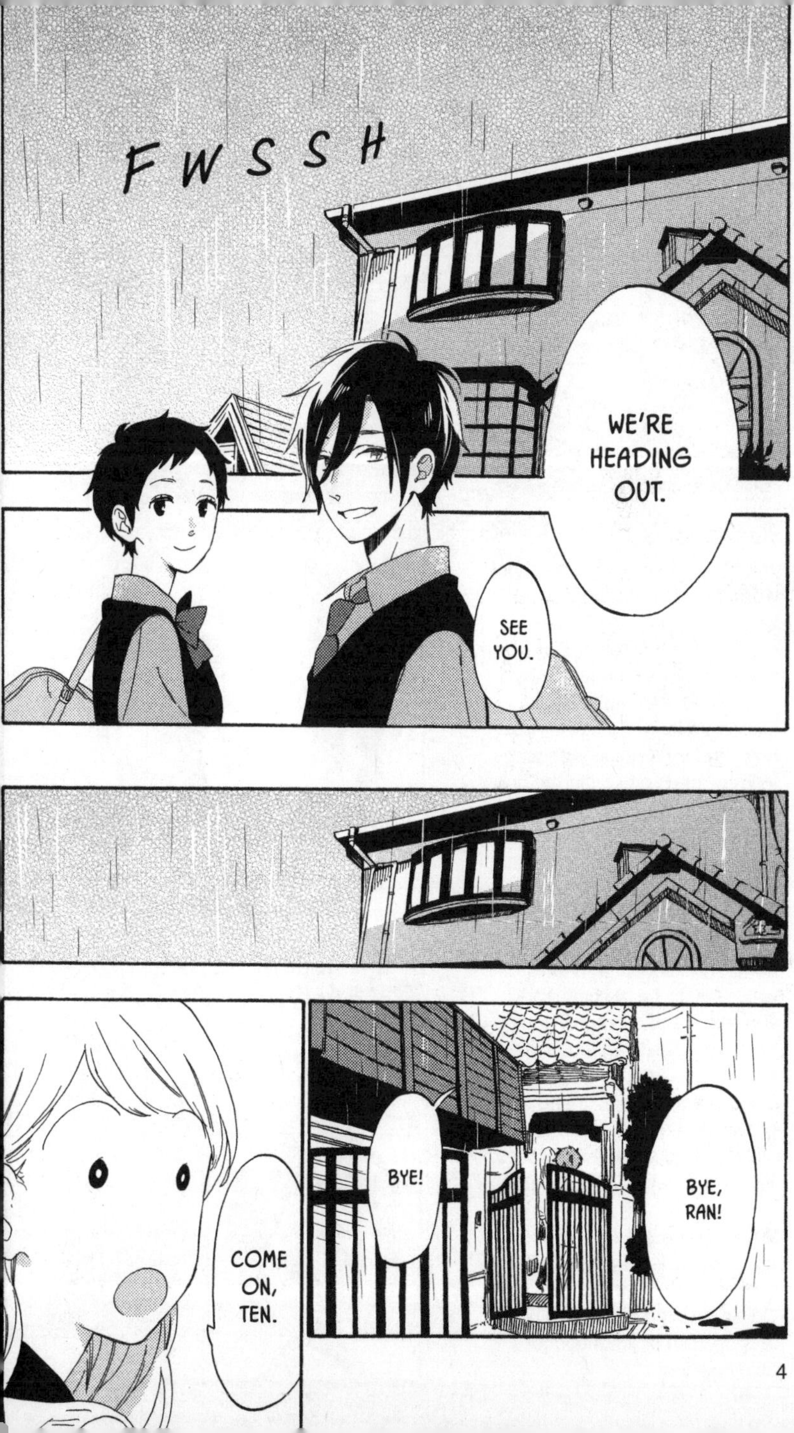
FWSSH
WE'RE HEADING OUT.
SEE YOU.
BYE, RAN!
BYE!
COME ON, TEN.

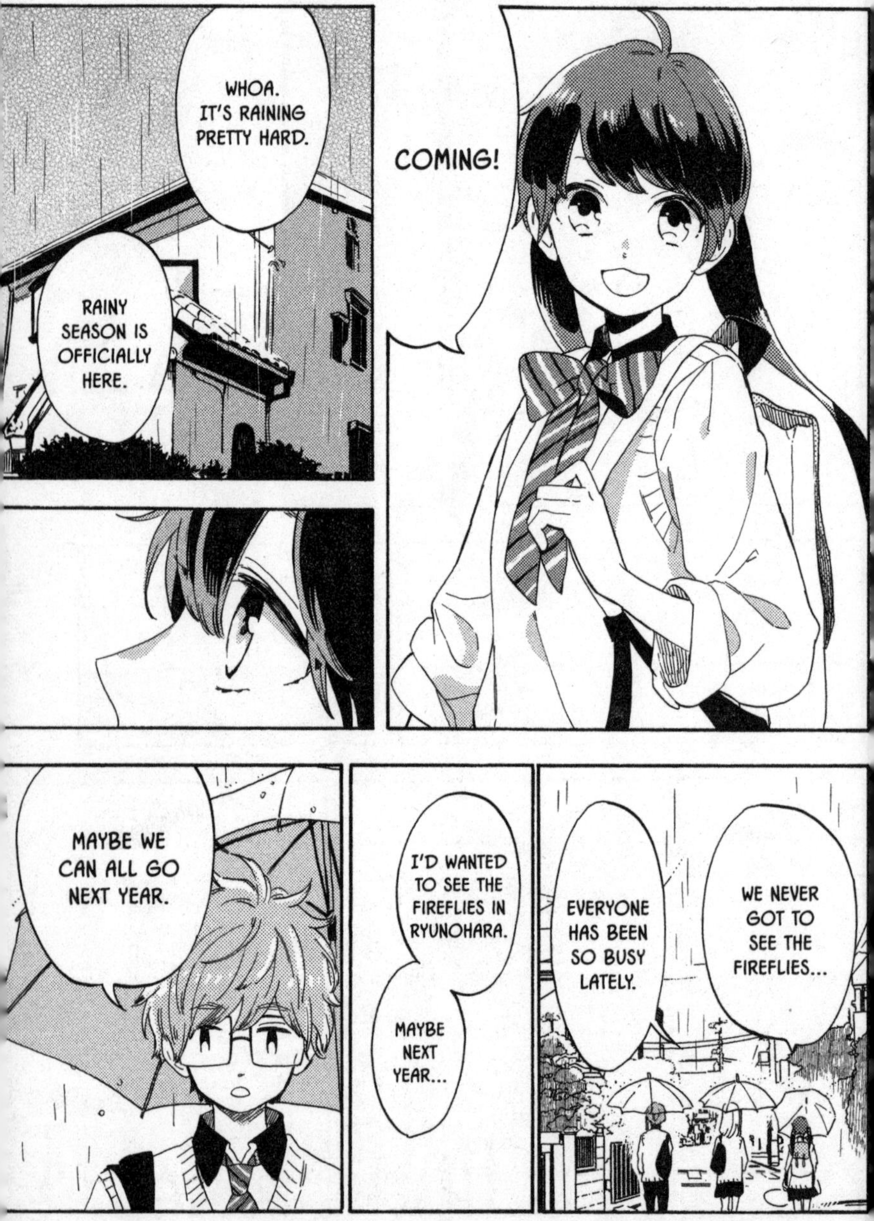
COMING!
WHOA. IT'S RAINING PRETTY HARD.
RAINY SEASON IS OFFICIALLY HERE.
WE NEVER GOT TO SEE THE FIREFLIES...
EVERYONE HAS BEEN SO BUSY LATELY.
I'D WANTED TO SEE THE FIREFLIES IN RYUNOHARA.
MAYBE NEXT YEAR...
MAYBE WE CAN ALL GO NEXT YEAR.

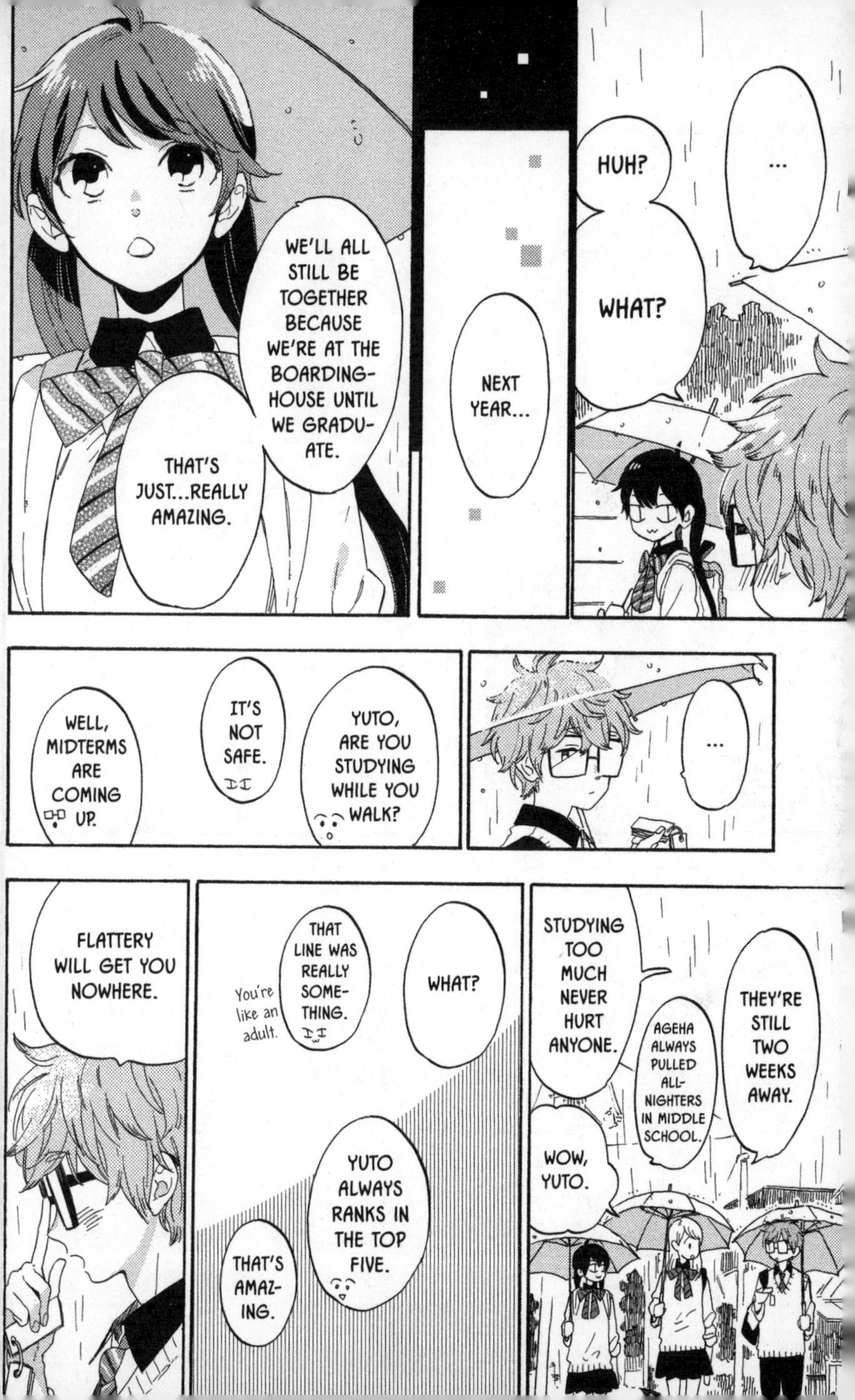
...
HUH?
WHAT?
NEXT YEAR...
WE'LL ALL STILL BE TOGETHER BECAUSE WE'RE AT THE BOARDING-HOUSE UNTIL WE GRADU-ATE.
THAT'S JUST...REALLY AMAZING.
...
YUTO, ARE YOU STUDYING WHILE YOU WALK?
IT'S NOT SAFE.
WELL, MIDTERMS ARE COMING UP.
THEY'RE STILL TWO WEEKS AWAY.
STUDYING TOO MUCH NEVER HURT ANYONE.
AGEHA ALWAYS PULLED ALL-NIGHTERS IN MIDDLE SCHOOL.
WOW, YUTO.
WHAT?
THAT LINE WAS REALLY SOME-THING.
You're like an adult.
YUTO ALWAYS RANKS IN THE TOP FIVE.
THAT'S AMAZ-ING.
FLATTERY WILL GET YOU NOWHERE.

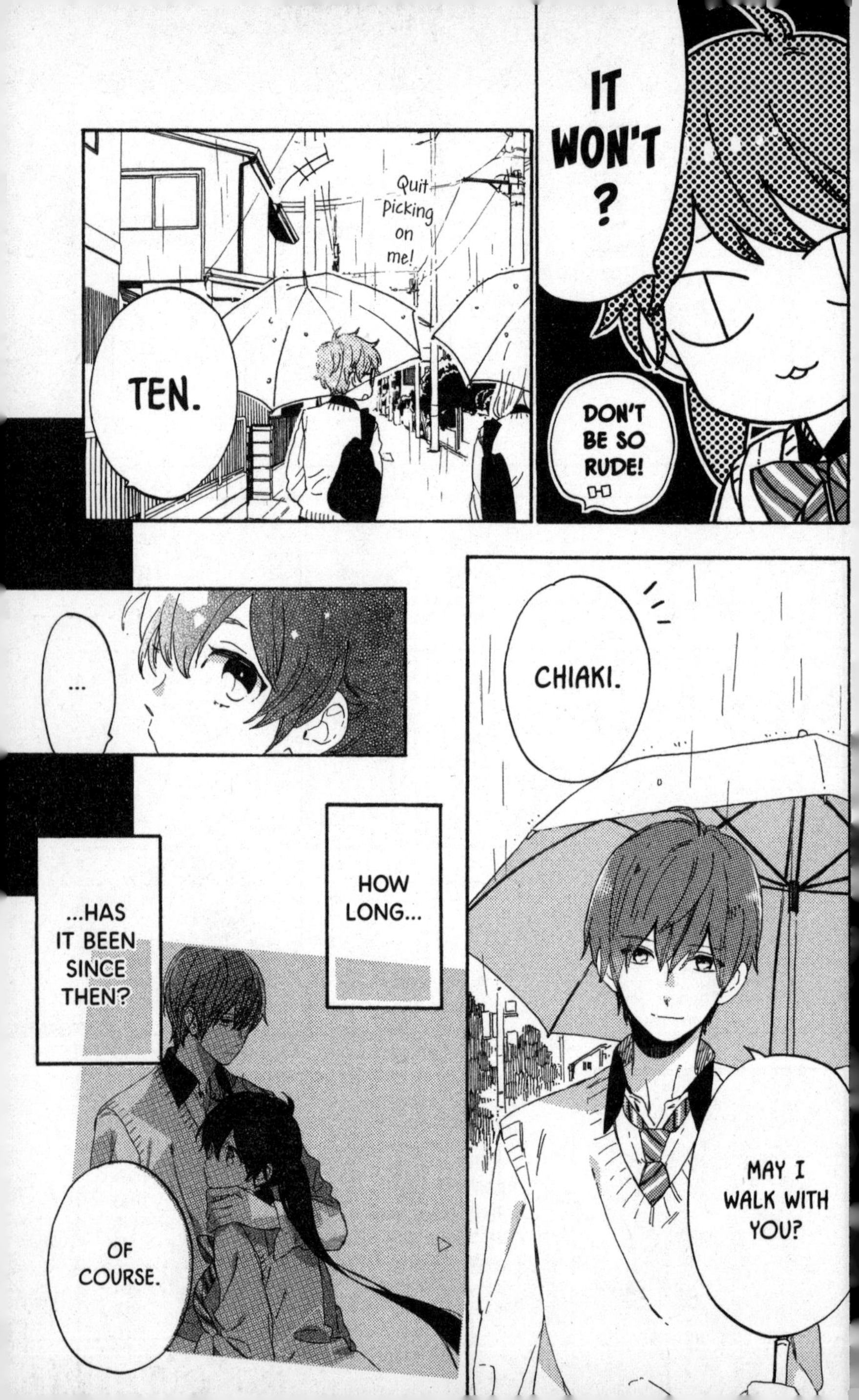
IT WON'T ?
DON'T BE SO RUDE!
Quit picking on me!
TEN.
CHIAKI.
MAY I WALK WITH YOU?
...
HOW LONG...
...HAS IT BEEN SINCE THEN?
OF COURSE.

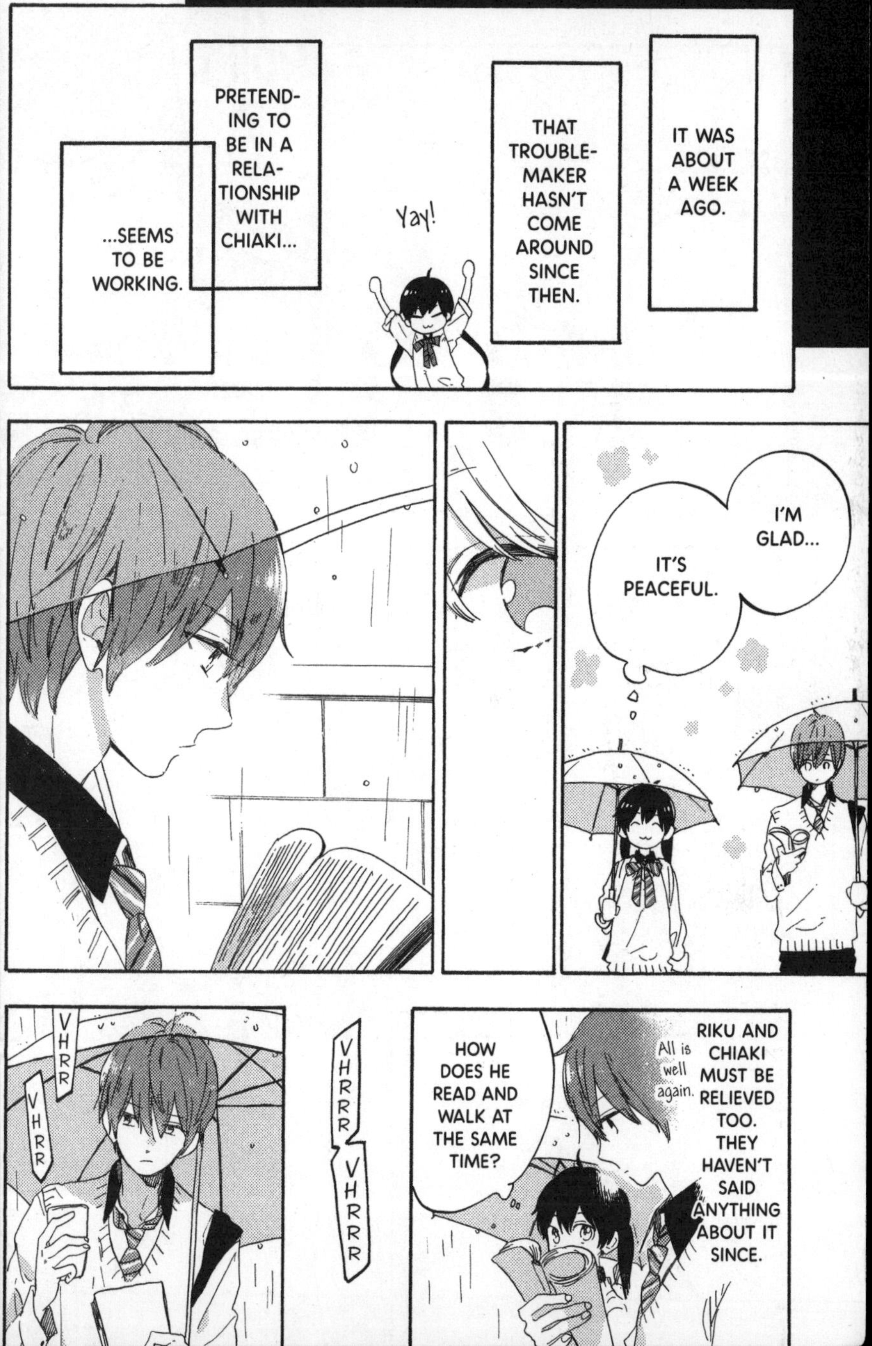
IT WAS ABOUT A WEEK AGO.
THAT TROUBLE-MAKER HASN'T COME AROUND SINCE THEN.
Yay!
PRETEND-ING TO BE IN A RELA-TIONSHIP WITH CHIAKI...
...SEEMS TO BE WORKING.
I'M GLAD... IT'S PEACEFUL.
RIKU AND CHIAKI MUST BE RELIEVED TOO. THEY HAVEN'T SAID ANYTHING ABOUT IT SINCE.
All is well again.
HOW DOES HE READ AND WALK AT THE SAME TIME?
VHRRR VHRRR
VHRR
VHRR

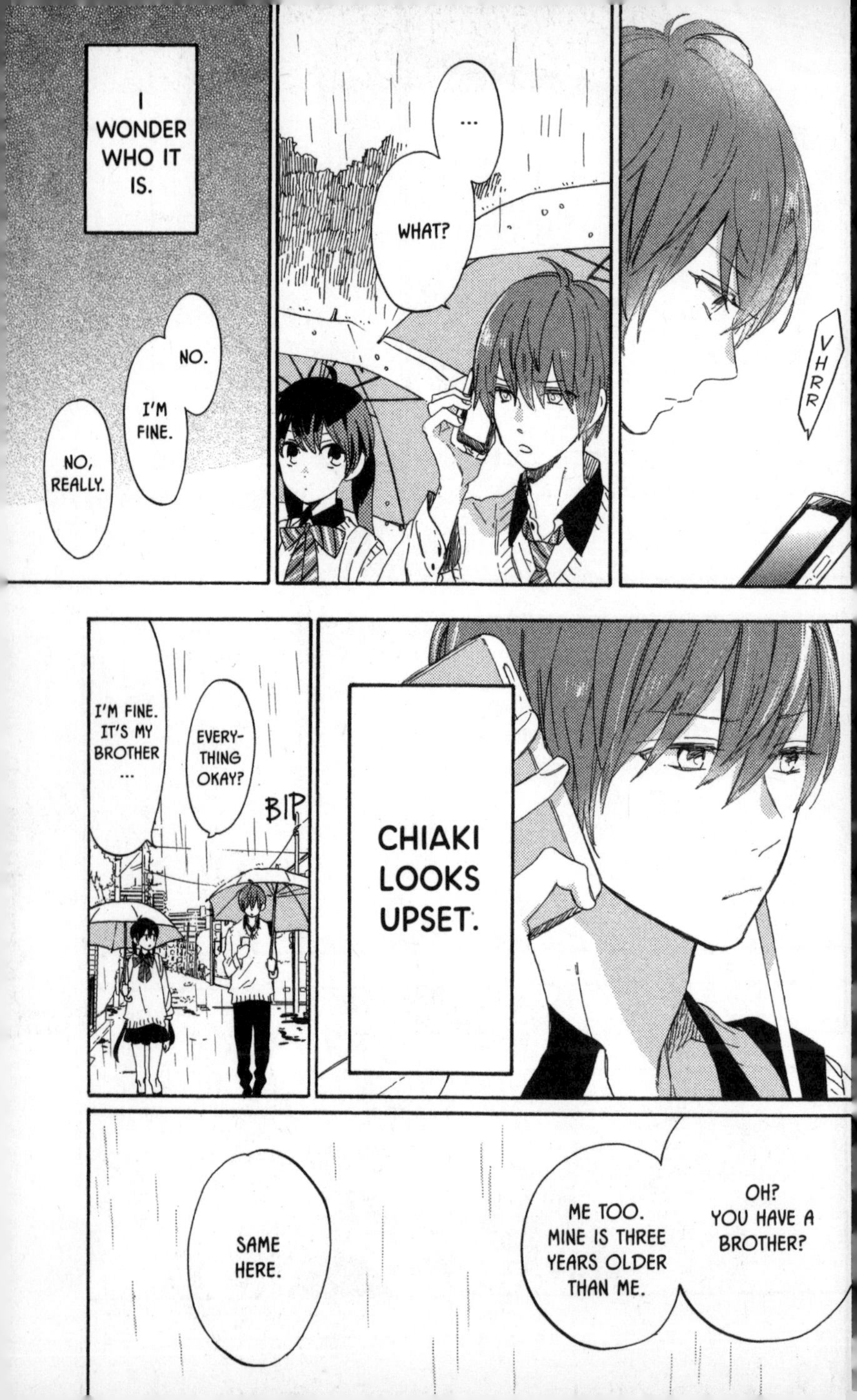
VHRR
...
WHAT?
I WONDER WHO IT IS.
NO.
I'M FINE.
NO, REALLY.
CHIAKI LOOKS UPSET.
EVERY-THING OKAY?
BIP
I'M FINE. IT'S MY BROTHER ...
OH? YOU HAVE A BROTHER?
ME TOO. MINE IS THREE YEARS OLDER THAN ME.
SAME HERE.

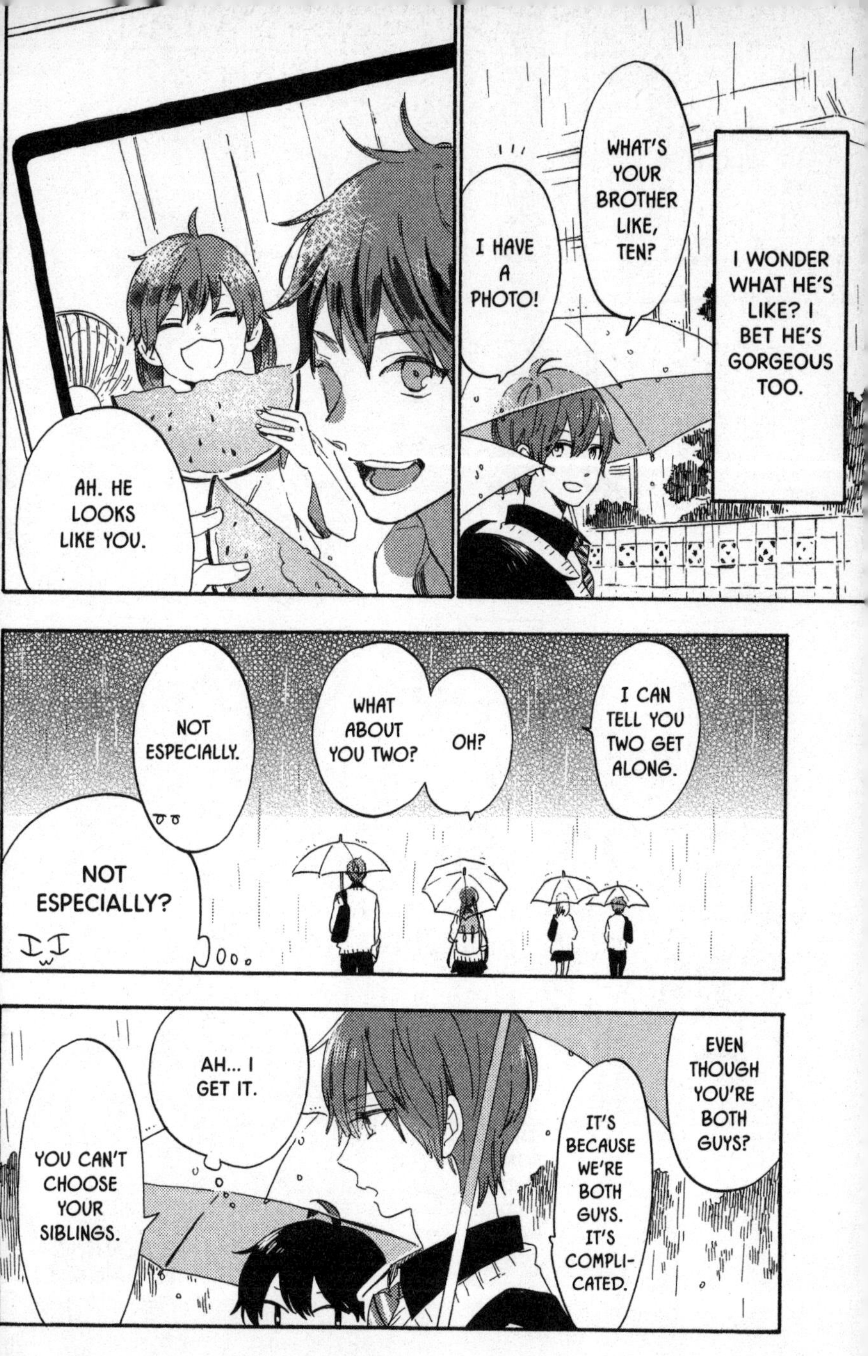
I WONDER WHAT HE'S LIKE? I BET HE'S GORGEOUS TOO.
WHAT'S YOUR BROTHER LIKE, TEN?
I HAVE A PHOTO!
AH. HE LOOKS LIKE YOU.
I CAN TELL YOU TWO GET ALONG.
OH?
WHAT ABOUT YOU TWO?
NOT ESPECIALLY.
NOT ESPECIALLY?
EVEN THOUGH YOU'RE BOTH GUYS?
IT'S BECAUSE WE'RE BOTH GUYS. IT'S COMPLICATED.
AH... I GET IT.
YOU CAN'T CHOOSE YOUR SIBLINGS.

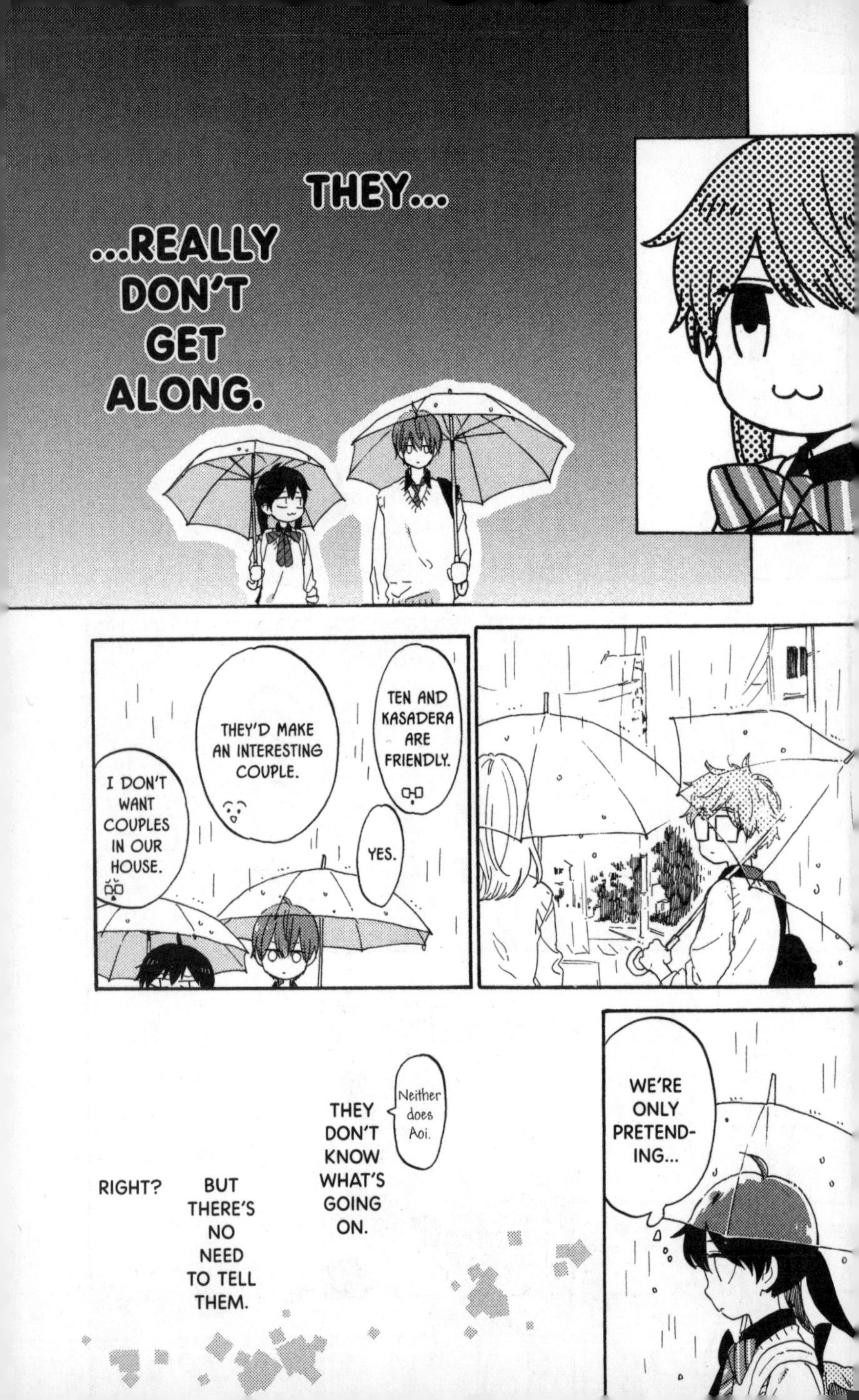
THEY...
...REALLY DON'T GET ALONG.
TEN AND KASADERA ARE FRIENDLY.
THEY'D MAKE AN INTERESTING COUPLE.
YES.
I DON'T WANT COUPLES IN OUR HOUSE.
WE'RE ONLY PRETEND-ING...
THEY DON'T KNOW WHAT'S GOING ON.
Neither does Aoi.
BUT THERE'S NO NEED TO TELL THEM.
RIGHT?

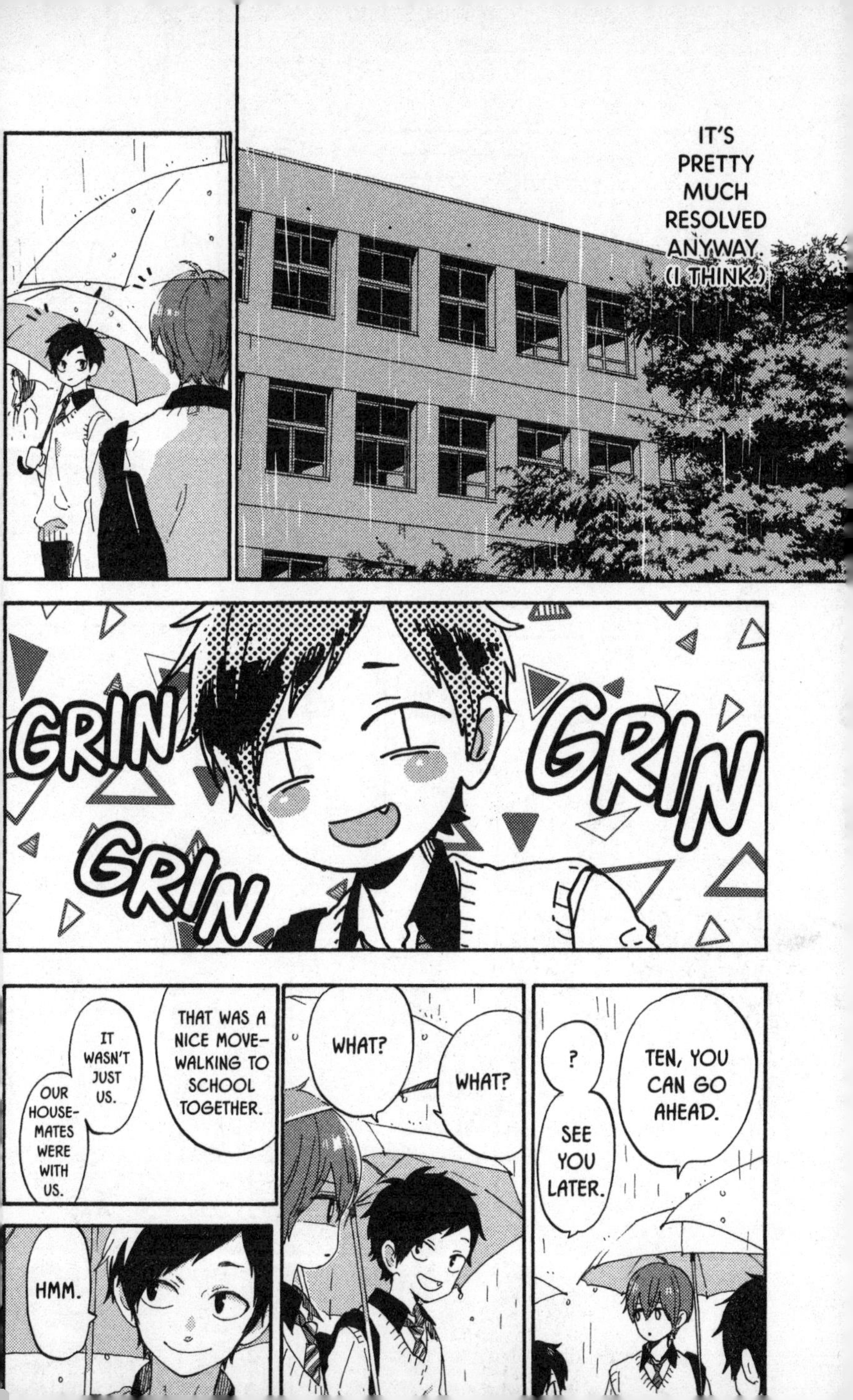
IT'S PRETTY MUCH RESOLVED ANYWAY. (I THINK.)
GRIN
GRIN
GRIN
TEN, YOU CAN GO AHEAD.
?
SEE YOU LATER.
WHAT?
WHAT?
THAT WAS A NICE MOVE—WALKING TO SCHOOL TOGETHER.
IT WASN'T JUST US.
OUR HOUSEMATES WERE WITH US.
HMM.

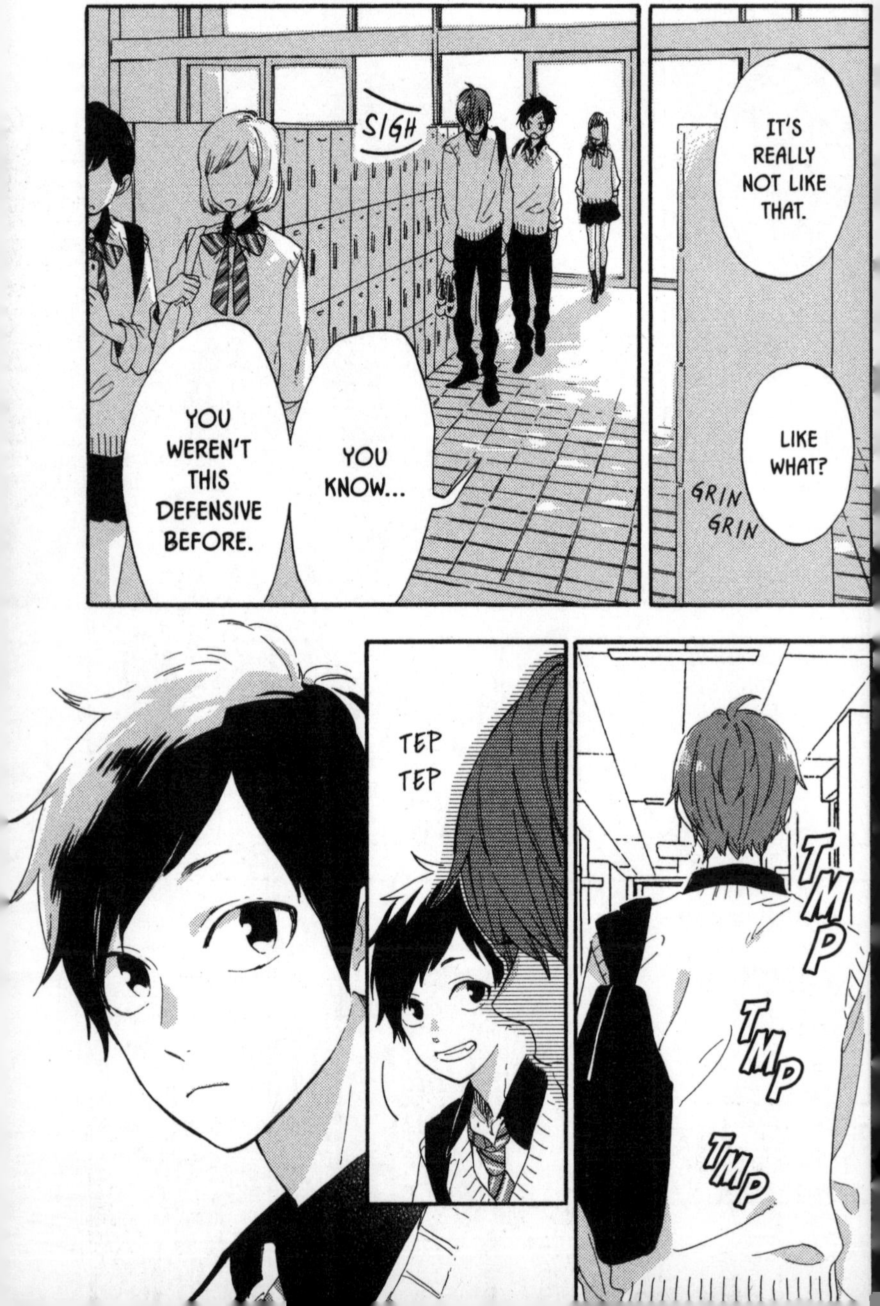
IT'S REALLY NOT LIKE THAT.
LIKE WHAT?
GRIN GRIN
SIGH
YOU KNOW...
YOU WEREN'T THIS DEFENSIVE BEFORE.
TMP
TMP
TMP
TEP TEP

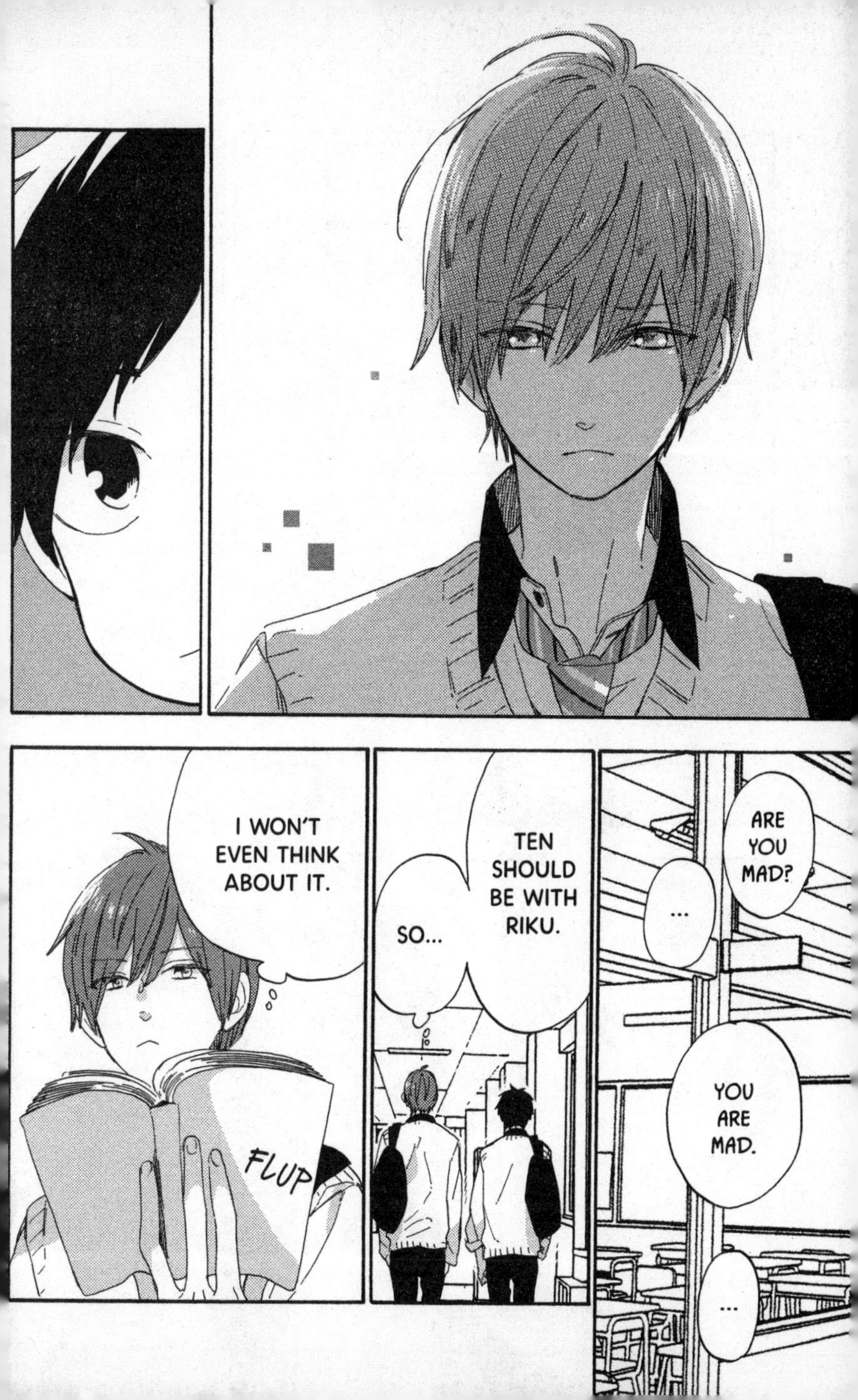
ARE YOU MAD?
...
YOU ARE MAD.
...
TEN SHOULD BE WITH RIKU.
SO...
I WON'T EVEN THINK ABOUT IT.
FLUP

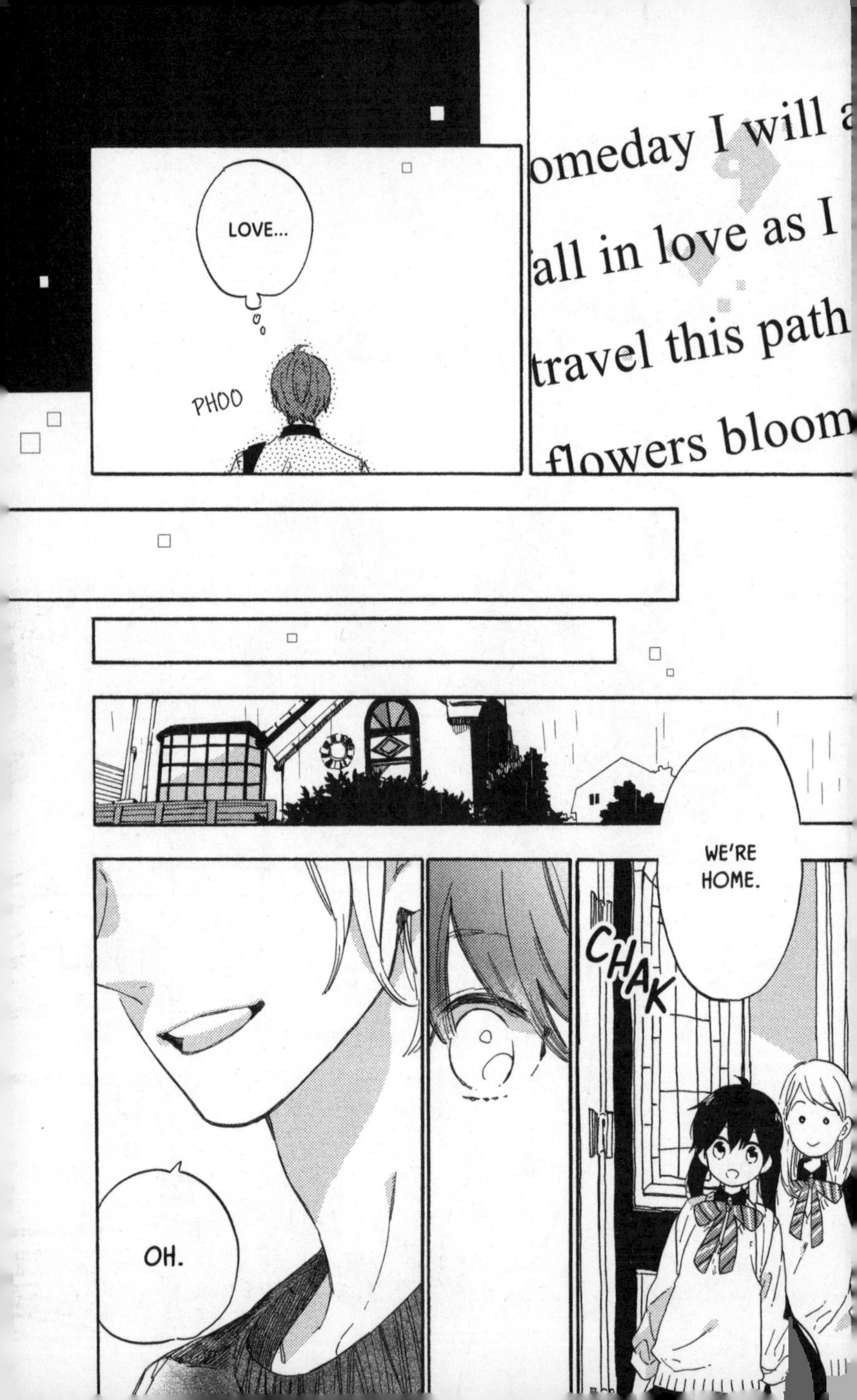

omeday I will a
all in love as I
travel this path
flowers bloom
LOVE...
PHOO
WE'RE HOME.
CHAK
OH.

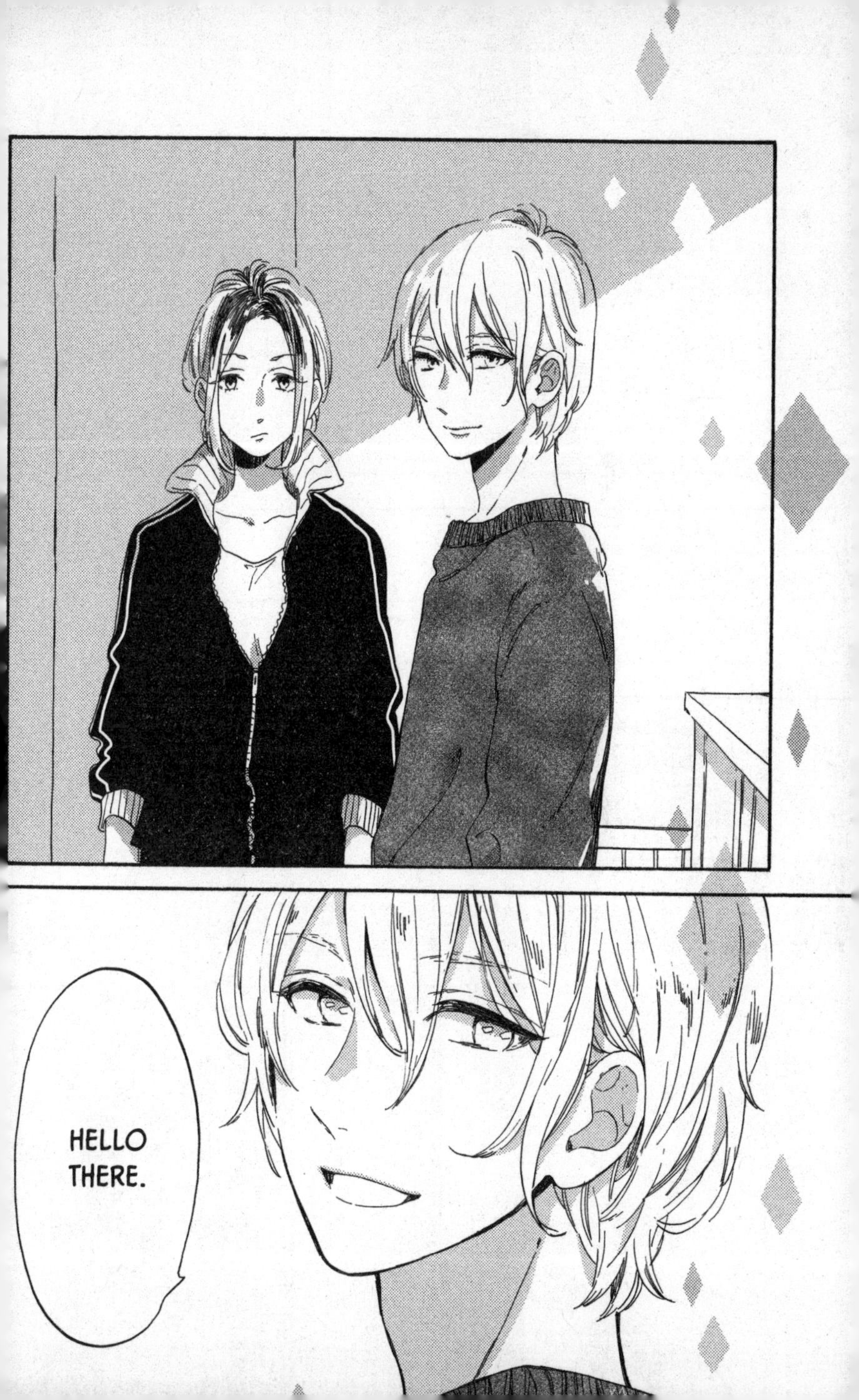
HELLO THERE.

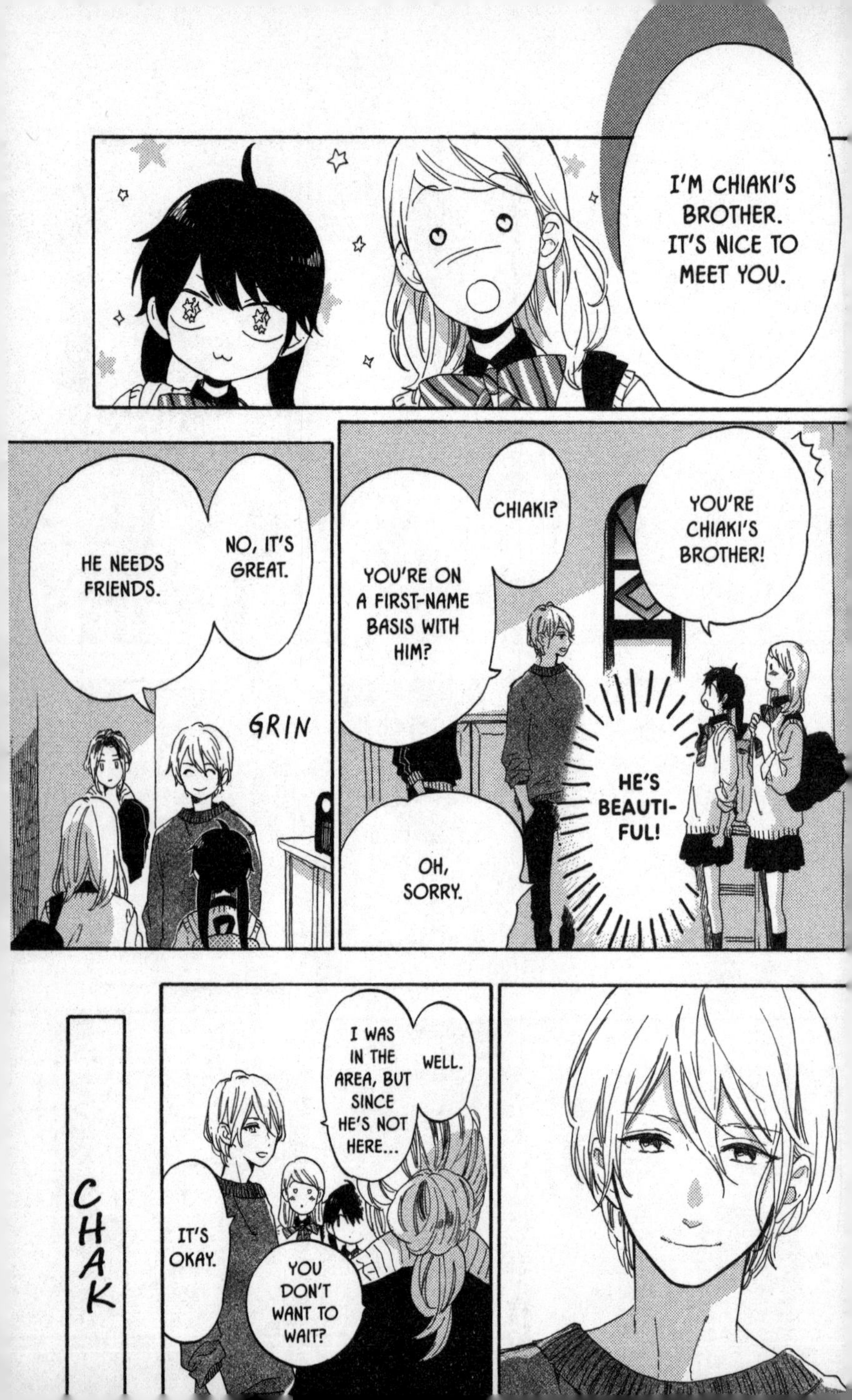
I'M CHIAKI'S BROTHER. IT'S NICE TO MEET YOU.
YOU'RE CHIAKI'S BROTHER!
HE'S BEAUTIFUL!
CHIAKI?
YOU'RE ON A FIRST-NAME BASIS WITH HIM?
OH, SORRY.
NO, IT'S GREAT.
HE NEEDS FRIENDS.
GRIN
WELL.
I WAS IN THE AREA, BUT SINCE HE'S NOT HERE...
YOU DON'T WANT TO WAIT?
IT'S OKAY.
CHAK

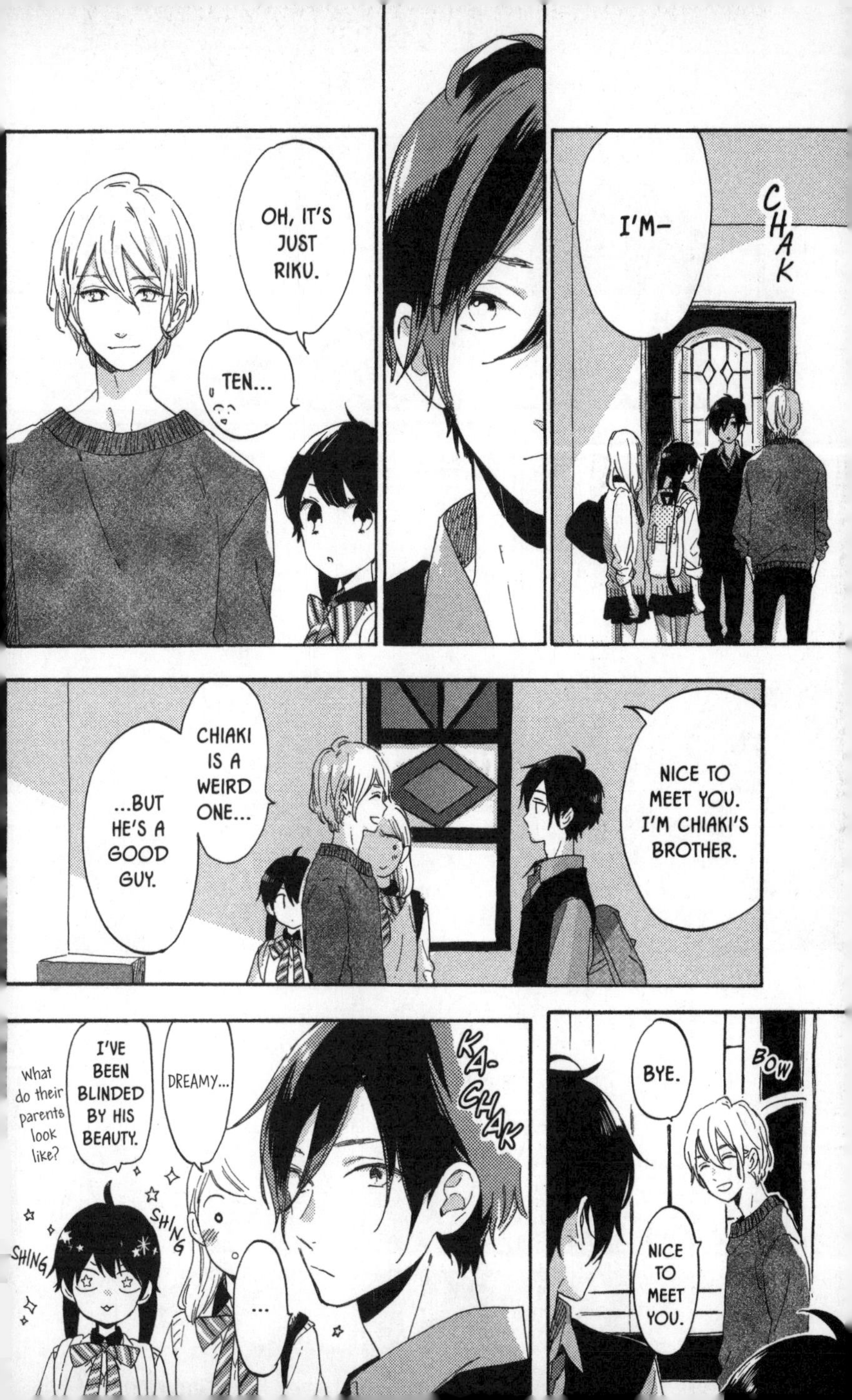
I'M—
CHAK
OH, IT'S JUST RIKU.
TEN...
NICE TO MEET YOU. I'M CHIAKI'S BROTHER.
CHIAKI IS A WEIRD ONE...
...BUT HE'S A GOOD GUY.
BYE.
BOW
NICE TO MEET YOU.
KA-CHAK
...
DREAMY...
I'VE BEEN BLINDED BY HIS BEAUTY.
What do their parents look like?
SHING
SHING

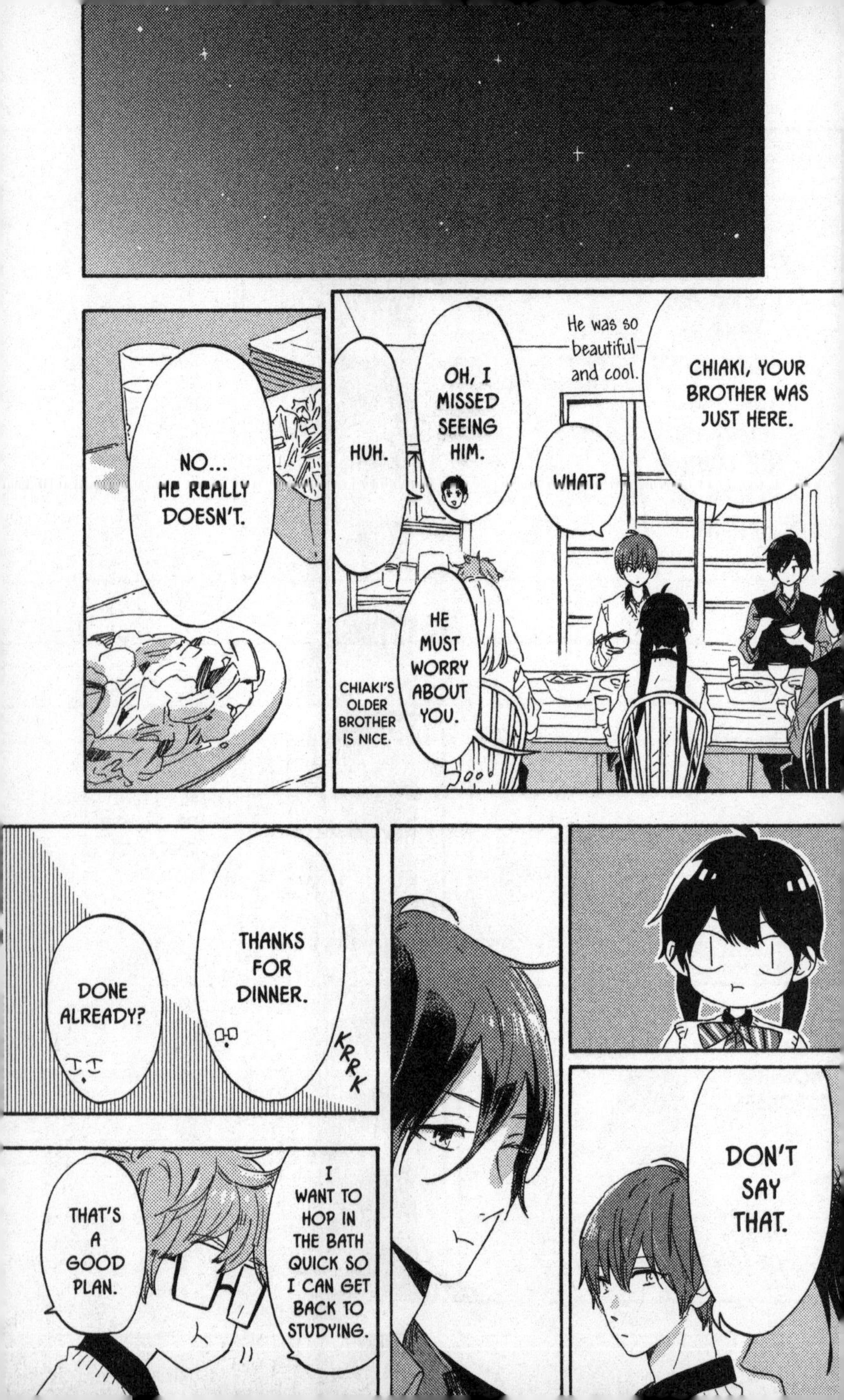
CHIAKI, YOUR BROTHER WAS JUST HERE.
He was so beautiful and cool.
WHAT?
OH, I MISSED SEEING HIM.
HUH.
HE MUST WORRY ABOUT YOU.
CHIAKI'S OLDER BROTHER IS NICE.
NO... HE REALLY DOESN'T.
DON'T SAY THAT.
THANKS FOR DINNER.
KRRK
DONE ALREADY?
I WANT TO HOP IN THE BATH QUICK SO I CAN GET BACK TO STUDYING.
THAT'S A GOOD PLAN.

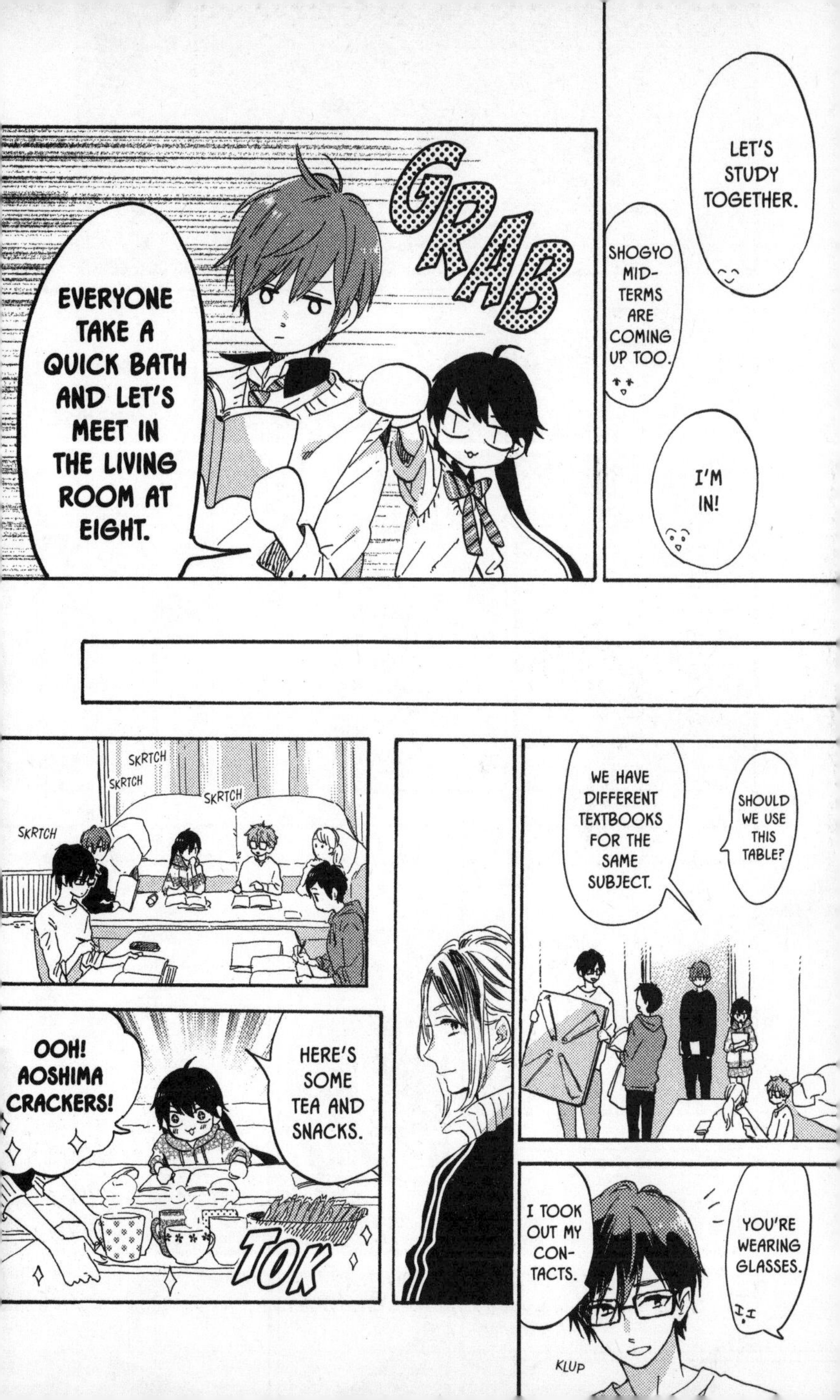
LET'S STUDY TOGETHER.
SHOGYO MID-TERMS ARE COMING UP TOO.
I'M IN!
GRAB
EVERYONE TAKE A QUICK BATH AND LET'S MEET IN THE LIVING ROOM AT EIGHT.
SHOULD WE USE THIS TABLE?
WE HAVE DIFFERENT TEXTBOOKS FOR THE SAME SUBJECT.
YOU'RE WEARING GLASSES.
I TOOK OUT MY CON-TACTS.
KLUP
SKRTCH
SKRTCH
SKRTCH
SKRTCH
HERE'S SOME TEA AND SNACKS.
OOH! AOSHIMA CRACKERS!
TOK

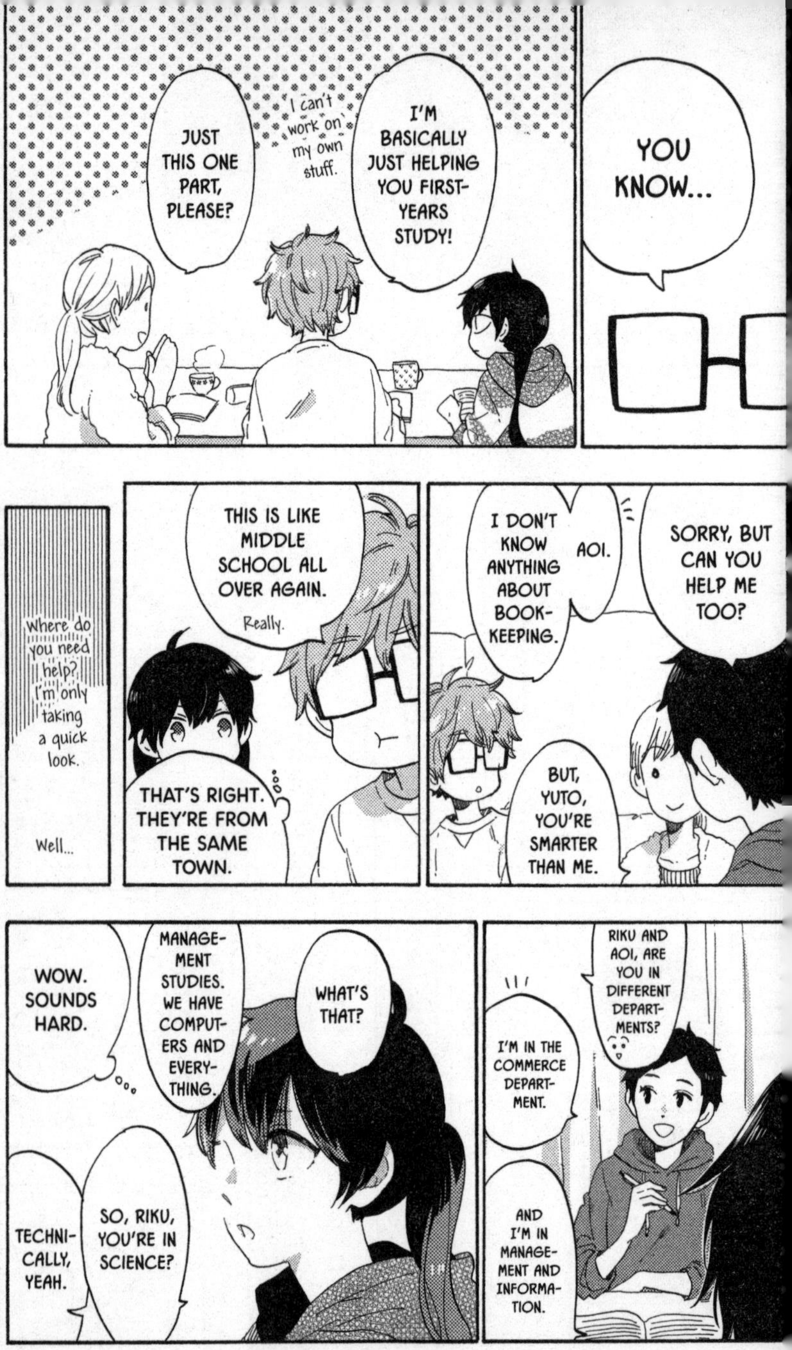
YOU KNOW...
I'M BASICALLY JUST HELPING YOU FIRST-YEARS STUDY!
I can't work on my own stuff.
JUST THIS ONE PART, PLEASE?
SORRY, BUT CAN YOU HELP ME TOO?
AOI.
I DON'T KNOW ANYTHING ABOUT BOOKKEEPING.
BUT, YUTO, YOU'RE SMARTER THAN ME.
THIS IS LIKE MIDDLE SCHOOL ALL OVER AGAIN.
Really.
THAT'S RIGHT. THEY'RE FROM THE SAME TOWN.
Where do you need help? I'm only taking a quick look.
Well...
RIKU AND AOI, ARE YOU IN DIFFERENT DEPARTMENTS?
I'M IN THE COMMERCE DEPARTMENT.
AND I'M IN MANAGEMENT AND INFORMATION.
WHAT'S THAT?
MANAGEMENT STUDIES. WE HAVE COMPUTERS AND EVERYTHING.
WOW. SOUNDS HARD.
SO, RIKU, YOU'RE IN SCIENCE?
TECHNICALLY, YEAH.

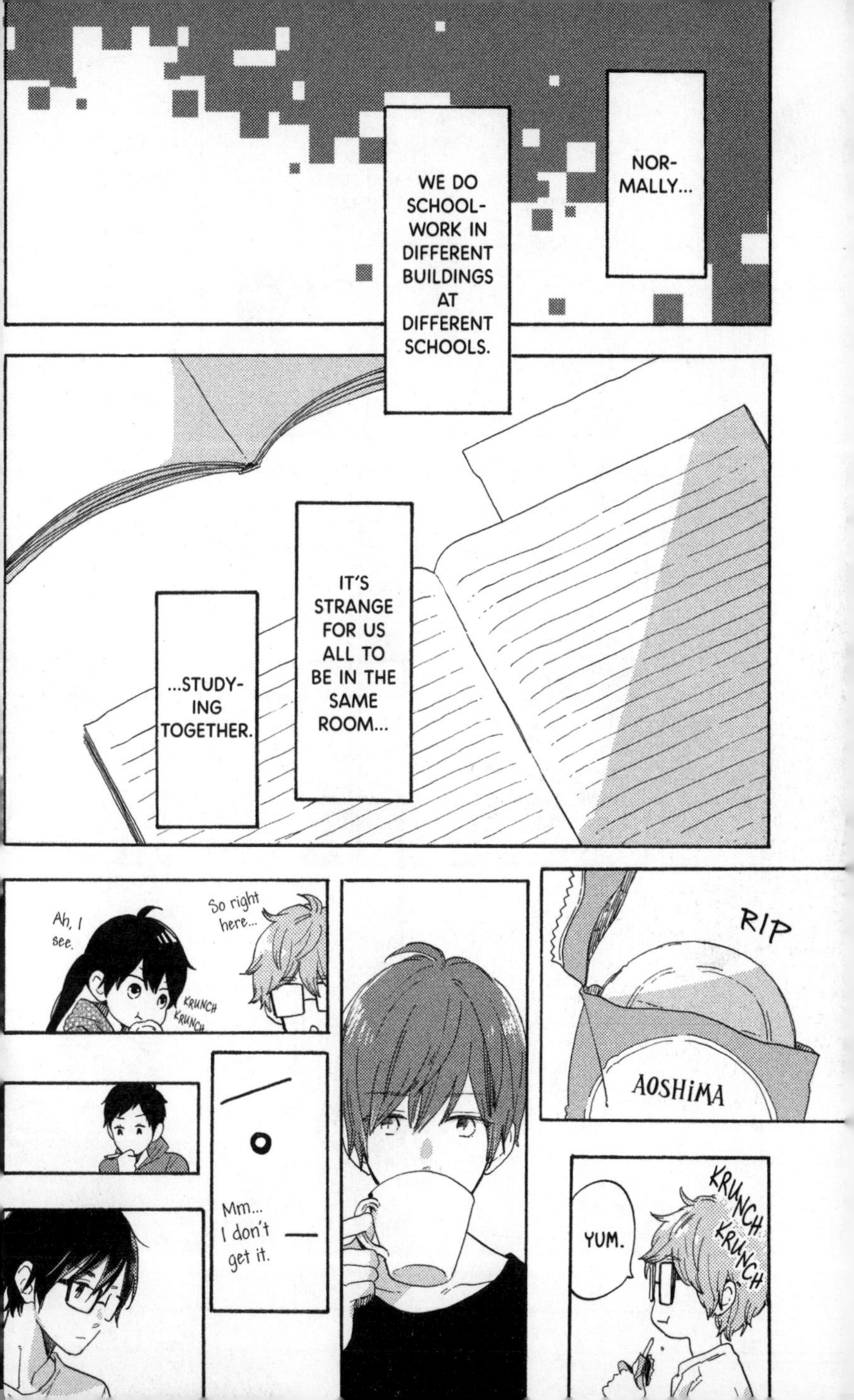
NOR-MALLY...
WE DO SCHOOL-WORK IN DIFFERENT BUILDINGS AT DIFFERENT SCHOOLS.
IT'S STRANGE FOR US ALL TO BE IN THE SAME ROOM...
...STUDYING TOGETHER.
RIP
AOSHIMA
KRUNCH KRUNCH
YUM.
So right here...
KRUNCH KRUNCH
Ah, I see.
Mm... I don't get it.

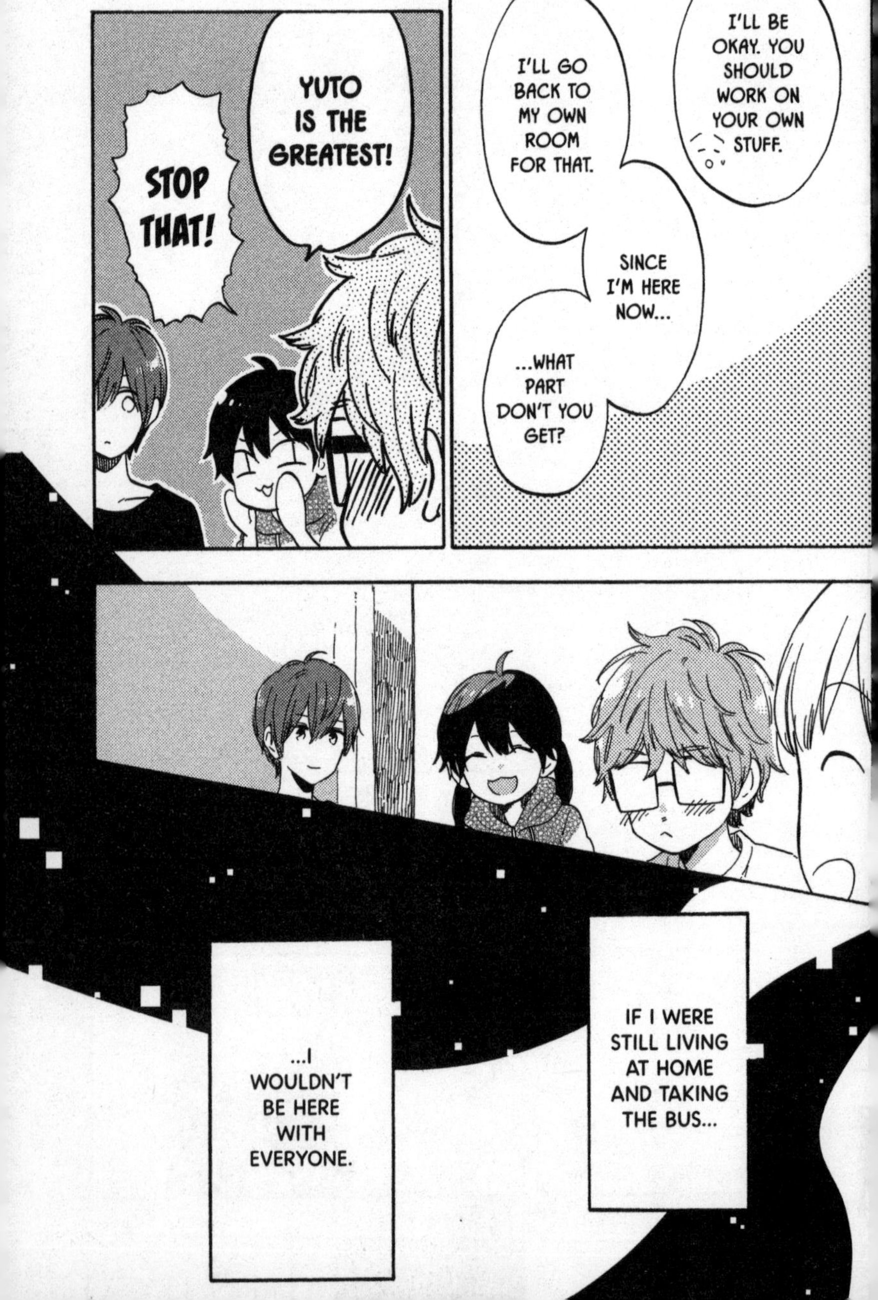
I'LL BE OKAY. YOU SHOULD WORK ON YOUR OWN STUFF.
I'LL GO BACK TO MY OWN ROOM FOR THAT.
SINCE I'M HERE NOW...
...WHAT PART DON'T YOU GET?
YUTO IS THE GREATEST!
STOP THAT!
IF I WERE STILL LIVING AT HOME AND TAKING THE BUS...
...I WOULDN'T BE HERE WITH EVERYONE.

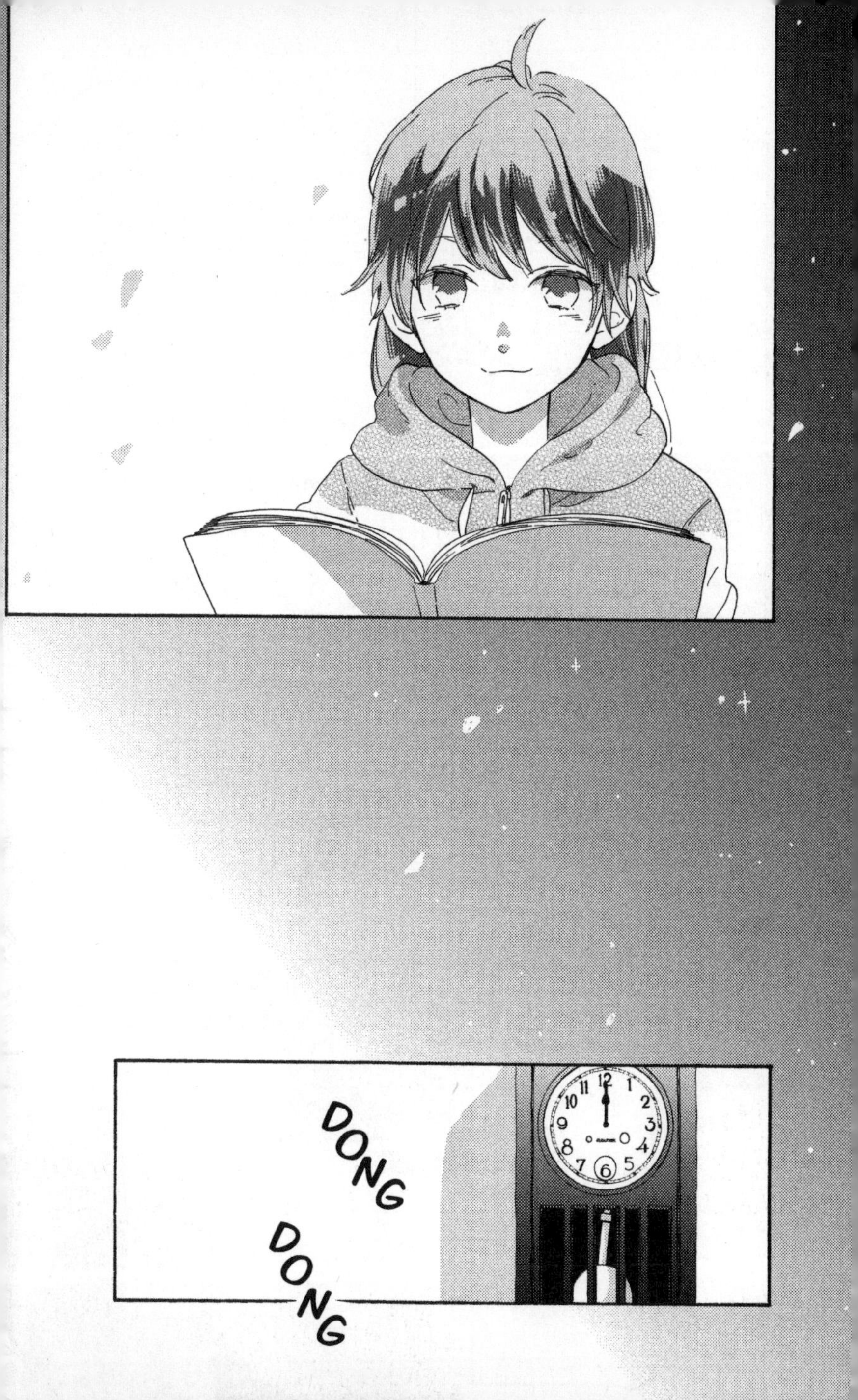
DONG
DONG

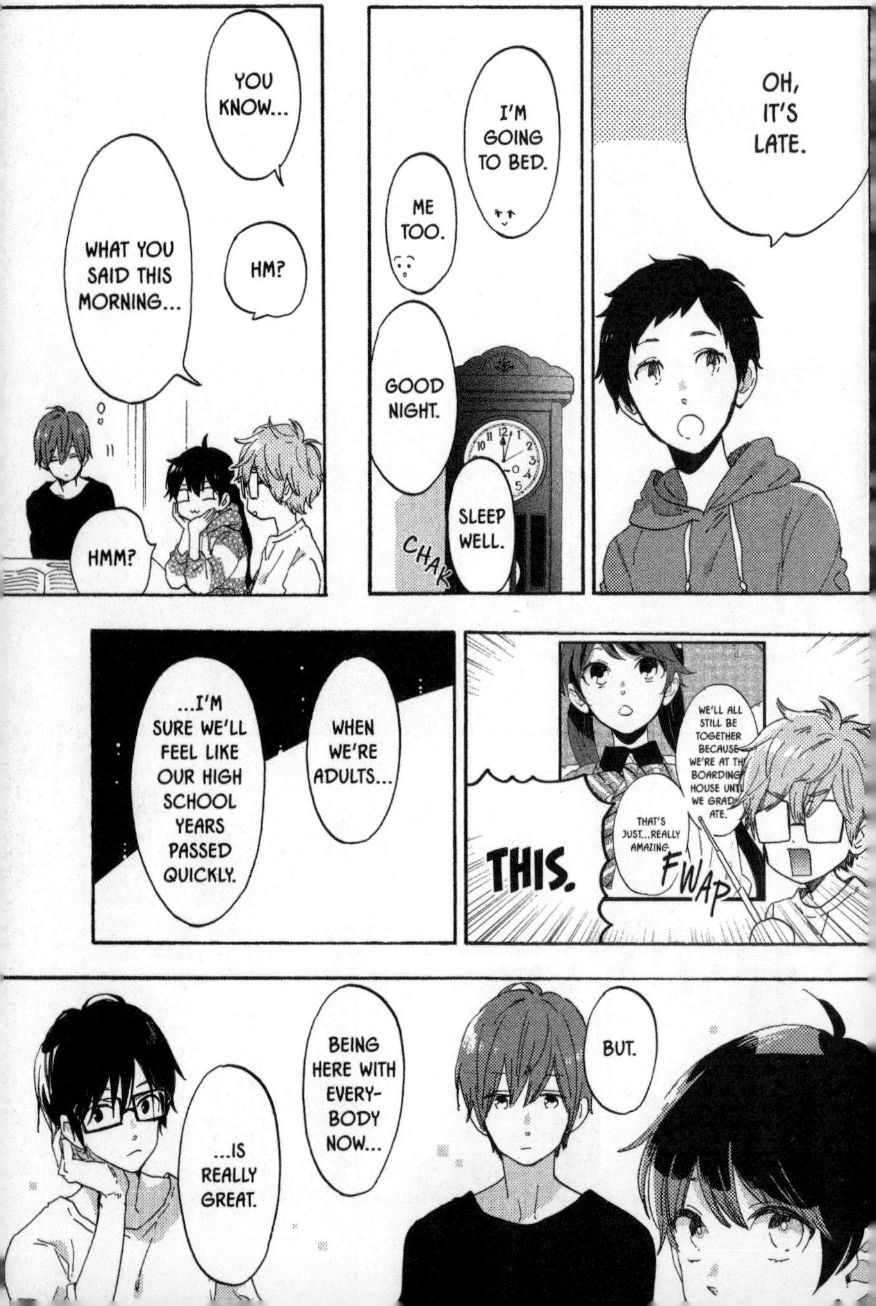
OH, IT'S LATE.
I'M GOING TO BED.
ME TOO.
GOOD NIGHT.
SLEEP WELL.
CHAK
YOU KNOW...
HM?
WHAT YOU SAID THIS MORNING...
HMM?
WE'LL ALL STILL BE TOGETHER BECAUSE WE'RE AT TH BOARDING HOUSE UNTI WE GRAD ATE.
THAT'S JUST...REALLY AMAZING
FWAP
THIS.
WHEN WE'RE ADULTS...
...I'M SURE WE'LL FEEL LIKE OUR HIGH SCHOOL YEARS PASSED QUICKLY.
BUT.
BEING HERE WITH EVERY-BODY NOW...
...IS REALLY GREAT.

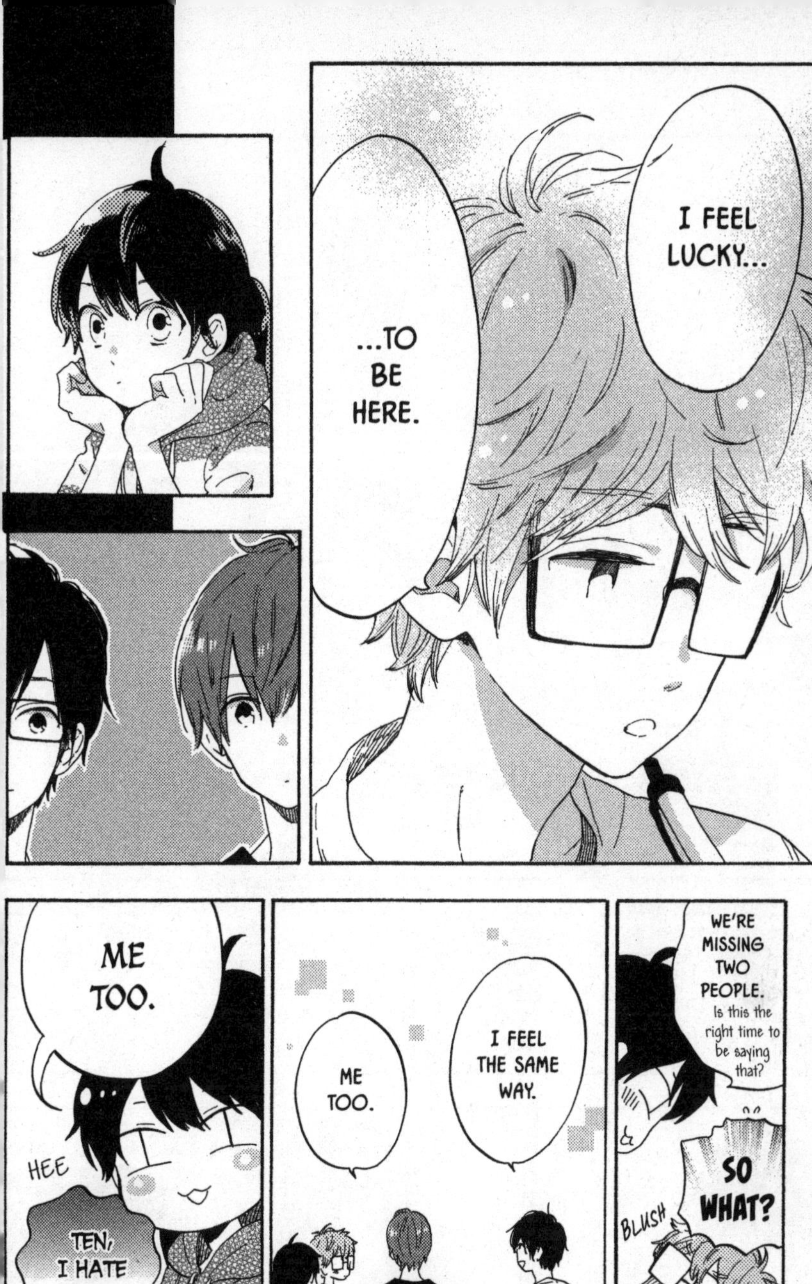
I FEEL LUCKY...
...TO BE HERE.
WE'RE MISSING TWO PEOPLE.
Is this the right time to be saying that?
SO WHAT?
BLUSH
I FEEL THE SAME WAY.
ME TOO.
ME TOO.
HEE
TEN, I HATE YOU...

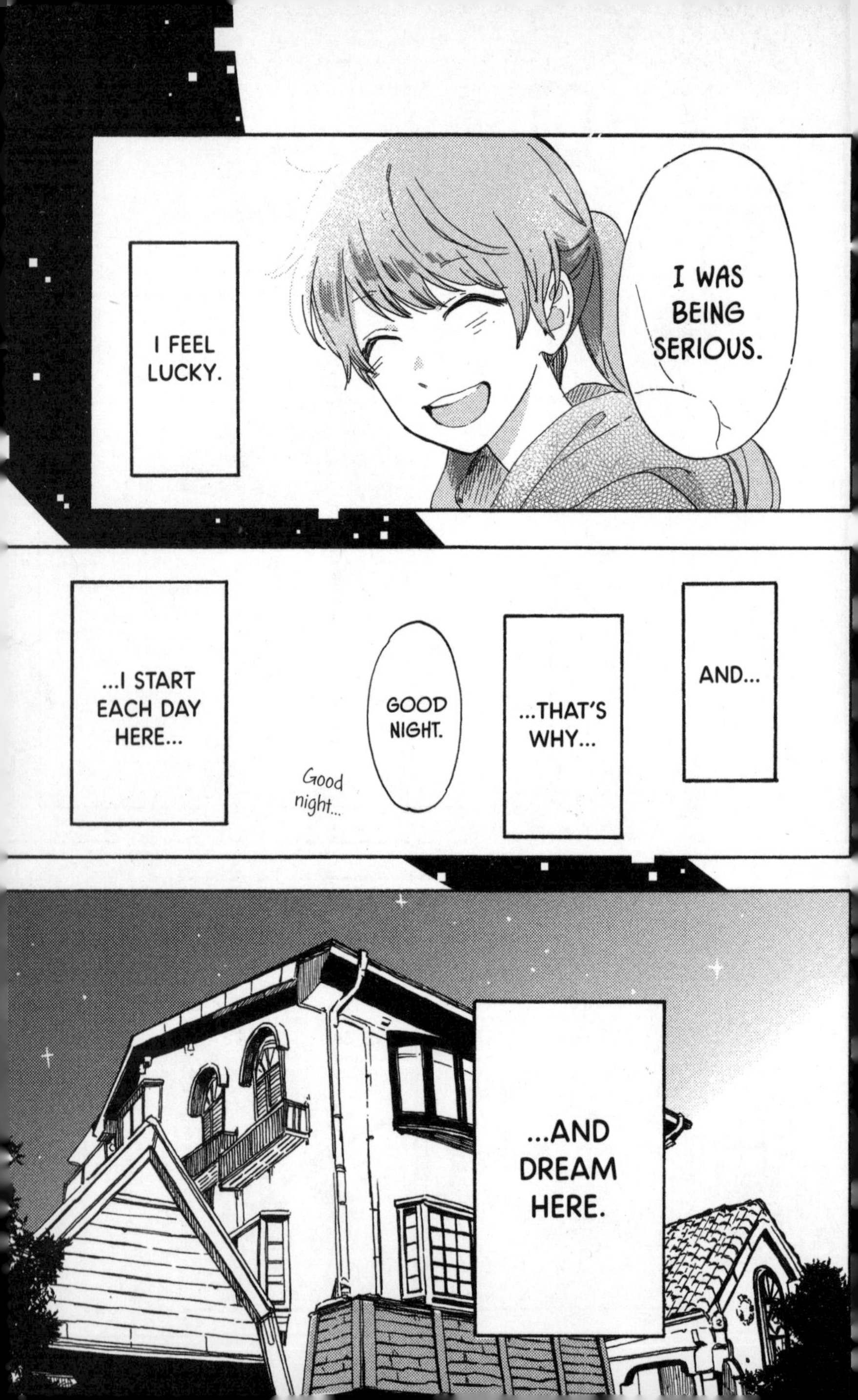
I WAS BEING SERIOUS.
I FEEL LUCKY.
AND...
...THAT'S WHY...
GOOD NIGHT.
Good night...
...I START EACH DAY HERE...
...AND DREAM HERE.

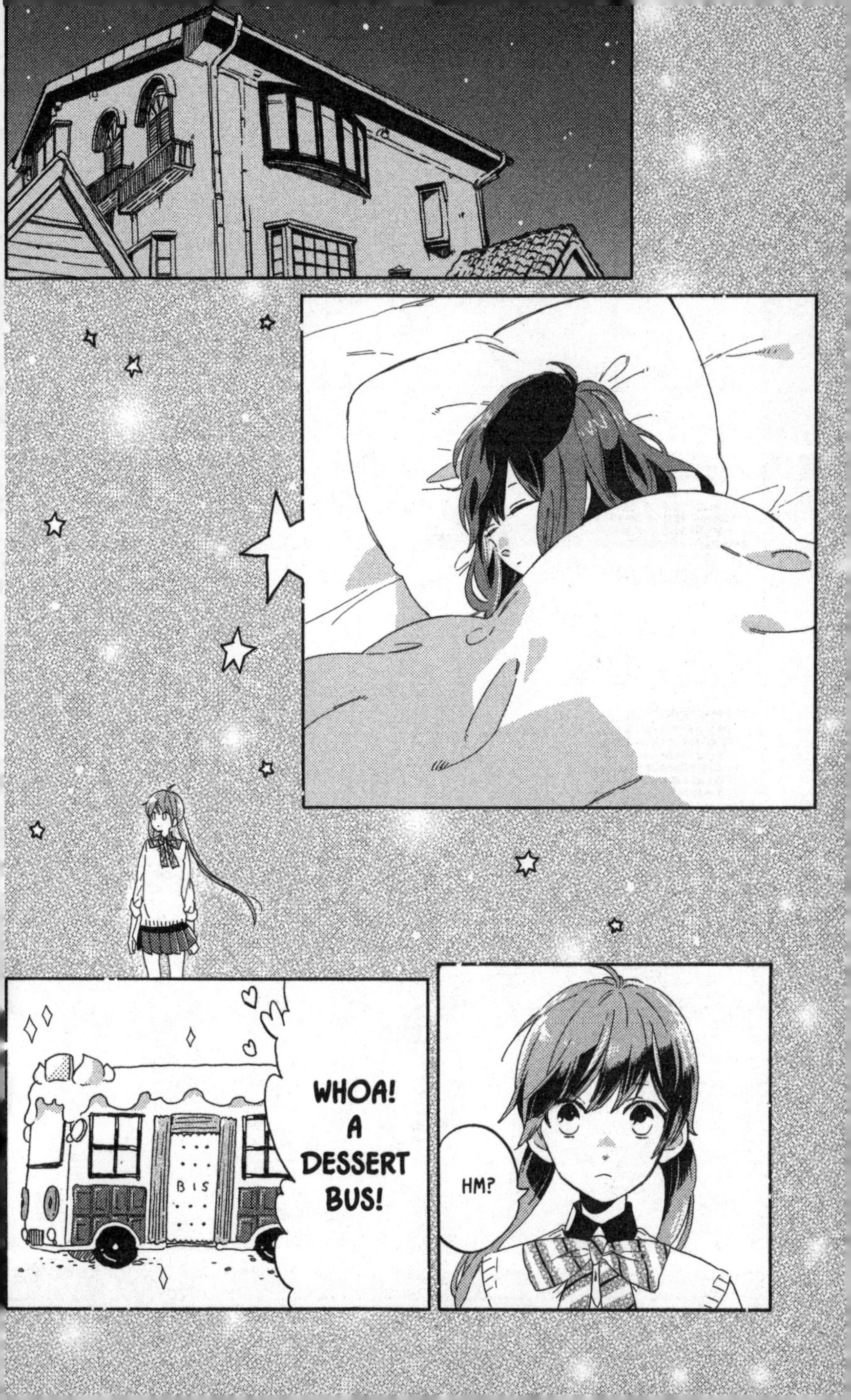
HM?
WHOA! A DESSERT BUS!
BIS

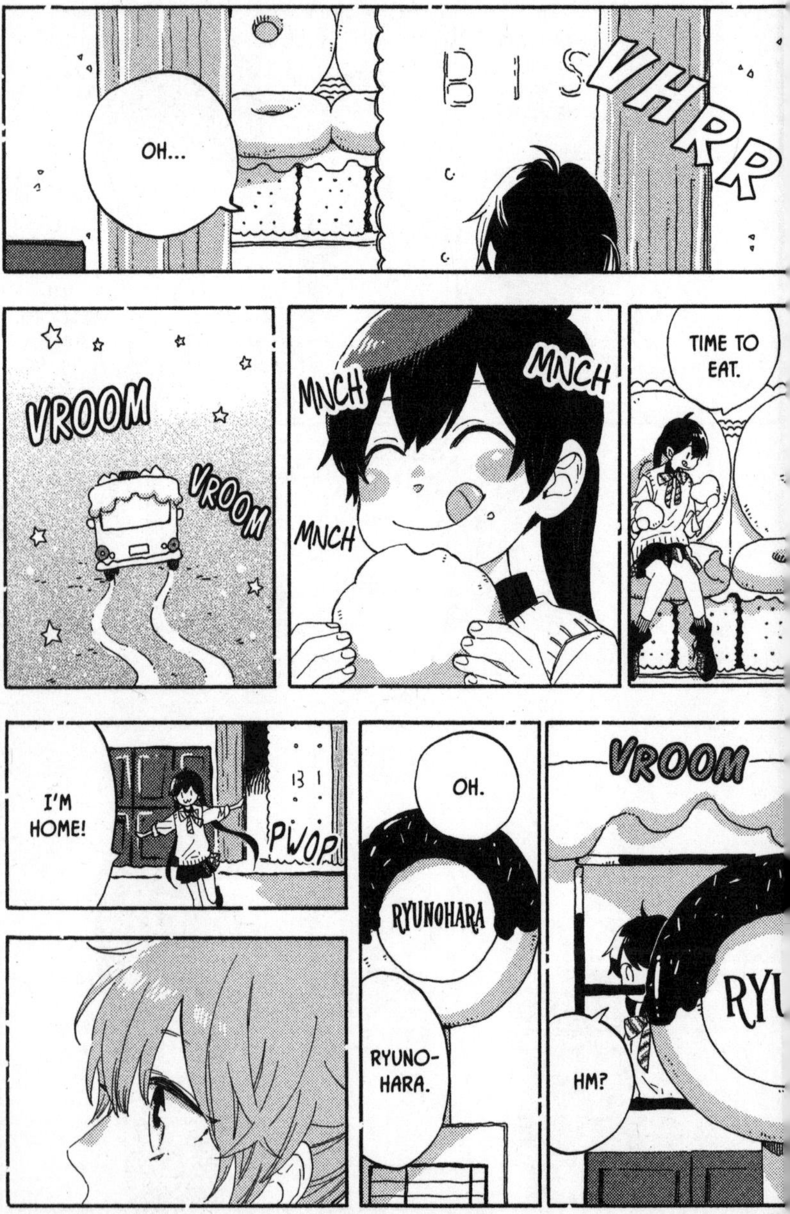
VHRR
B I S
OH...
TIME TO EAT.
MNCH
MNCH
MNCH
VROOM
VROOM
VROOM
RYU
HM?
OH.
RYUNOHARA
RYUNO-HARA.
I'M HOME!
B I
PWOP

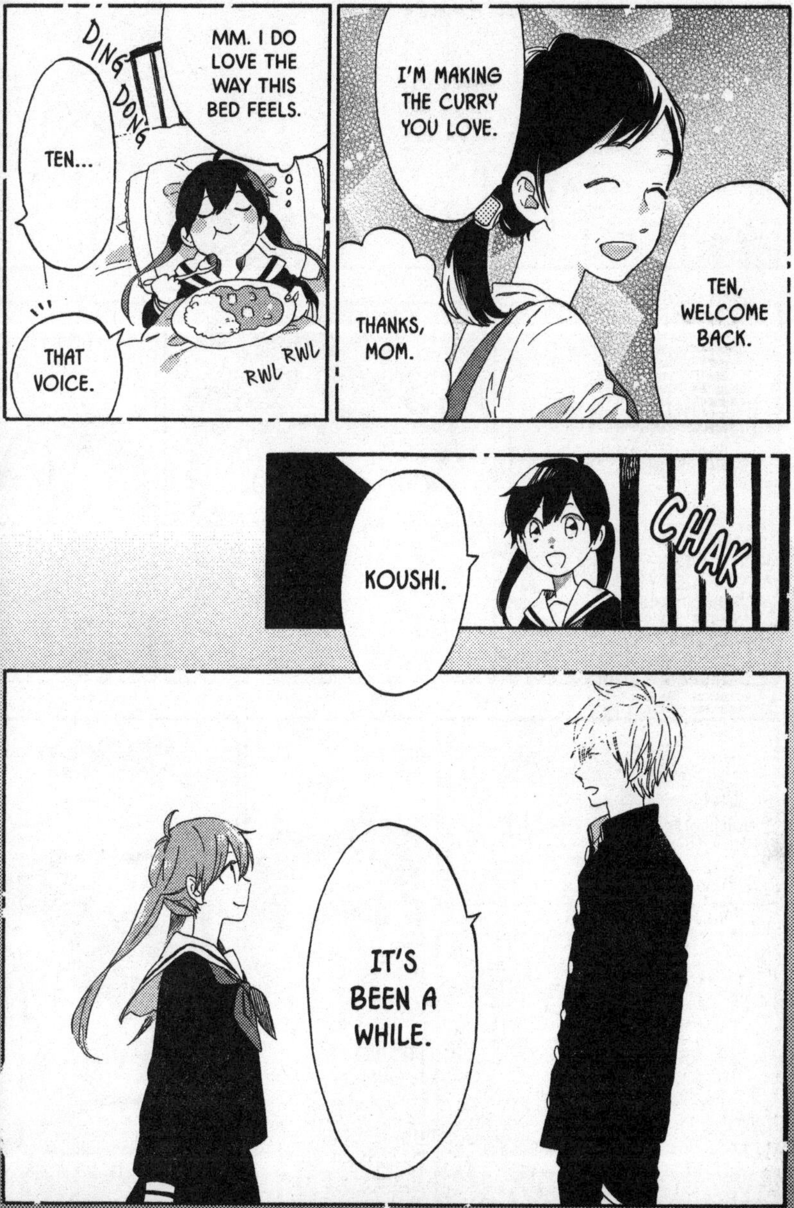
TEN, WELCOME BACK.
I'M MAKING THE CURRY YOU LOVE.
THANKS, MOM.
MM. I DO LOVE THE WAY THIS BED FEELS.
DING DONG
TEN...
THAT VOICE.
RWL RWL
CHAK
KOUSHI.
IT'S BEEN A WHILE.

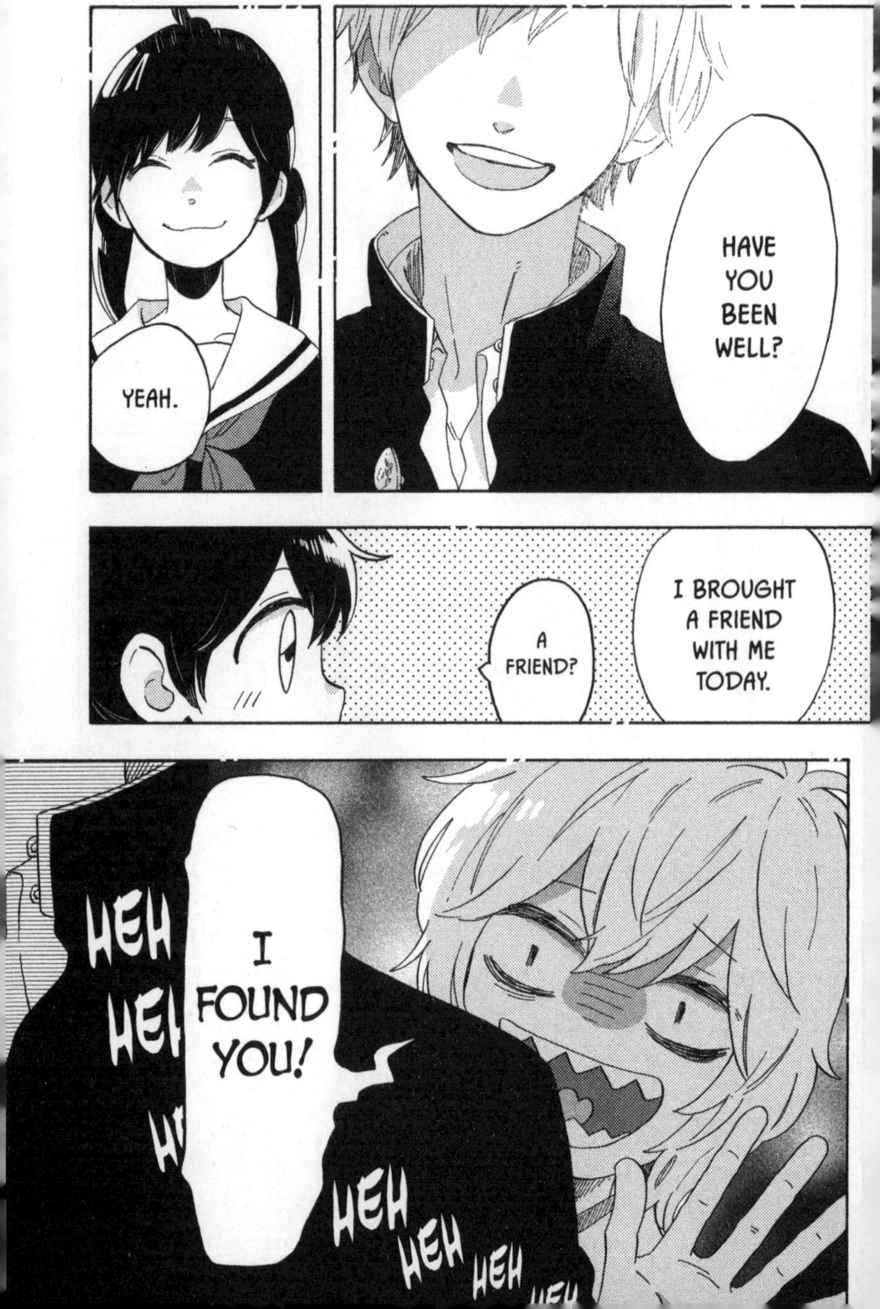
HAVE YOU BEEN WELL?
YEAH.
I BROUGHT A FRIEND WITH ME TODAY.
A FRIEND?
I FOUND YOU!
HEH
HEH
HEH HEH HEH

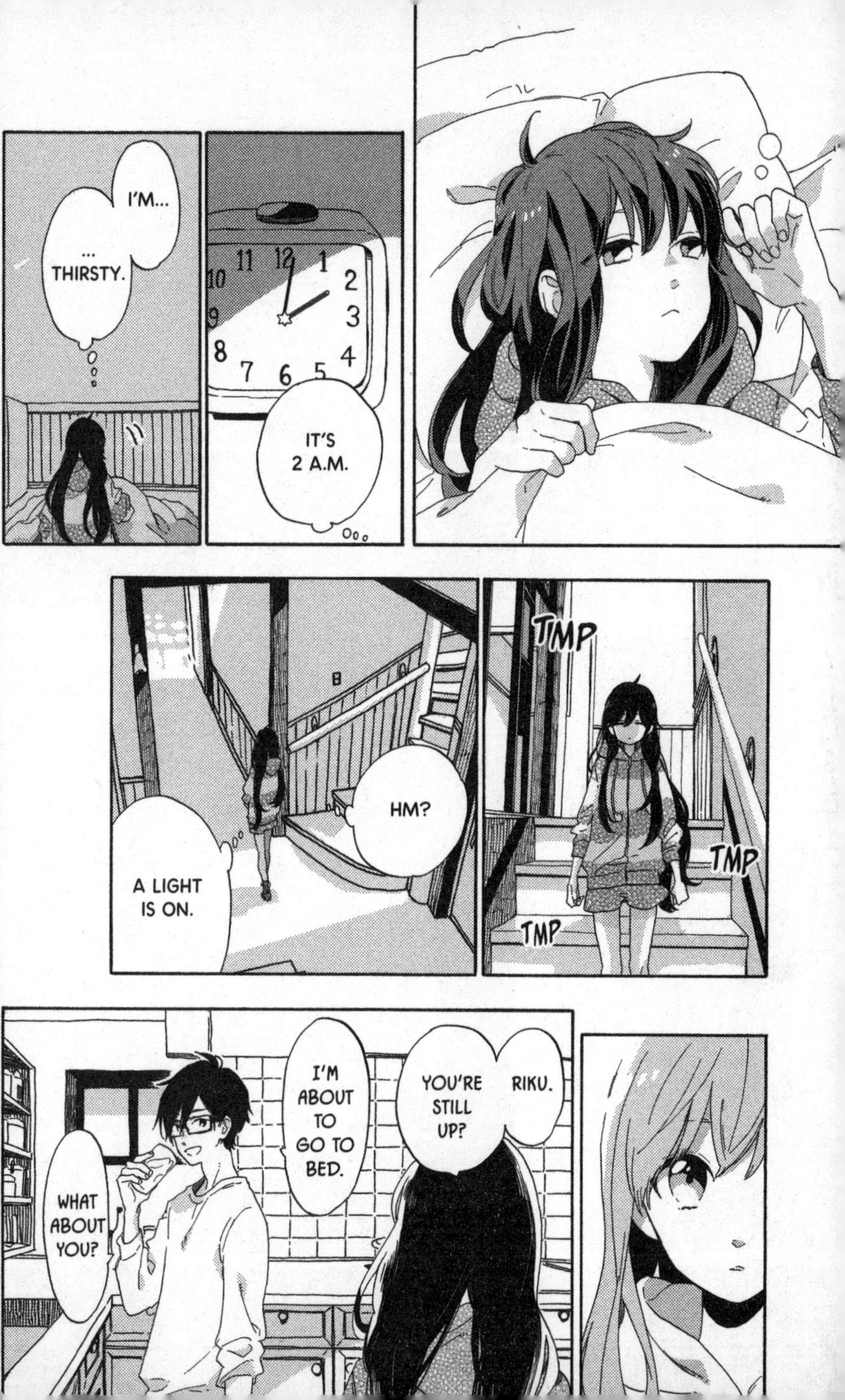
IT'S 2 A.M.
I'M...
... THIRSTY.
TMP
TMP
TMP
HM?
A LIGHT IS ON.
RIKU.
YOU'RE STILL UP?
I'M ABOUT TO GO TO BED.
WHAT ABOUT YOU?

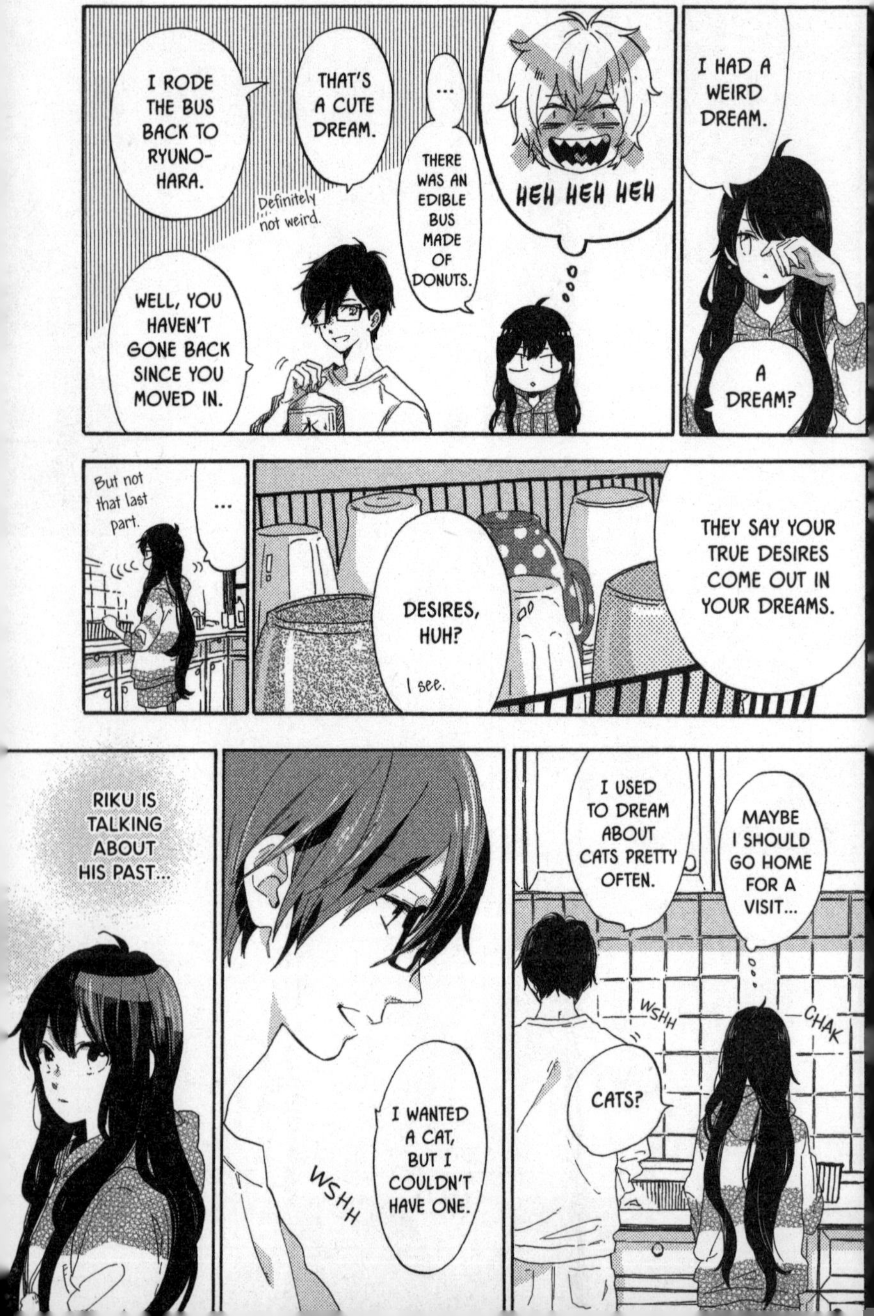
I HAD A WEIRD DREAM.
A DREAM?
HEH HEH HEH
...
THERE WAS AN EDIBLE BUS MADE OF DONUTS.
THAT'S A CUTE DREAM.
I RODE THE BUS BACK TO RYUNO-HARA.
Definitely not weird.
WELL, YOU HAVEN'T GONE BACK SINCE YOU MOVED IN.
THEY SAY YOUR TRUE DESIRES COME OUT IN YOUR DREAMS.
DESIRES, HUH?
I see.
...
But not that last part.
MAYBE I SHOULD GO HOME FOR A VISIT...
I USED TO DREAM ABOUT CATS PRETTY OFTEN.
CHAK
WSHH
CATS?
I WANTED A CAT, BUT I COULDN'T HAVE ONE.
WSHH
RIKU IS TALKING ABOUT HIS PAST...

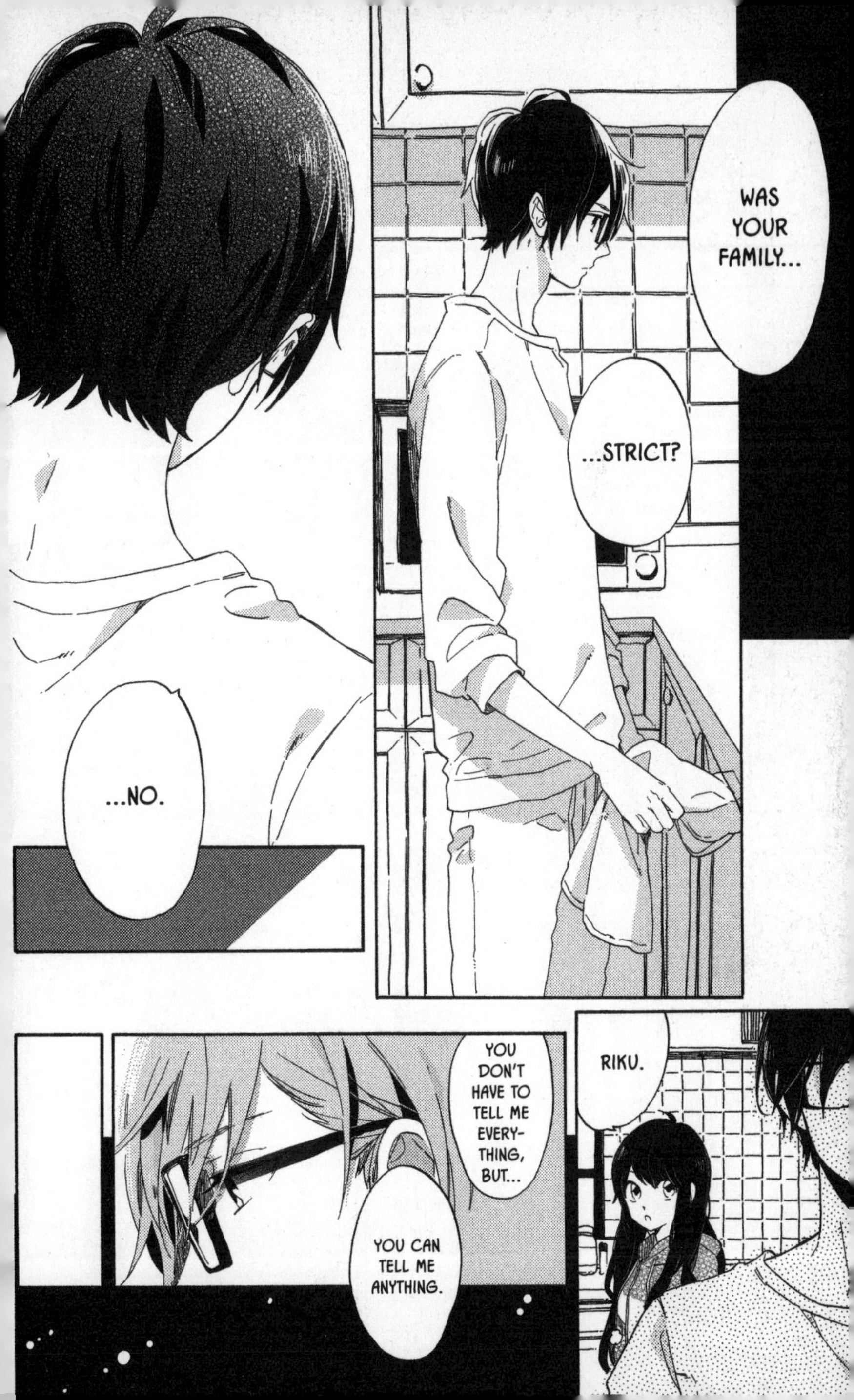
WAS YOUR FAMILY...
...STRICT?
...NO.
RIKU.
YOU DON'T HAVE TO TELL ME EVERY-THING, BUT...
YOU CAN TELL ME ANYTHING.

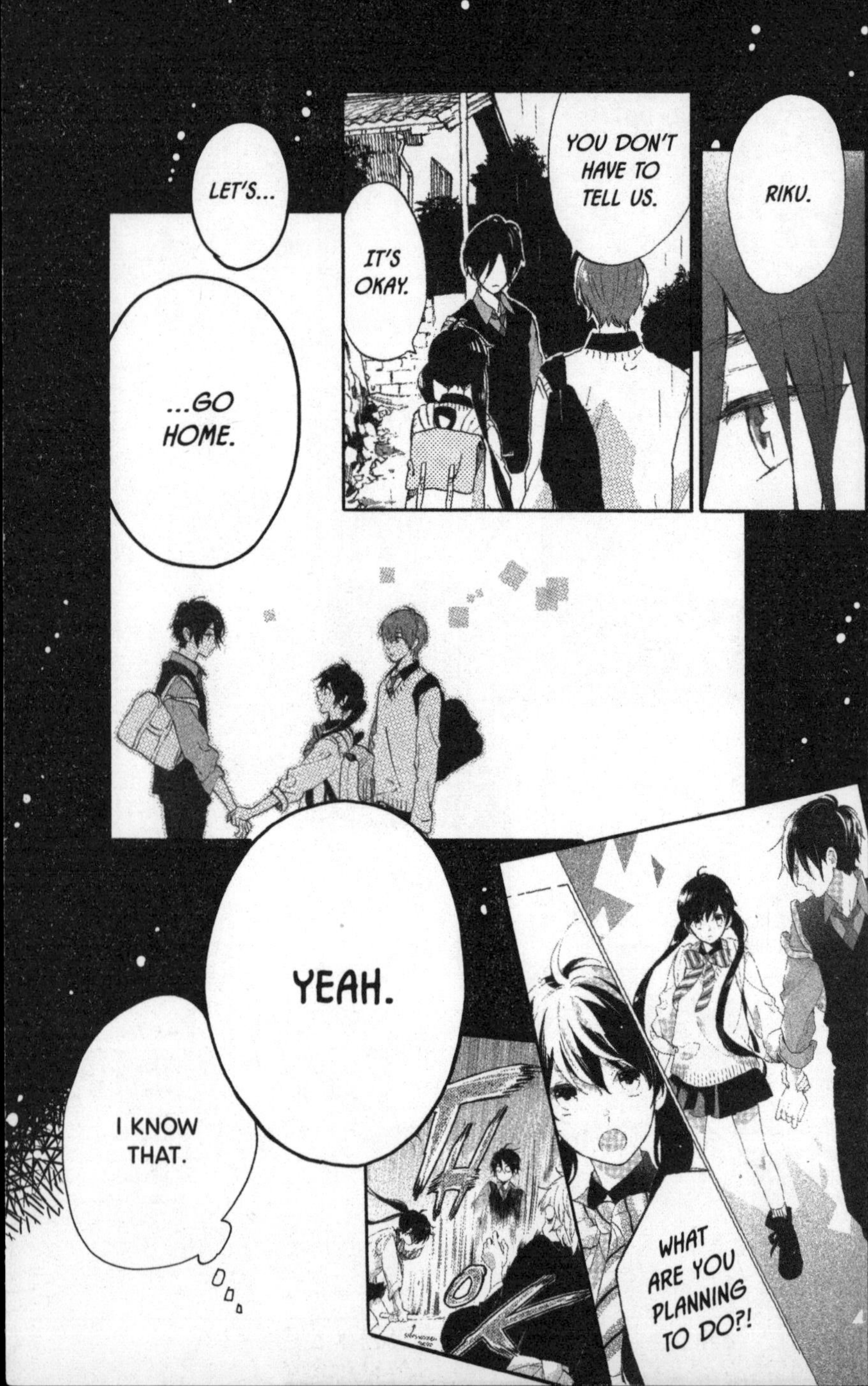
RIKU.
YOU DON'T HAVE TO TELL US.
IT'S OKAY.
LET'S...
...GO HOME.
WHAT ARE YOU PLANNING TO DO?!
YEAH.
I KNOW THAT.

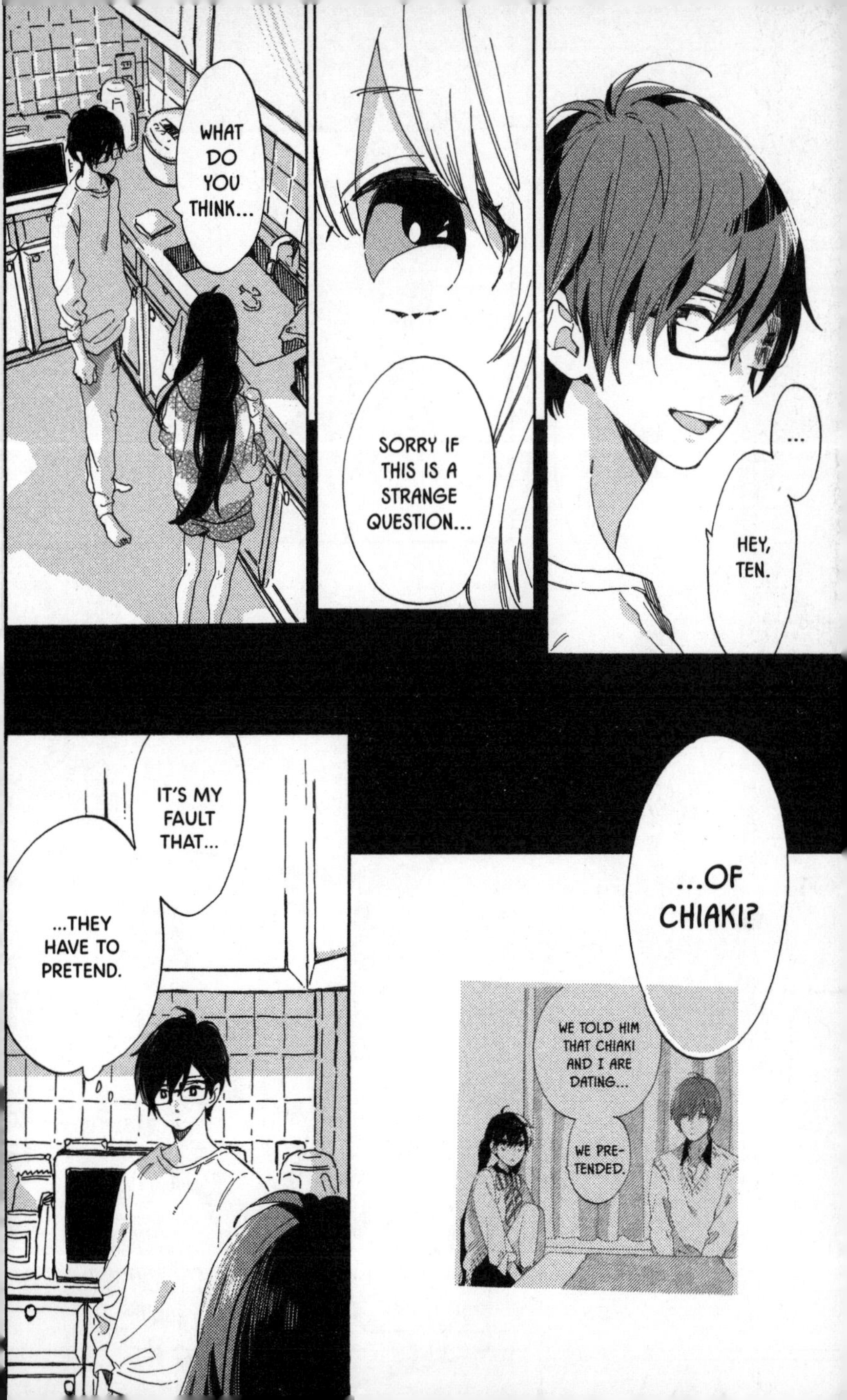
...
HEY, TEN.
SORRY IF THIS IS A STRANGE QUESTION...
WHAT DO YOU THINK...
...OF CHIAKI?
WE TOLD HIM THAT CHIAKI AND I ARE DATING...
WE PRE-TENDED.
IT'S MY FAULT THAT...
...THEY HAVE TO PRETEND.

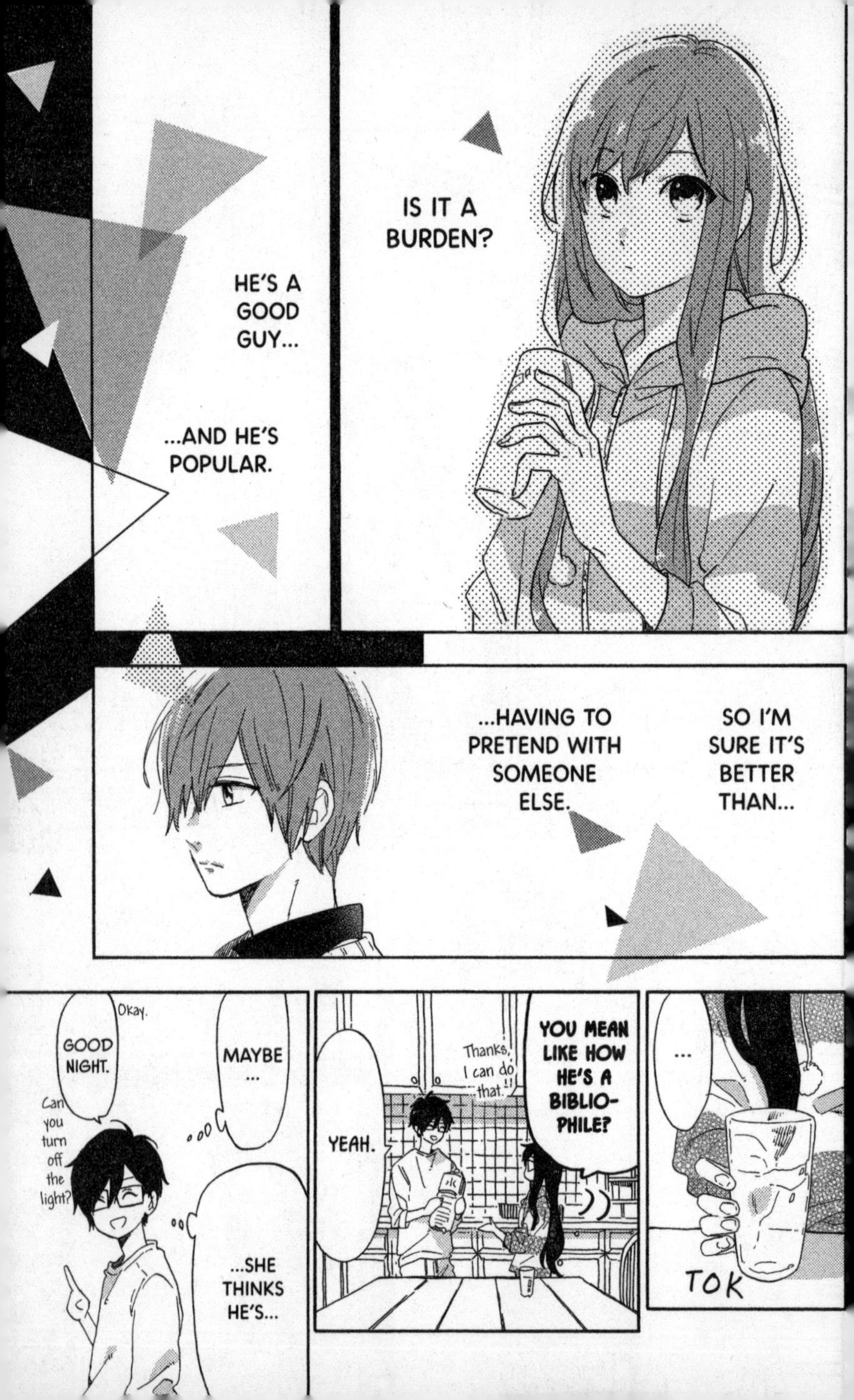
IS IT A BURDEN?
HE'S A GOOD GUY...
...AND HE'S POPULAR.
SO I'M SURE IT'S BETTER THAN...
...HAVING TO PRETEND WITH SOMEONE ELSE.
...
TOK
YOU MEAN LIKE HOW HE'S A BIBLIO-PHILE?
Thanks, I can do that.
YEAH.
MAYBE ...
Okay.
GOOD NIGHT.
Can you turn off the light?
...SHE THINKS HE'S...

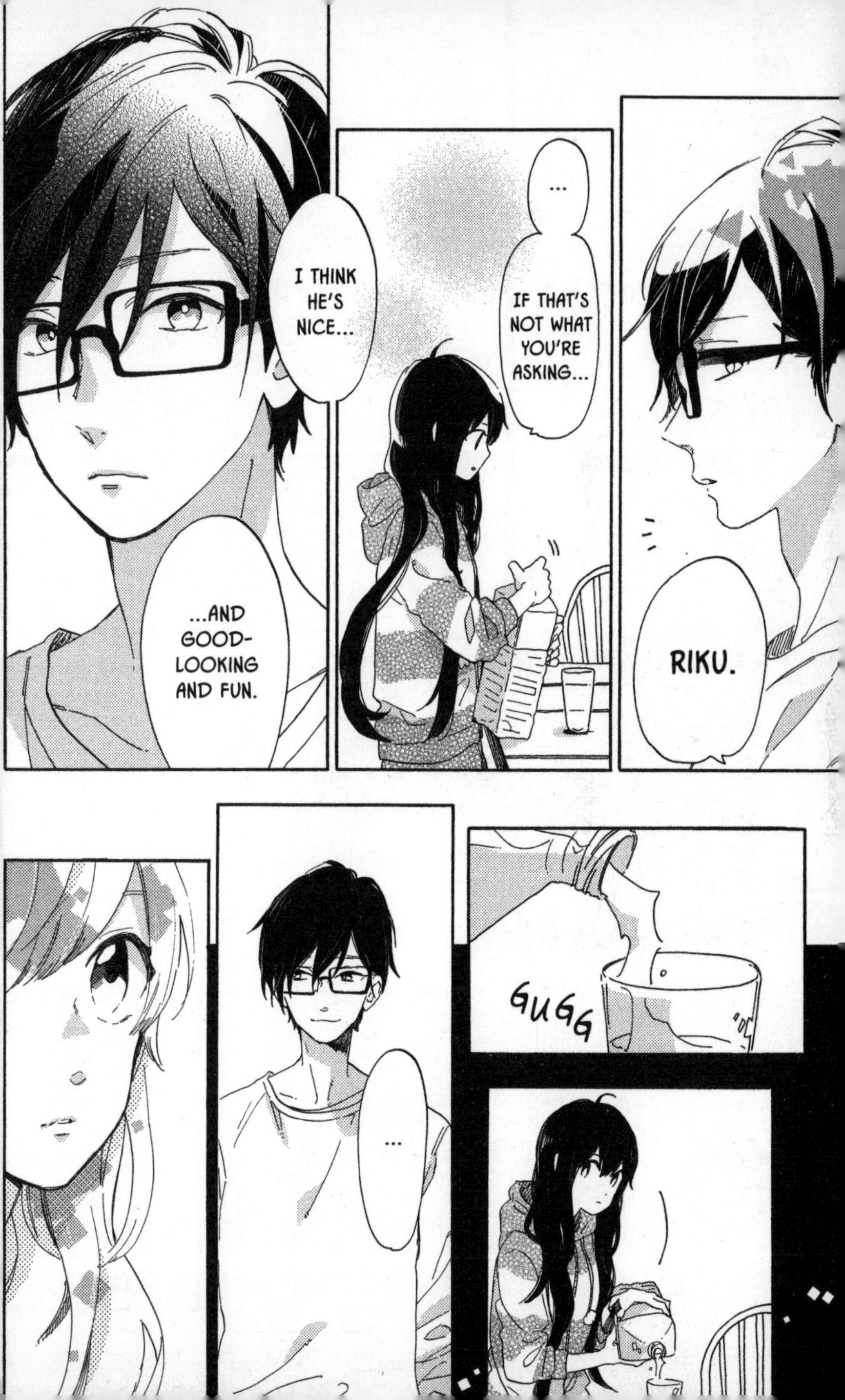
RIKU.
...
IF THAT'S NOT WHAT YOU'RE ASKING...
I THINK HE'S NICE...
...AND GOOD-LOOKING AND FUN.
GUGG
...

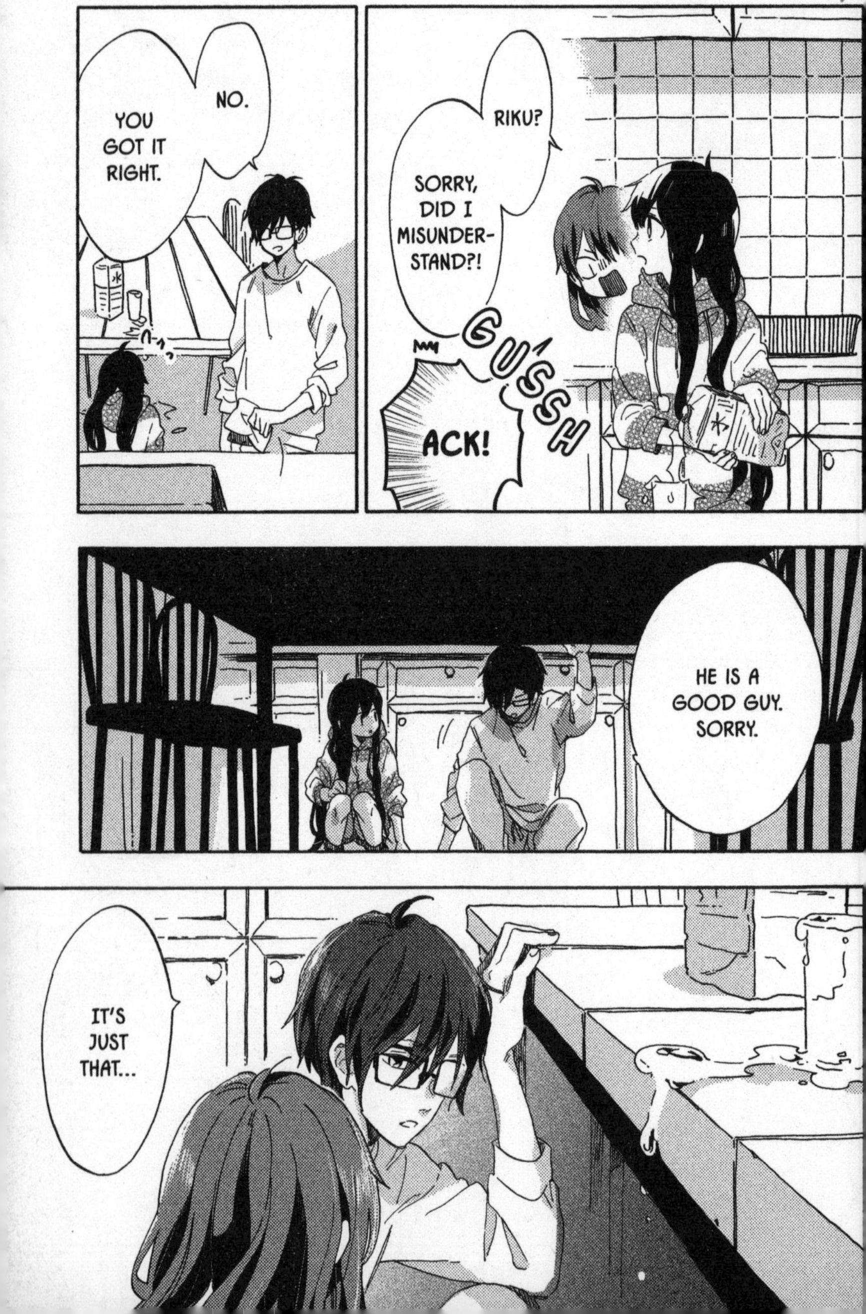
RIKU?
SORRY, DID I MISUNDERSTAND?!
GUSSH
ACK!
NO.
YOU GOT IT RIGHT.
HE IS A GOOD GUY. SORRY.
IT'S JUST THAT...

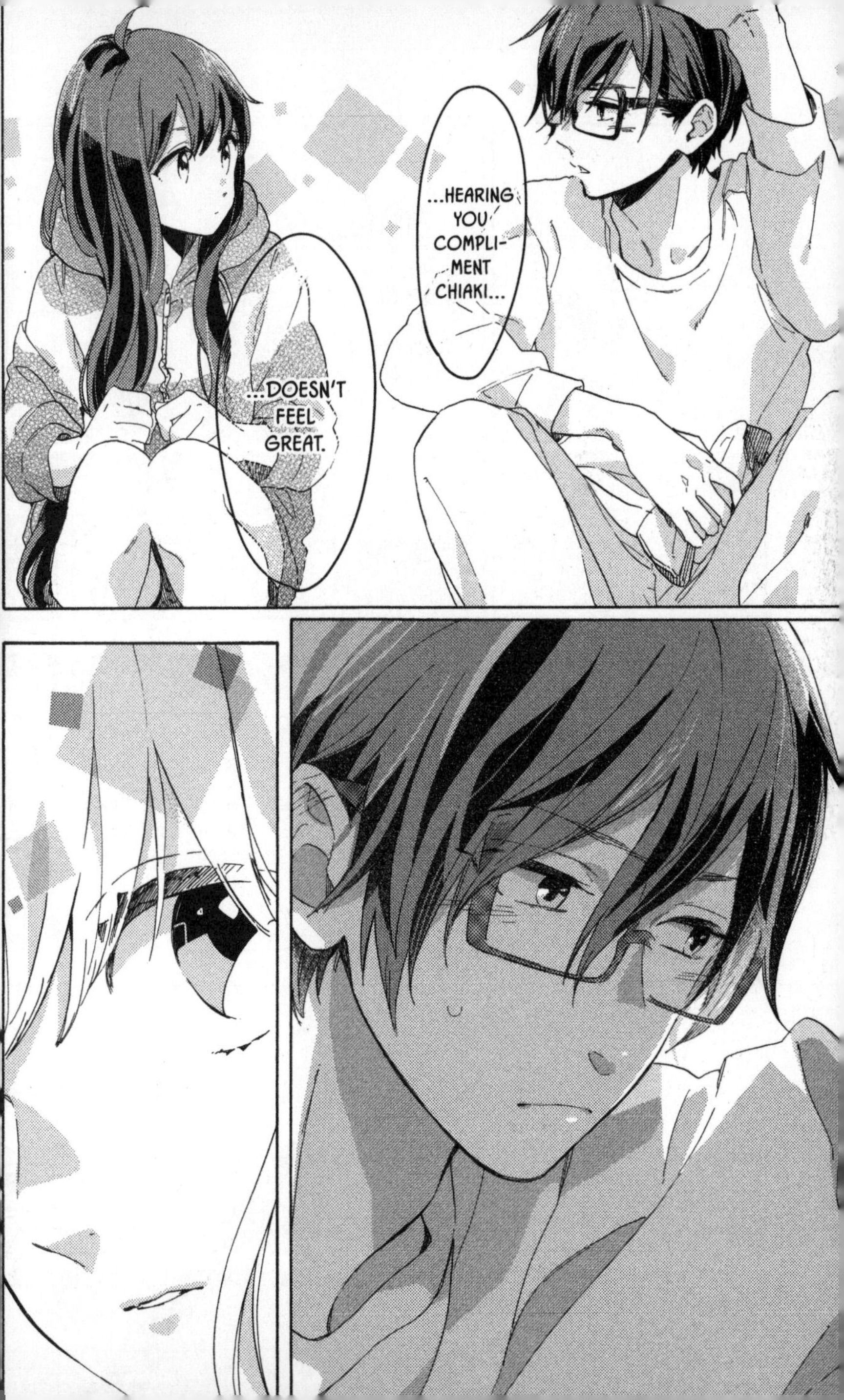
...HEARING YOU COMPLI-MENT CHIAKI...
...DOESN'T FEEL GREAT.

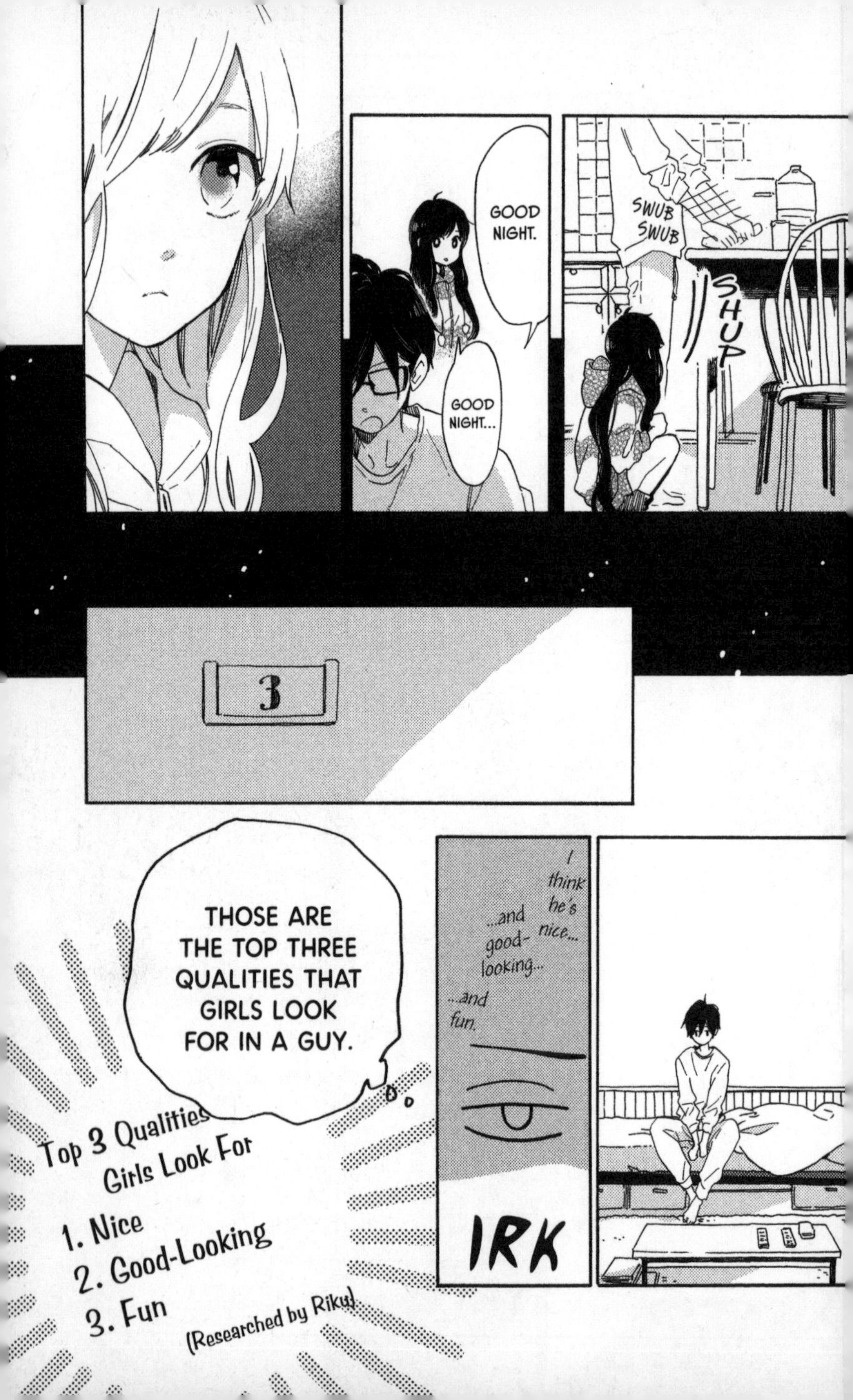
SWUB SWUB
SHUP
GOOD NIGHT.
GOOD NIGHT...
3
I think he's nice...
...and good-looking...
...and fun.
IRK
THOSE ARE THE TOP THREE QUALITIES THAT GIRLS LOOK FOR IN A GUY.
Top 3 Qualities Girls Look For
1. Nice
2. Good-Looking
3. Fun
(Researched by Riku)

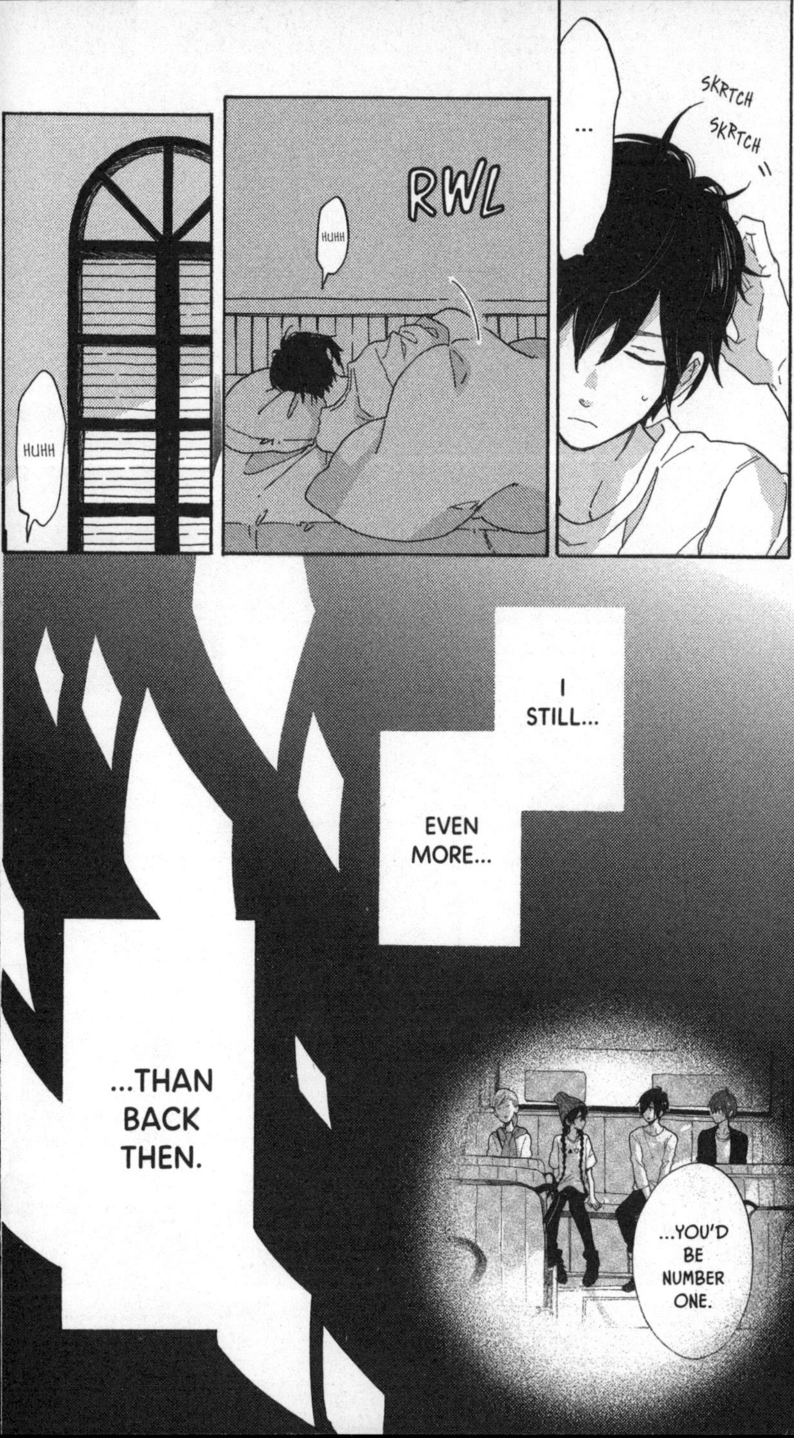

SKRTCH
SKRTCH
...
RWL
HUHH
HUHH
I STILL...
EVEN MORE...
...THAN BACK THEN.
...YOU'D BE NUMBER ONE.

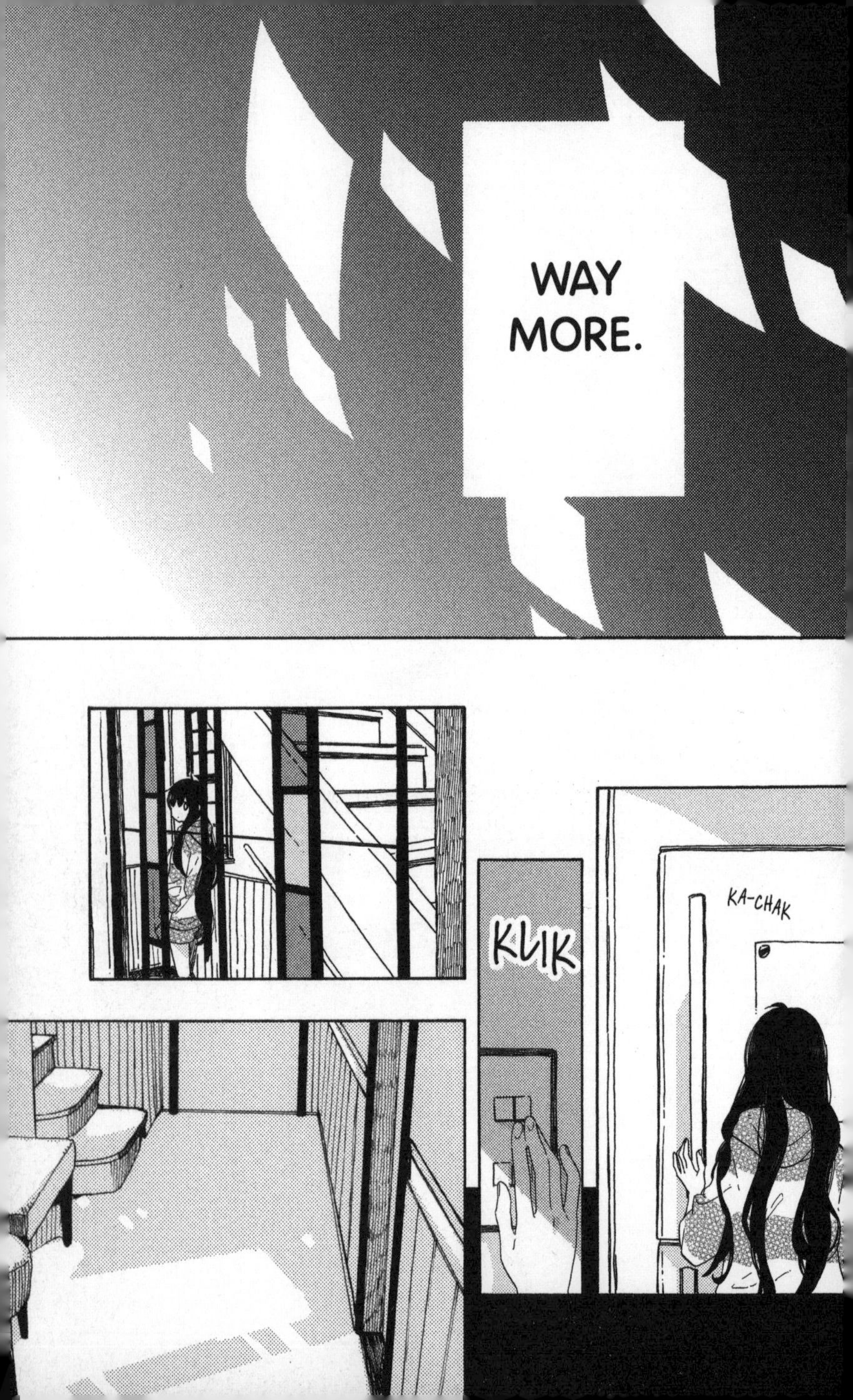
WAY MORE.
KA-CHAK
KLIK

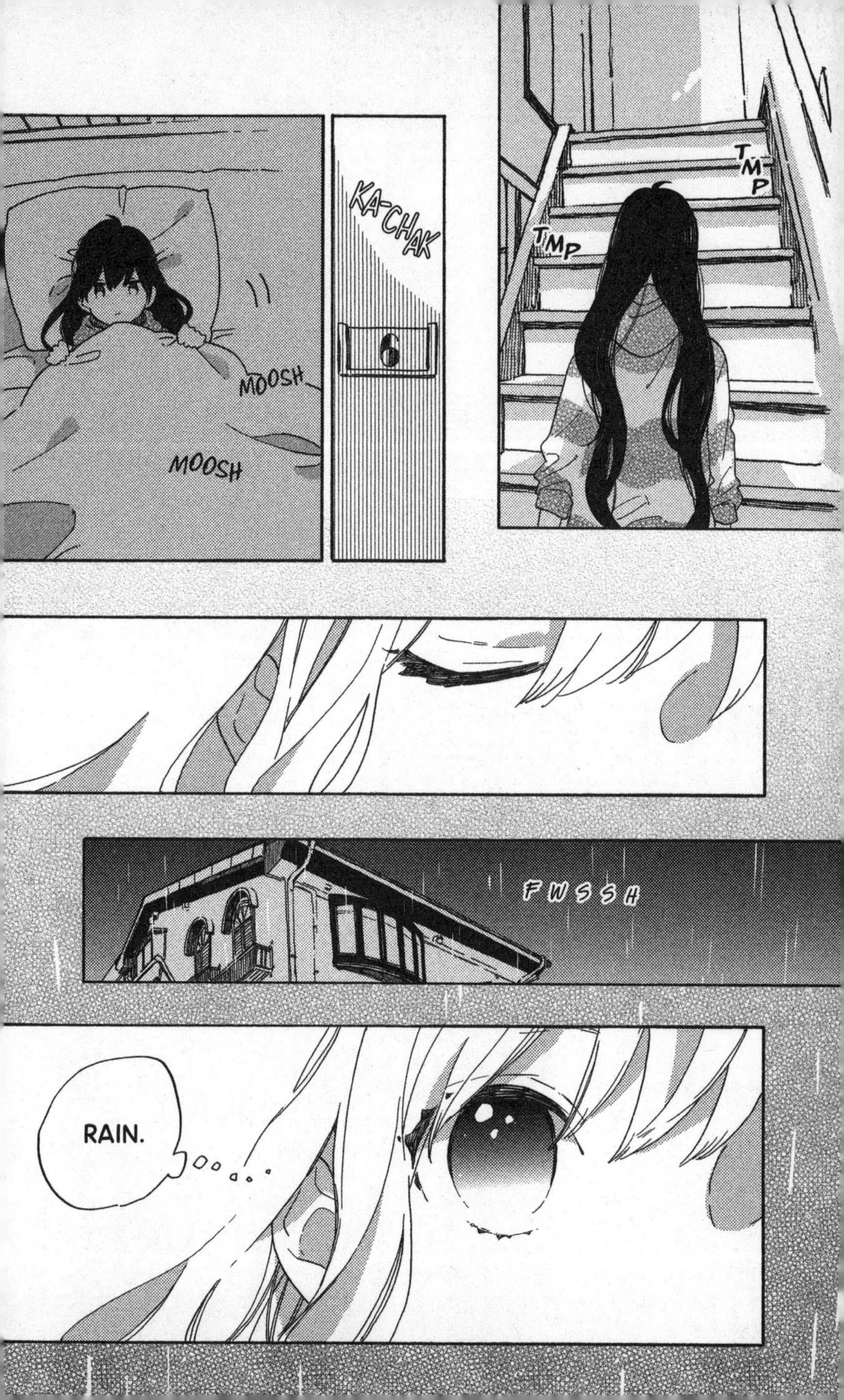
TMP
TMP
KA-CHAK
MOOSH
MOOSH
FWSSH
RAIN.

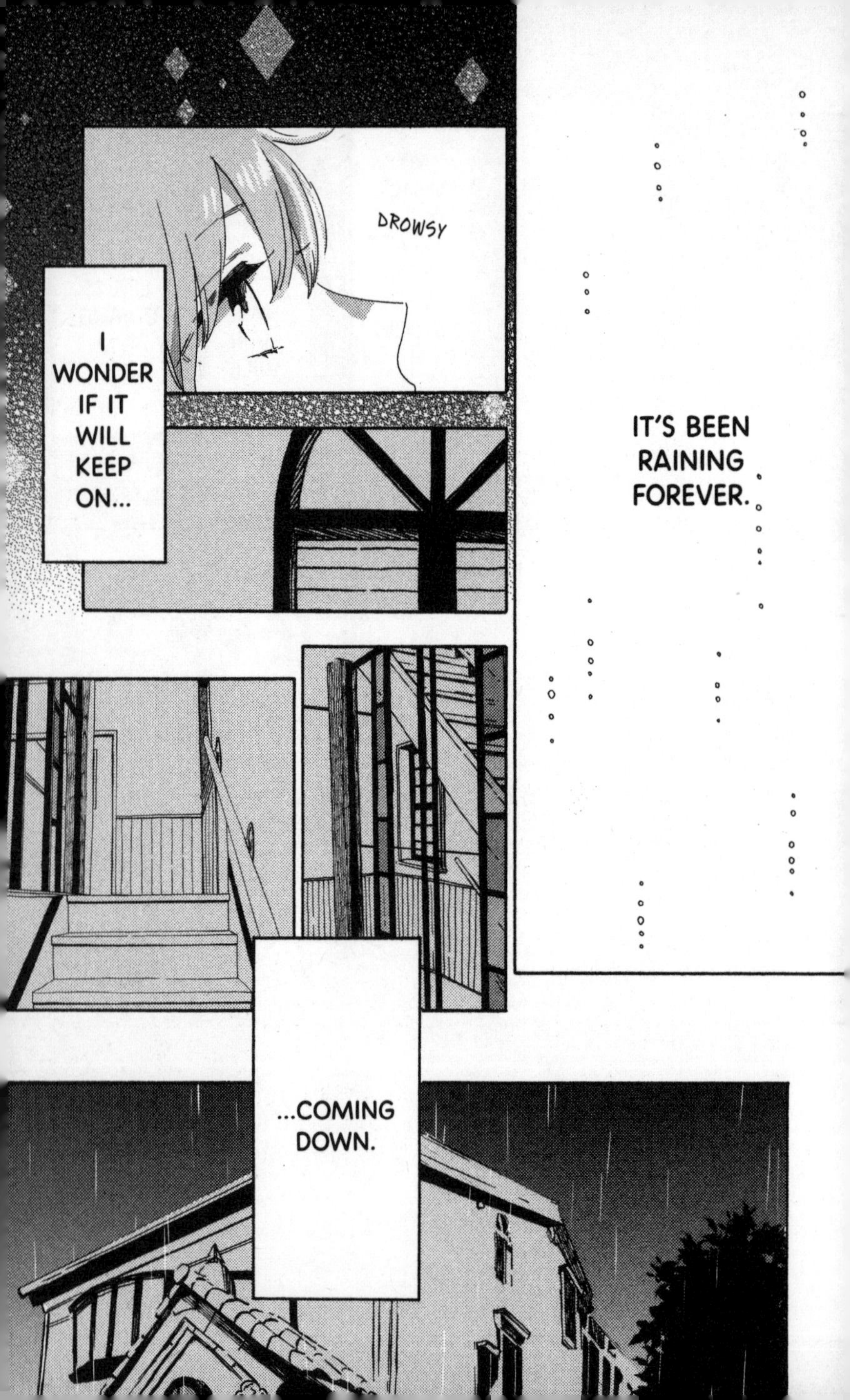
IT'S BEEN RAINING FOREVER.
DROWSY
I WONDER IF IT WILL KEEP ON...
...COMING DOWN.

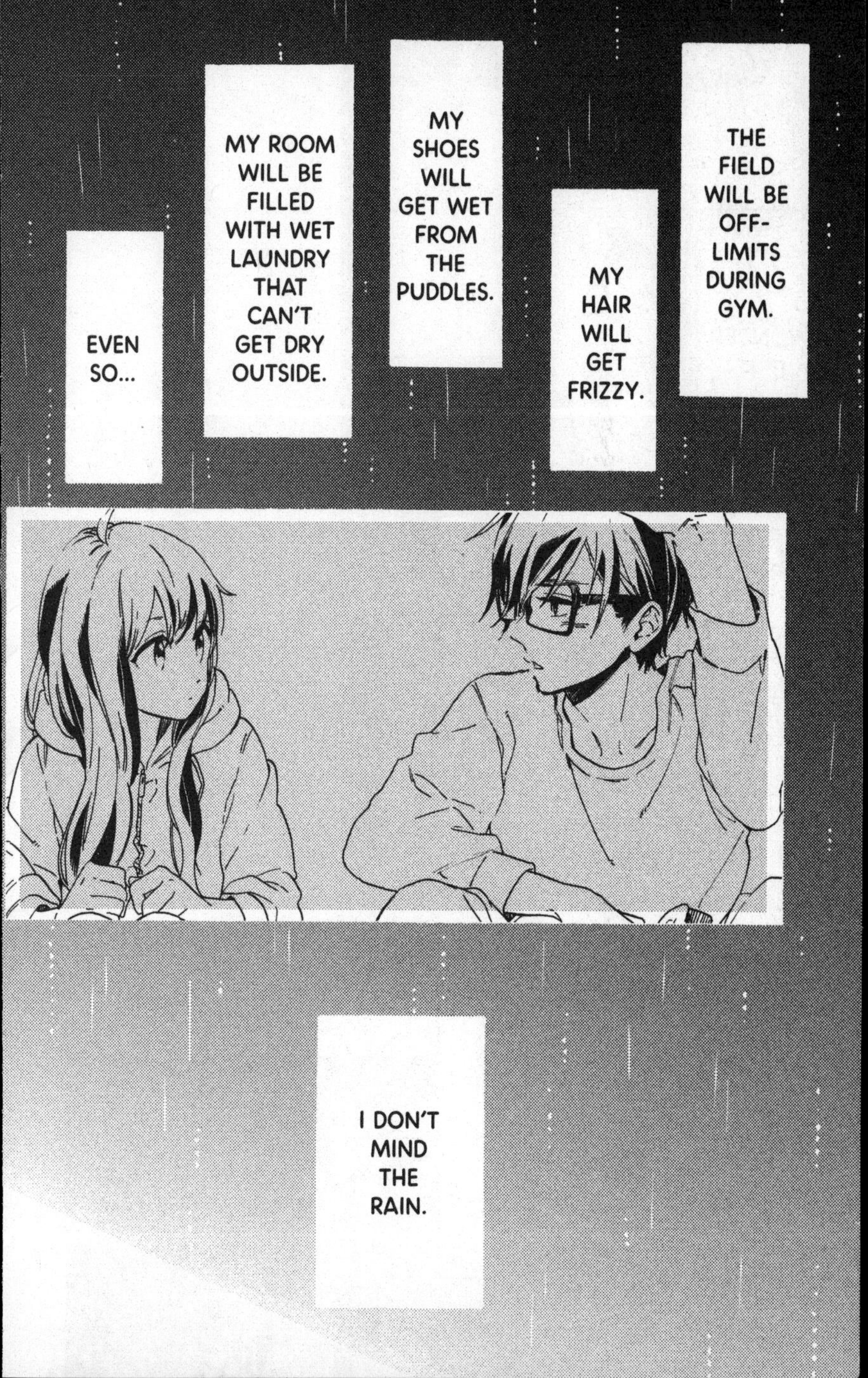
THE FIELD WILL BE OFF-LIMITS DURING GYM.
MY HAIR WILL GET FRIZZY.
MY SHOES WILL GET WET FROM THE PUDDLES.
MY ROOM WILL BE FILLED WITH WET LAUNDRY THAT CAN'T GET DRY OUTSIDE.
EVEN SO...
I DON'T MIND THE RAIN.

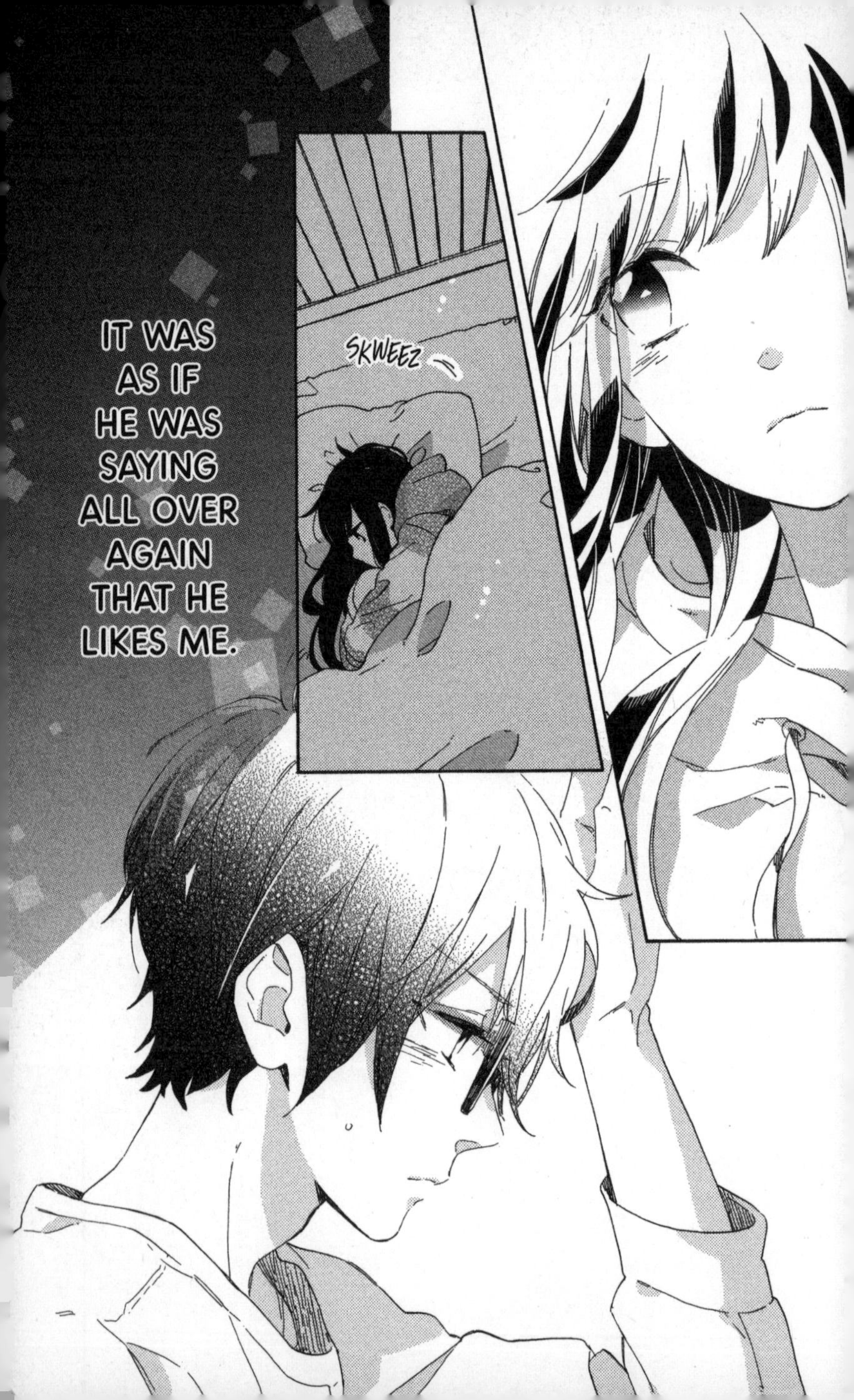
SKWEEZ
IT WAS AS IF HE WAS SAYING ALL OVER AGAIN THAT HE LIKES ME.

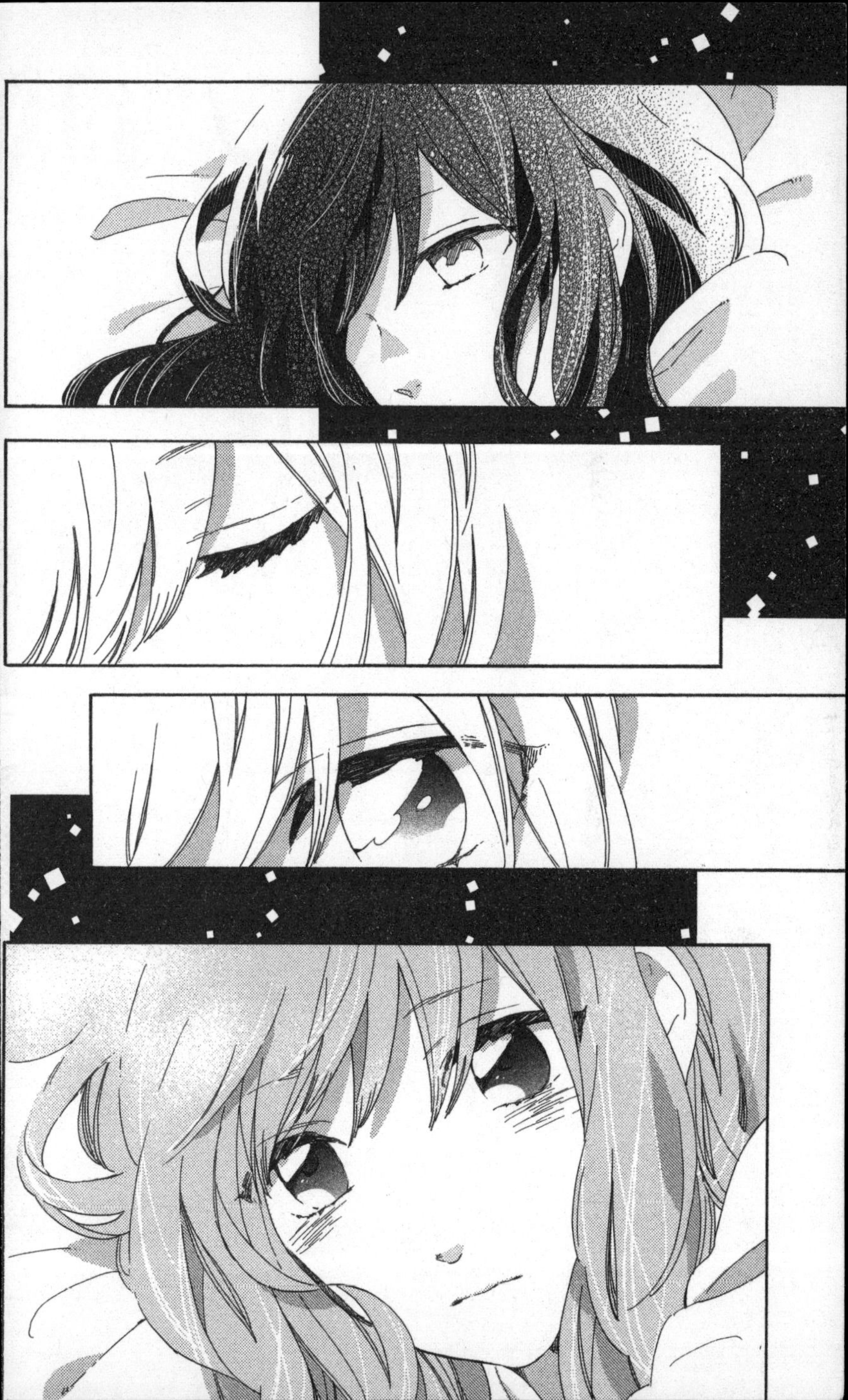

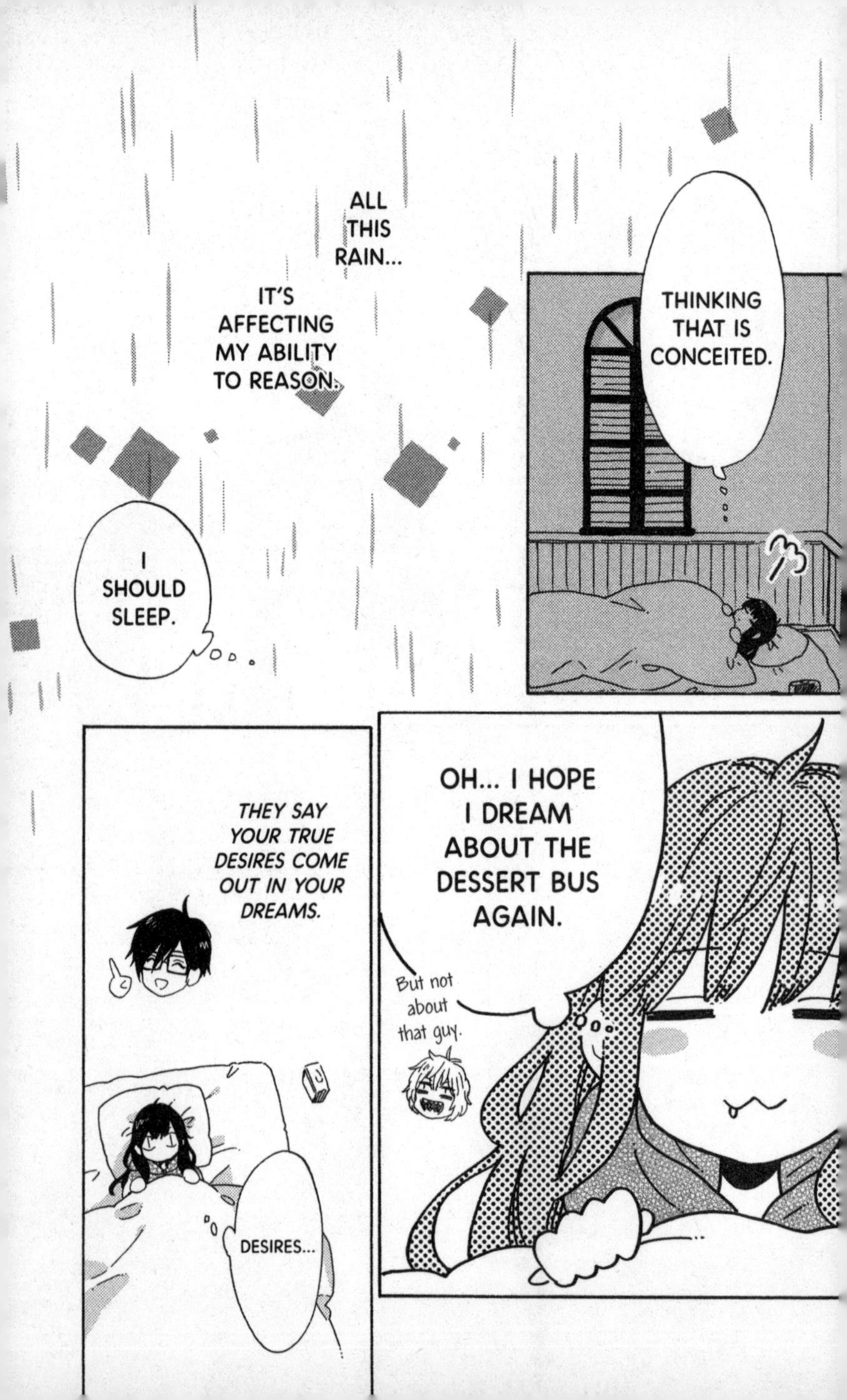
THINKING THAT IS CONCEITED.
ALL THIS RAIN...
IT'S AFFECTING MY ABILITY TO REASON.
I SHOULD SLEEP.
OH... I HOPE I DREAM ABOUT THE DESSERT BUS AGAIN.
But not about that guy.
THEY SAY YOUR TRUE DESIRES COME OUT IN YOUR DREAMS.
DESIRES...

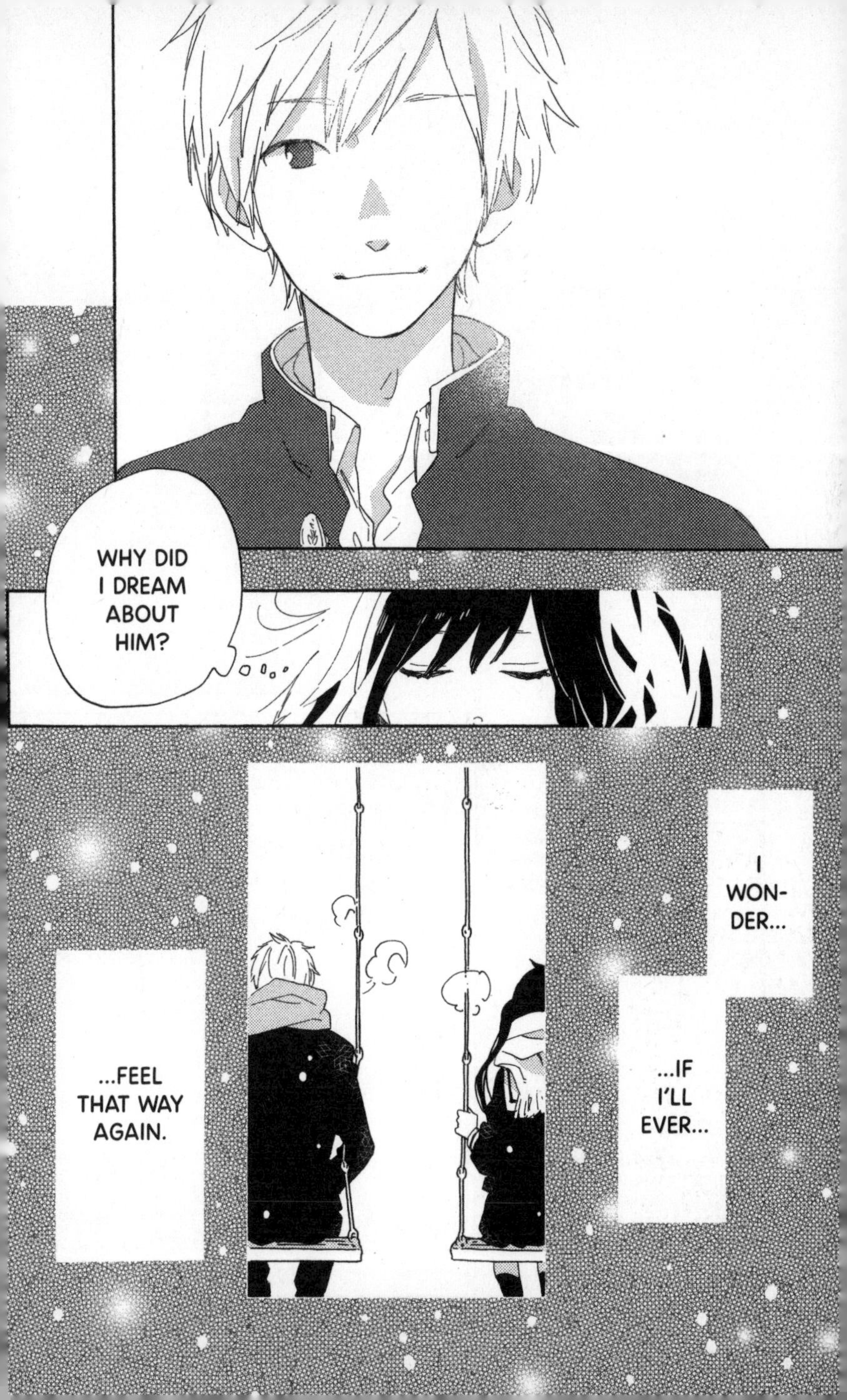
WHY DID I DREAM ABOUT HIM?
I WONDER...
...IF I'LL EVER...
...FEEL THAT WAY AGAIN.

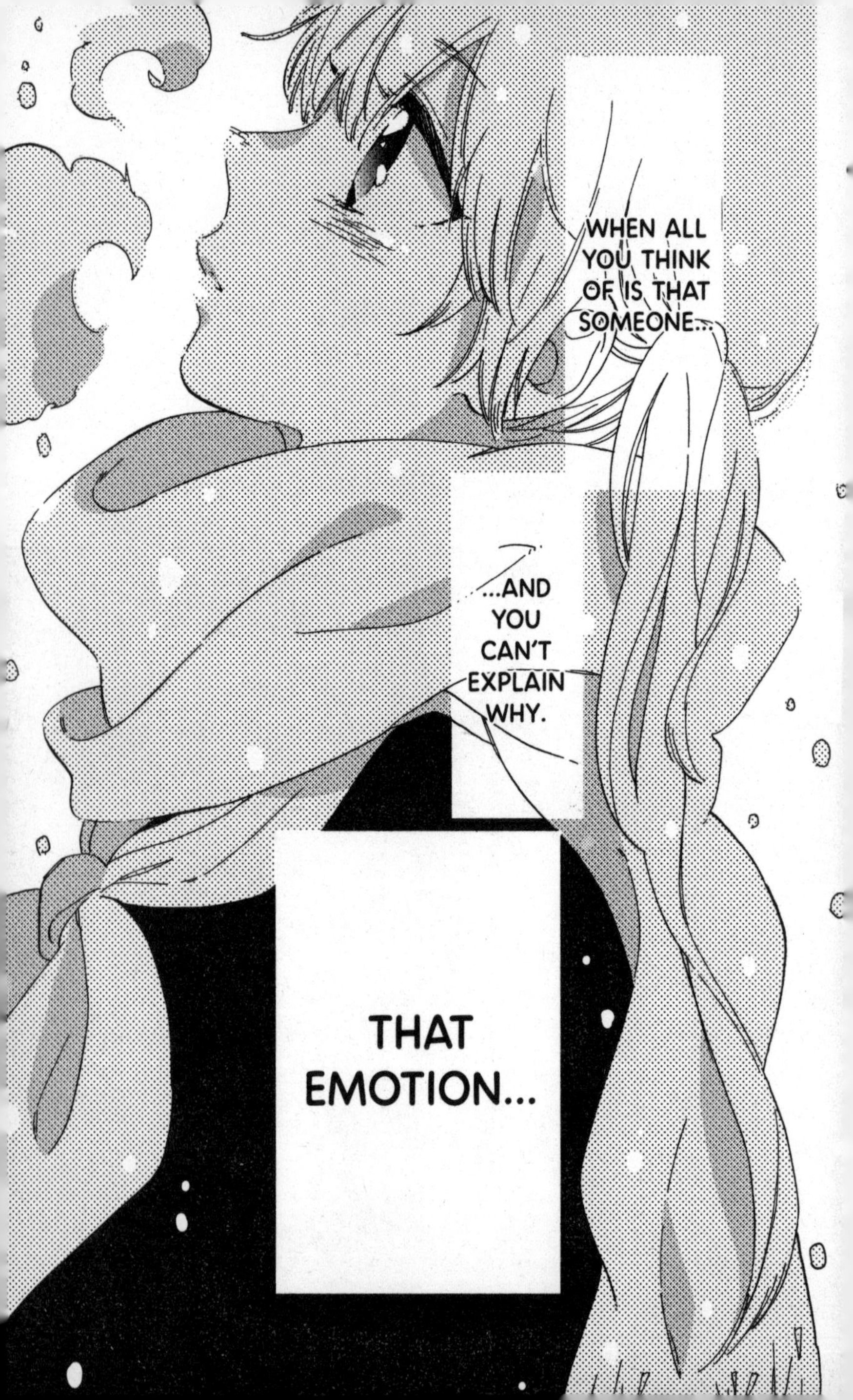
WHEN ALL YOU THINK OF IS THAT SOMEONE...
...AND YOU CAN'T EXPLAIN WHY.
THAT EMOTION...

I've been waiting for you!
THE DREAM CONTINUES
MORNING
I feel like...
...I had a bad dream...

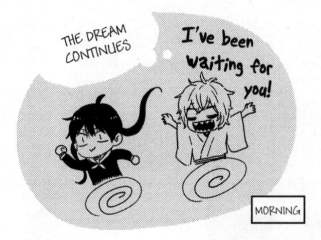

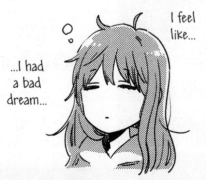

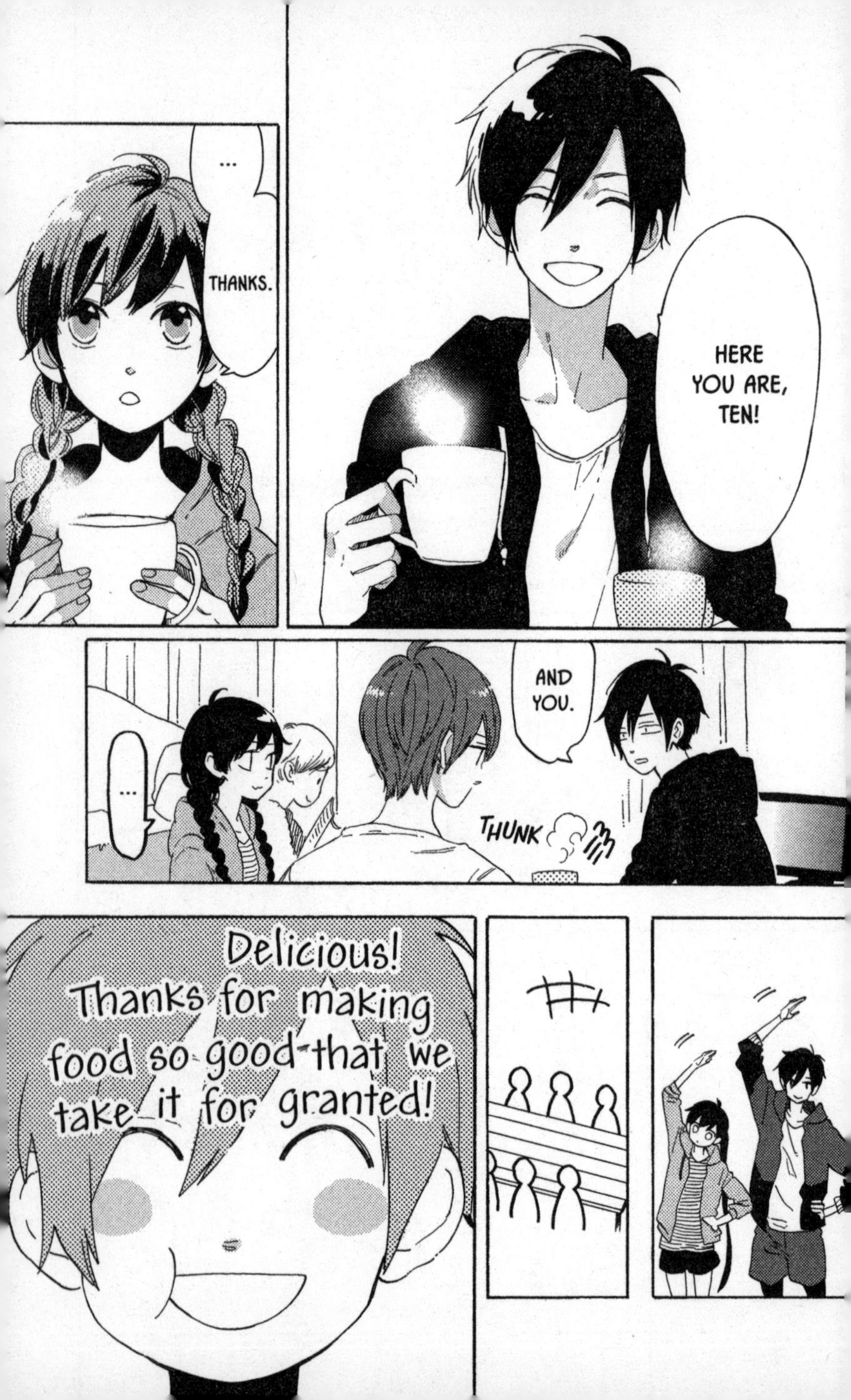
HERE YOU ARE, TEN!
...
THANKS.
AND YOU.
THUNK
...
Delicious! Thanks for making food so good that we take it for granted!

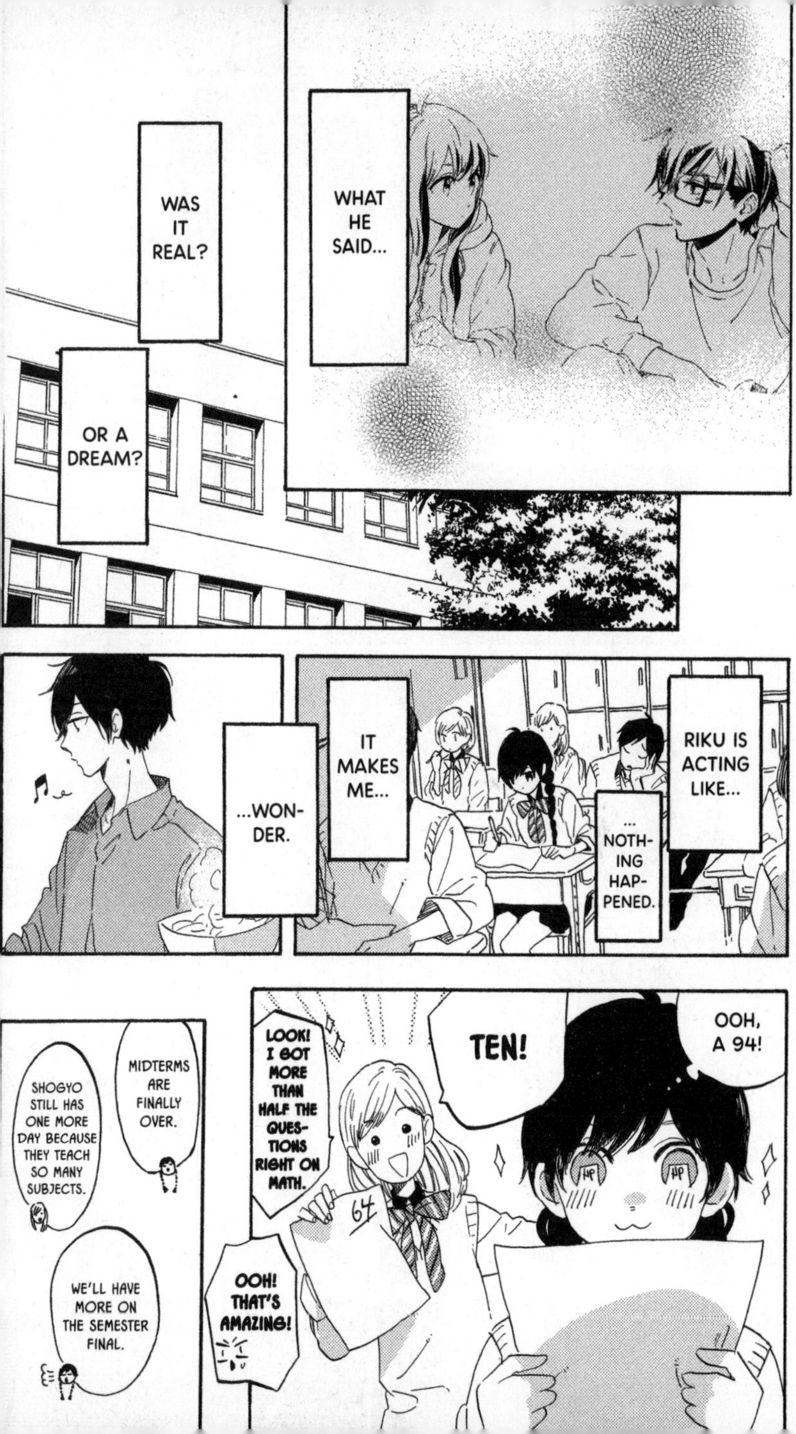
WHAT HE SAID...
WAS IT REAL?
OR A DREAM?
RIKU IS ACTING LIKE...
...NOTH-ING HAP-PENED.
IT MAKES ME...
...WON-DER.
OOH, A 94!
TEN!
LOOK! I GOT MORE THAN HALF THE QUES-TIONS RIGHT ON MATH.
OOH! THAT'S AMAZING!
MIDTERMS ARE FINALLY OVER.
SHOGYO STILL HAS ONE MORE DAY BECAUSE THEY TEACH SO MANY SUBJECTS.
WE'LL HAVE MORE ON THE SEMESTER FINAL.
64

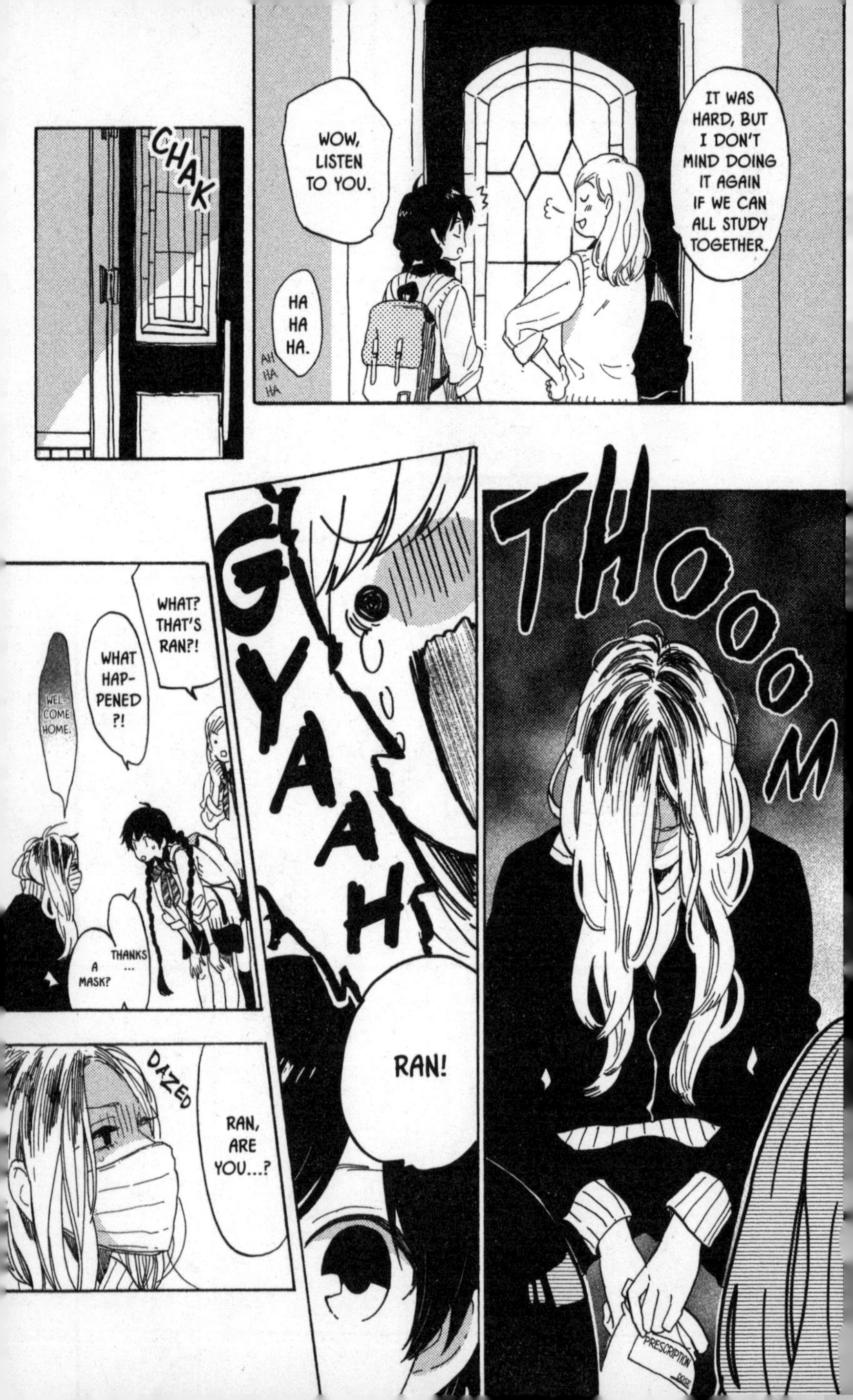
IT WAS HARD, BUT I DON'T MIND DOING IT AGAIN IF WE CAN ALL STUDY TOGETHER.
WOW, LISTEN TO YOU.
HA HA HA.
AH HA HA
CHAK
THOOOM
PRESCRIPTION
DOSE
GYAAAH
RAN!
WHAT? THAT'S RAN?!
WHAT HAP-PENED ?!
WEL-COME HOME.
THANKS ...
A MASK?
DAZED
RAN, ARE YOU...?

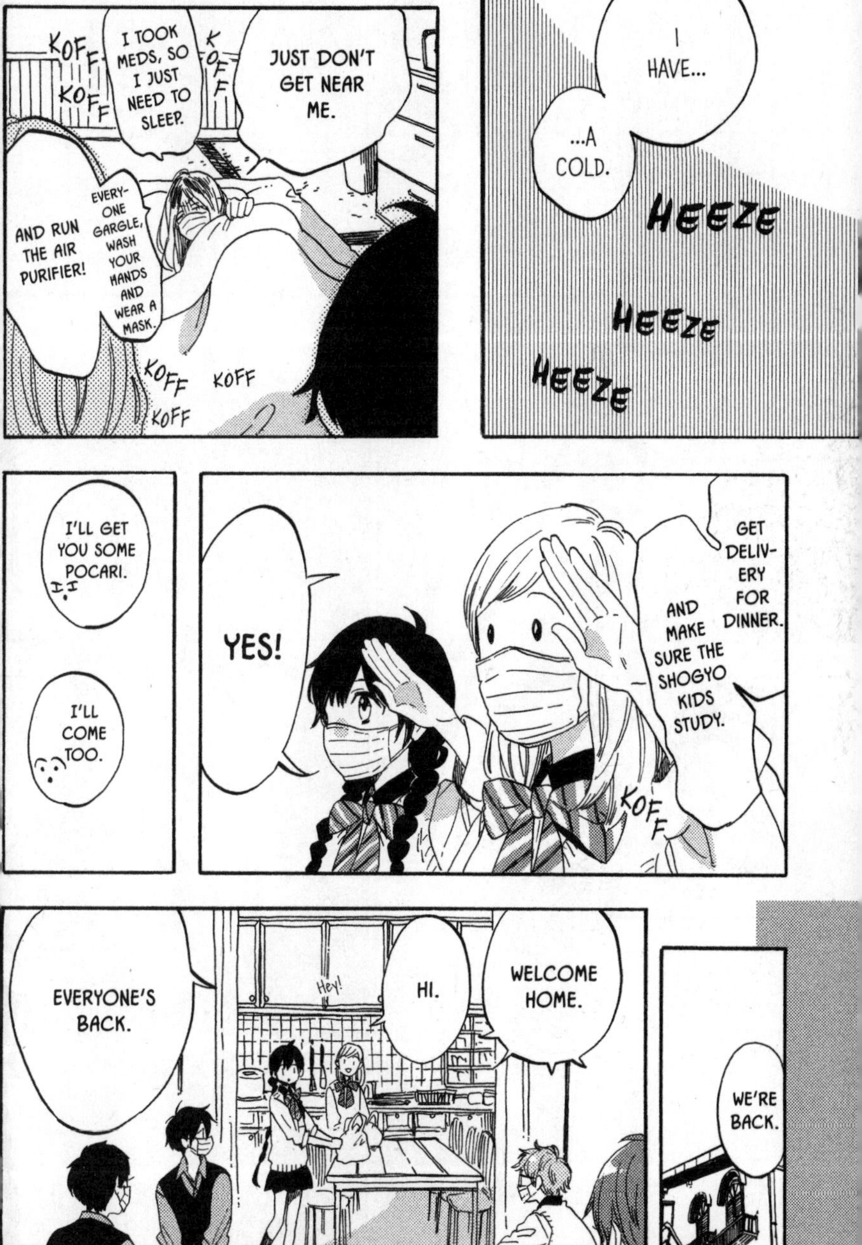
I HAVE...
...A COLD.
HEEZE
HEEZE
HEEZE
JUST DON'T GET NEAR ME.
KOFF
I TOOK MEDS, SO I JUST NEED TO SLEEP.
KOFF
KOFF
EVERYONE GARGLE, WASH YOUR HANDS AND WEAR A MASK.
AND RUN THE AIR PURIFIER!
KOFF
KOFF
KOFF
GET DELIVERY FOR DINNER.
AND MAKE SURE THE SHOGYO KIDS STUDY.
KOFF
YES!
I'LL GET YOU SOME POCARI.
I'LL COME TOO.
WE'RE BACK.
WELCOME HOME.
HI.
Hey!
EVERYONE'S BACK.

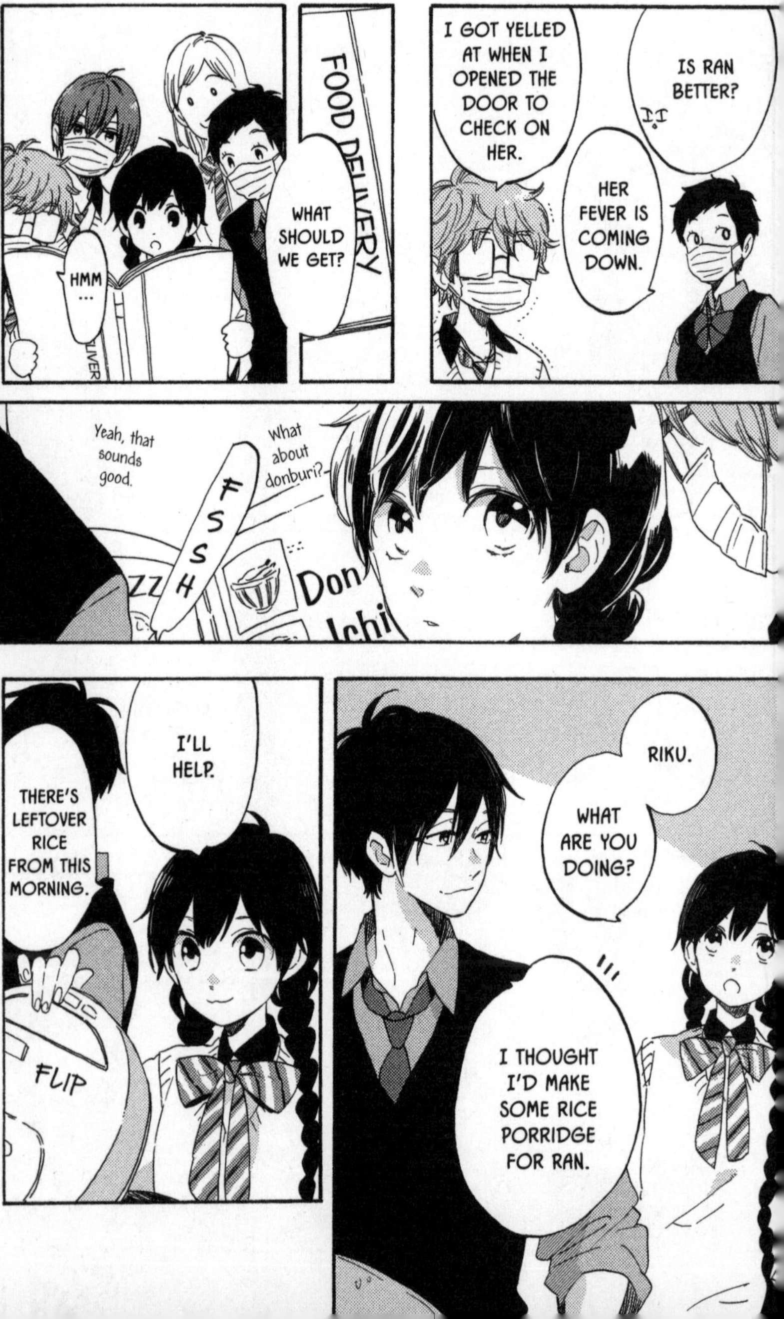
IS RAN BETTER?
HER FEVER IS COMING DOWN.
I GOT YELLED AT WHEN I OPENED THE DOOR TO CHECK ON HER.
FOOD DELIVERY
WHAT SHOULD WE GET?
HMM...
What about donburi?
Yeah, that sounds good.
FSSH
Don Ichi
RIKU.
WHAT ARE YOU DOING?
I THOUGHT I'D MAKE SOME RICE PORRIDGE FOR RAN.
I'LL HELP.
THERE'S LEFTOVER RICE FROM THIS MORNING.
FLIP

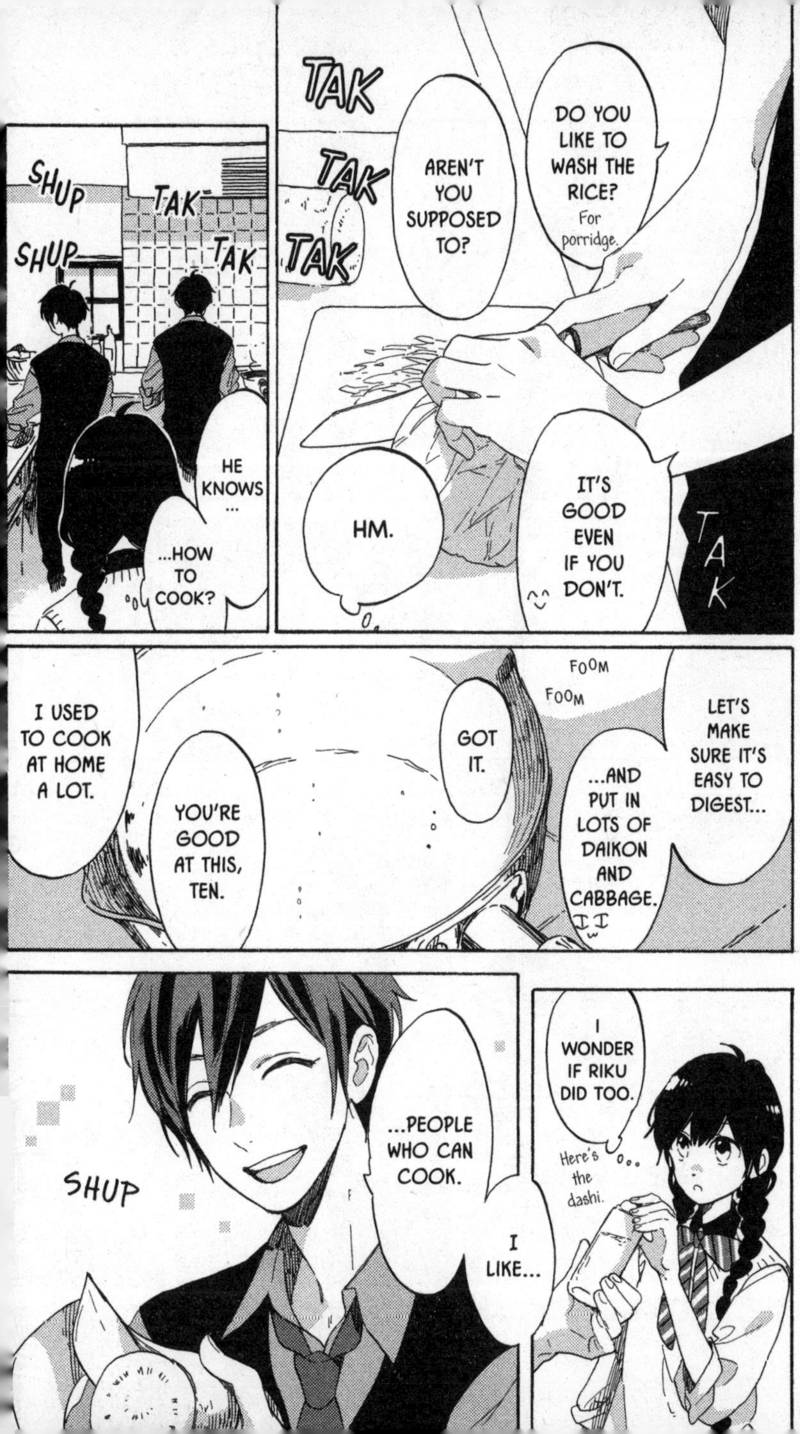
TAK
TAK
TAK
DO YOU LIKE TO WASH THE RICE?
For porridge.
AREN'T YOU SUPPOSED TO?
IT'S GOOD EVEN IF YOU DON'T.
HM.
TAK
SHUP
SHUP
TAK
TAK
HE KNOWS...
...HOW TO COOK?
LET'S MAKE SURE IT'S EASY TO DIGEST...
...AND PUT IN LOTS OF DAIKON AND CABBAGE.
FOOM
FOOM
GOT IT.
YOU'RE GOOD AT THIS, TEN.
I USED TO COOK AT HOME A LOT.
I WONDER IF RIKU DID TOO.
Here's the dashi.
I LIKE...
...PEOPLE WHO CAN COOK.
SHUP

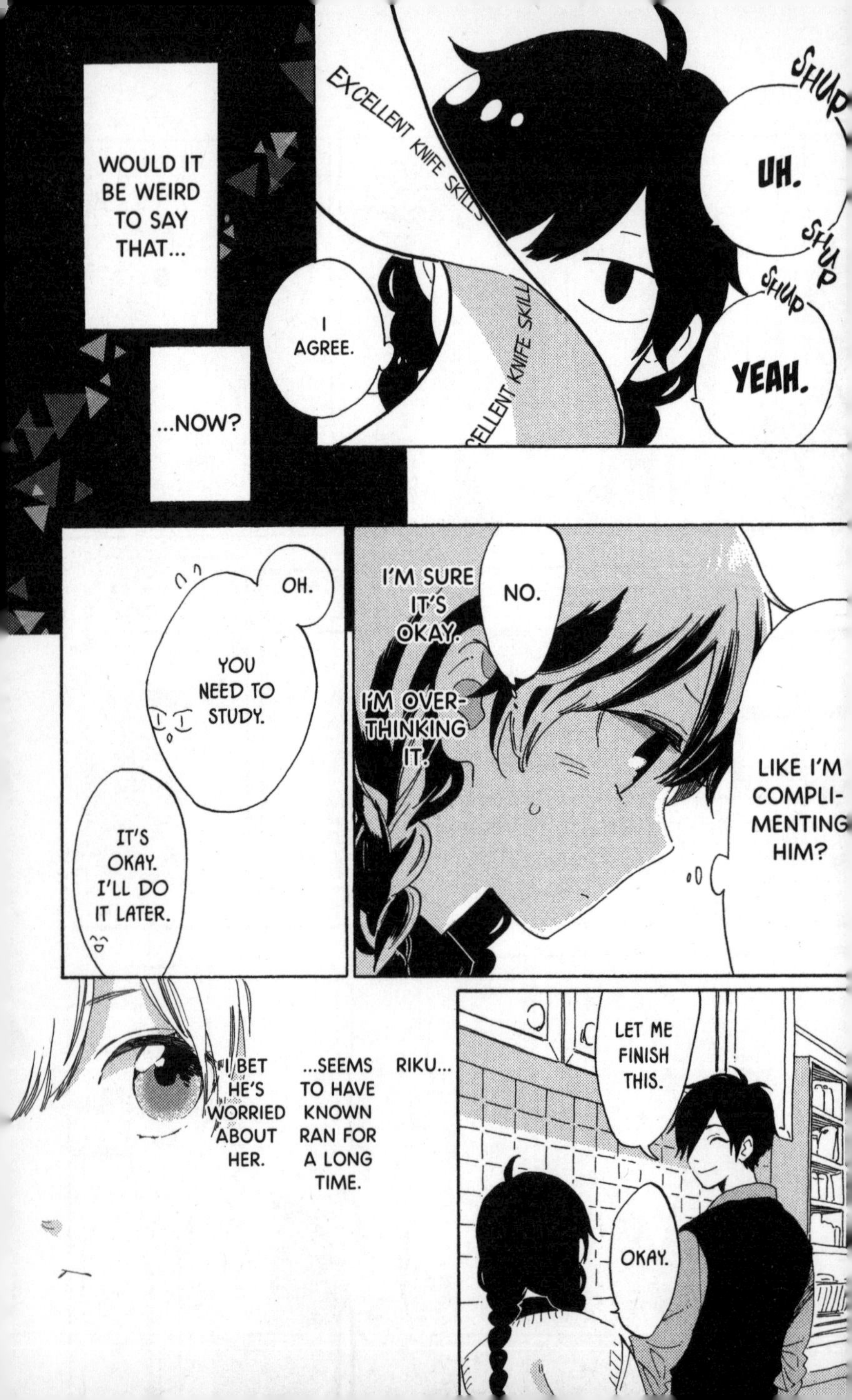
SHUP
UH.
SHUP
SHUP
YEAH.
I AGREE.
EXCELLENT KNIFE SKILLS
EXCELLENT KNIFE SKILL
WOULD IT BE WEIRD TO SAY THAT...
...NOW?
LIKE I'M COMPLIMENTING HIM?
NO.
I'M SURE IT'S OKAY.
I'M OVERTHINKING IT.
OH.
YOU NEED TO STUDY.
IT'S OKAY. I'LL DO IT LATER.
LET ME FINISH THIS.
OKAY.
RIKU...
...SEEMS TO HAVE KNOWN RAN FOR A LONG TIME.
I BET HE'S WORRIED ABOUT HER.

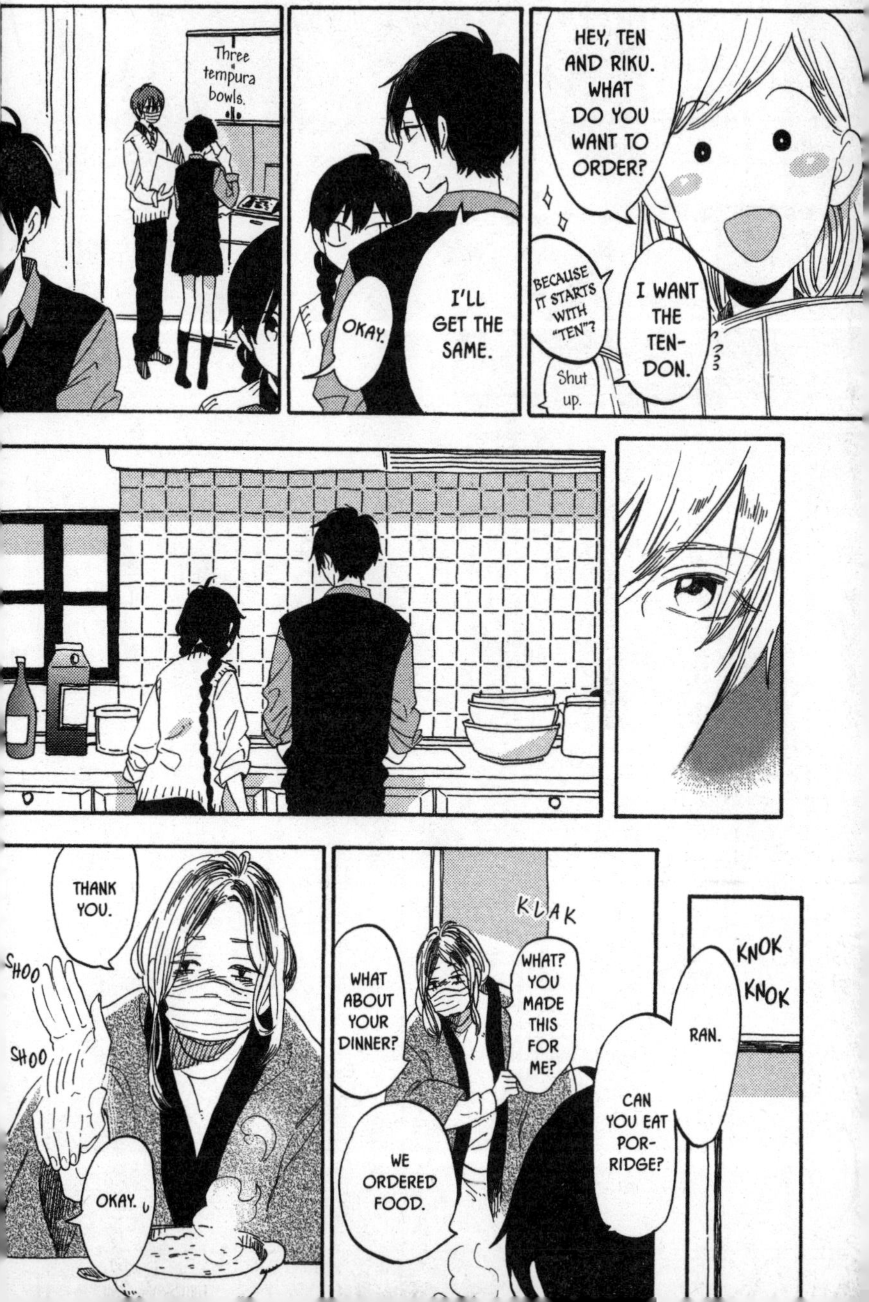
HEY, TEN AND RIKU. WHAT DO YOU WANT TO ORDER?
I WANT THE TEN-DON.
BECAUSE IT STARTS WITH "TEN"?
Shut up.
I'LL GET THE SAME.
OKAY.
Three tempura bowls.
KNOK KNOK
RAN.
CAN YOU EAT POR-RIDGE?
KLAK
WHAT? YOU MADE THIS FOR ME?
WHAT ABOUT YOUR DINNER?
WE ORDERED FOOD.
THANK YOU.
SHOO
SHOO
OKAY.

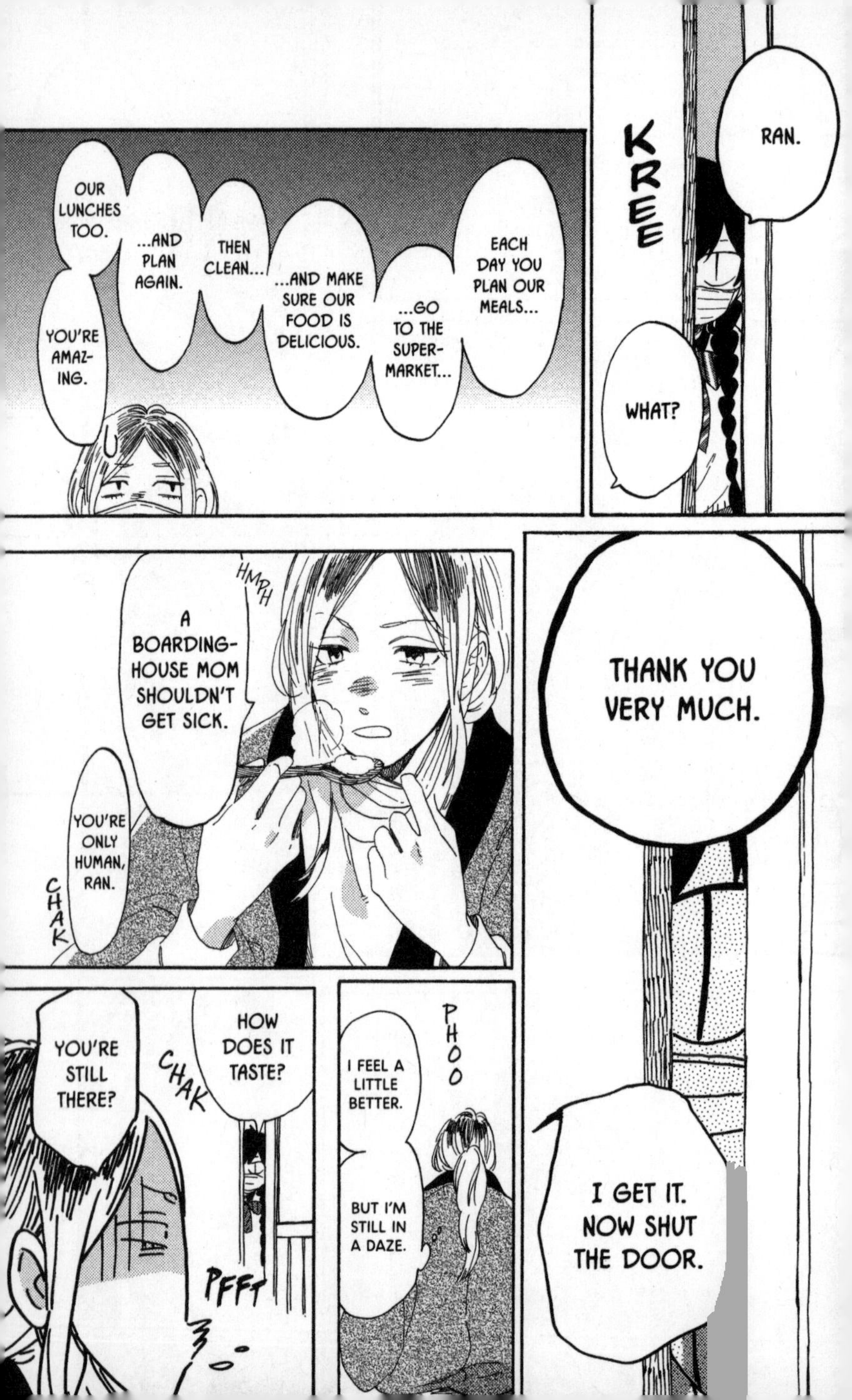
RAN.
KREE
WHAT?
EACH DAY YOU PLAN OUR MEALS...
...GO TO THE SUPER-MARKET...
...AND MAKE SURE OUR FOOD IS DELICIOUS.
THEN CLEAN...
...AND PLAN AGAIN.
OUR LUNCHES TOO.
YOU'RE AMAZ-ING.
THANK YOU VERY MUCH.
I GET IT. NOW SHUT THE DOOR.
HMPH
A BOARDING-HOUSE MOM SHOULDN'T GET SICK.
YOU'RE ONLY HUMAN, RAN.
CHAK
PHOO
I FEEL A LITTLE BETTER.
BUT I'M STILL IN A DAZE.
HOW DOES IT TASTE?
CHAK
YOU'RE STILL THERE?
PFFT

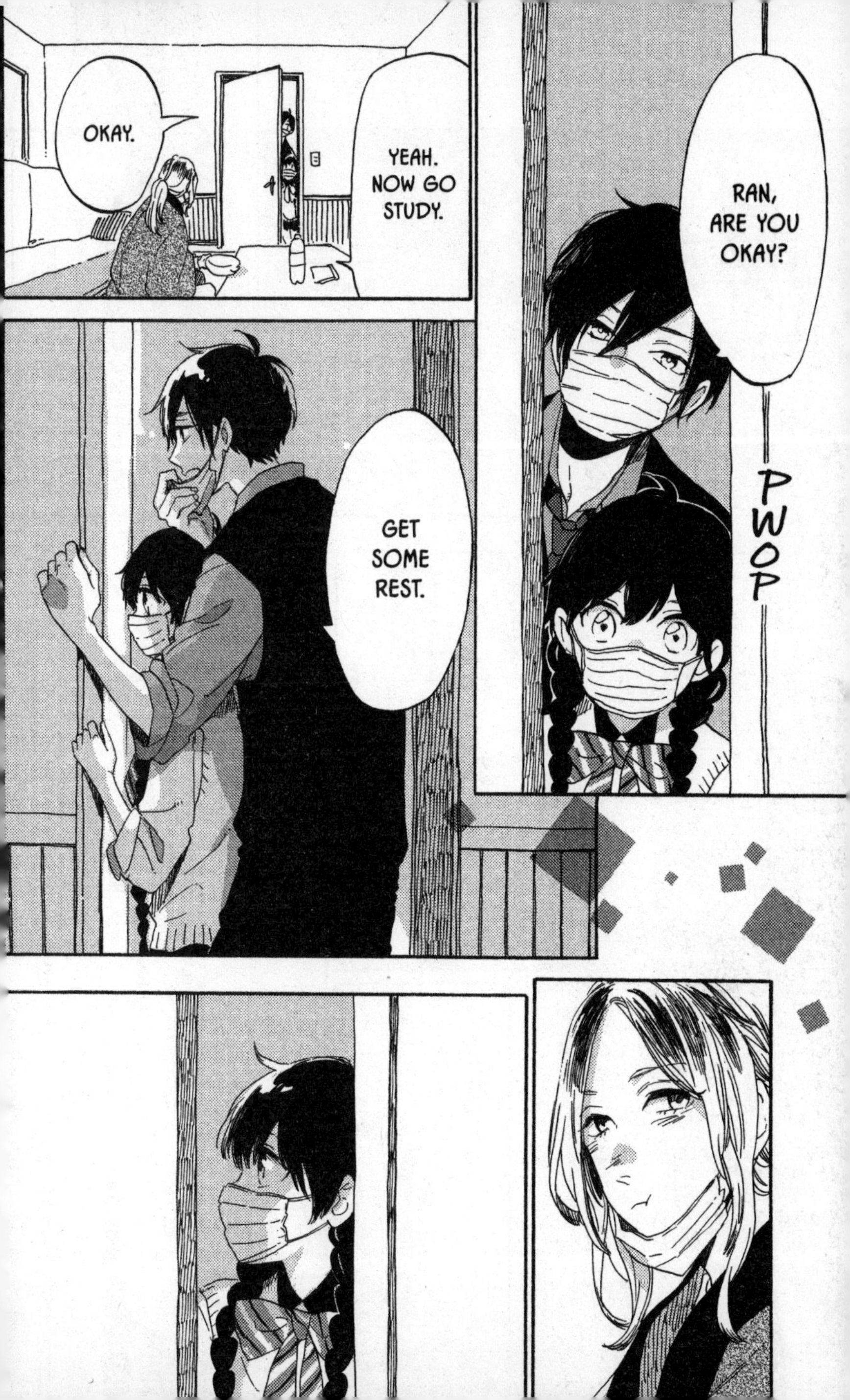
RAN, ARE YOU OKAY?
PWOP
YEAH. NOW GO STUDY.
OKAY.
GET SOME REST.

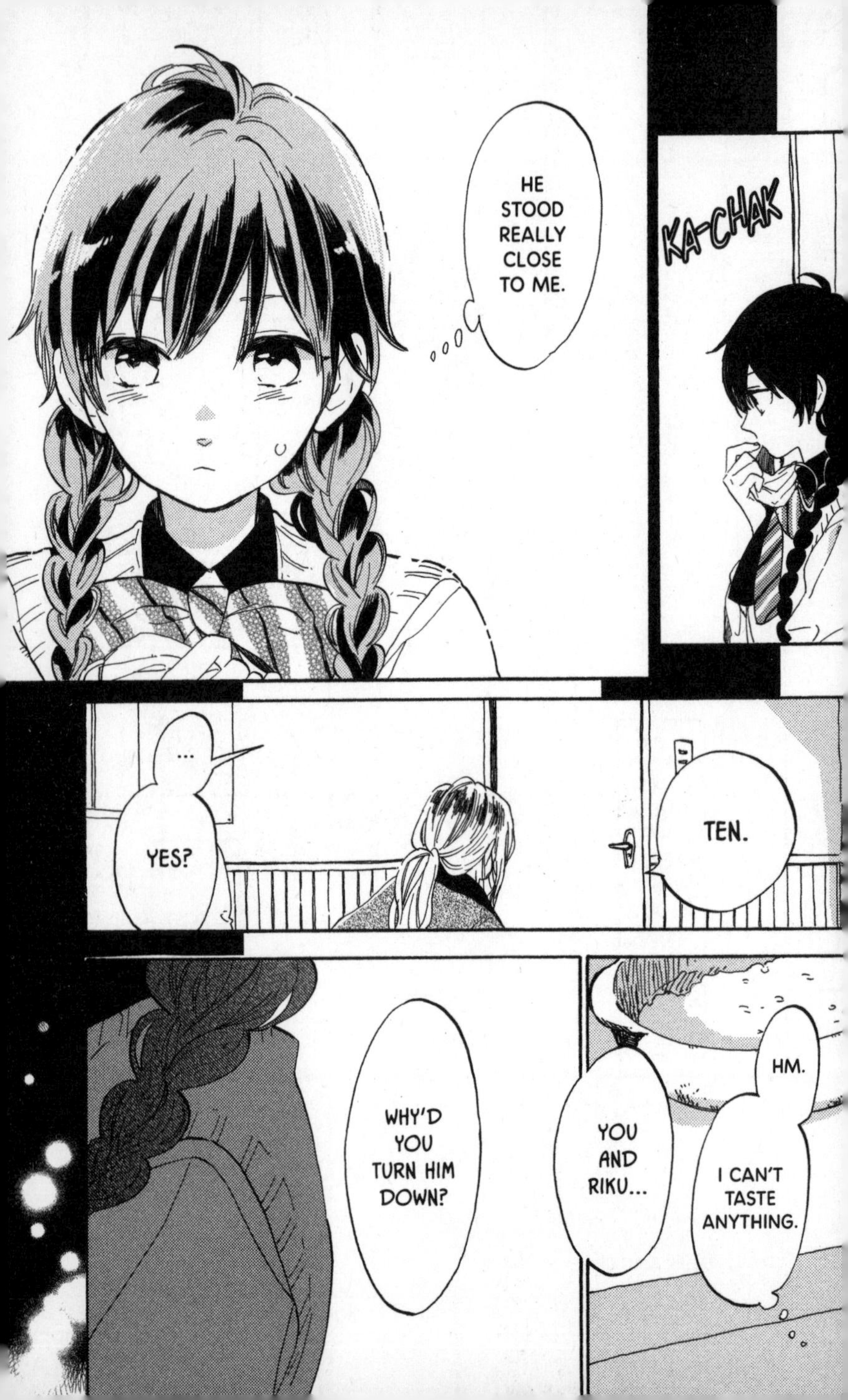
KA-CHAK
HE STOOD REALLY CLOSE TO ME.
TEN.
...
YES?
HM.
I CAN'T TASTE ANYTHING.
YOU AND RIKU...
WHY'D YOU TURN HIM DOWN?

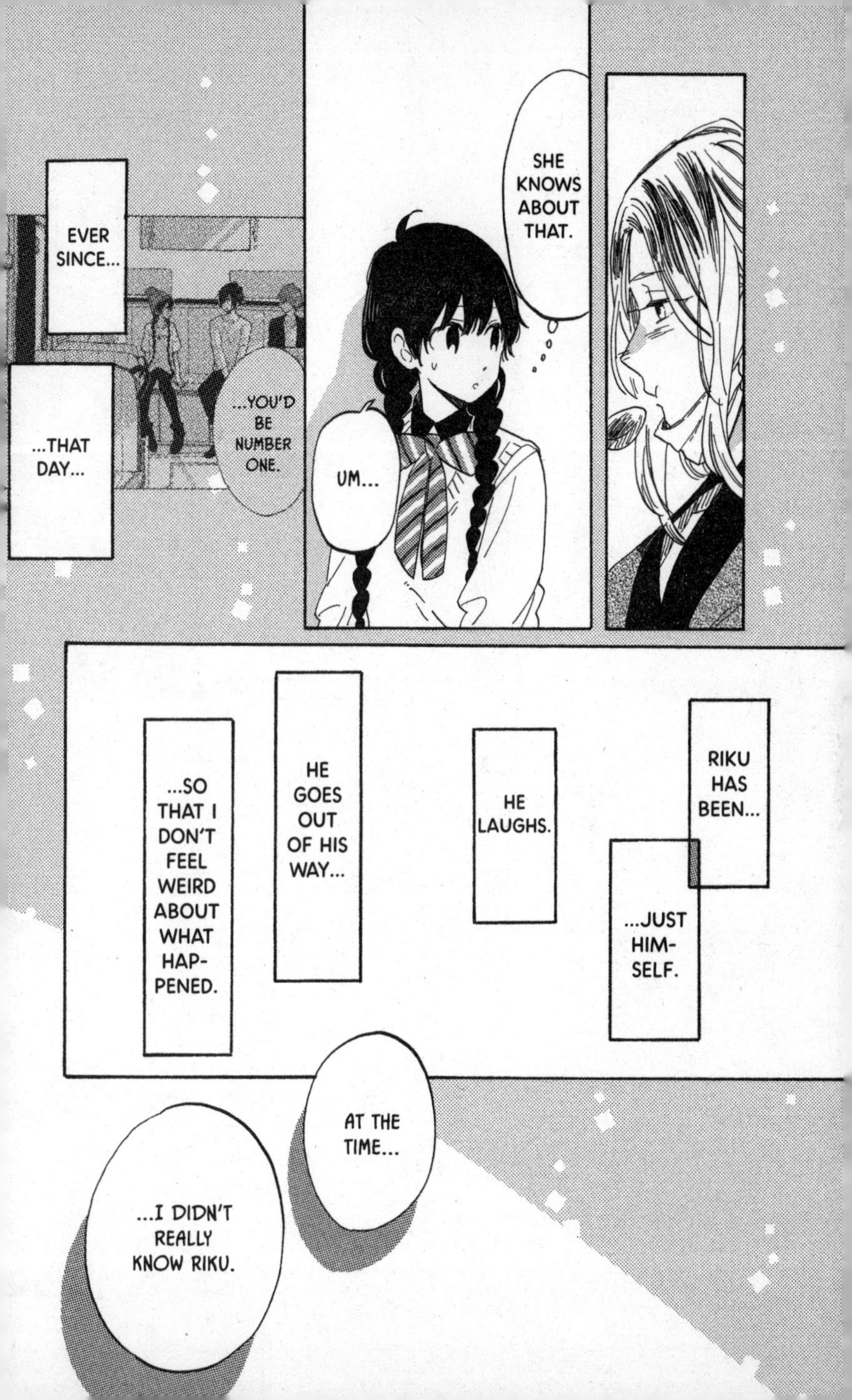
SHE KNOWS ABOUT THAT.
UM...
EVER SINCE...
...YOU'D BE NUMBER ONE.
...THAT DAY...
RIKU HAS BEEN...
...JUST HIMSELF.
HE LAUGHS.
HE GOES OUT OF HIS WAY...
...SO THAT I DON'T FEEL WEIRD ABOUT WHAT HAPPENED.
AT THE TIME...
...I DIDN'T REALLY KNOW RIKU.

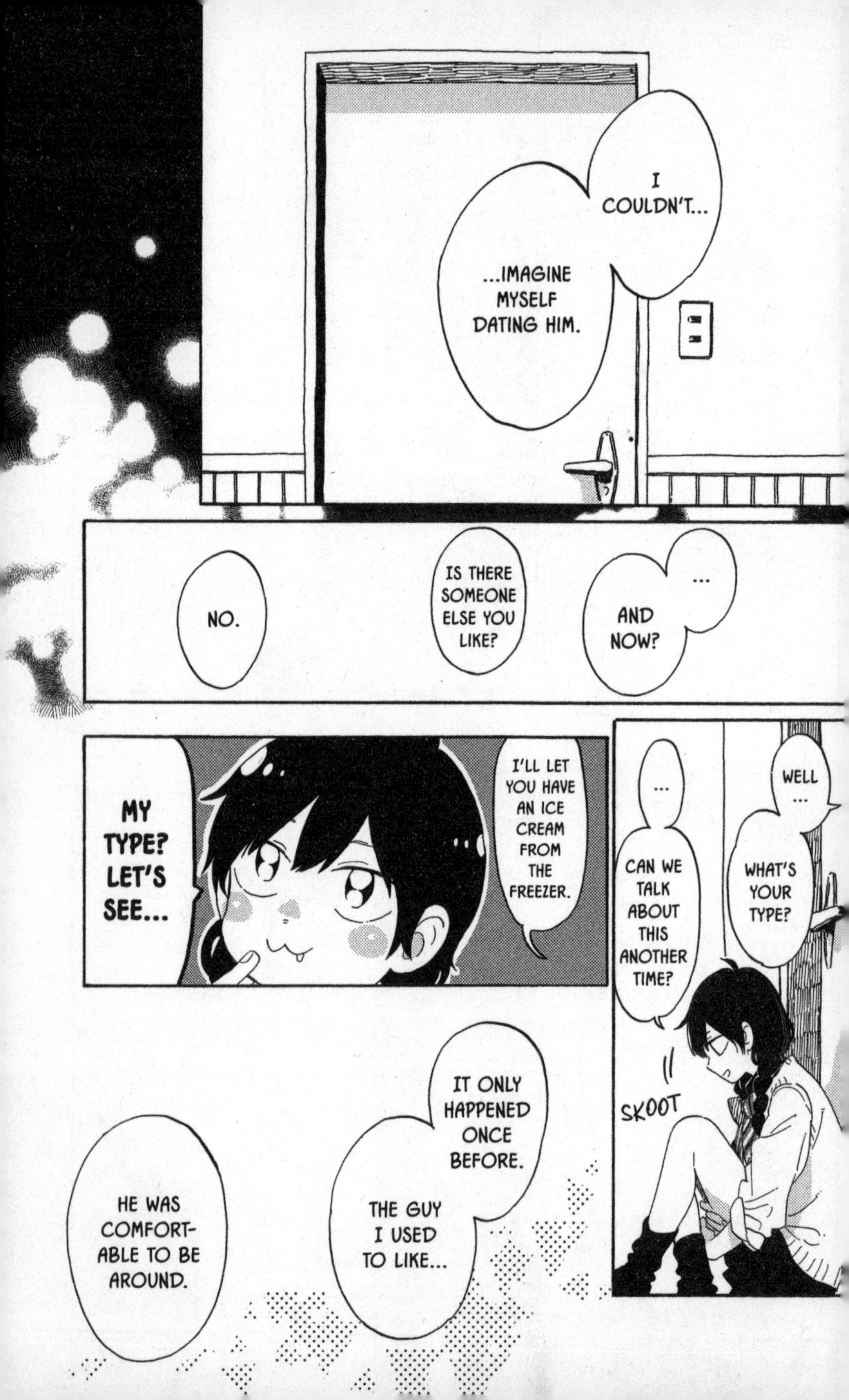
I COULDN'T...
...IMAGINE MYSELF DATING HIM.
...
AND NOW?
IS THERE SOMEONE ELSE YOU LIKE?
NO.
WELL ...
WHAT'S YOUR TYPE?
...
CAN WE TALK ABOUT THIS ANOTHER TIME?
SKOOT
I'LL LET YOU HAVE AN ICE CREAM FROM THE FREEZER.
MY TYPE? LET'S SEE...
IT ONLY HAPPENED ONCE BEFORE.
THE GUY I USED TO LIKE...
HE WAS COMFORT-ABLE TO BE AROUND.

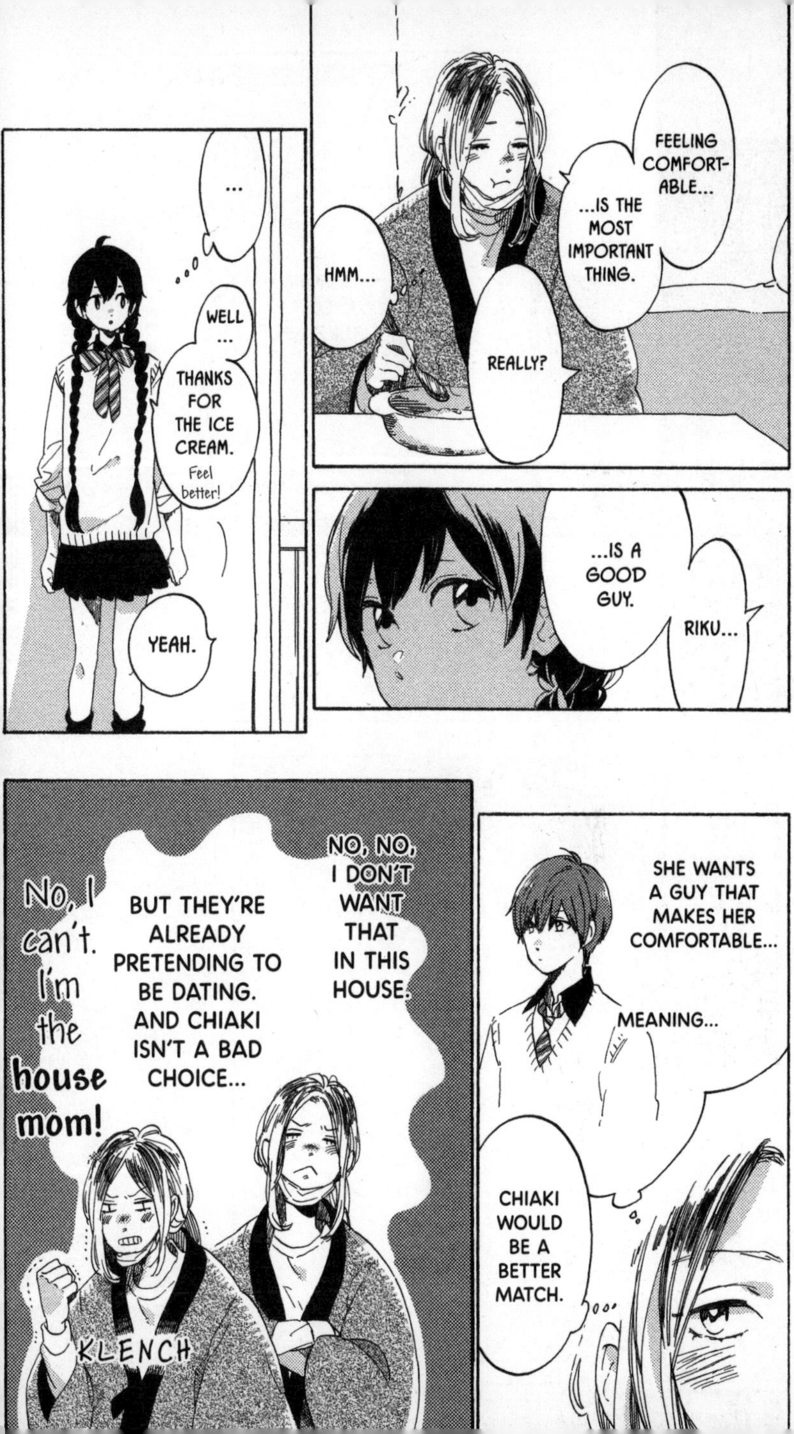
FEELING COMFORTABLE...
...IS THE MOST IMPORTANT THING.
HMM...
REALLY?
RIKU...
...IS A GOOD GUY.
...
WELL...
THANKS FOR THE ICE CREAM.
Feel better!
YEAH.
SHE WANTS A GUY THAT MAKES HER COMFORTABLE...
MEANING...
CHIAKI WOULD BE A BETTER MATCH.
NO, NO, I DON'T WANT THAT IN THIS HOUSE.
BUT THEY'RE ALREADY PRETENDING TO BE DATING. AND CHIAKI ISN'T A BAD CHOICE...
No, I can't. I'm the house mom!
KLENCH

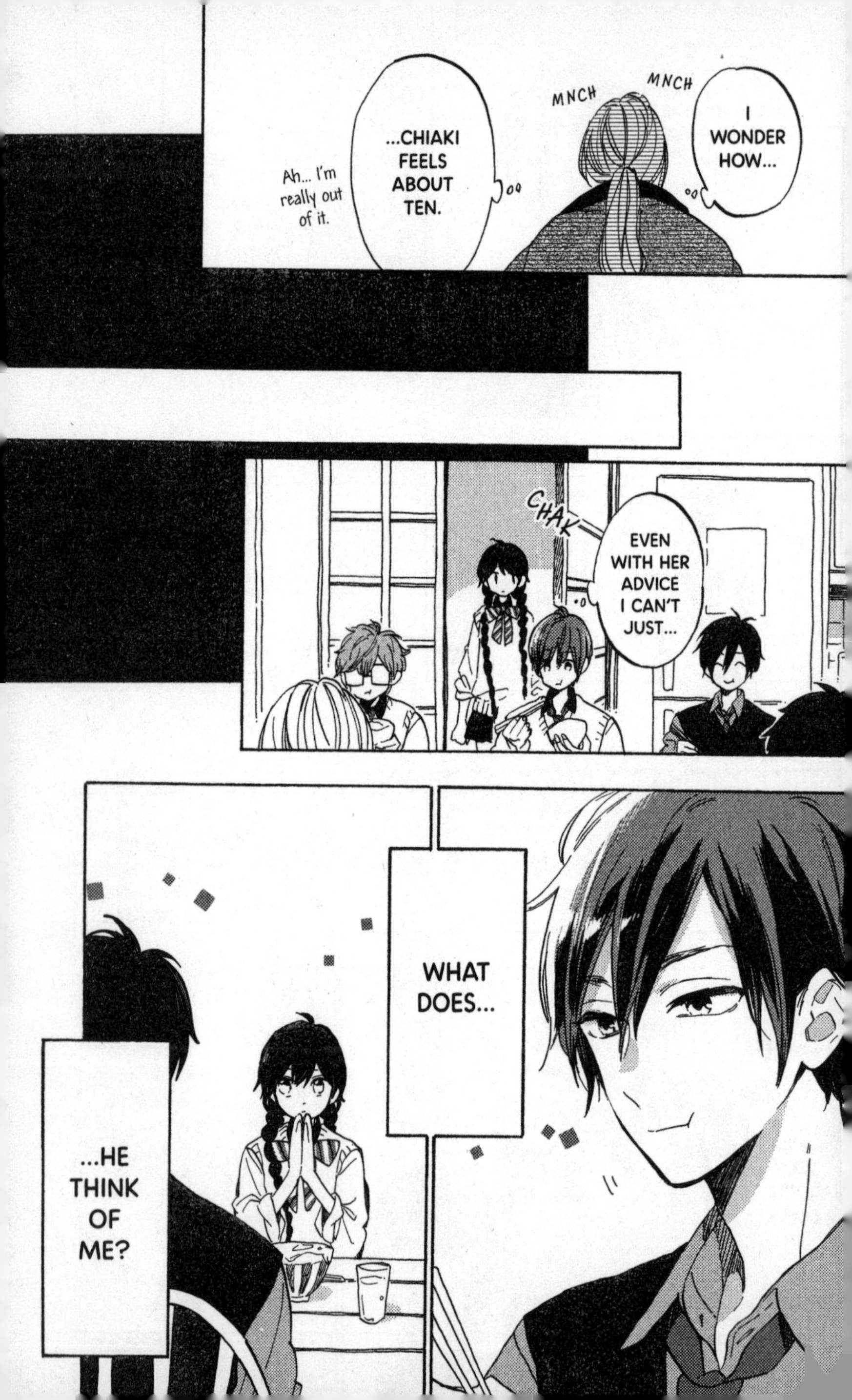
MNCH
MNCH
I WONDER HOW...
...CHIAKI FEELS ABOUT TEN.
Ah... I'm really out of it.
CHAK
EVEN WITH HER ADVICE I CAN'T JUST...
WHAT DOES...
...HE THINK OF ME?

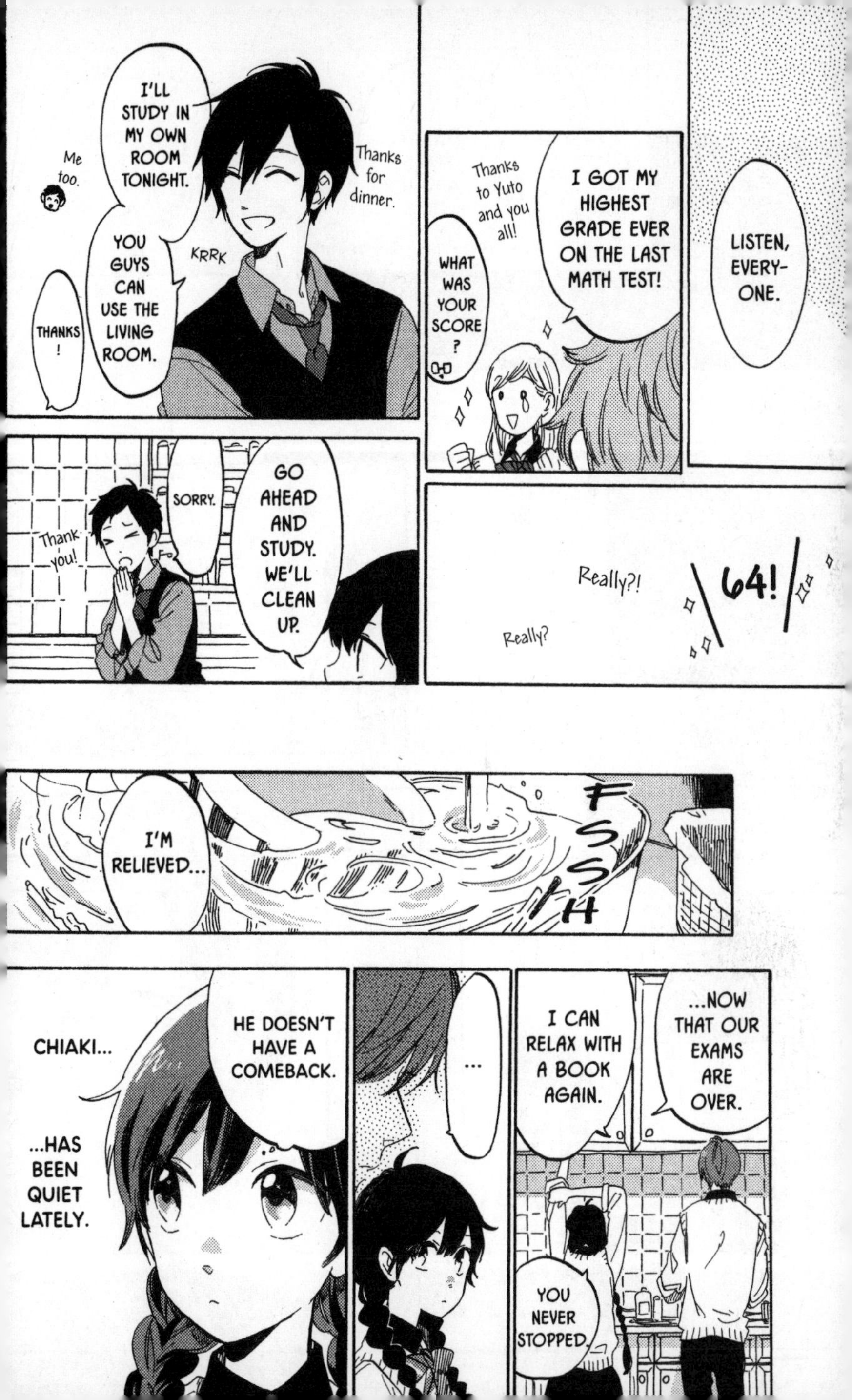
LISTEN, EVERYONE.
I GOT MY HIGHEST GRADE EVER ON THE LAST MATH TEST!
Thanks to Yuto and you all!
WHAT WAS YOUR SCORE?
64!
Really?!
Really?
I'LL STUDY IN MY OWN ROOM TONIGHT.
Thanks for dinner.
KRRK
YOU GUYS CAN USE THE LIVING ROOM.
Me too.
THANKS!
GO AHEAD AND STUDY. WE'LL CLEAN UP.
SORRY.
Thank you!
FSSSH
I'M RELIEVED...
...NOW THAT OUR EXAMS ARE OVER.
I CAN RELAX WITH A BOOK AGAIN.
YOU NEVER STOPPED.
...
HE DOESN'T HAVE A COMEBACK.
CHIAKI...
...HAS BEEN QUIET LATELY.

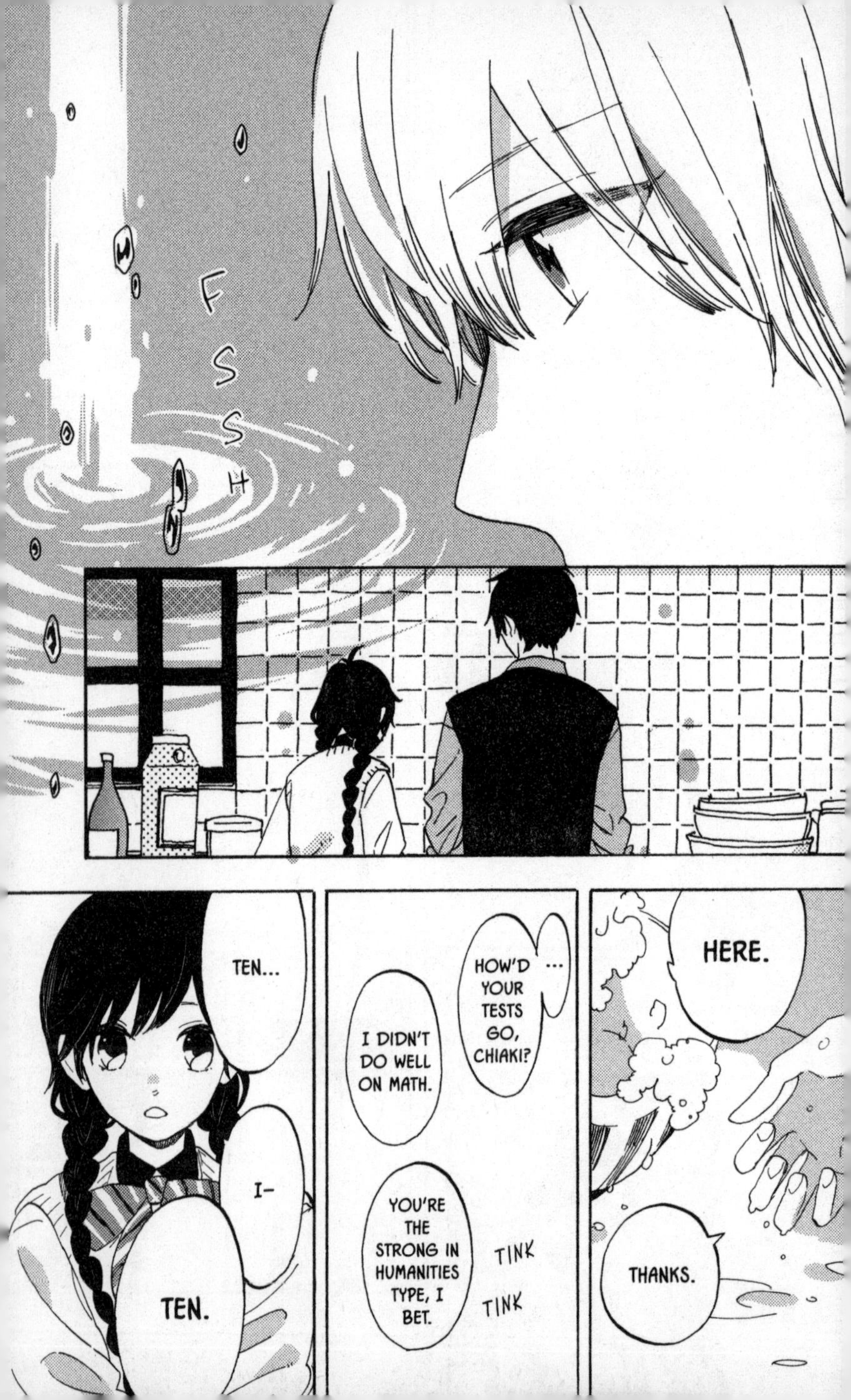
FSSH
HERE.
THANKS.
...
HOW'D YOUR TESTS GO, CHIAKI?
I DIDN'T DO WELL ON MATH.
TINK
YOU'RE THE STRONG IN HUMANITIES TYPE, I BET.
TINK
TEN...
I-
TEN.

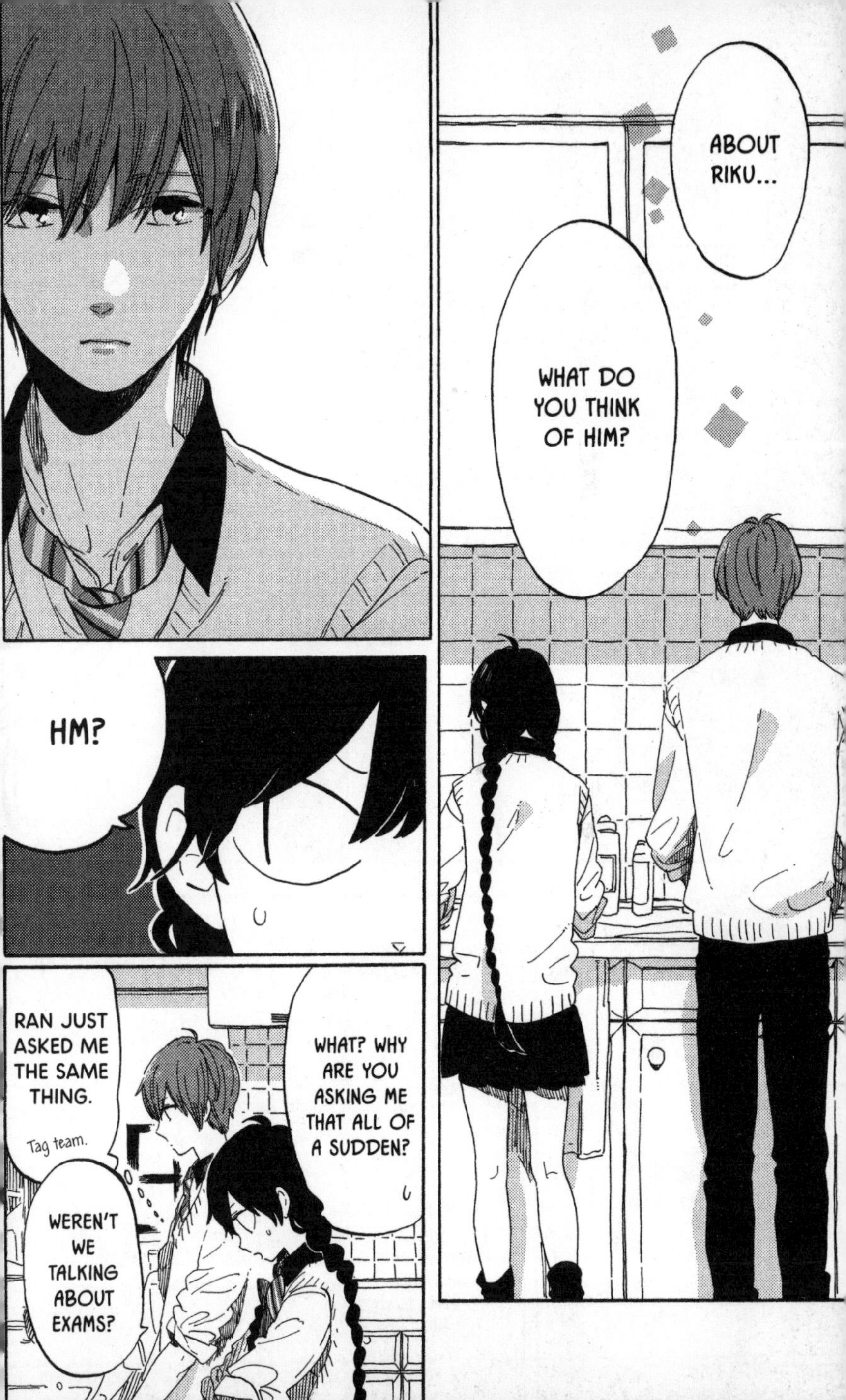
ABOUT RIKU...
WHAT DO YOU THINK OF HIM?
HM?
WHAT? WHY ARE YOU ASKING ME THAT ALL OF A SUDDEN?
RAN JUST ASKED ME THE SAME THING.
Tag team.
WEREN'T WE TALKING ABOUT EXAMS?

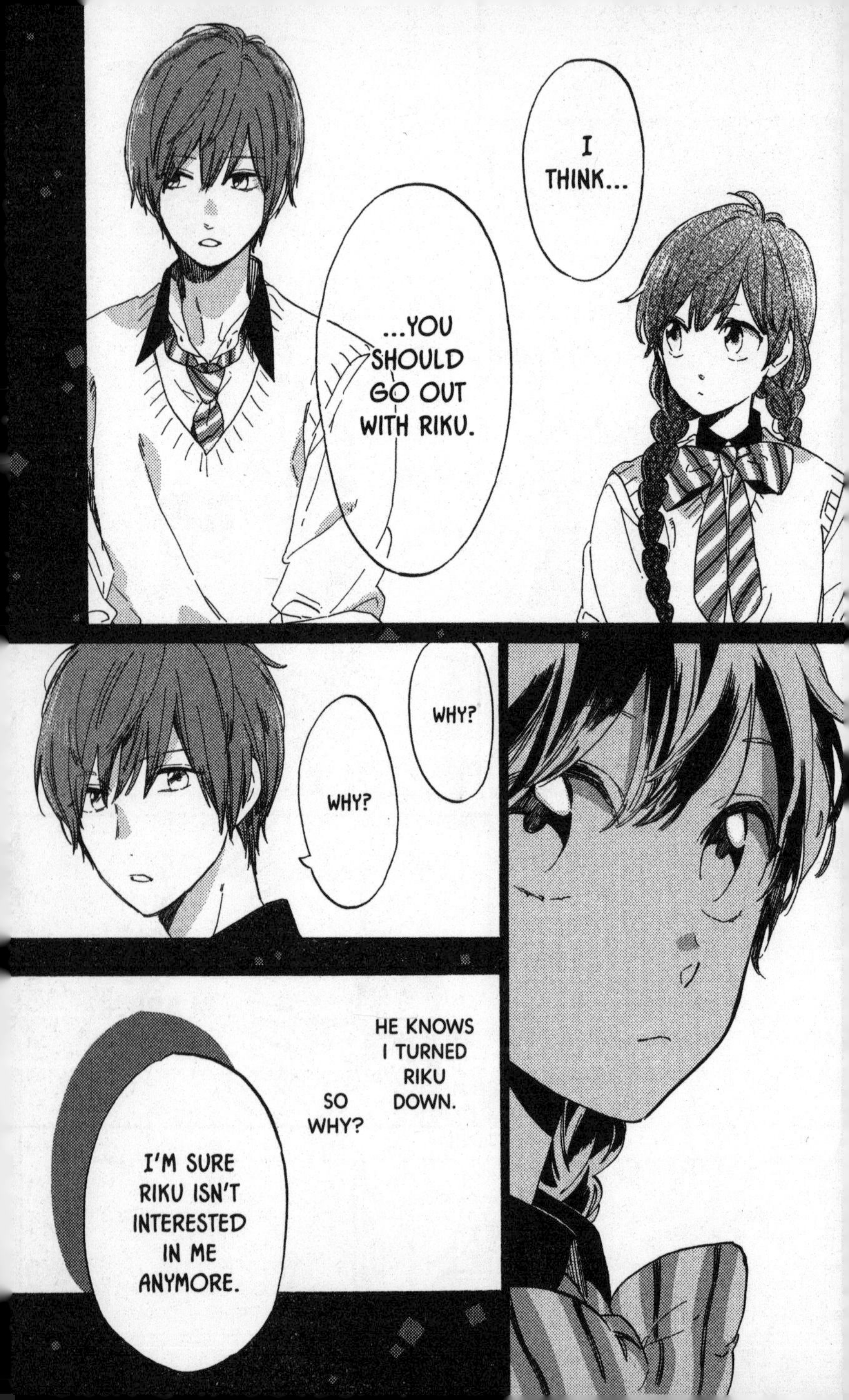
I THINK...
...YOU SHOULD GO OUT WITH RIKU.
WHY?
WHY?
HE KNOWS I TURNED RIKU DOWN.
SO WHY?
I'M SURE RIKU ISN'T INTERESTED IN ME ANYMORE.

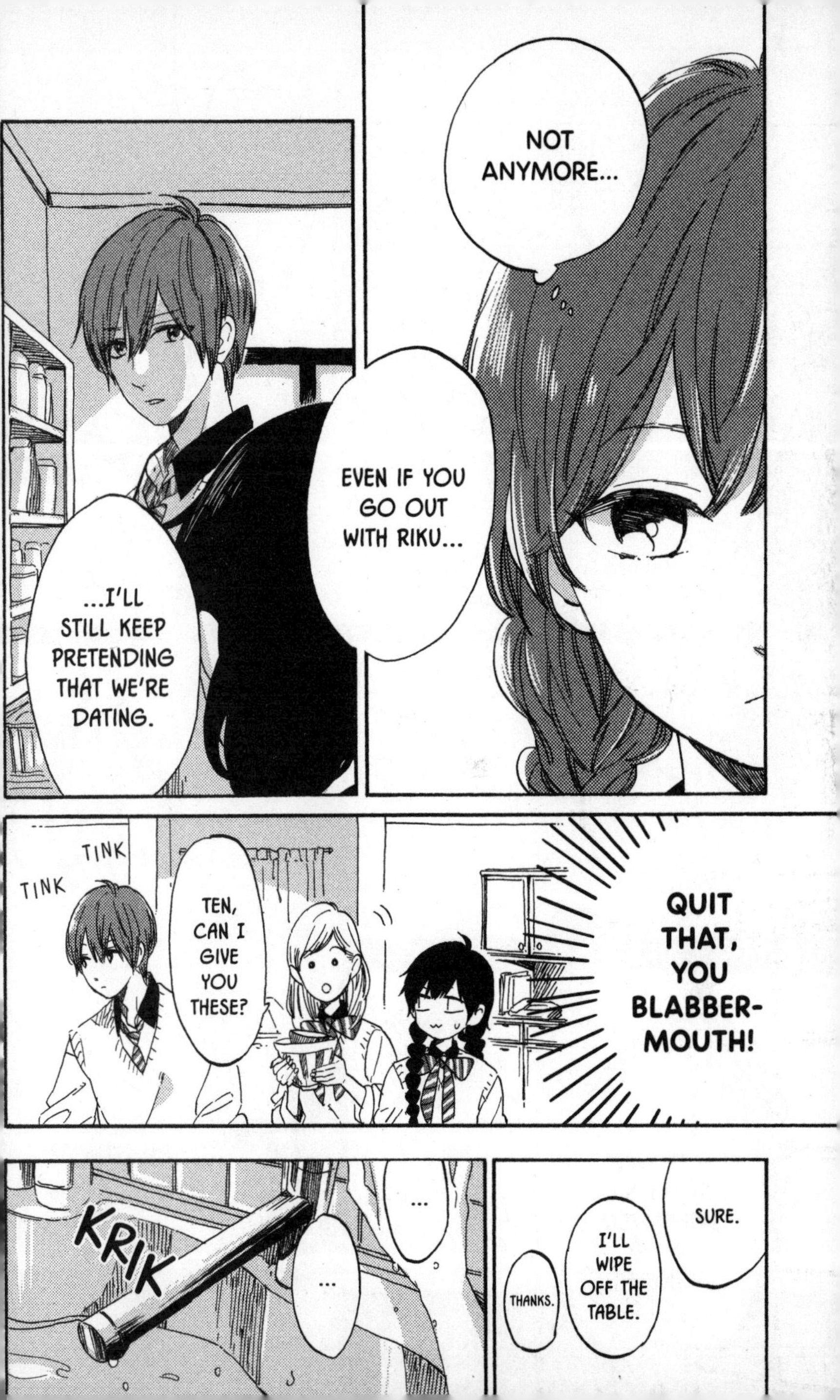
NOT ANYMORE...
EVEN IF YOU GO OUT WITH RIKU...
...I'LL STILL KEEP PRETENDING THAT WE'RE DATING.
QUIT THAT, YOU BLABBER-MOUTH!
TINK
TINK
TEN, CAN I GIVE YOU THESE?
SURE.
I'LL WIPE OFF THE TABLE.
THANKS.
...
...
KRIK

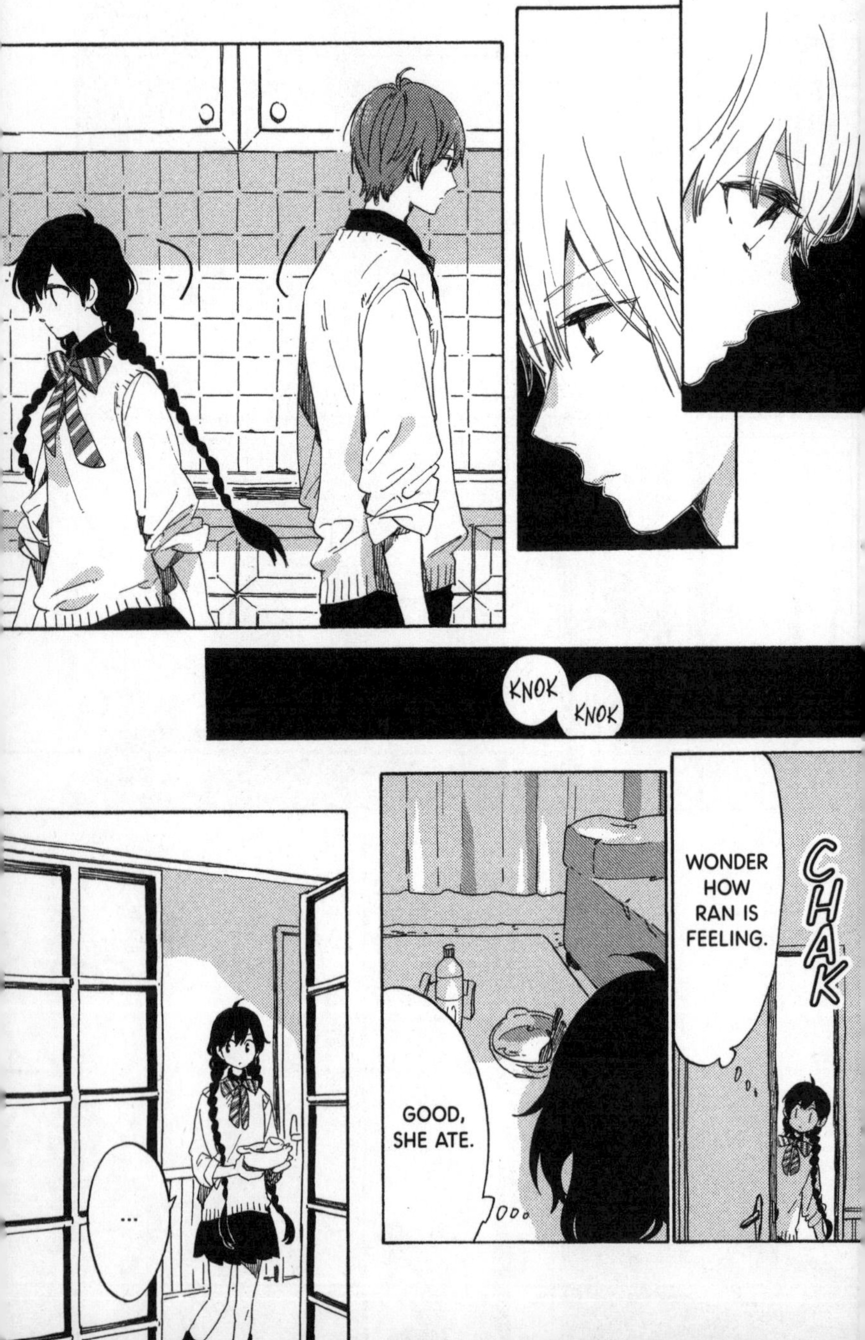
KNOK
KNOK
CHAK
WONDER HOW RAN IS FEELING.
GOOD, SHE ATE.
...

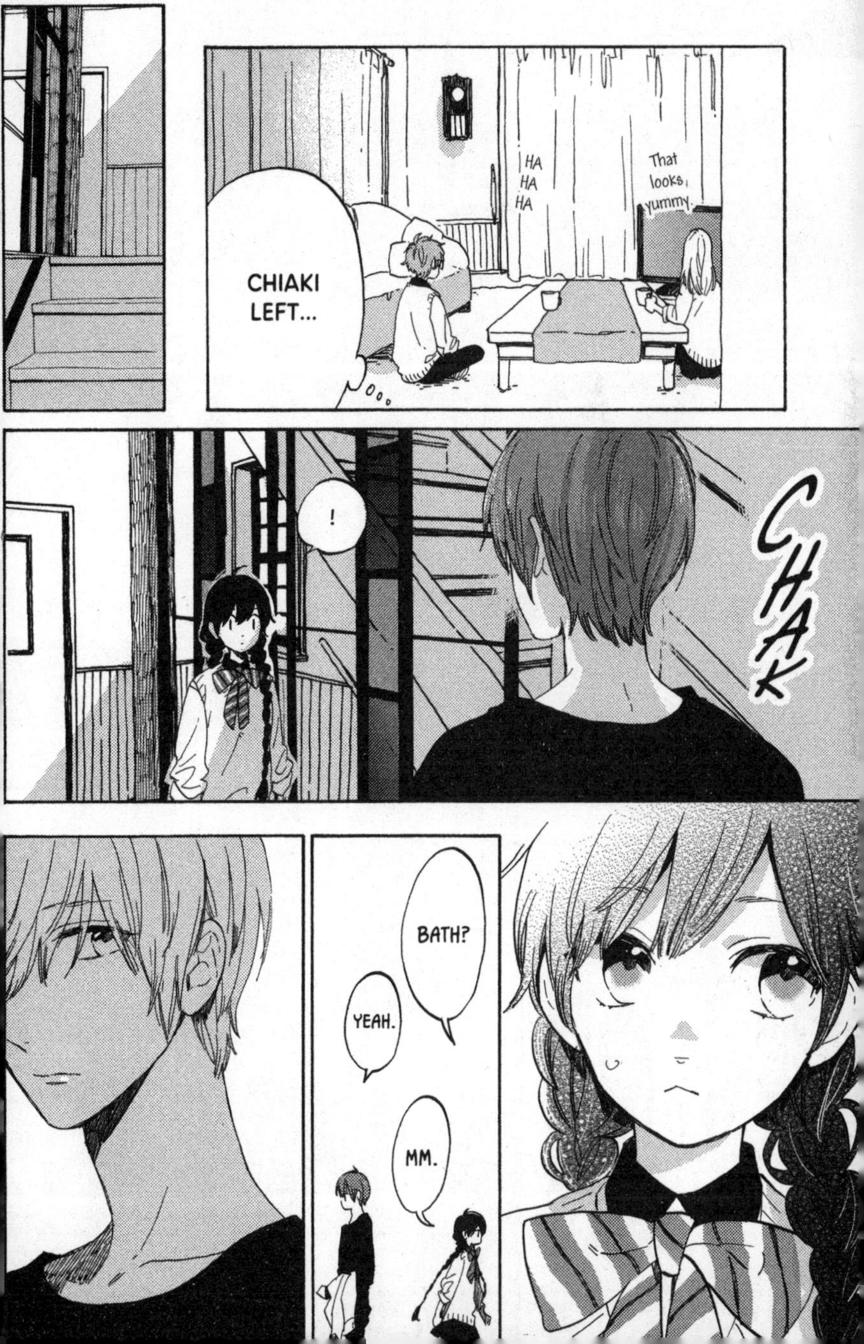
That looks yummy.
HA HA HA
CHIAKI LEFT...
CHAK
!
BATH?
YEAH.
MM.

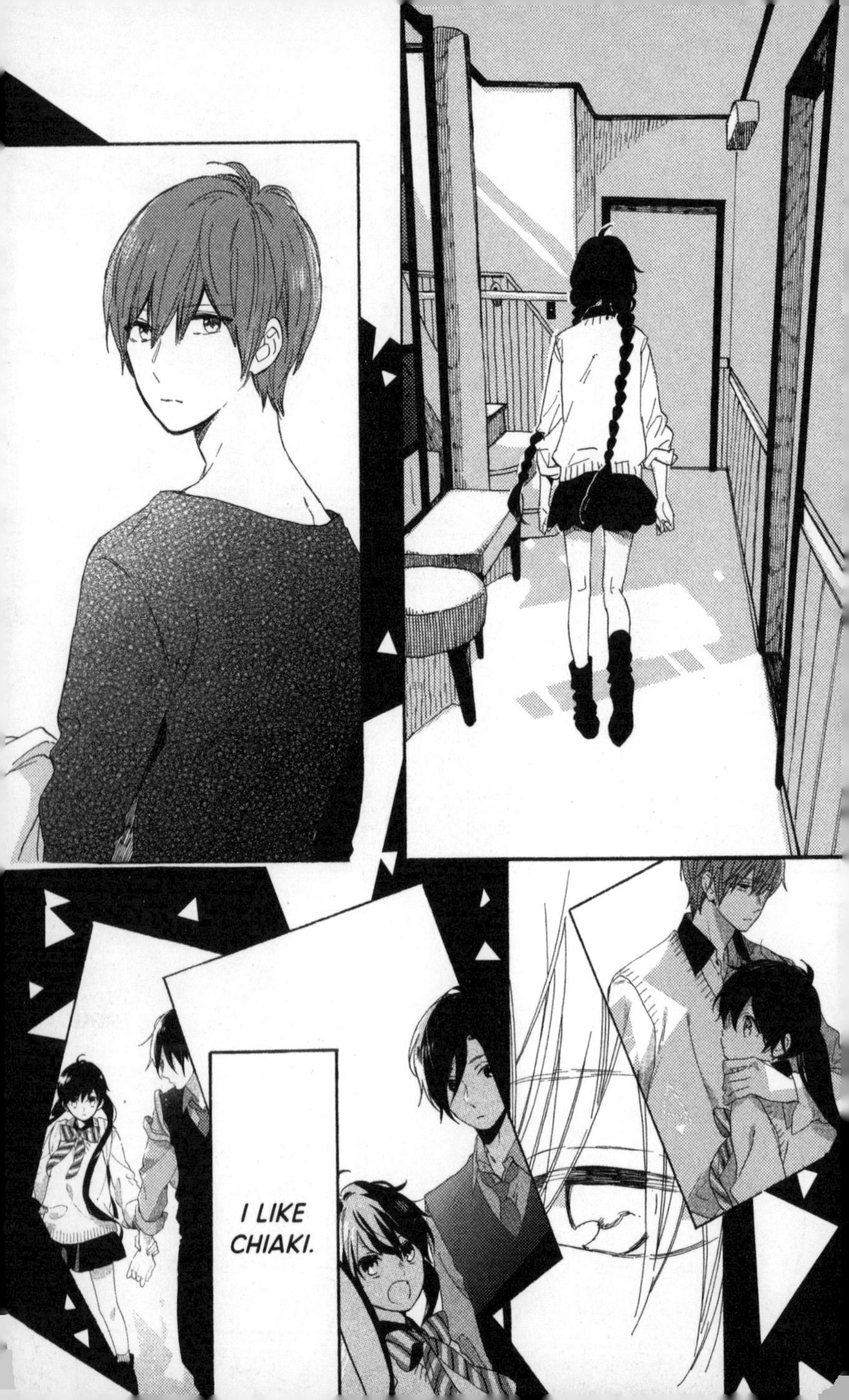
I LIKE CHIAKI.

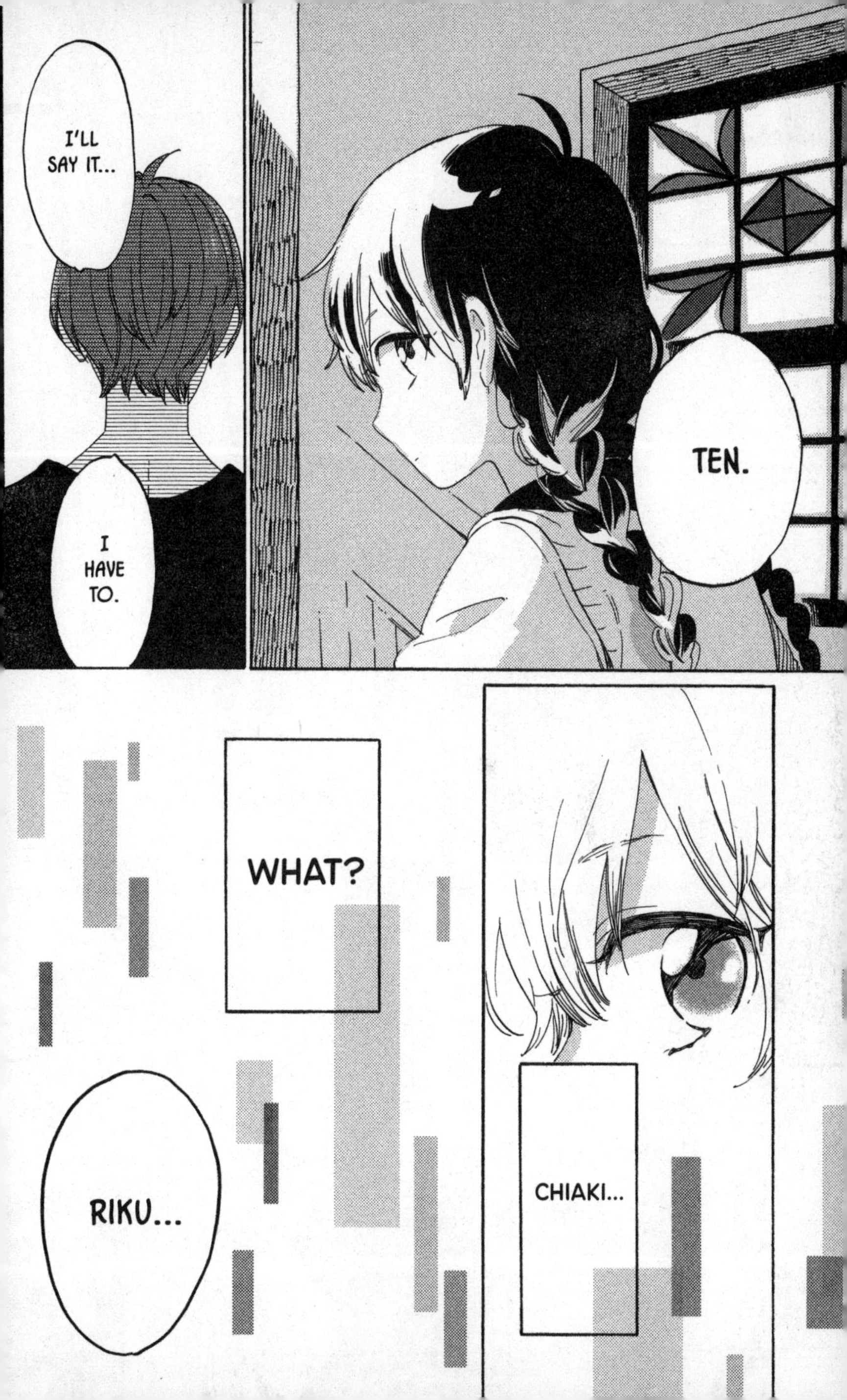
TEN.
I'LL SAY IT...
I HAVE TO.
CHIAKI...
WHAT?
RIKU...

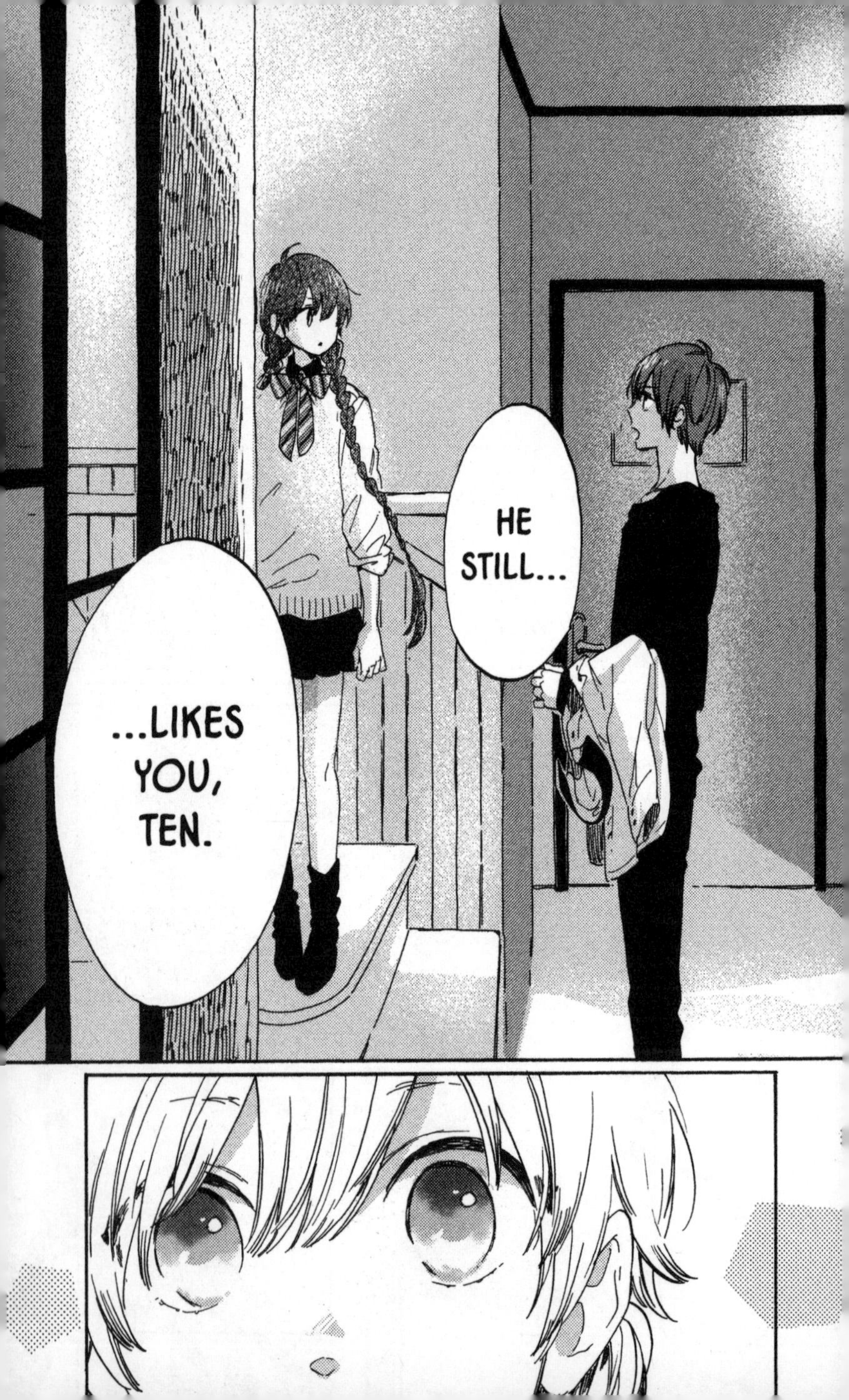
HE STILL...
...LIKES YOU, TEN.

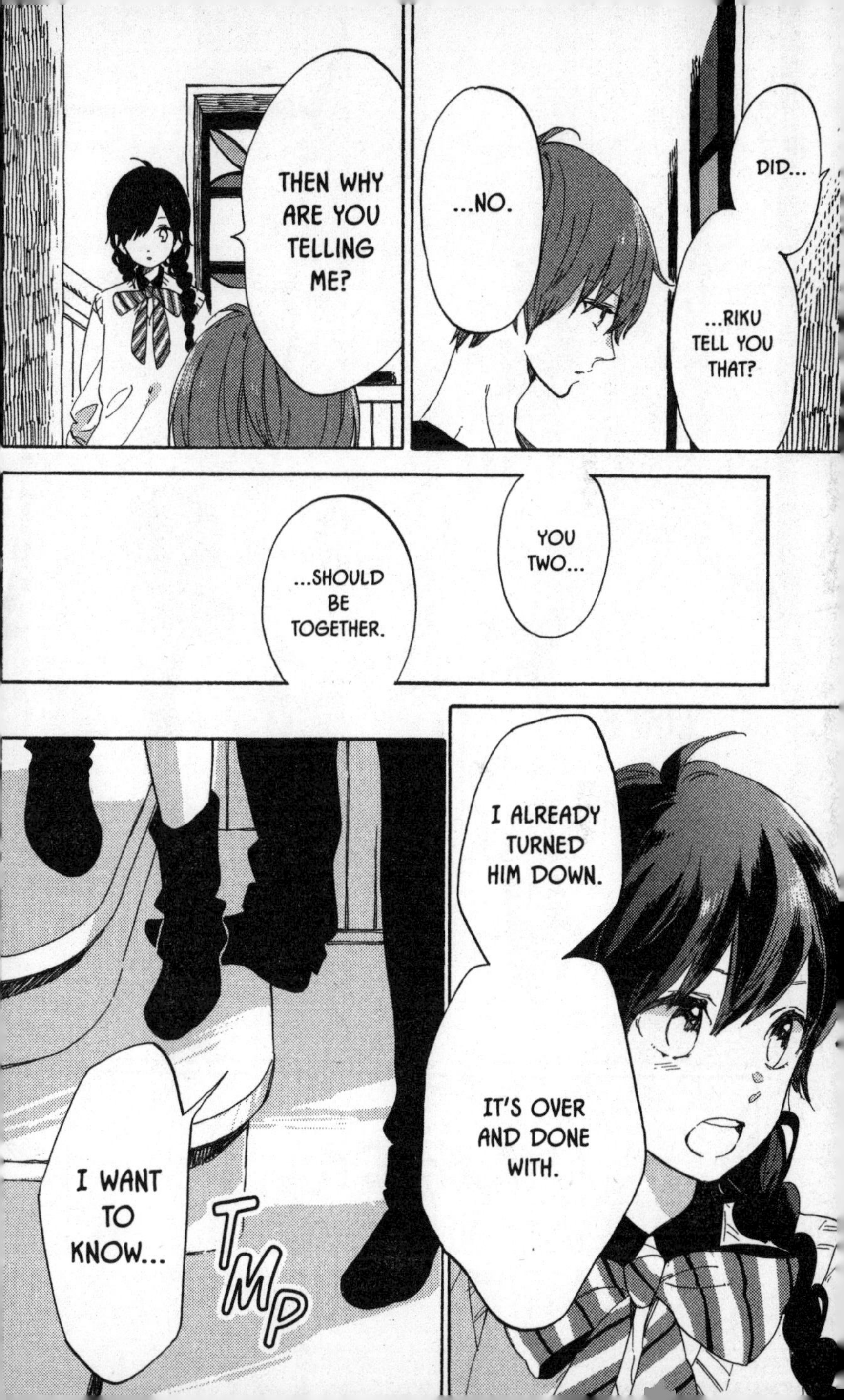
DID...
...RIKU TELL YOU THAT?
...NO.
THEN WHY ARE YOU TELLING ME?
YOU TWO...
...SHOULD BE TOGETHER.
I ALREADY TURNED HIM DOWN.
IT'S OVER AND DONE WITH.
I WANT TO KNOW...
TMP

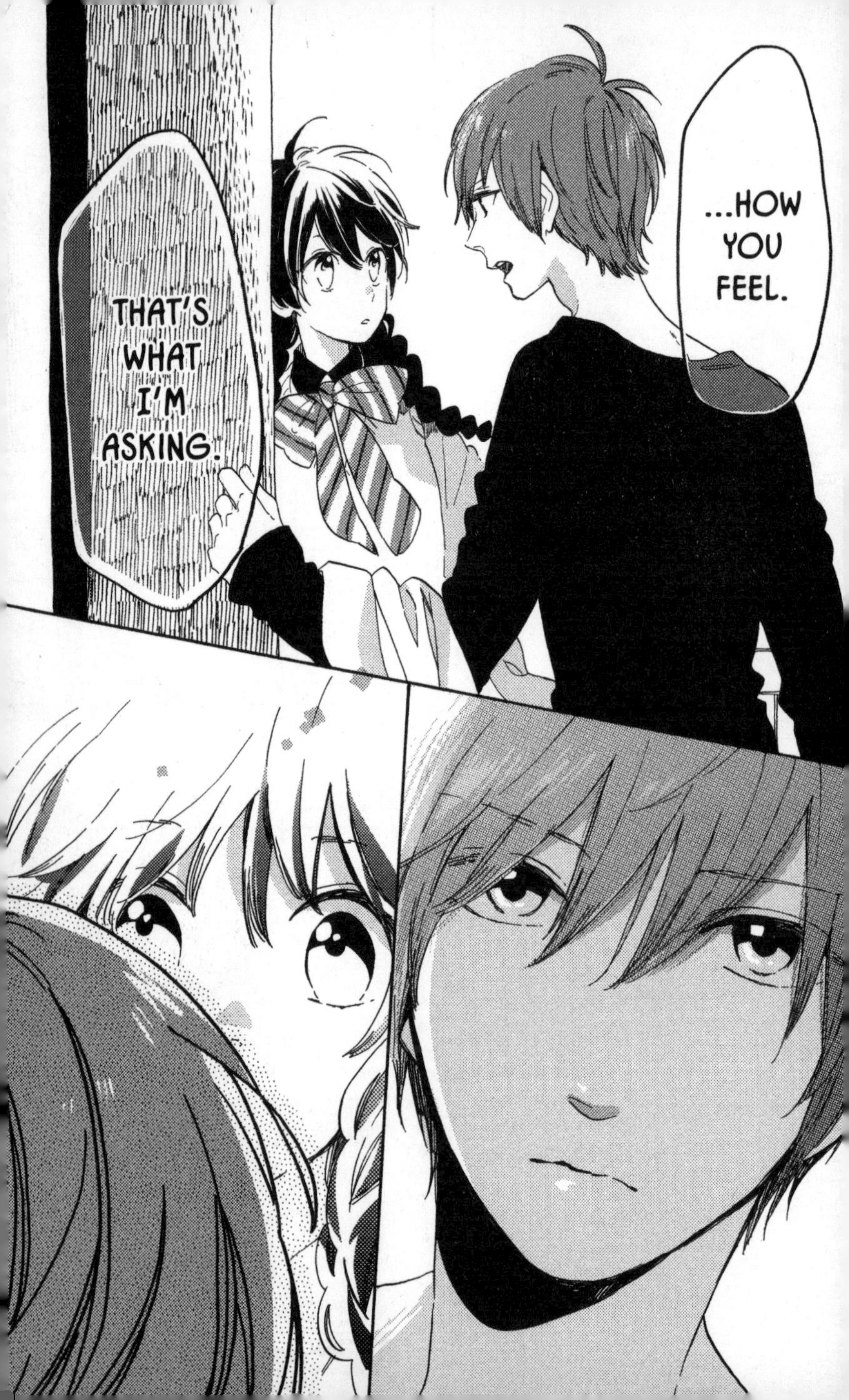
...HOW YOU FEEL.
THAT'S WHAT I'M ASKING.

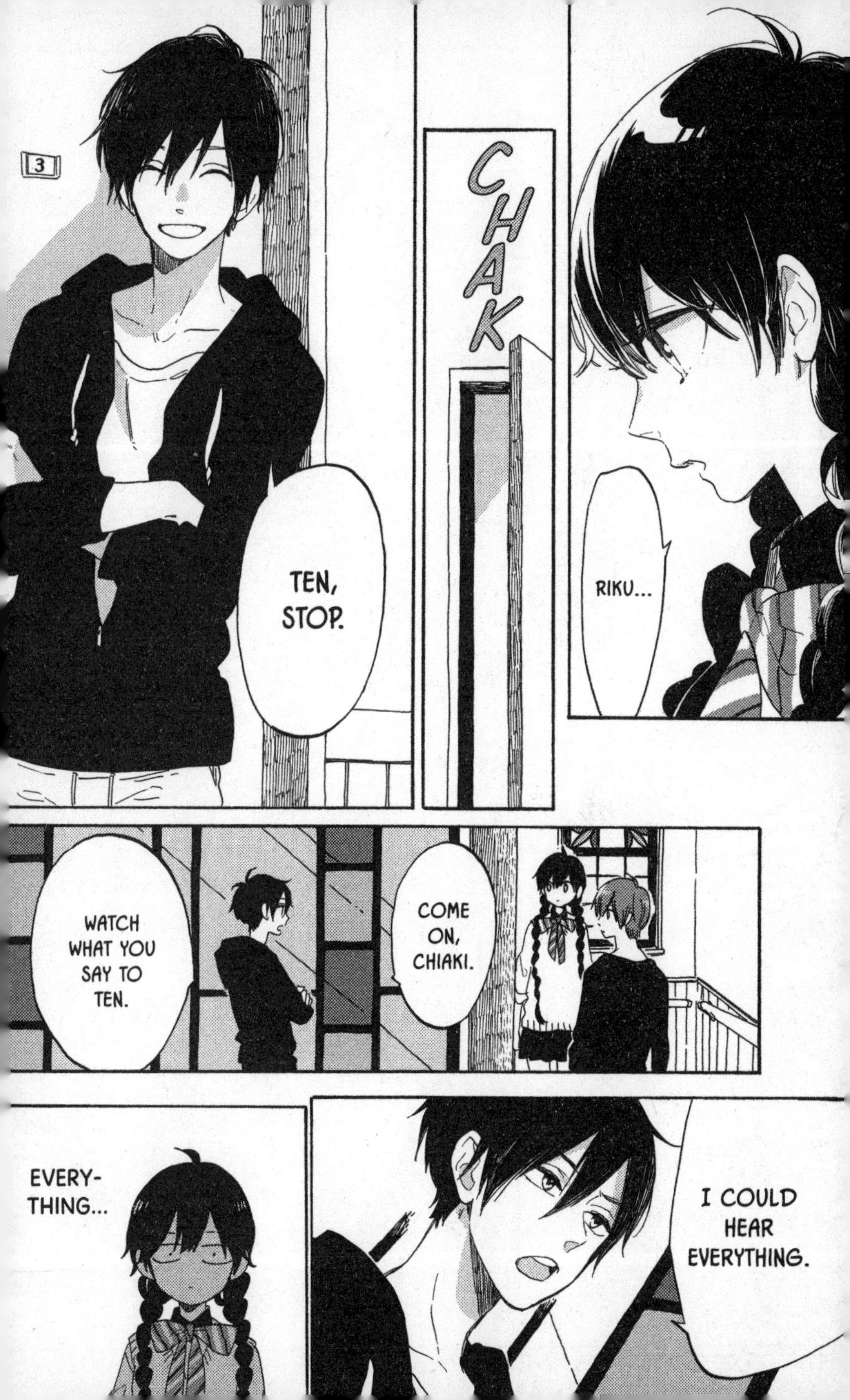
3
RIKU...
CHAK
TEN, STOP.
COME ON, CHIAKI.
WATCH WHAT YOU SAY TO TEN.
I COULD HEAR EVERYTHING.
EVERY-THING...

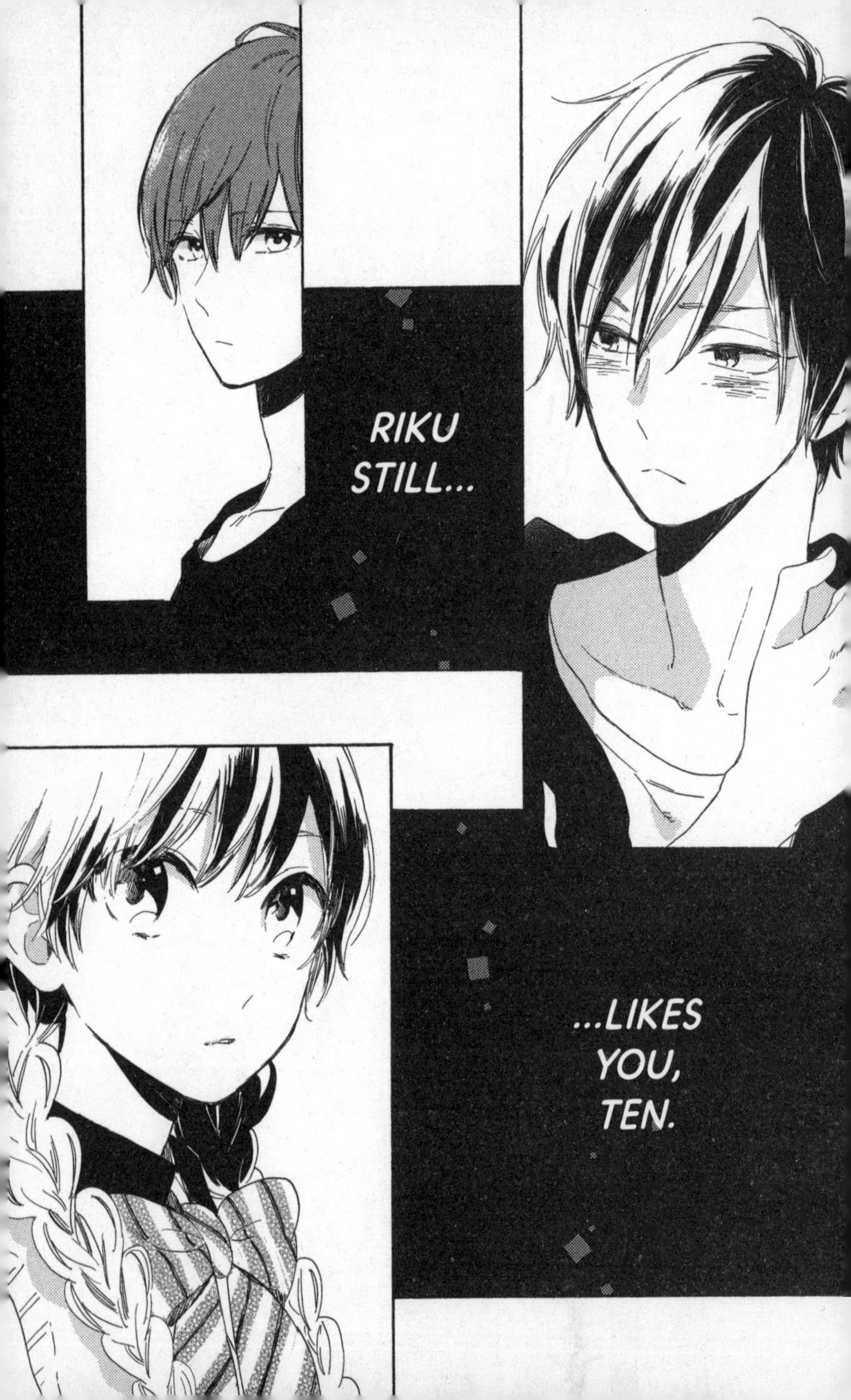
RIKU STILL...
...LIKES YOU, TEN.

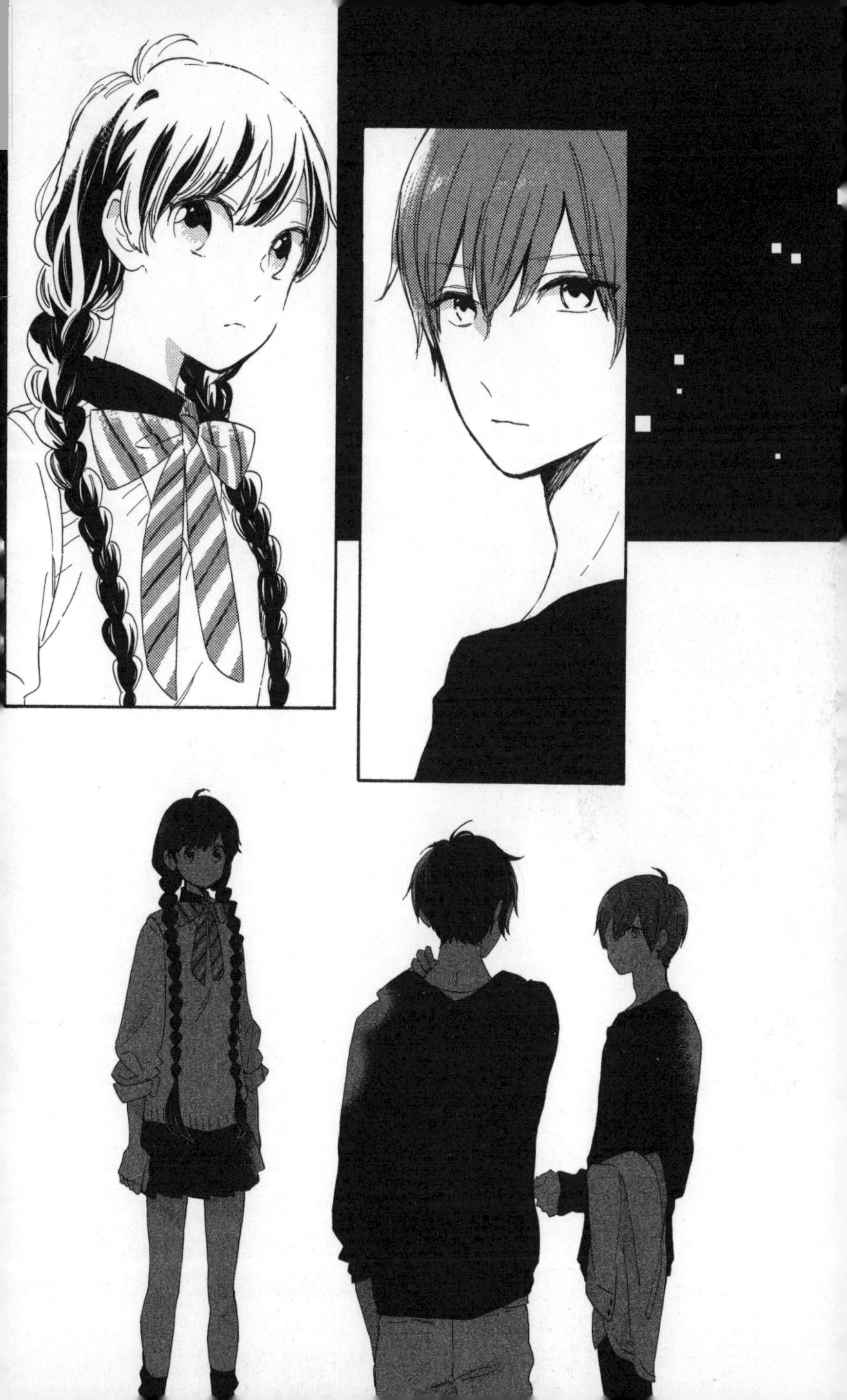

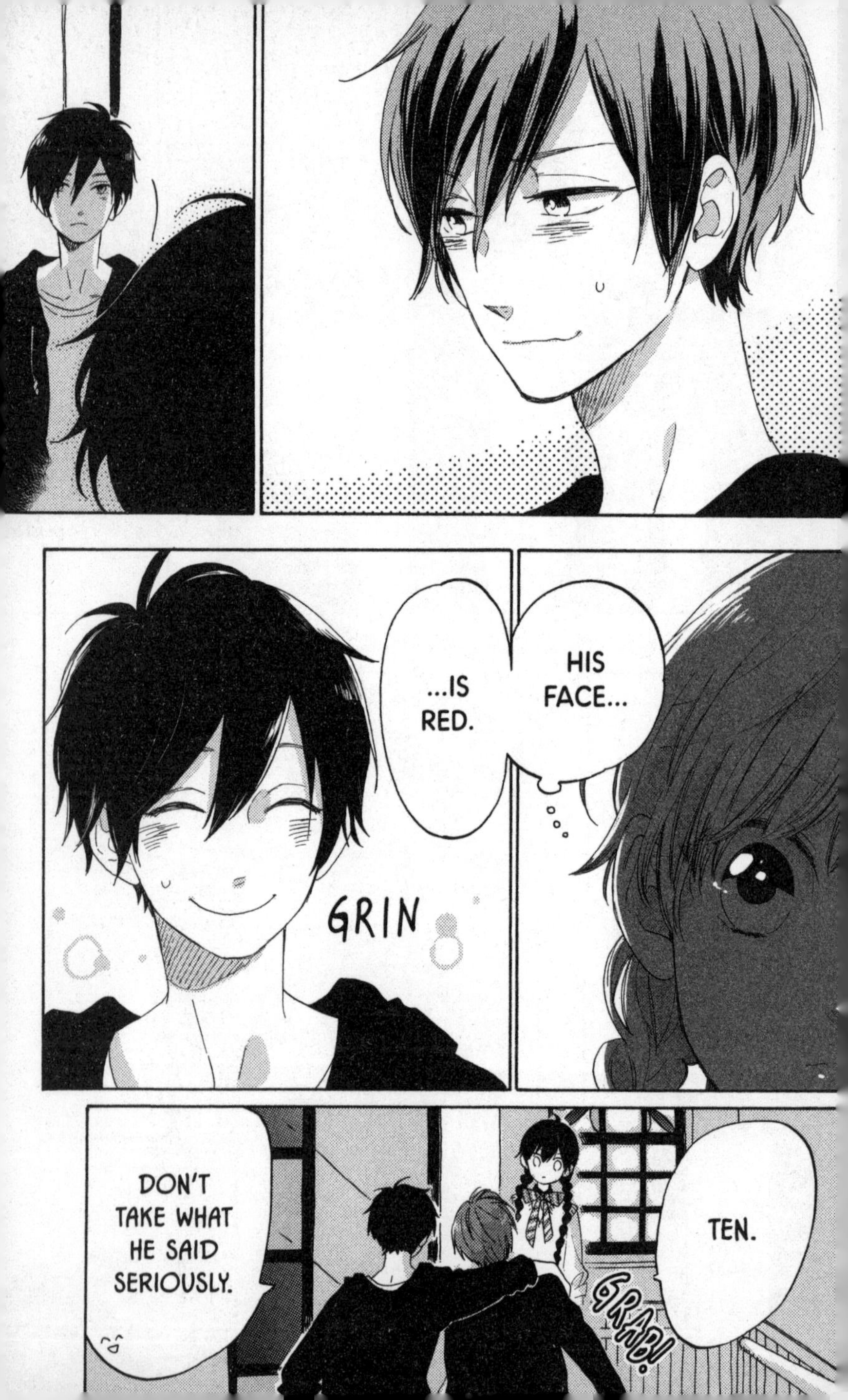
HIS FACE...
...IS RED.
GRIN
TEN.
GRAB!
DON'T TAKE WHAT HE SAID SERIOUSLY.

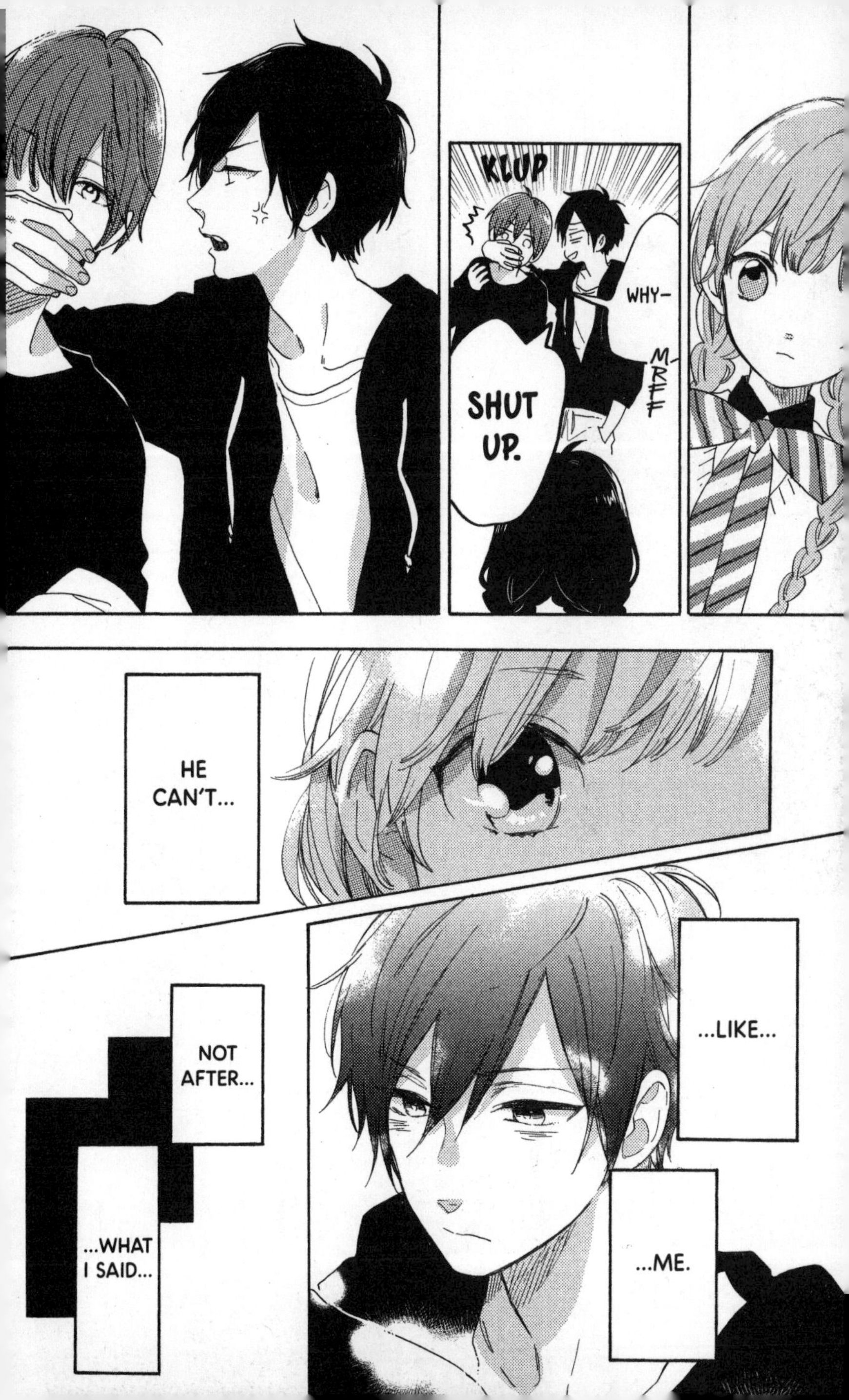
KLUP
WHY-
MRFF
SHUT UP.
HE CAN'T...
...LIKE...
...ME.
NOT AFTER...
...WHAT I SAID...

I'M SORRY, BUT I DON'T...

SORRY.

TMP

TMP

TMP

TMP

HE...

TMP

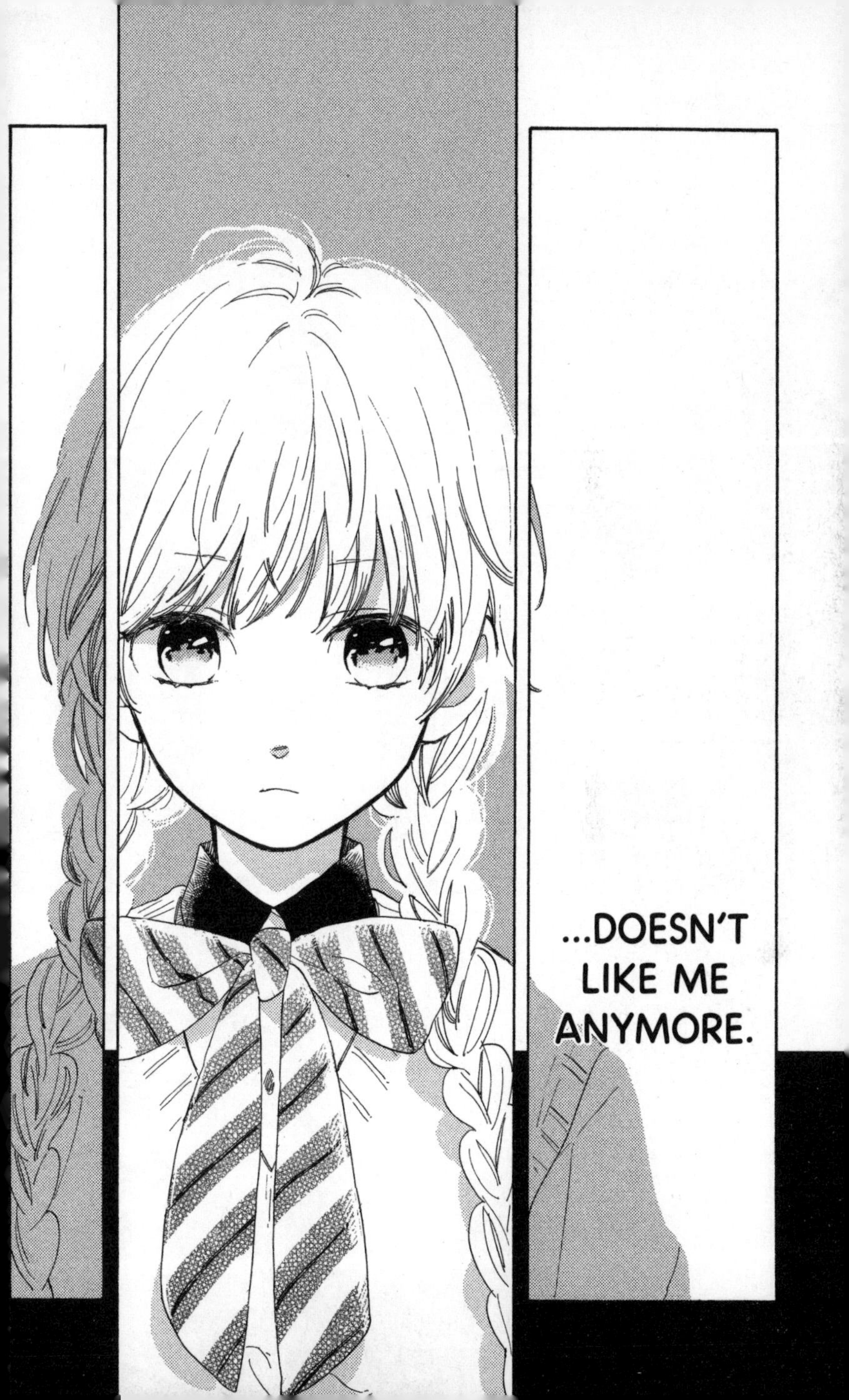
...DOESN'T LIKE ME ANYMORE.

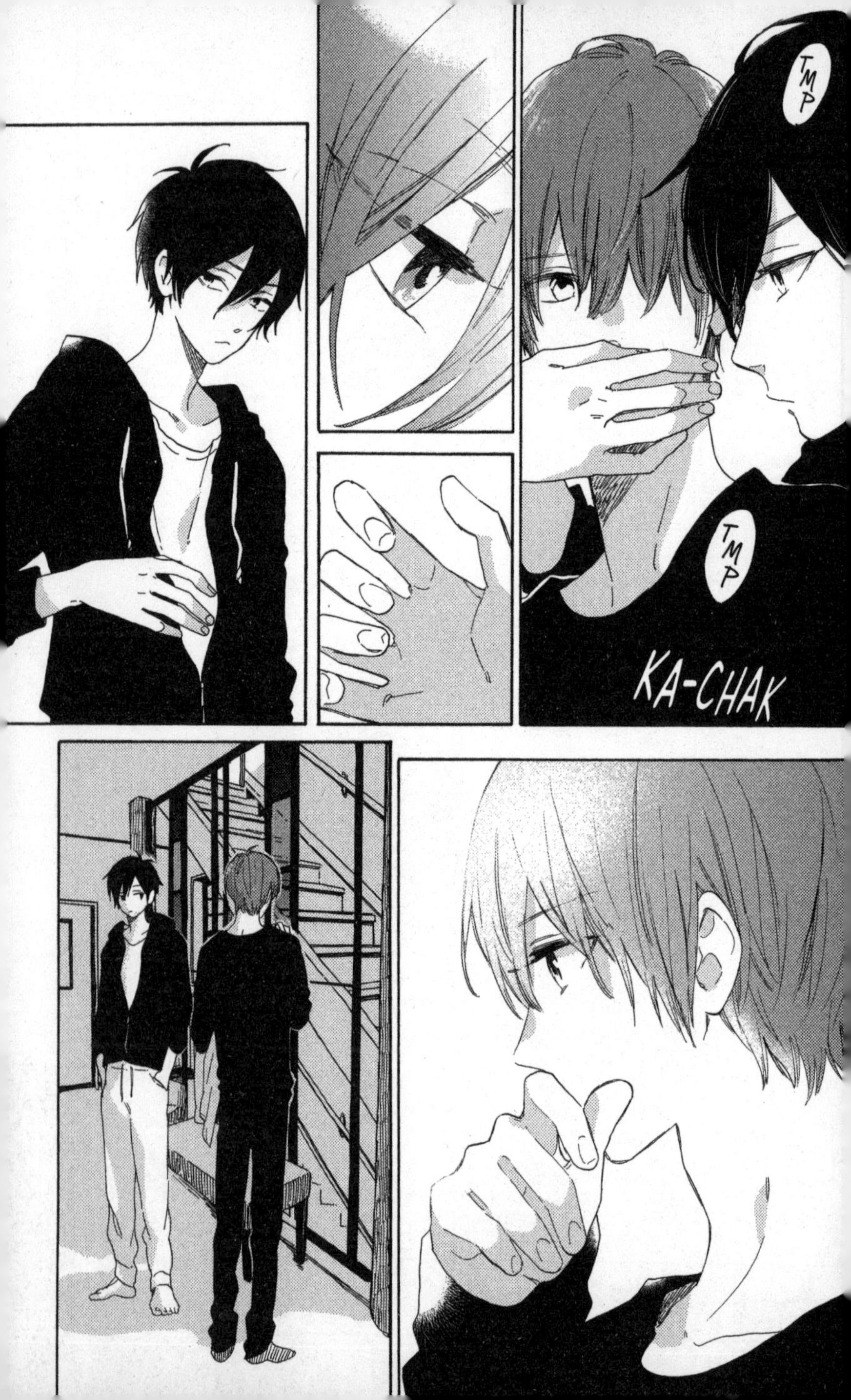
TMP
TMP
KA-CHAK

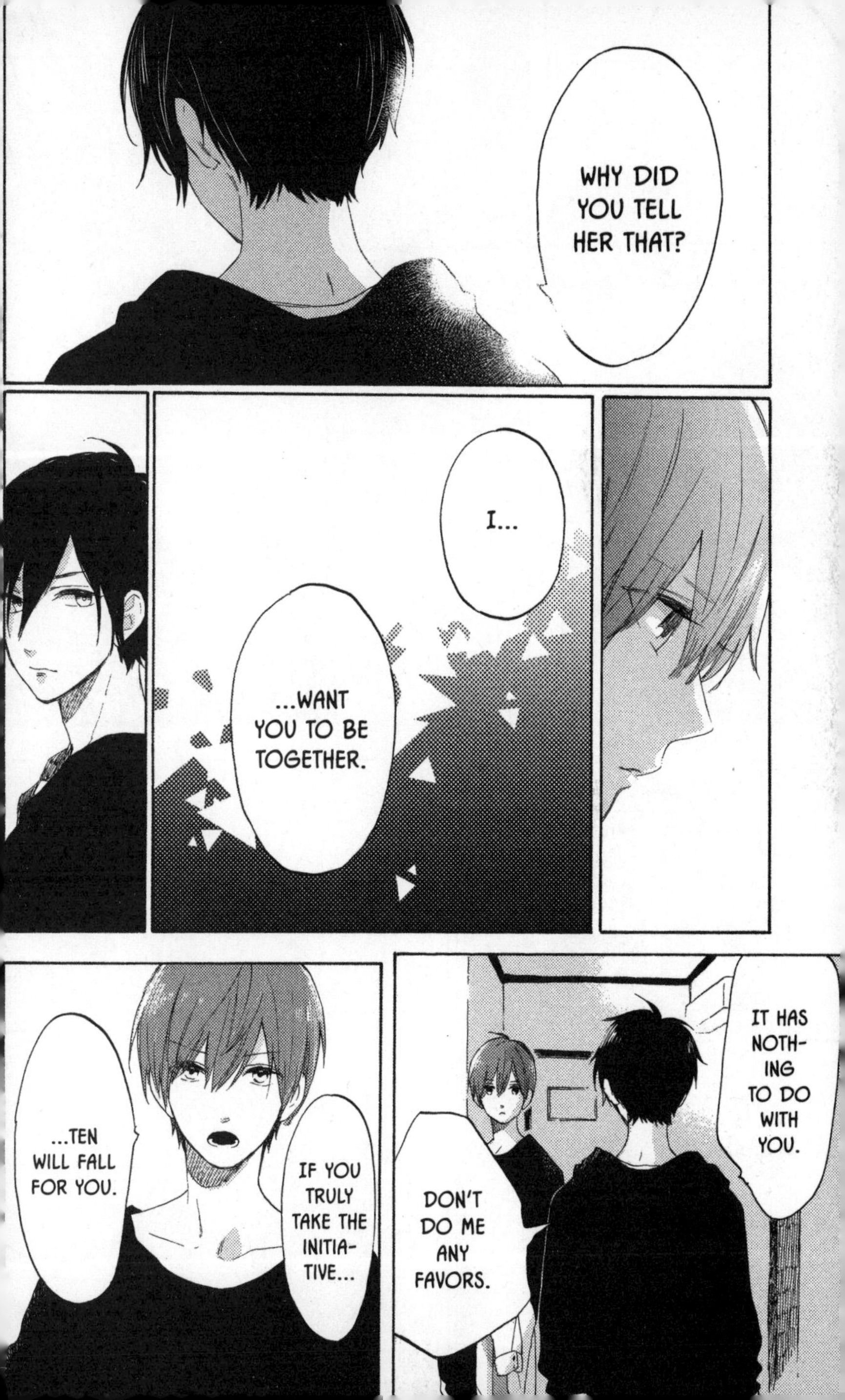
WHY DID YOU TELL HER THAT?
I...
...WANT YOU TO BE TOGETHER.
IT HAS NOTHING TO DO WITH YOU.
DON'T DO ME ANY FAVORS.
IF YOU TRULY TAKE THE INITIATIVE...
...TEN WILL FALL FOR YOU.

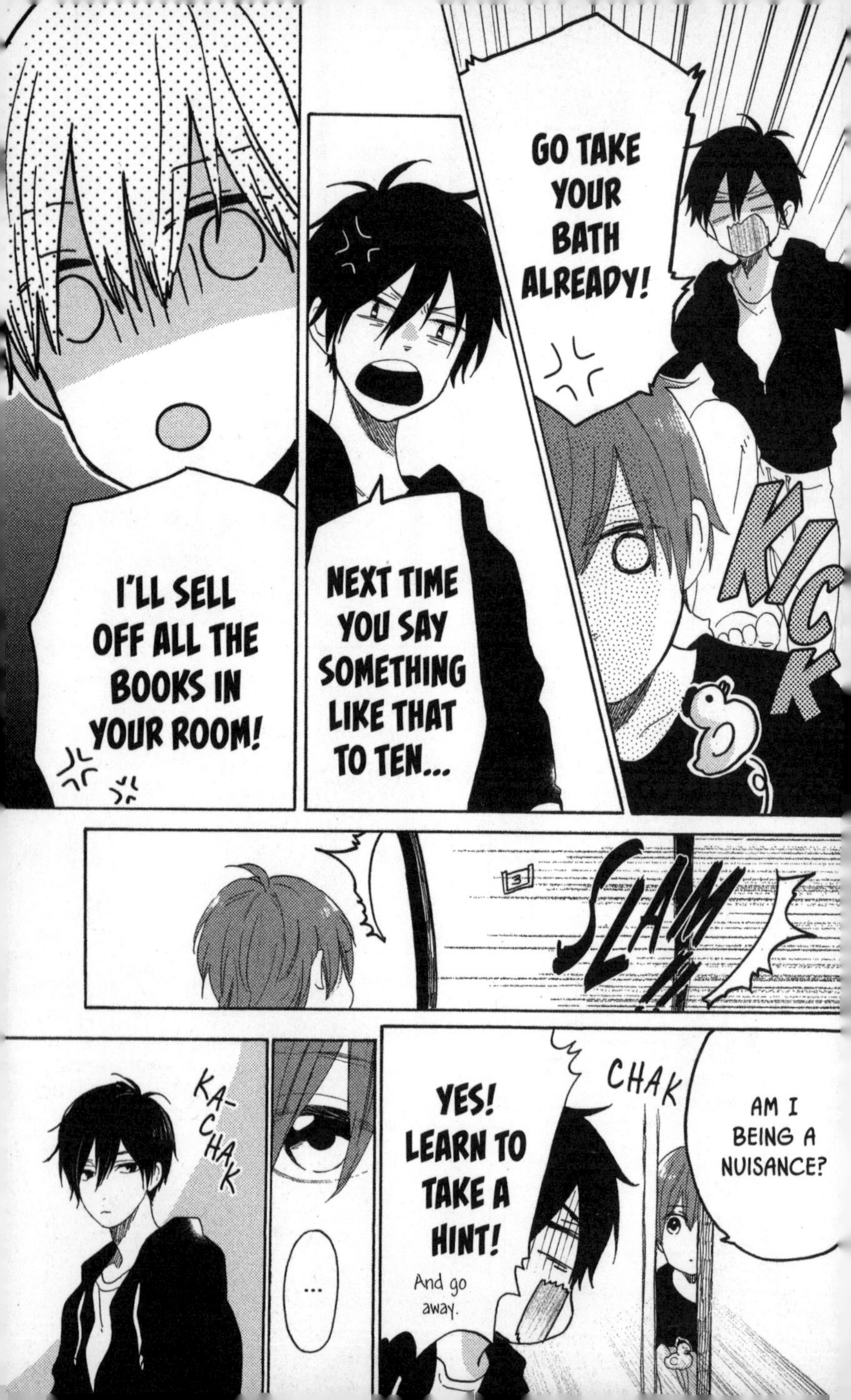
GO TAKE YOUR BATH ALREADY!
KICK
NEXT TIME YOU SAY SOMETHING LIKE THAT TO TEN...
I'LL SELL OFF ALL THE BOOKS IN YOUR ROOM!
SLAM
AM I BEING A NUISANCE?
CHAK
YES! LEARN TO TAKE A HINT!
And go away.
...
KA-CHAK

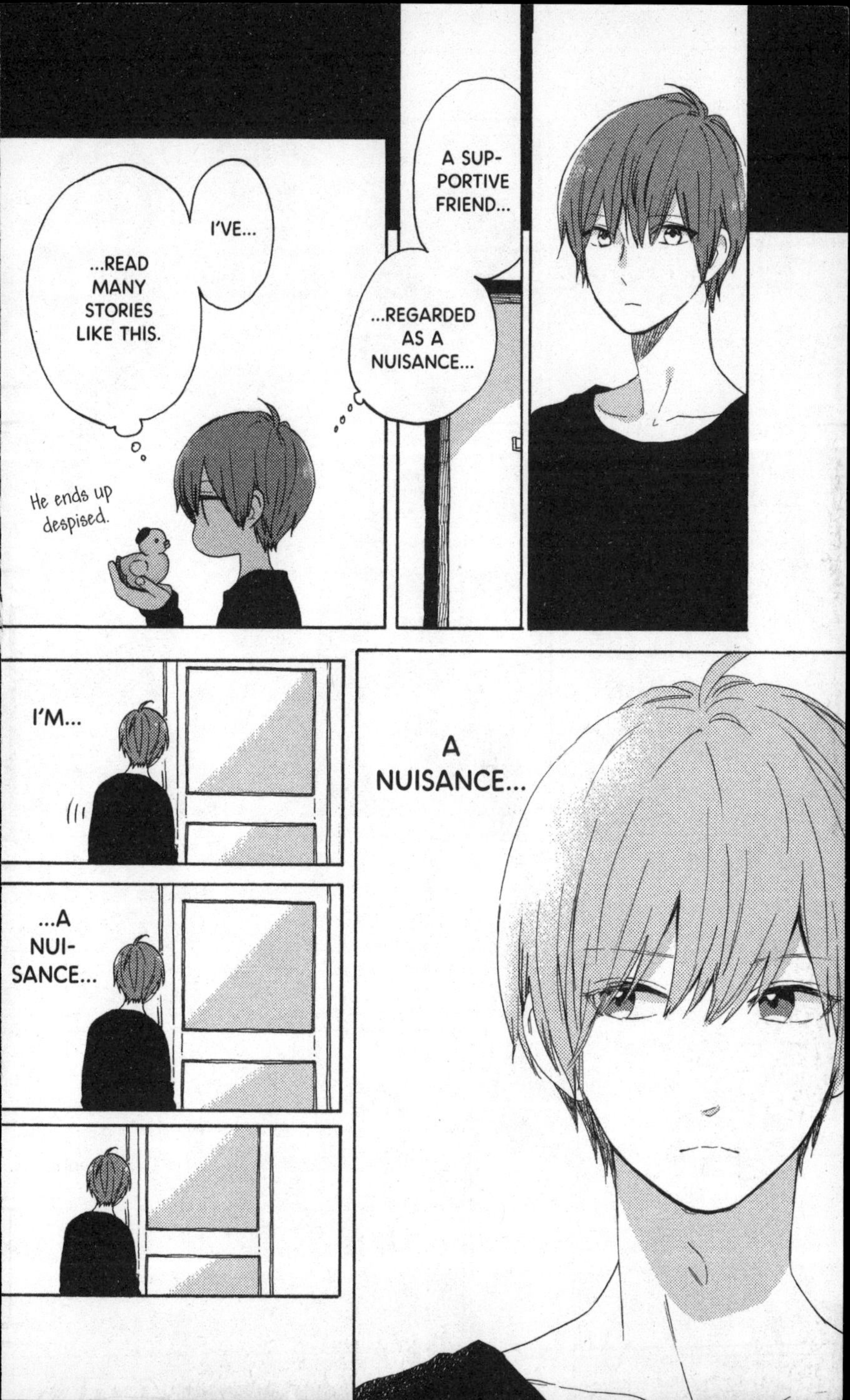
A SUP-PORTIVE FRIEND...
...REGARDED AS A NUISANCE...
I'VE...
...READ MANY STORIES LIKE THIS.
He ends up despised.
A NUISANCE...
I'M...
...A NUI-SANCE...

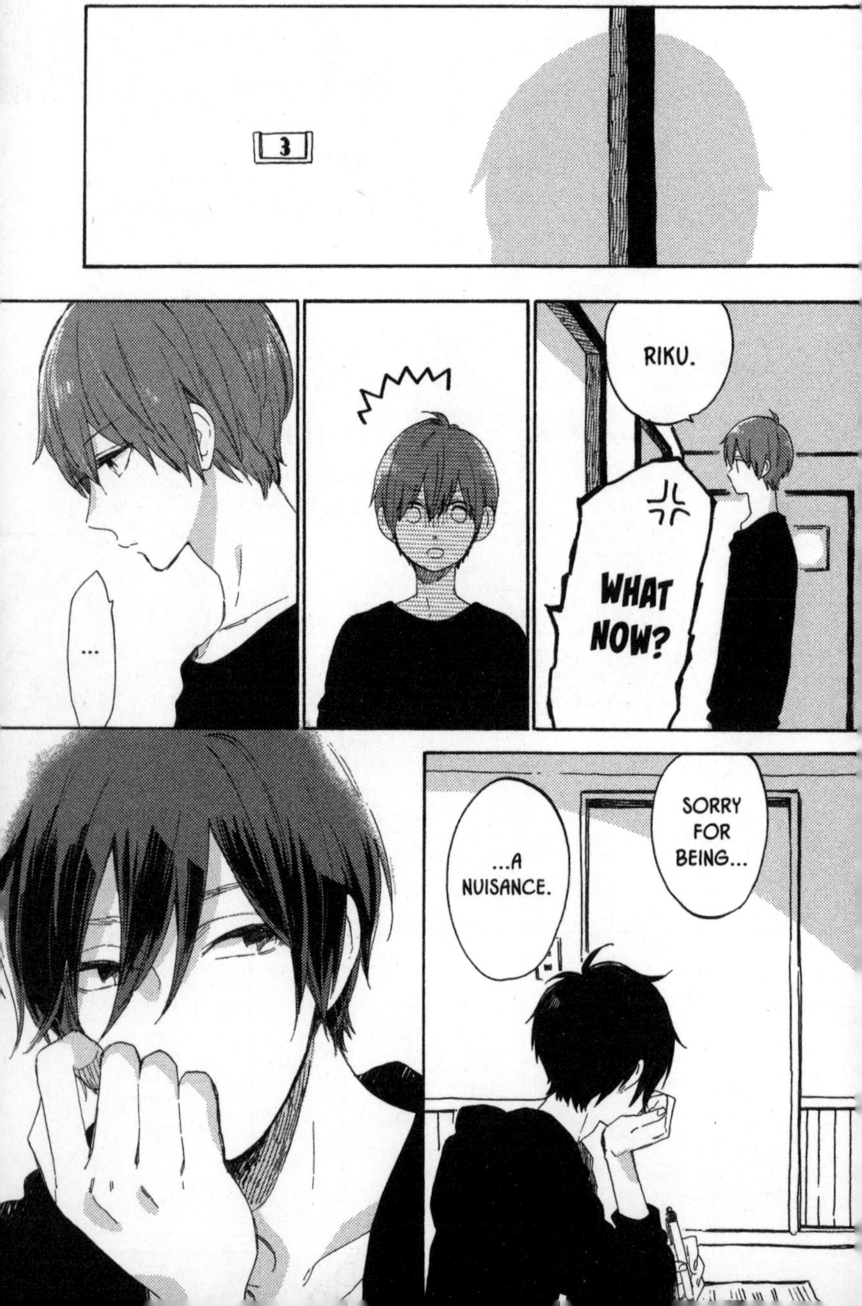
RIKU.
WHAT NOW?
...
SORRY FOR BEING...
...A NUISANCE.

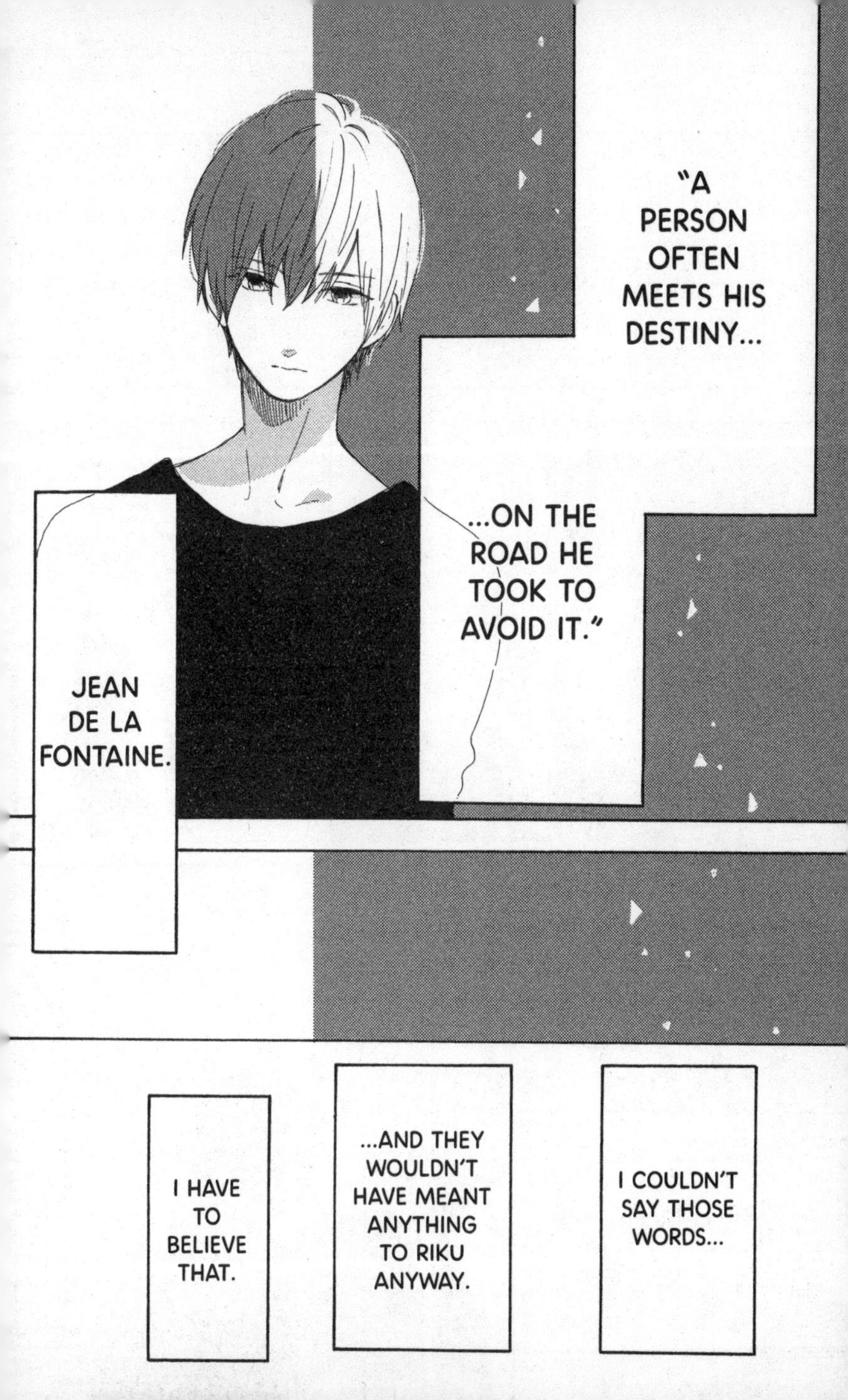
"A PERSON OFTEN MEETS HIS DESTINY...
...ON THE ROAD HE TOOK TO AVOID IT."
JEAN DE LA FONTAINE.
I COULDN'T SAY THOSE WORDS...
...AND THEY WOULDN'T HAVE MEANT ANYTHING TO RIKU ANYWAY.
I HAVE TO BELIEVE THAT.

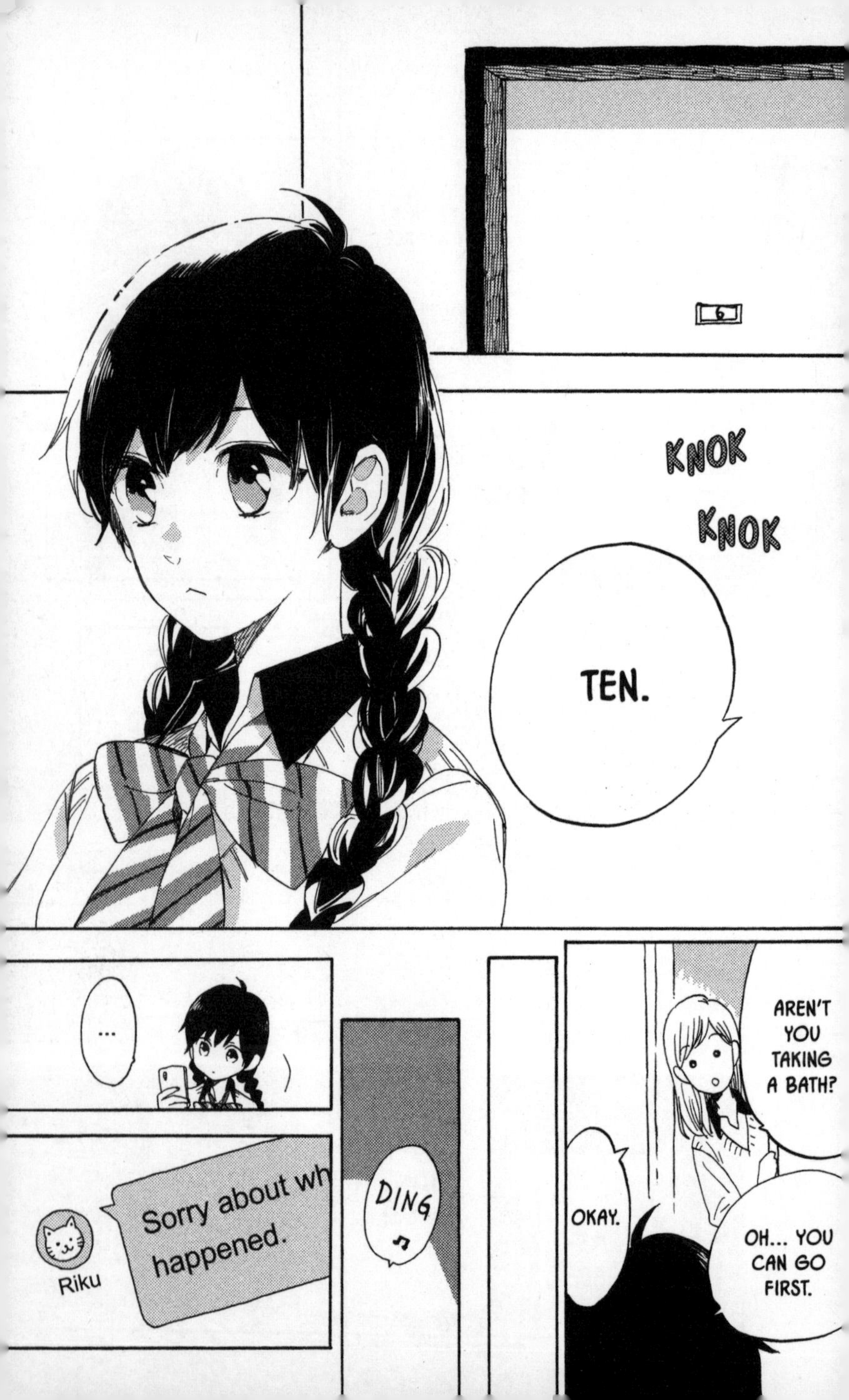
KNOK
KNOK
TEN.
AREN'T YOU TAKING A BATH?
OH... YOU CAN GO FIRST.
OKAY.
DING ♫
...
Sorry about wh happened.
Riku

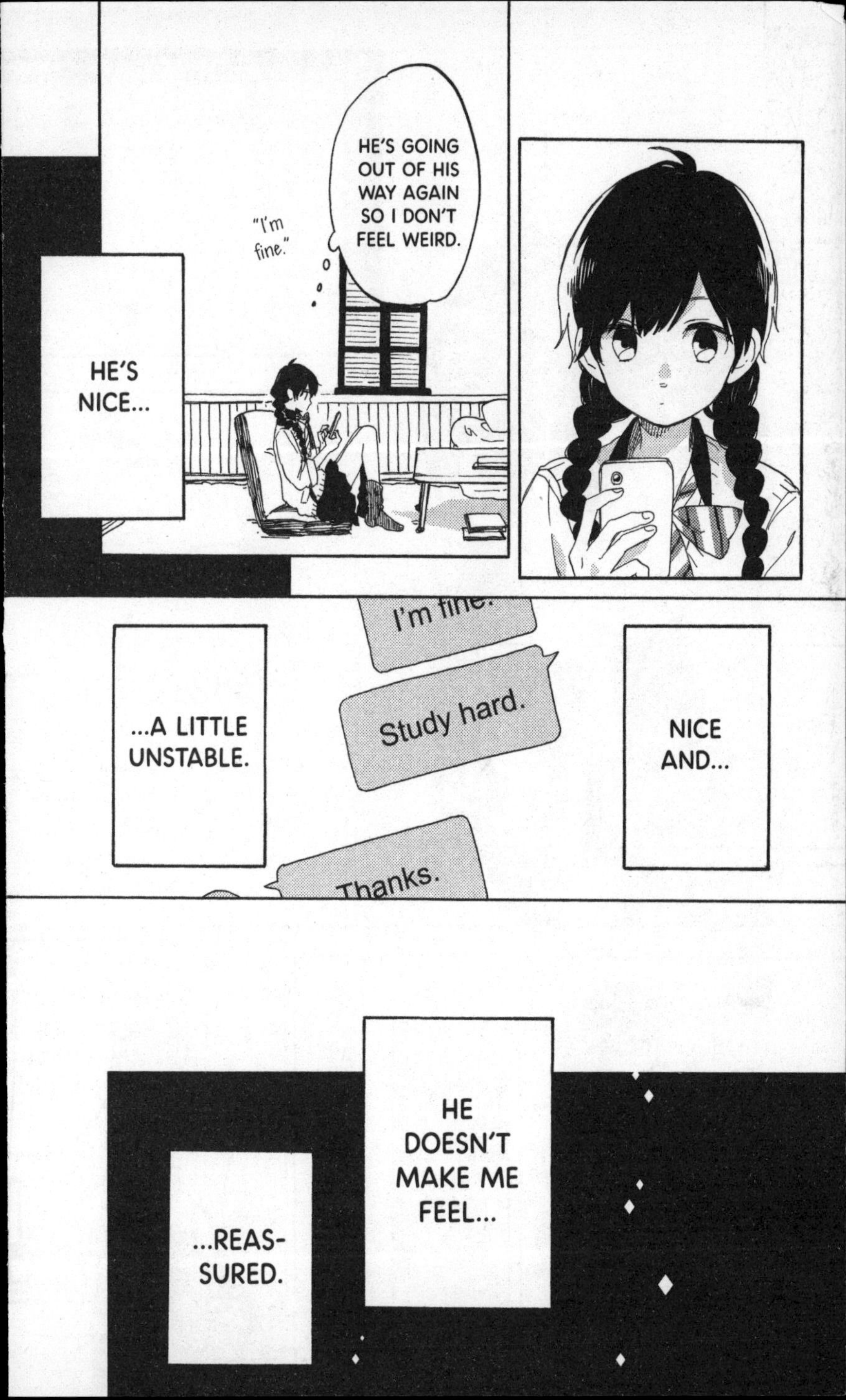
HE'S GOING OUT OF HIS WAY AGAIN SO I DON'T FEEL WEIRD.
"I'm fine."
HE'S NICE...
NICE AND...
I'm fine.
Study hard.
Thanks.
...A LITTLE UNSTABLE.
HE DOESN'T MAKE ME FEEL...
...REAS-SURED.

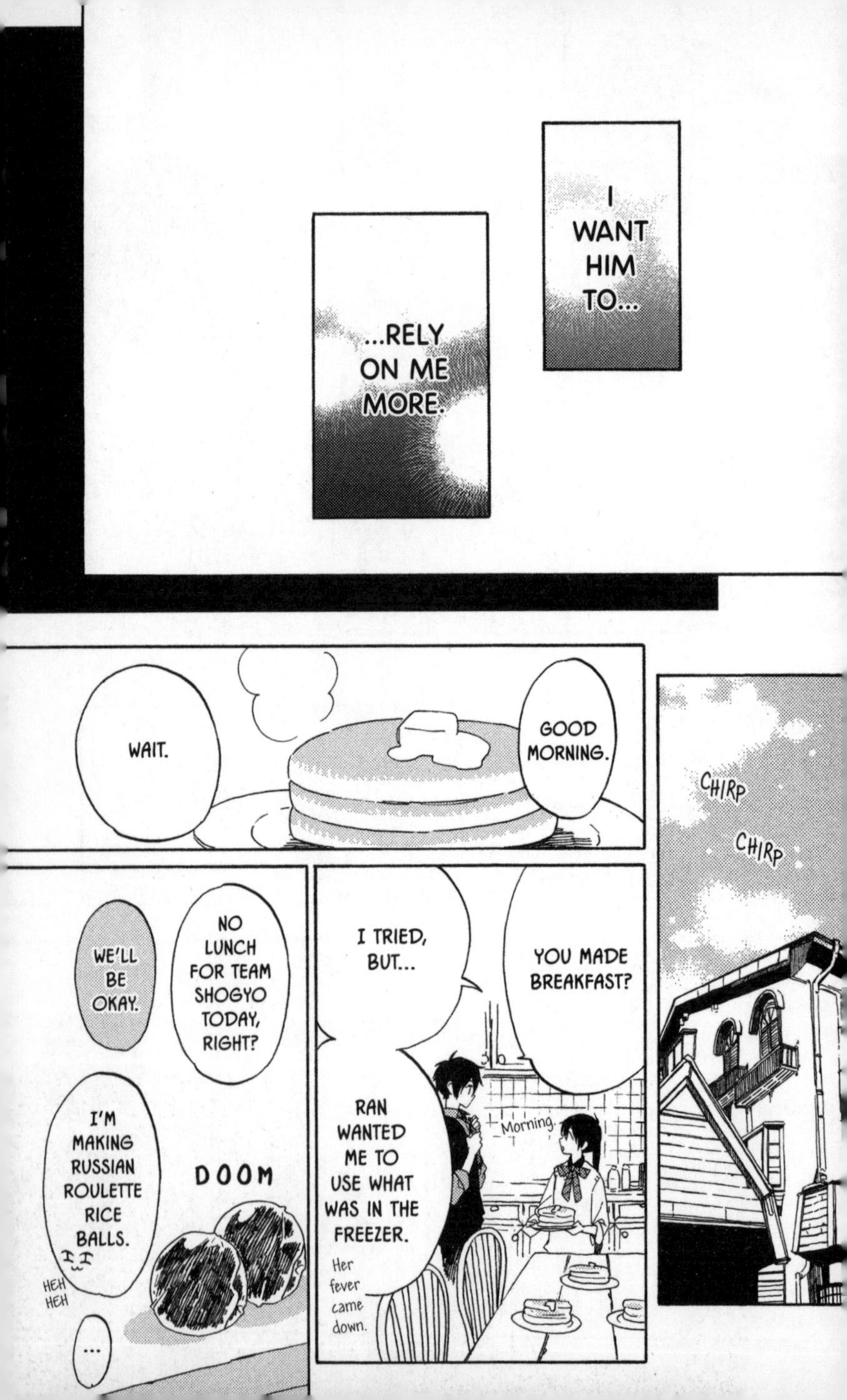
I WANT HIM TO...
...RELY ON ME MORE.
CHIRP
CHIRP
GOOD MORNING.
WAIT.
YOU MADE BREAKFAST?
I TRIED, BUT...
Morning.
RAN WANTED ME TO USE WHAT WAS IN THE FREEZER.
Her fever came down.
NO LUNCH FOR TEAM SHOGYO TODAY, RIGHT?
WE'LL BE OKAY.
I'M MAKING RUSSIAN ROULETTE RICE BALLS.
DOOM
HEH HEH
...

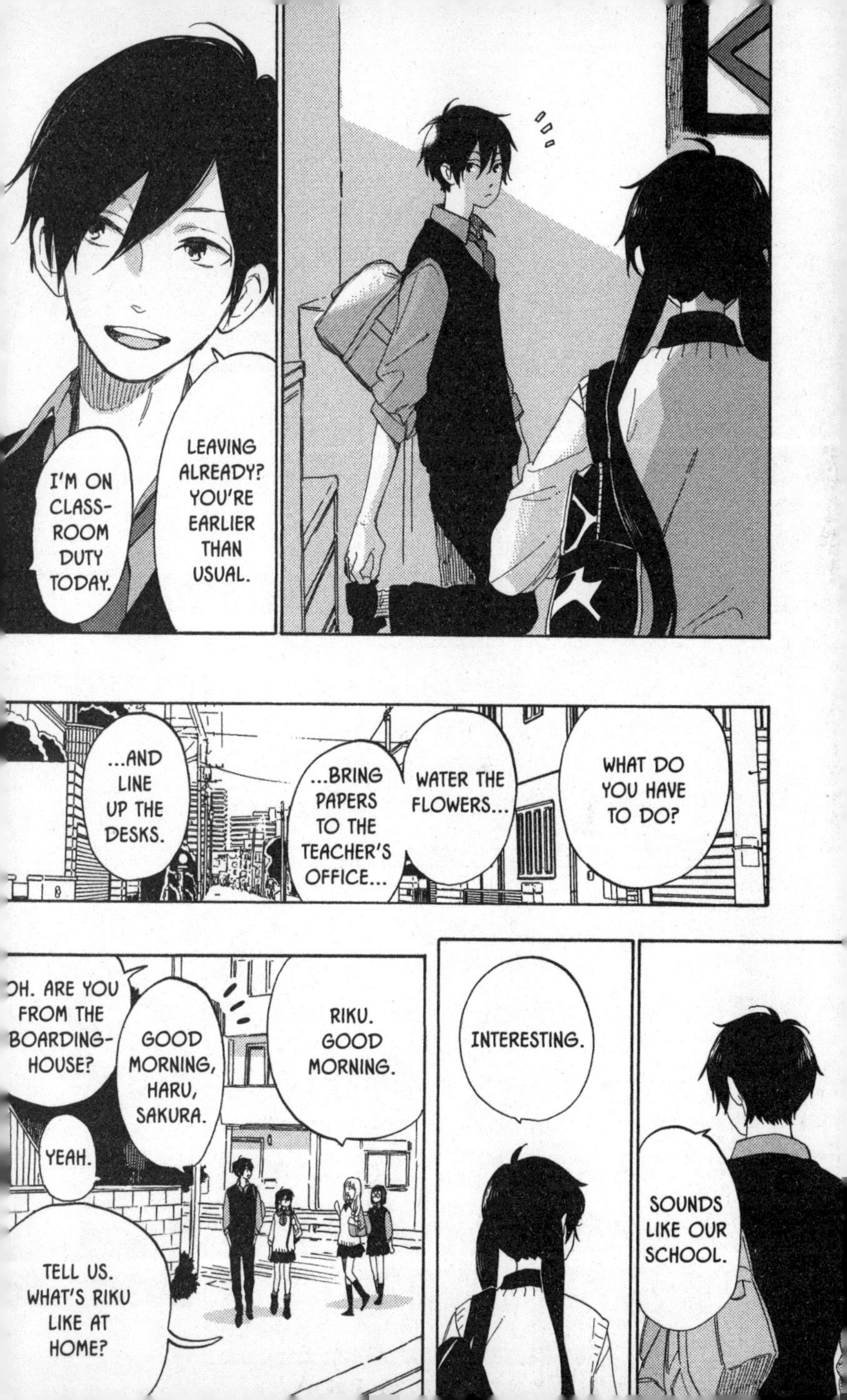
LEAVING ALREADY? YOU'RE EARLIER THAN USUAL.
I'M ON CLASS-ROOM DUTY TODAY.
WHAT DO YOU HAVE TO DO?
WATER THE FLOWERS...
...BRING PAPERS TO THE TEACHER'S OFFICE...
...AND LINE UP THE DESKS.
SOUNDS LIKE OUR SCHOOL.
INTERESTING.
RIKU. GOOD MORNING.
GOOD MORNING, HARU, SAKURA.
OH. ARE YOU FROM THE BOARDING-HOUSE?
YEAH.
TELL US. WHAT'S RIKU LIKE AT HOME?

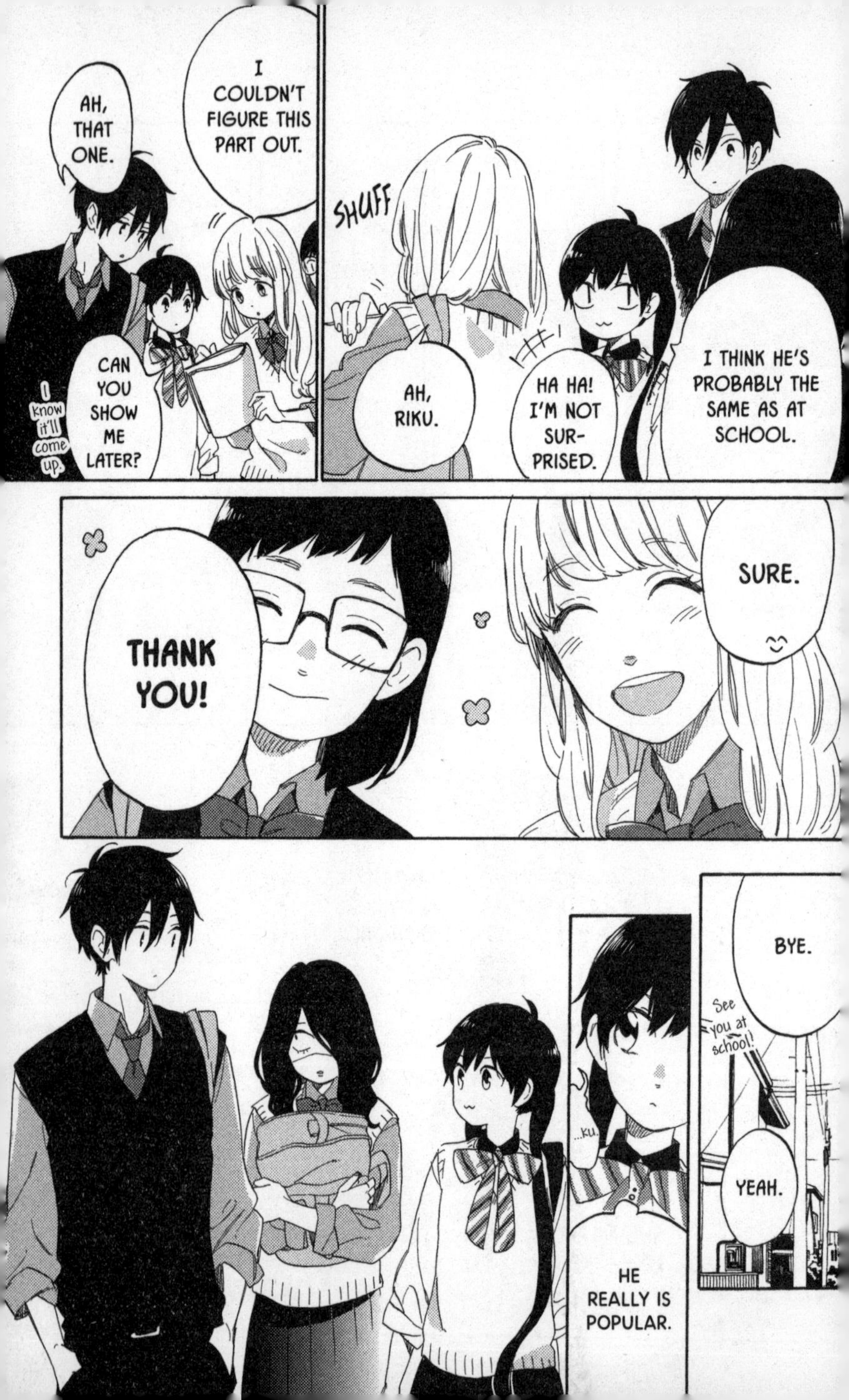
I THINK HE'S PROBABLY THE SAME AS AT SCHOOL.
HA HA! I'M NOT SUR-PRISED.
AH, RIKU.
SHUFF
I COULDN'T FIGURE THIS PART OUT.
AH, THAT ONE.
CAN YOU SHOW ME LATER?
I know it'll come up.
SURE.
THANK YOU!
BYE.
See you at school!
YEAH.
...ku.
HE REALLY IS POPULAR.

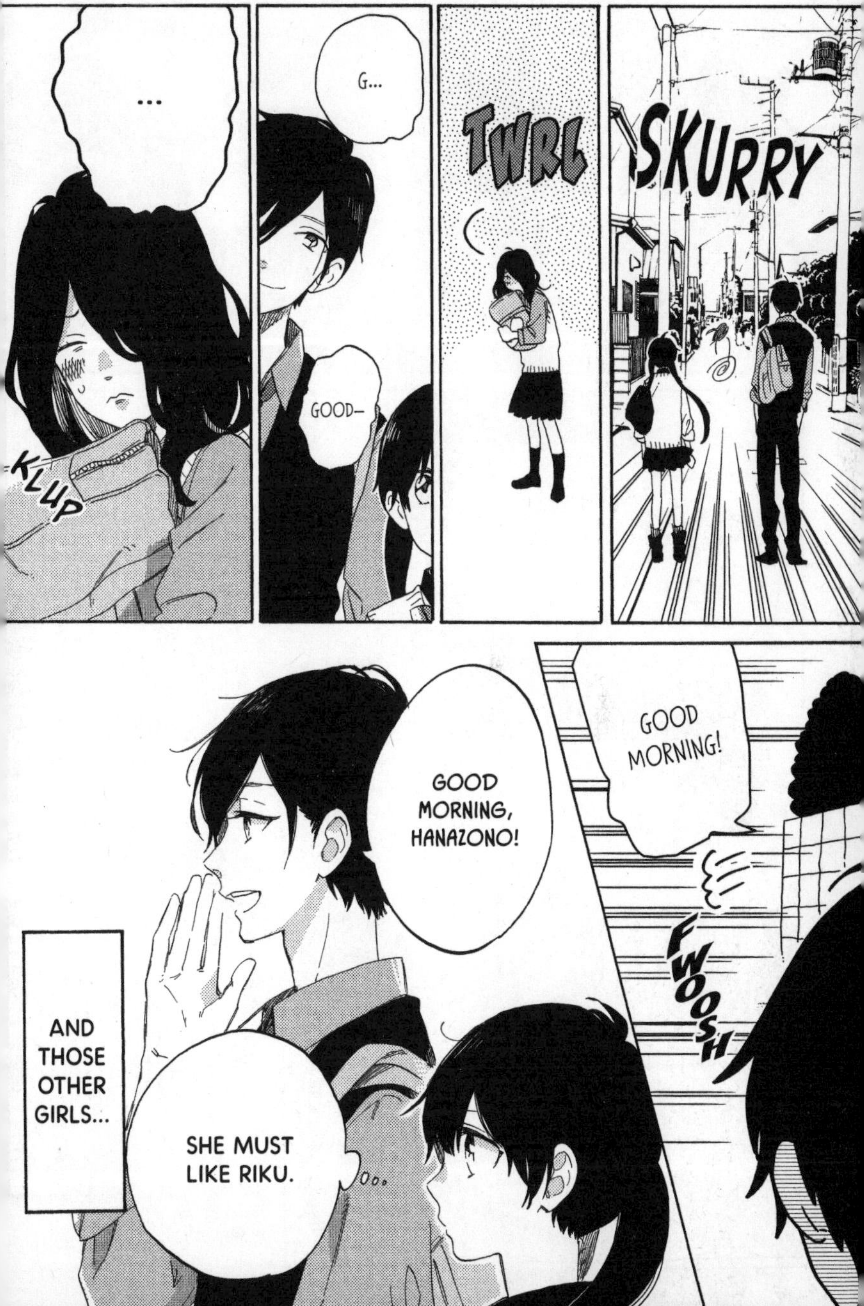
SKURRY
TWRL
G...
GOOD—
...
KLUP
GOOD MORNING!
FWOOSH
GOOD MORNING, HANAZONO!
SHE MUST LIKE RIKU.
AND THOSE OTHER GIRLS...

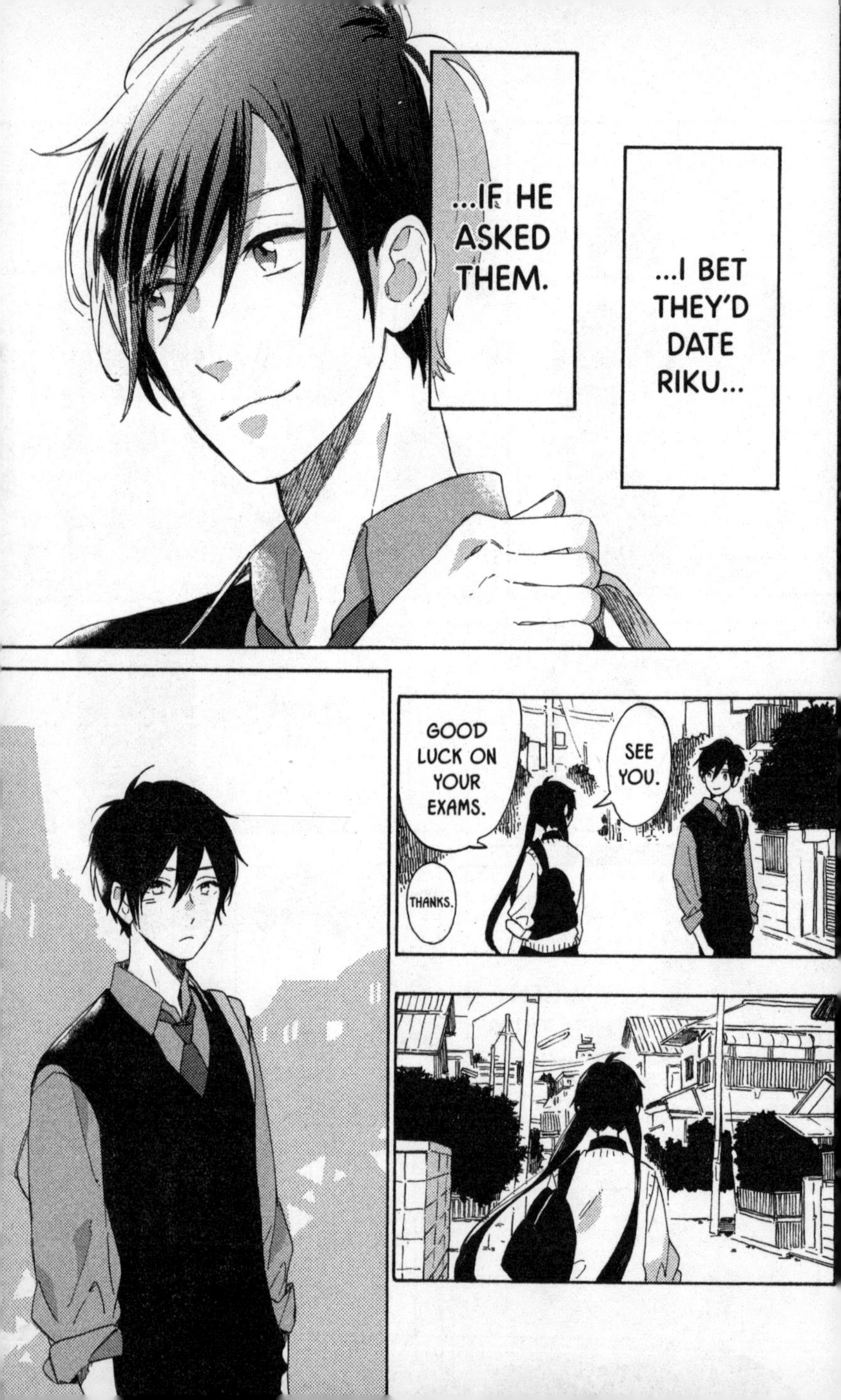
...I BET THEY'D DATE RIKU...
...IF HE ASKED THEM.
SEE YOU.
GOOD LUCK ON YOUR EXAMS.
THANKS.

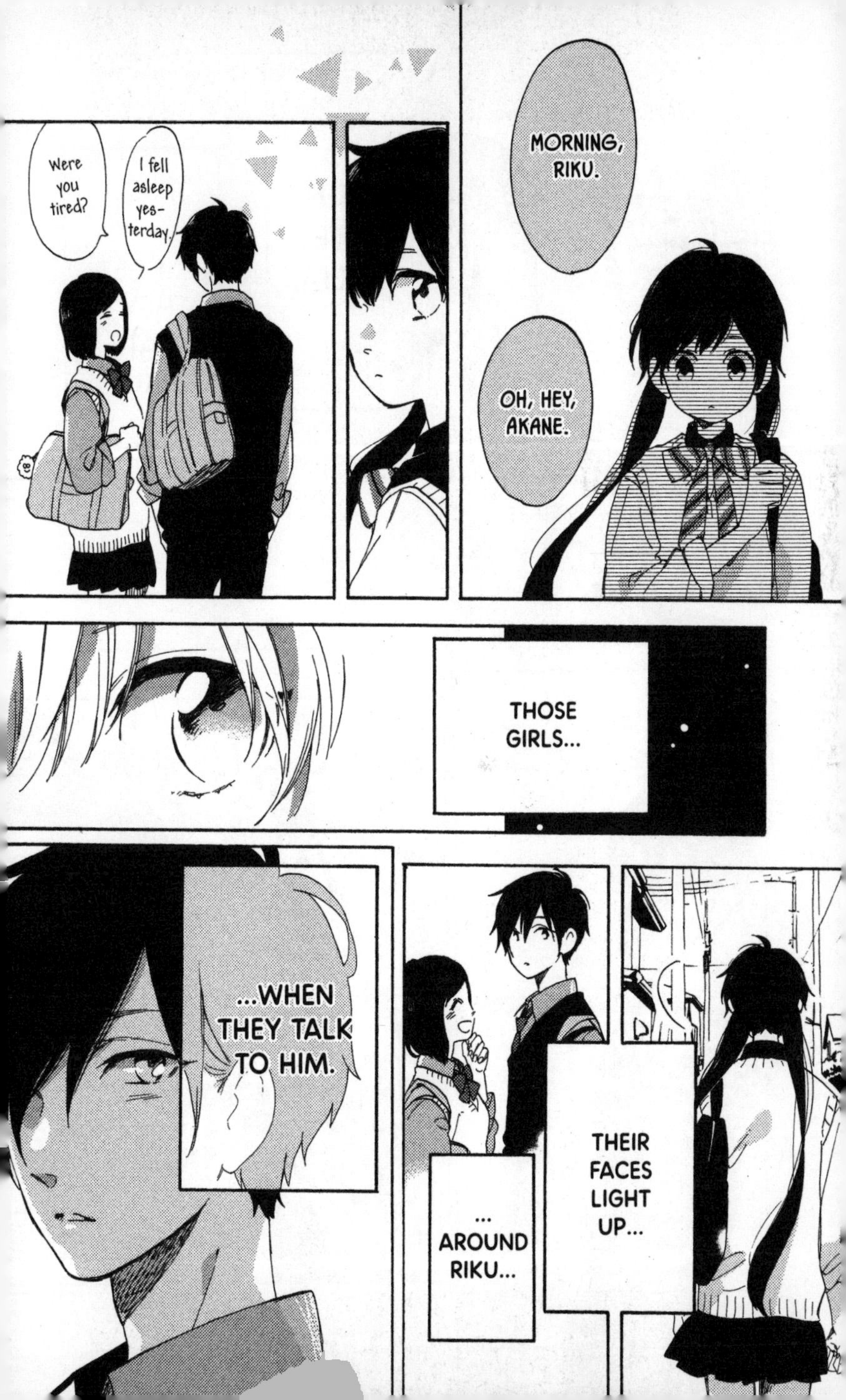
MORNING, RIKU.
OH, HEY, AKANE.
I fell asleep yes-terday.
Were you tired?
THOSE GIRLS...
THEIR FACES LIGHT UP...
...AROUND RIKU...
...WHEN THEY TALK TO HIM.

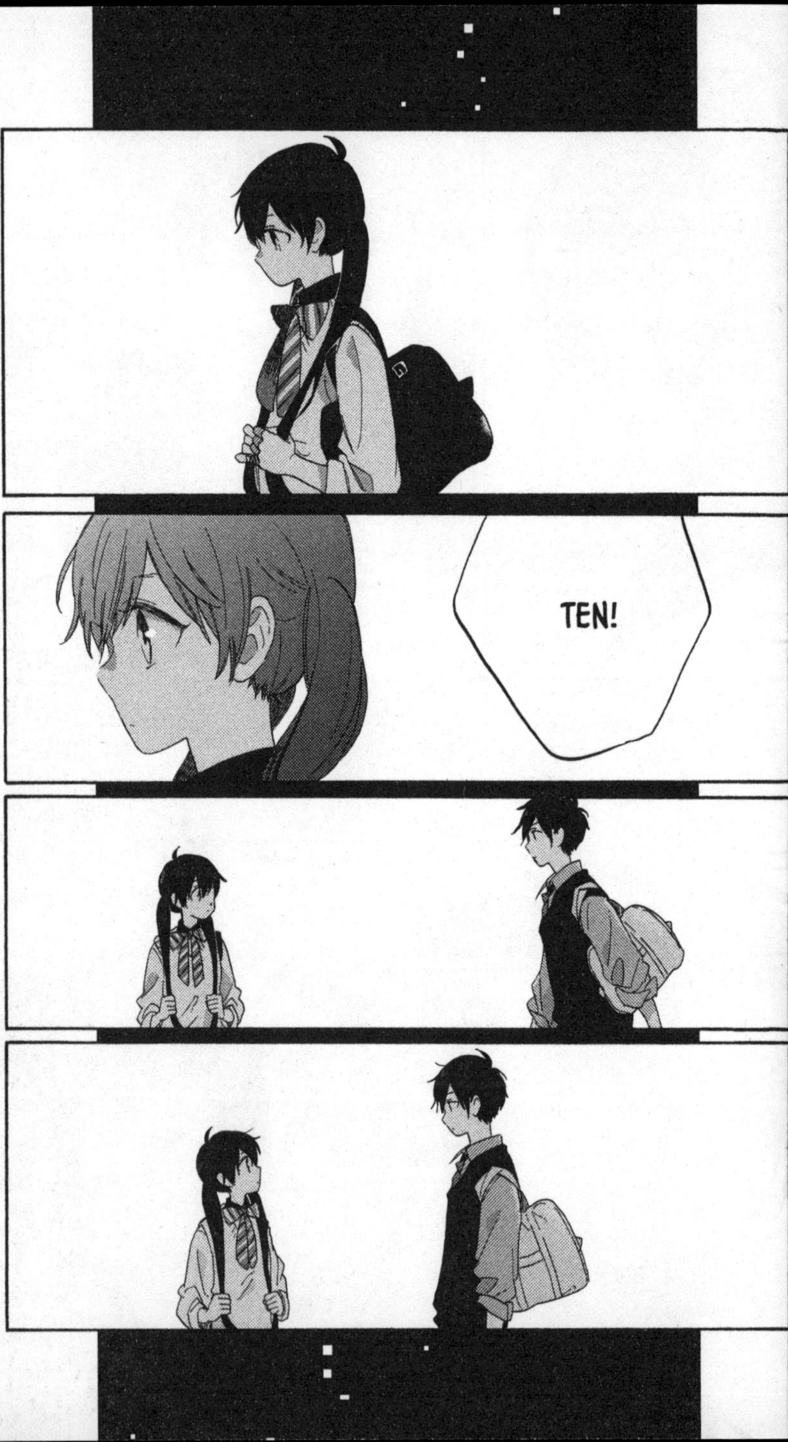
TEN!

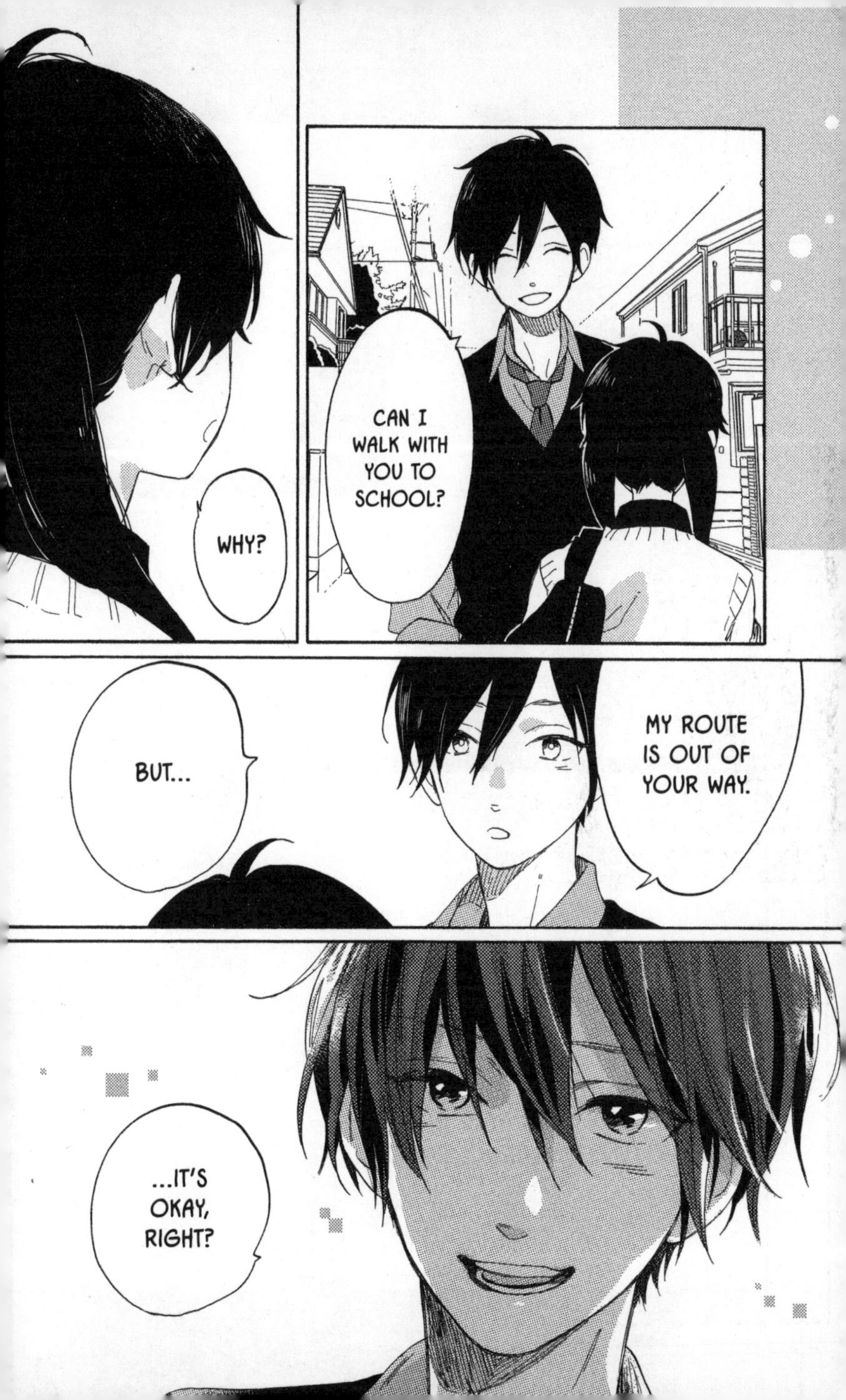
CAN I WALK WITH YOU TO SCHOOL?
WHY?
MY ROUTE IS OUT OF YOUR WAY.
BUT...
...IT'S OKAY, RIGHT?

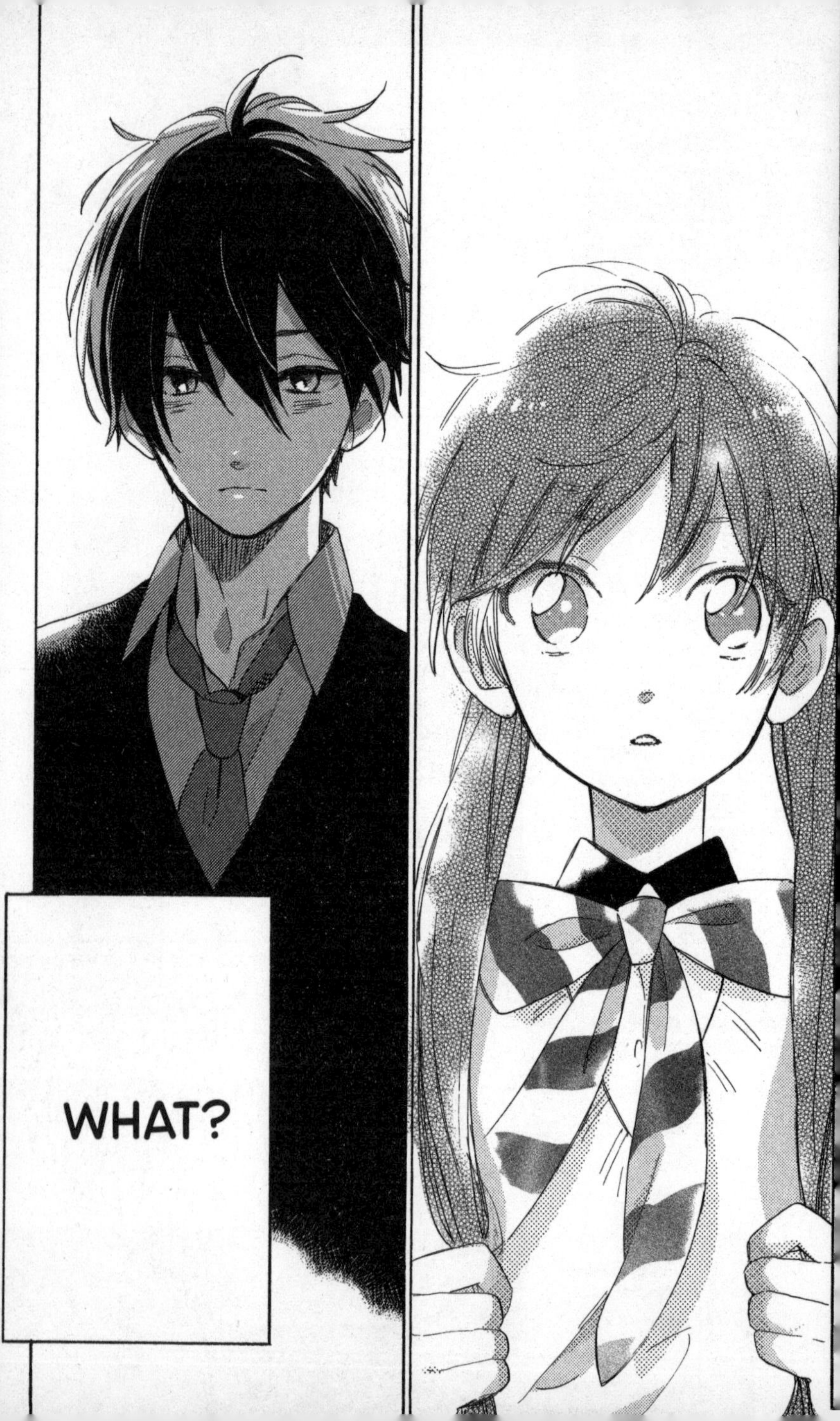
WHAT?

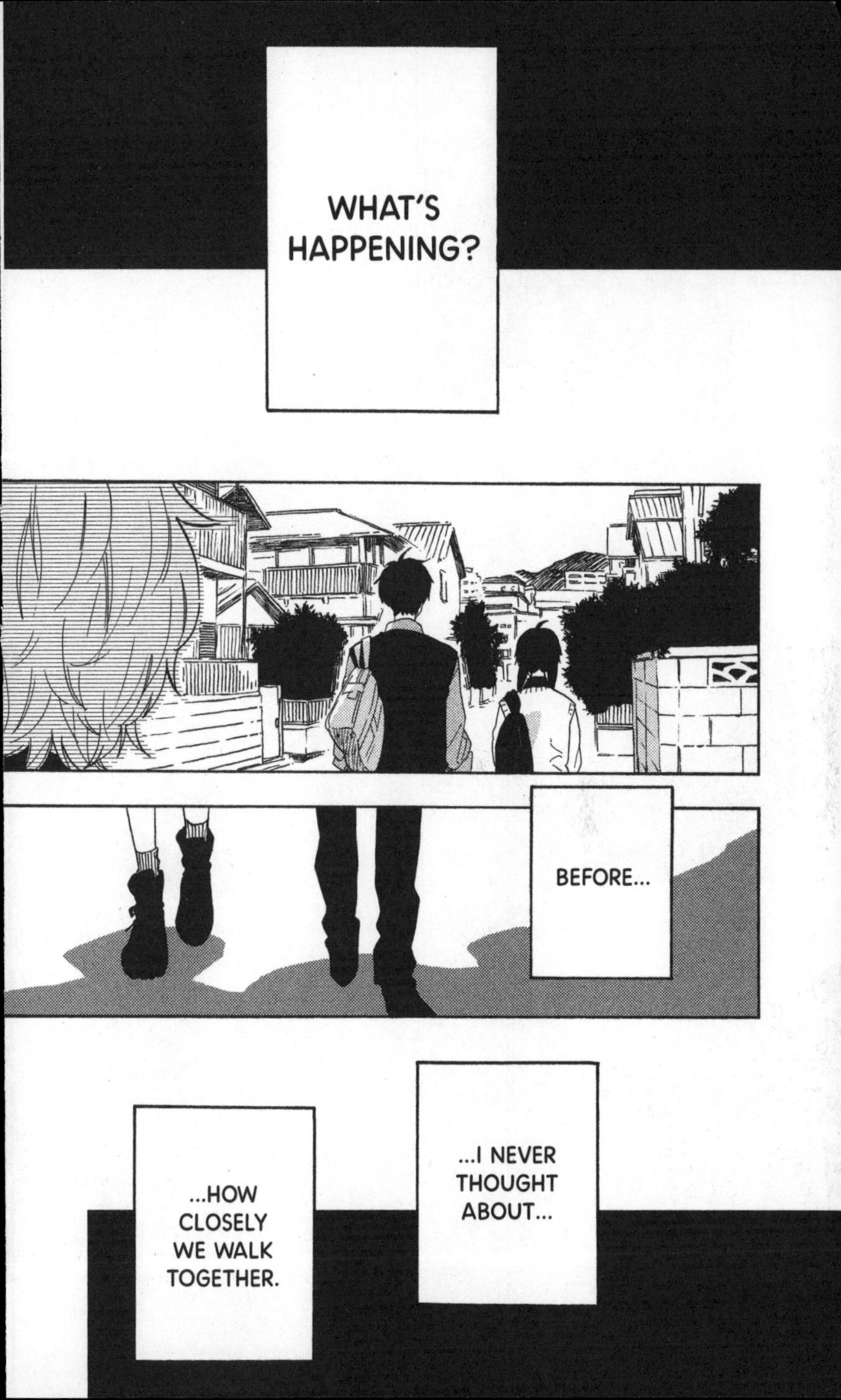
WHAT'S HAPPENING?
BEFORE...
...I NEVER THOUGHT ABOUT...
...HOW CLOSELY WE WALK TOGETHER.

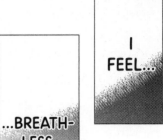

I FEEL...

...BREATH-
LESS.

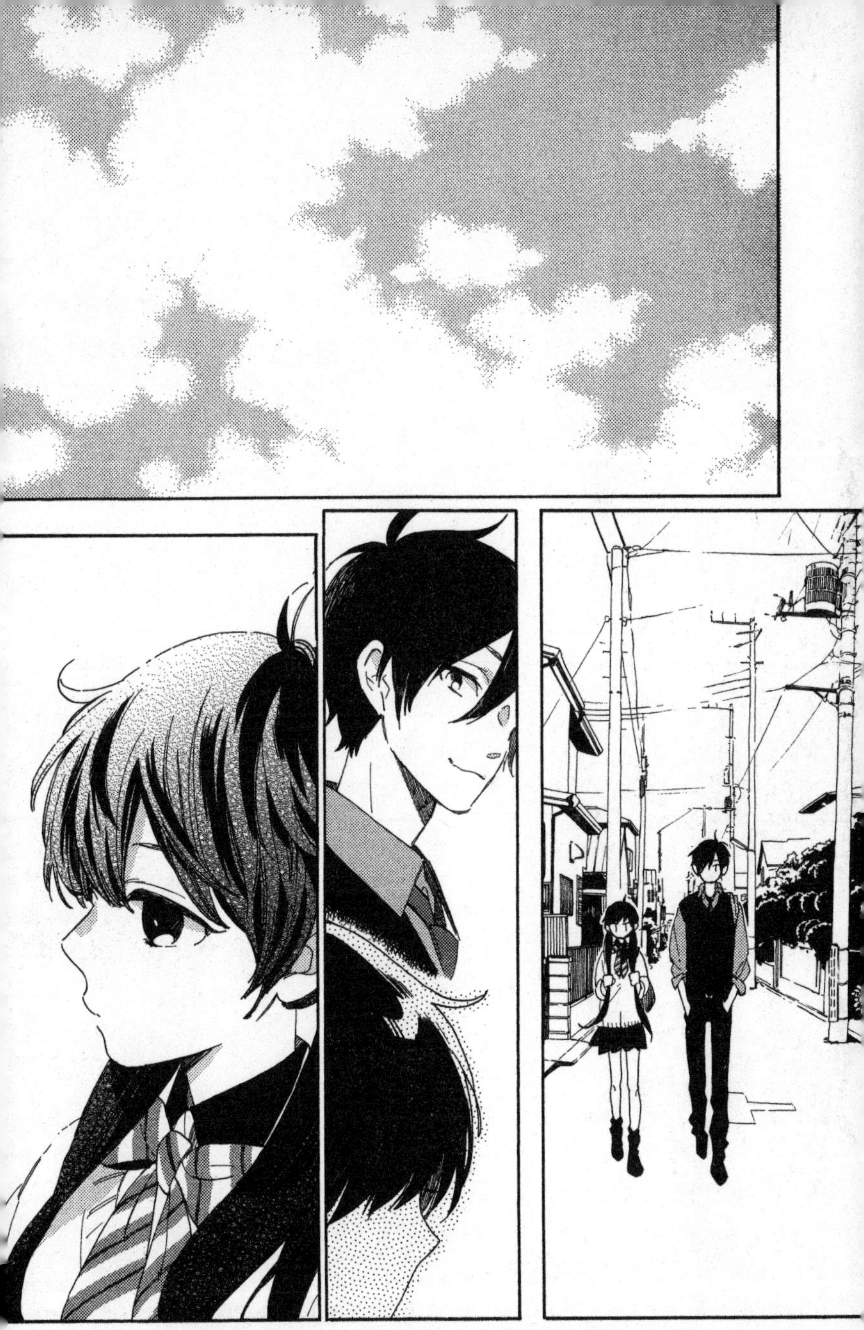

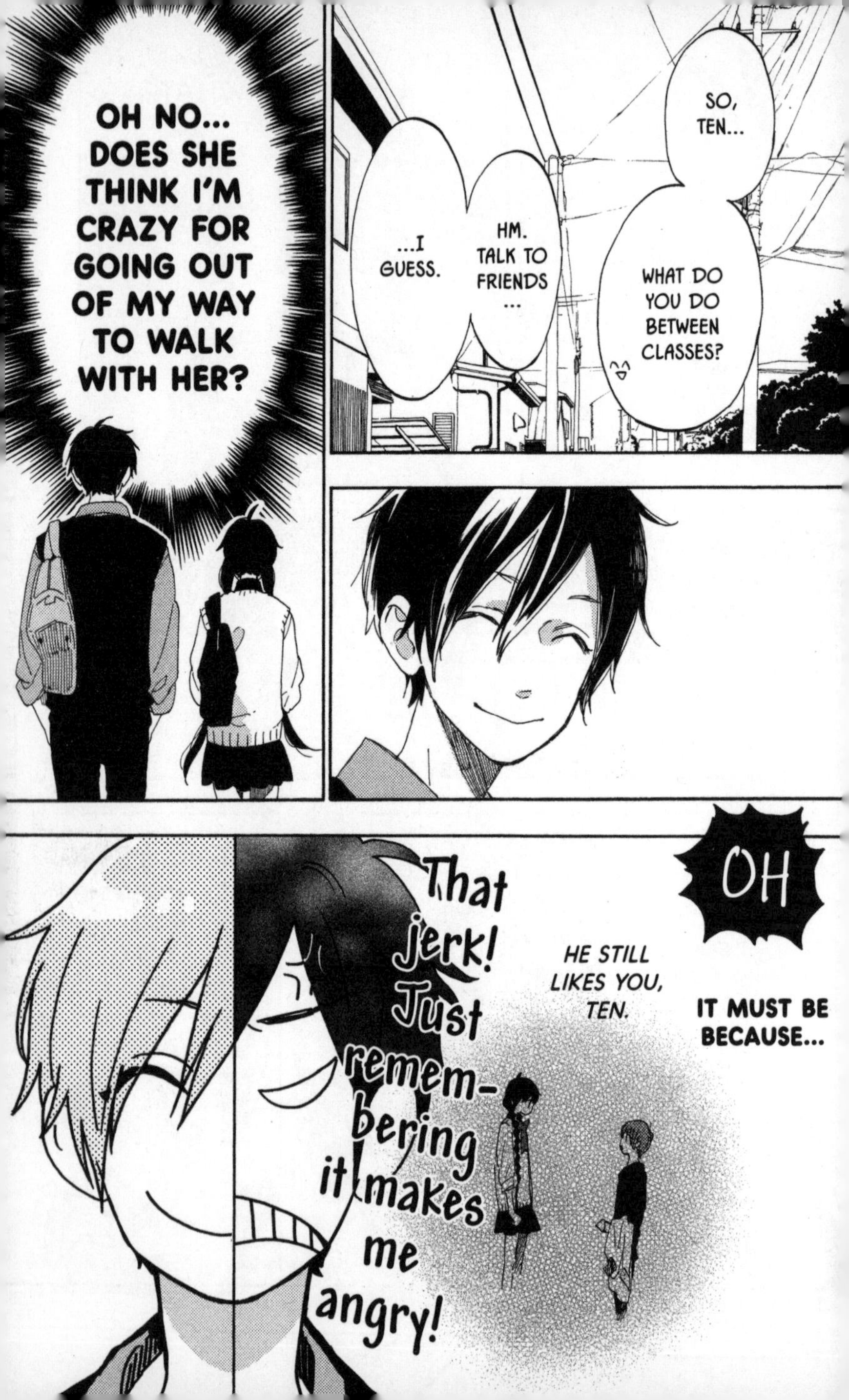
SO, TEN...
WHAT DO YOU DO BETWEEN CLASSES?
HM. TALK TO FRIENDS...
...I GUESS.
OH NO... DOES SHE THINK I'M CRAZY FOR GOING OUT OF MY WAY TO WALK WITH HER?
OH
IT MUST BE BECAUSE...
HE STILL LIKES YOU, TEN.
That jerk! Just remem-bering it makes me angry!

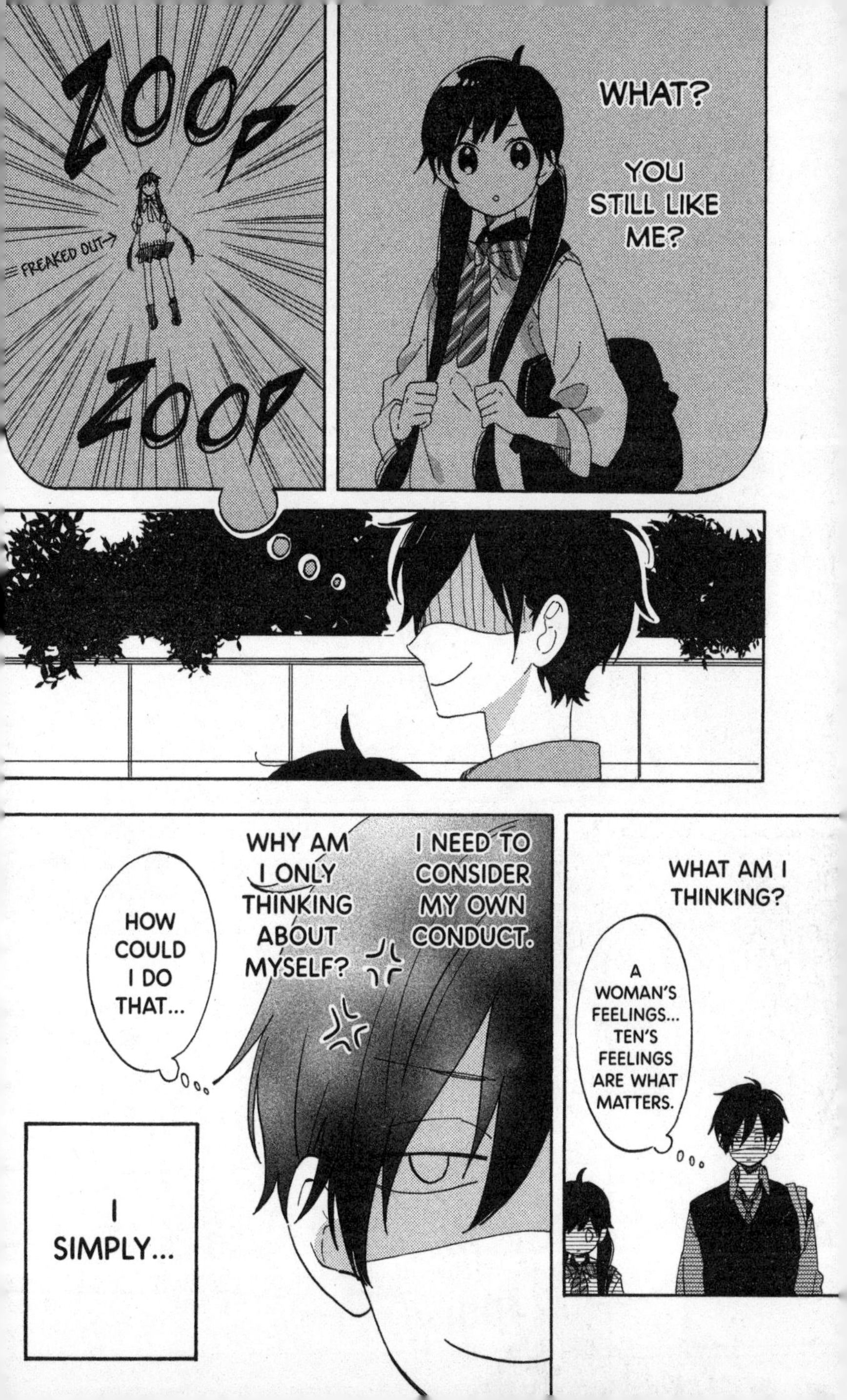
WHAT?
YOU STILL LIKE ME?
ZOOP
FREAKED OUT
ZOOP
WHAT AM I THINKING?
A WOMAN'S FEELINGS... TEN'S FEELINGS ARE WHAT MATTERS.
I NEED TO CONSIDER MY OWN CONDUCT.
WHY AM I ONLY THINKING ABOUT MYSELF?
HOW COULD I DO THAT...
I SIMPLY...

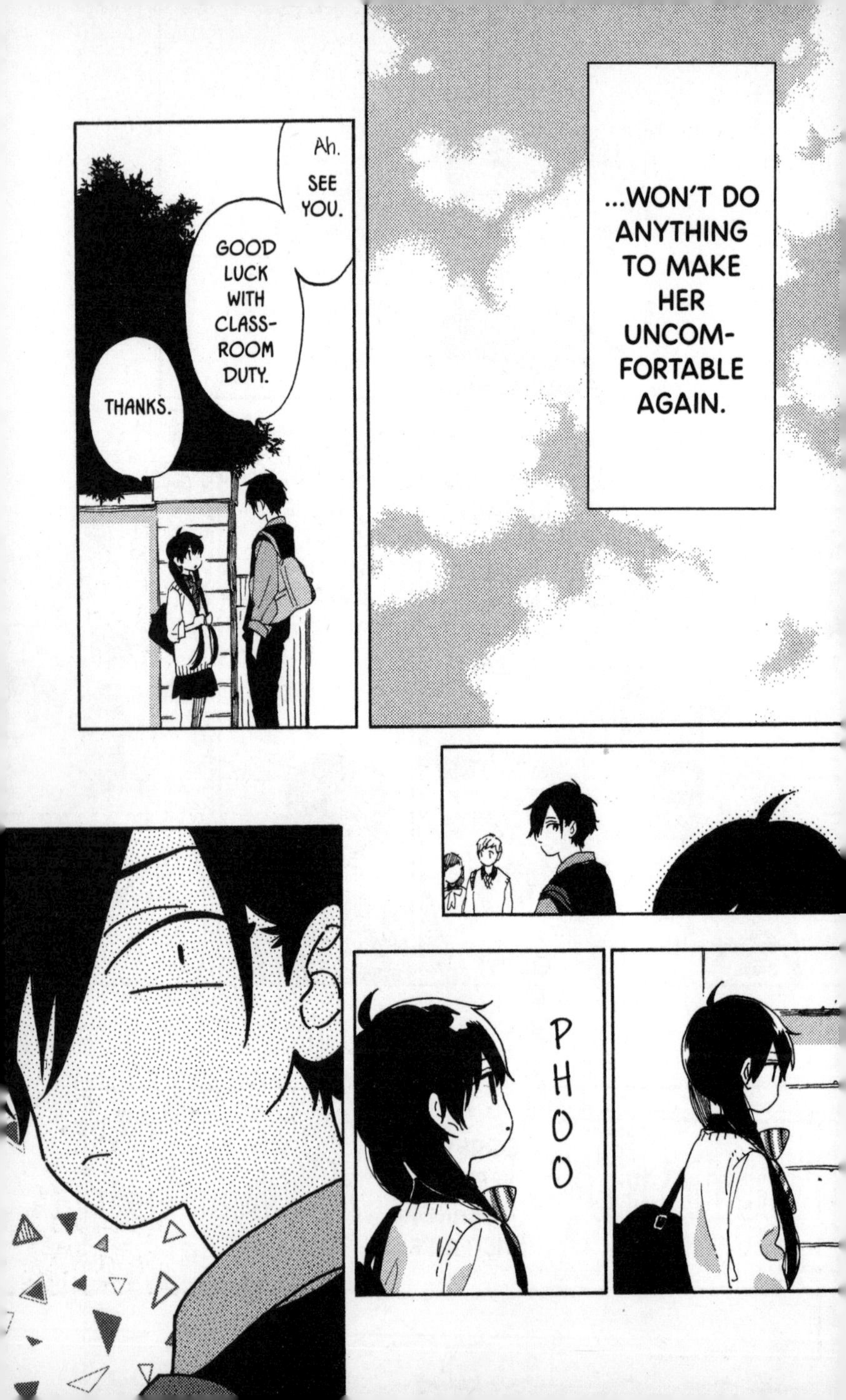
...WON'T DO ANYTHING TO MAKE HER UNCOMFORTABLE AGAIN.
Ah. SEE YOU.
GOOD LUCK WITH CLASSROOM DUTY.
THANKS.
PHOO

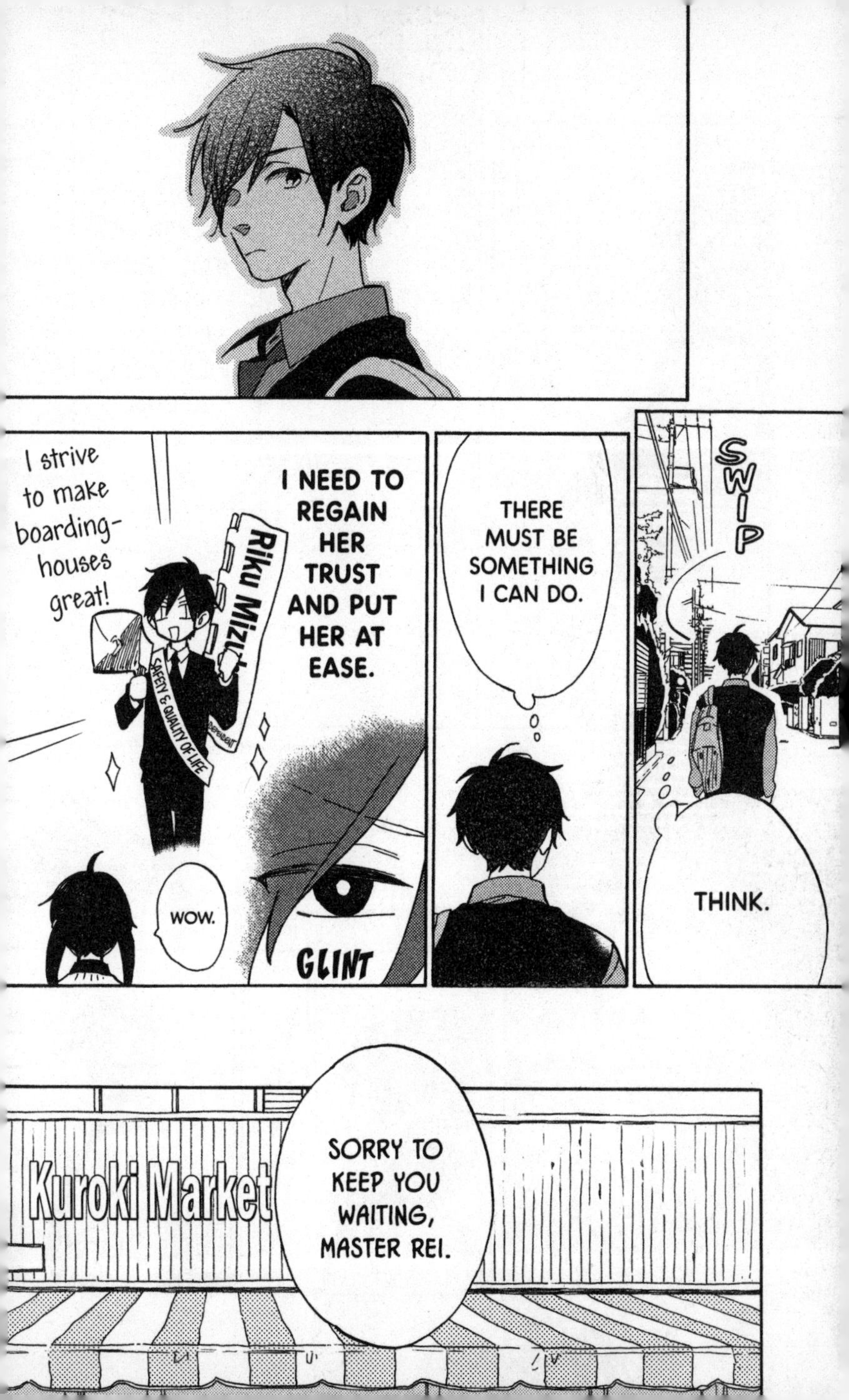

SWIP
THINK.
THERE MUST BE SOMETHING I CAN DO.
I NEED TO REGAIN HER TRUST AND PUT HER AT EASE.
I strive to make boarding-houses great!
Riku Mizu
SAFETY & QUALITY OF LIFE
WOW.
GLINT
Kuroki Market
SORRY TO KEEP YOU WAITING, MASTER REI.

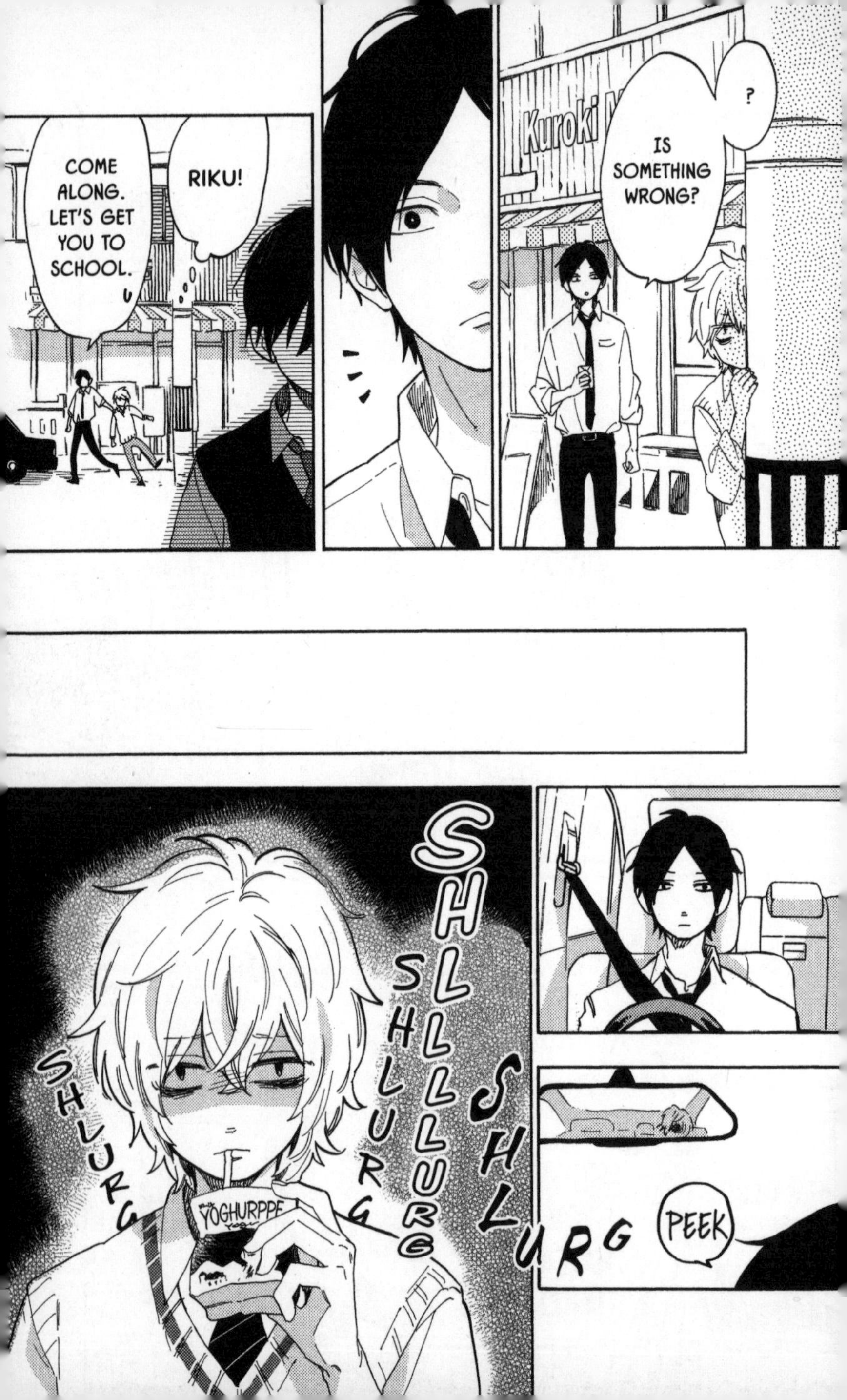
Kuroki M
?
IS SOMETHING WRONG?
RIKU!
COME ALONG. LET'S GET YOU TO SCHOOL.
PEEK
SHLURG
SHLLLLURG
SHLLURG
SHLURG
YOGHURPPE

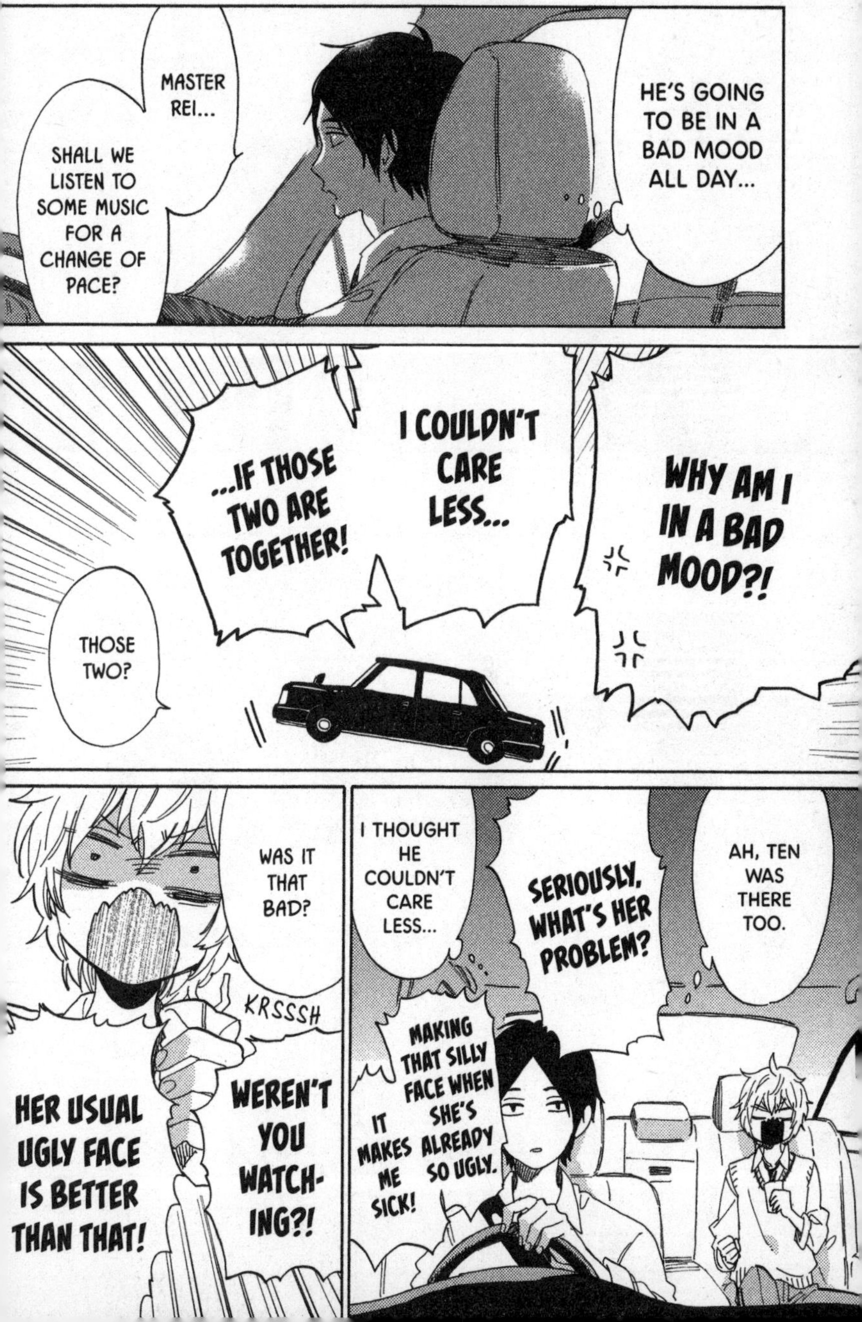
HE'S GOING TO BE IN A BAD MOOD ALL DAY...
MASTER REI...
SHALL WE LISTEN TO SOME MUSIC FOR A CHANGE OF PACE?
WHY AM I IN A BAD MOOD?!
I COULDN'T CARE LESS...
...IF THOSE TWO ARE TOGETHER!
THOSE TWO?
AH, TEN WAS THERE TOO.
SERIOUSLY, WHAT'S HER PROBLEM?
I THOUGHT HE COULDN'T CARE LESS...
MAKING THAT SILLY FACE WHEN SHE'S ALREADY SO UGLY.
IT MAKES ME SICK!
WAS IT THAT BAD?
KRSSSH
WEREN'T YOU WATCHING?!
HER USUAL UGLY FACE IS BETTER THAN THAT!

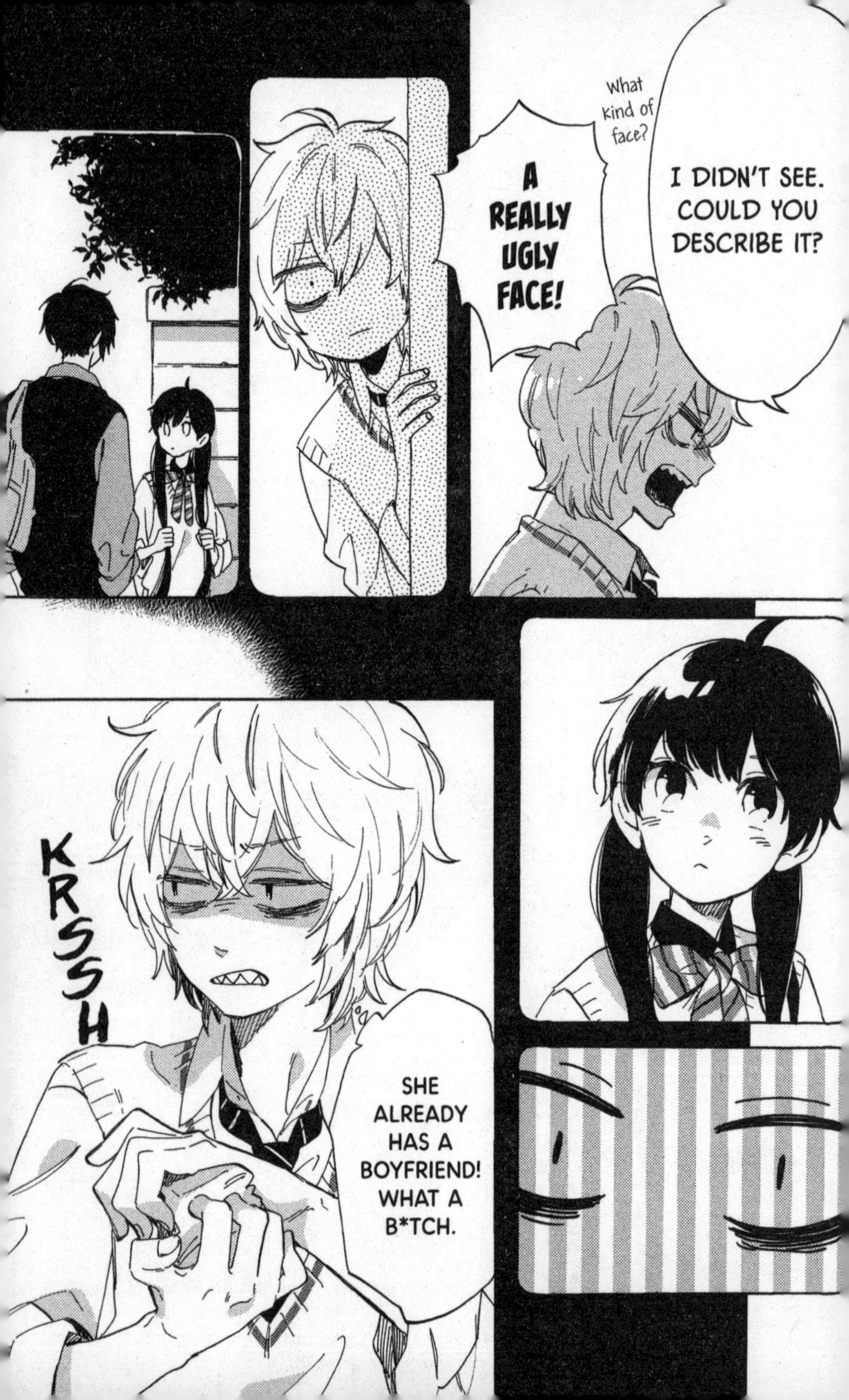
I DIDN'T SEE. COULD YOU DESCRIBE IT?
What kind of face?
A REALLY UGLY FACE!
SHE ALREADY HAS A BOYFRIEND! WHAT A B*TCH.
KRSSH

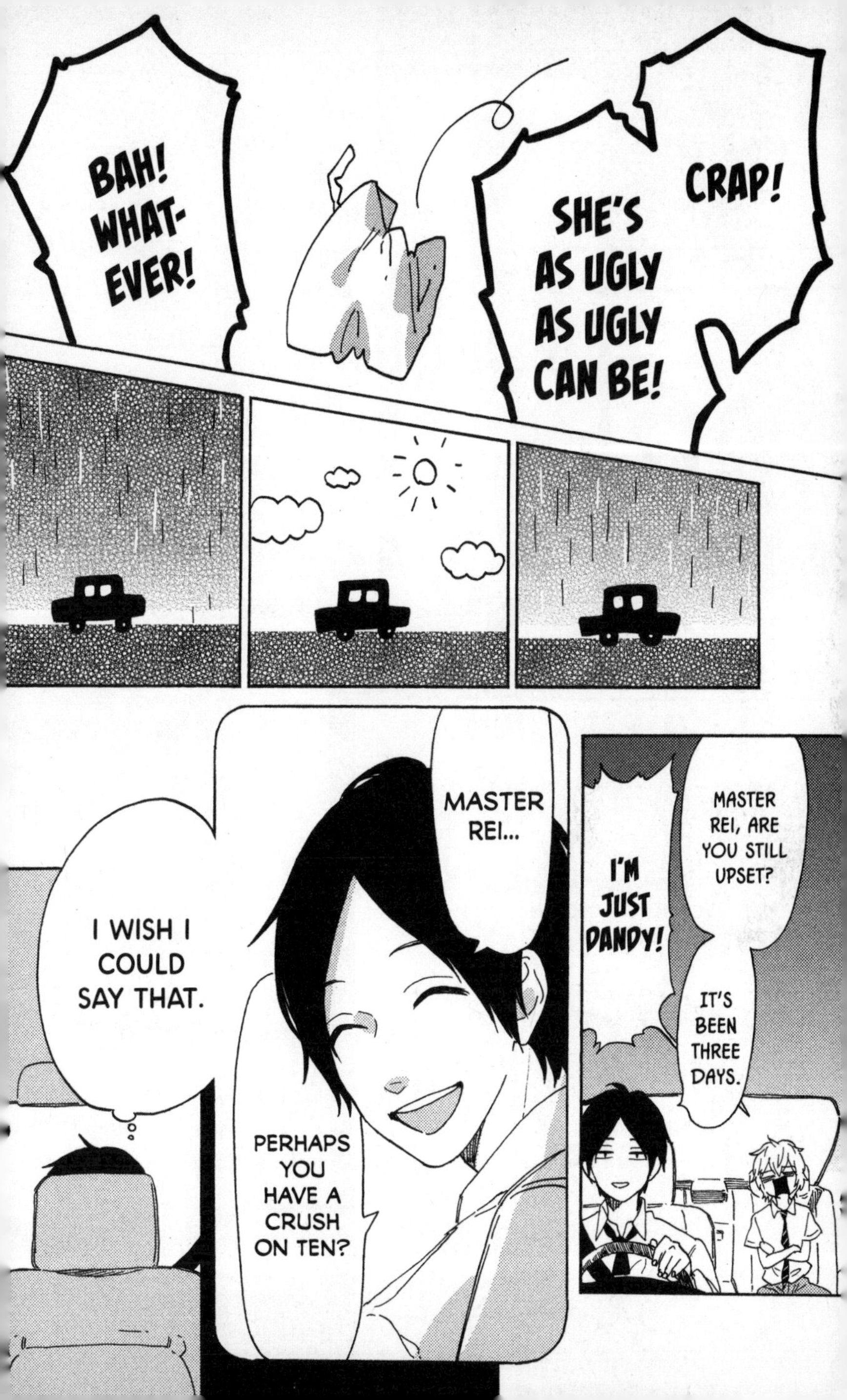
CRAP!
SHE'S AS UGLY AS UGLY CAN BE!
BAH! WHAT-EVER!
MASTER REI, ARE YOU STILL UPSET?
I'M JUST DANDY!
IT'S BEEN THREE DAYS.
MASTER REI...
PERHAPS YOU HAVE A CRUSH ON TEN?
I WISH I COULD SAY THAT.

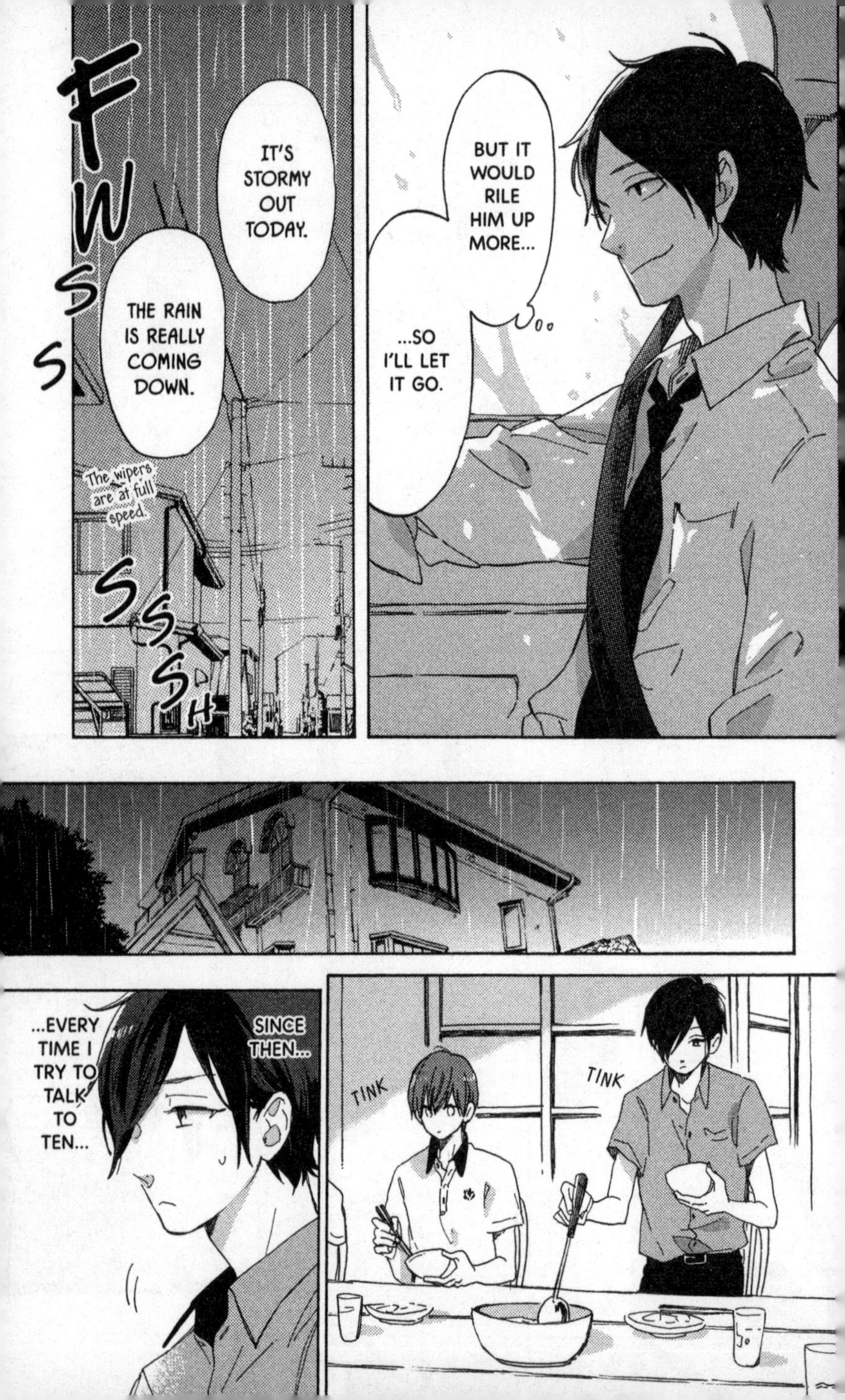
BUT IT WOULD RILE HIM UP MORE...
...SO I'LL LET IT GO.
IT'S STORMY OUT TODAY.
FWSS
THE RAIN IS REALLY COMING DOWN.
S
The wipers are at full speed.
SSSSH
TINK
TINK
SINCE THEN...
...EVERY TIME I TRY TO TALK TO TEN...

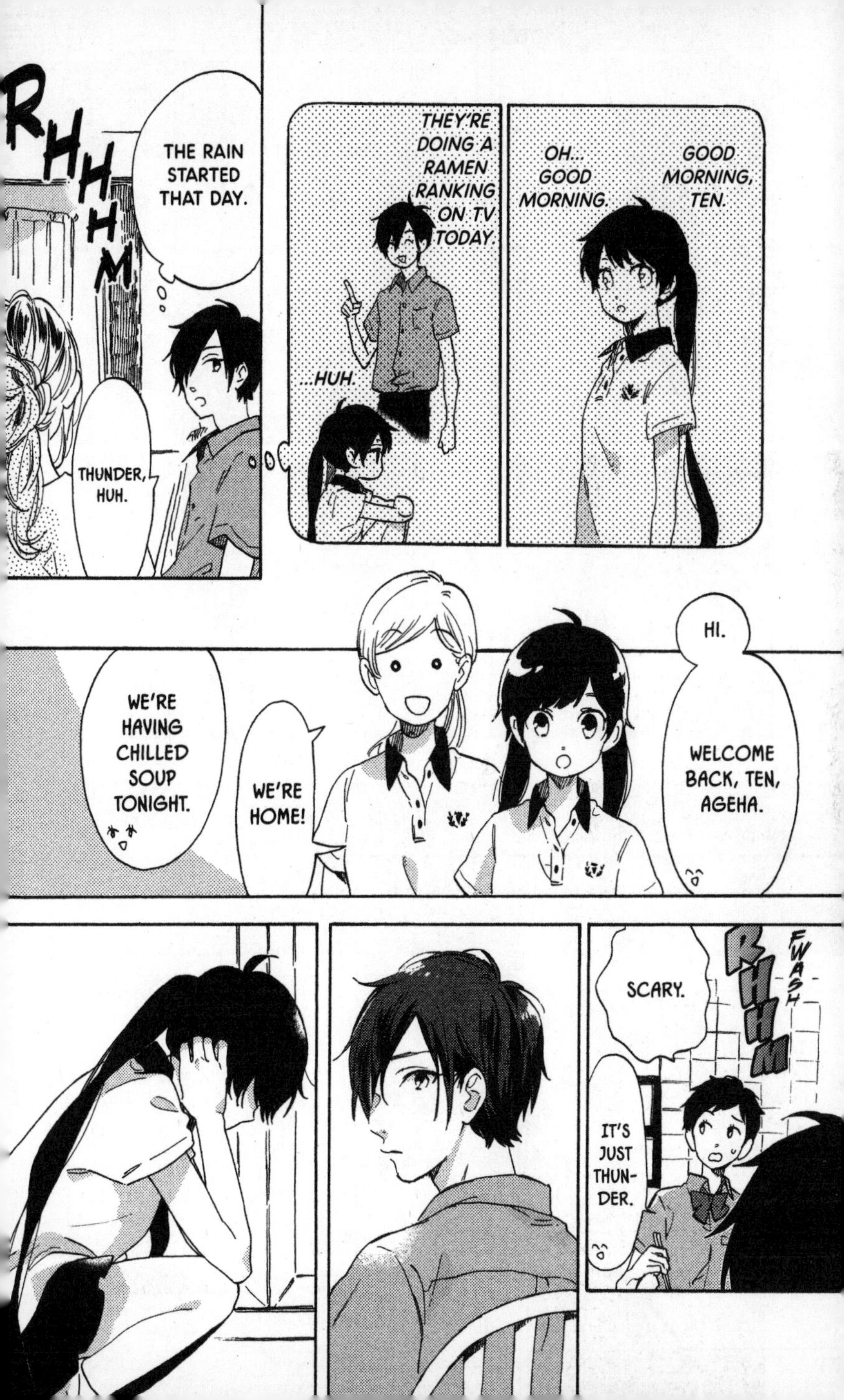
GOOD MORNING, TEN.
OH... GOOD MORNING.
THEY'RE DOING A RAMEN RANKING ON TV TODAY.
...HUH.
RHHHM
THE RAIN STARTED THAT DAY.
THUNDER, HUH.
HI.
WELCOME BACK, TEN, AGEHA.
WE'RE HOME!
WE'RE HAVING CHILLED SOUP TONIGHT.
RHHHM
FWASH
SCARY.
IT'S JUST THUNDER.

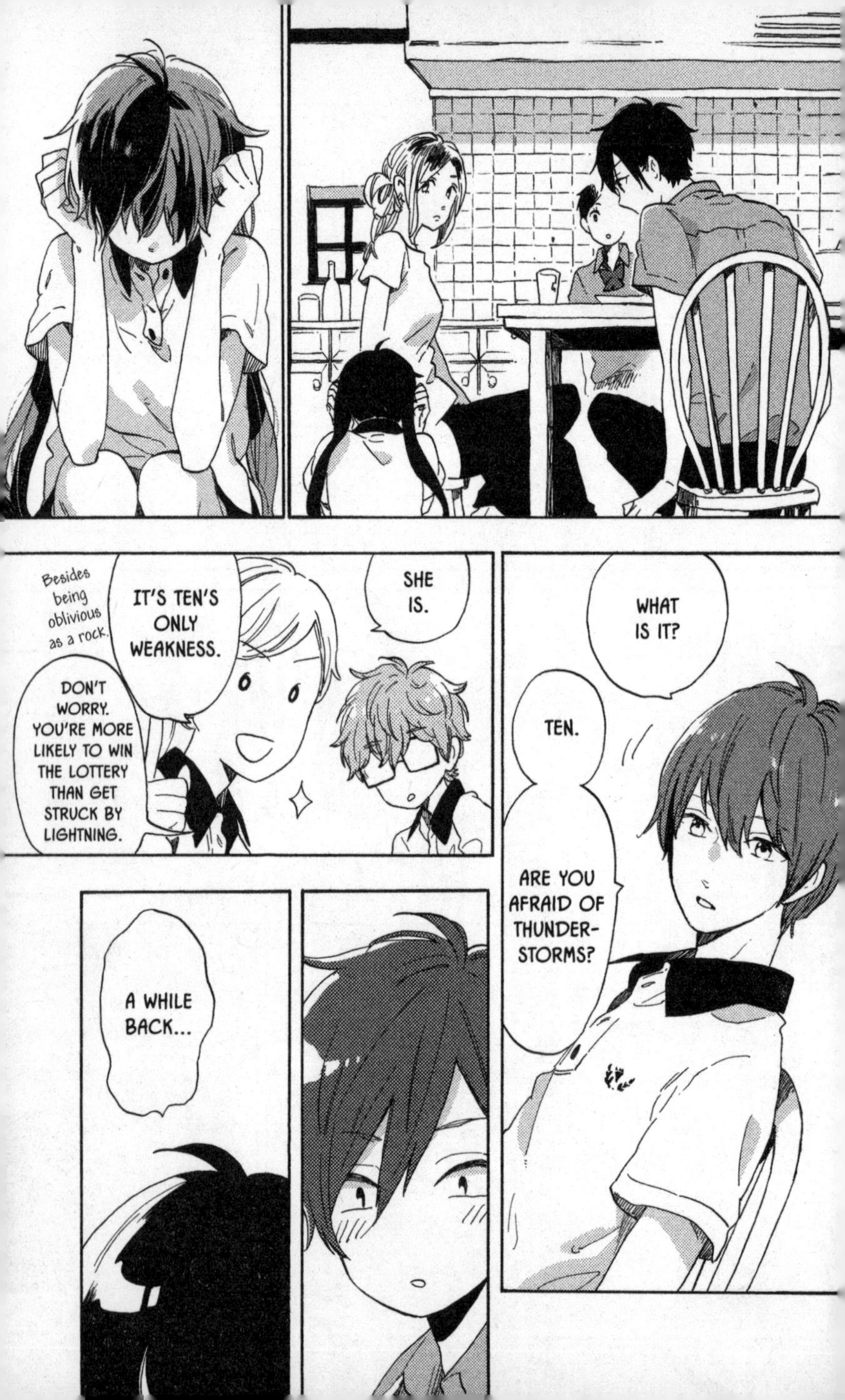
WHAT IS IT?
TEN.
ARE YOU AFRAID OF THUNDER-STORMS?
SHE IS.
IT'S TEN'S ONLY WEAKNESS.
Besides being oblivious as a rock.
DON'T WORRY. YOU'RE MORE LIKELY TO WIN THE LOTTERY THAN GET STRUCK BY LIGHTNING.
A WHILE BACK...

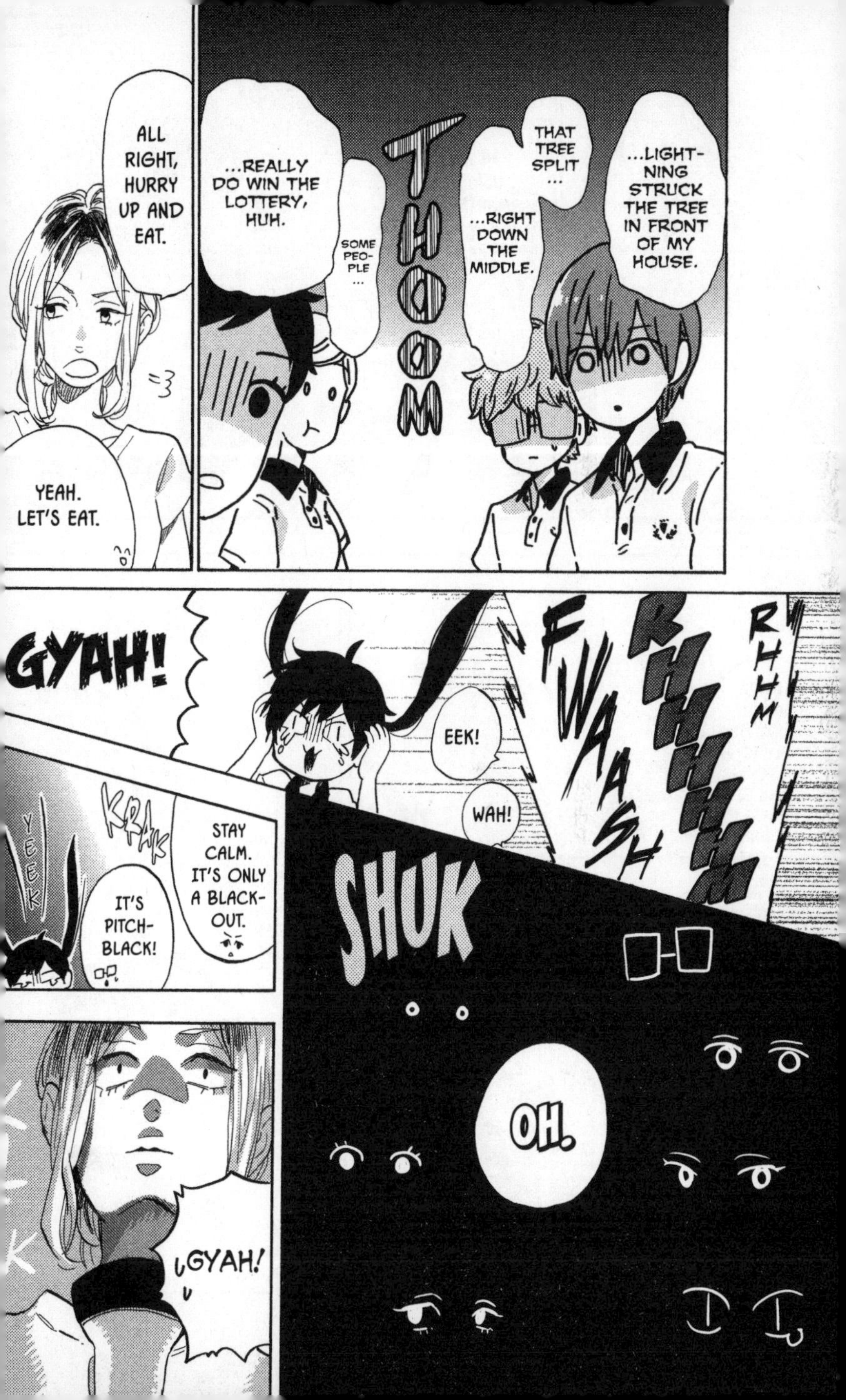
...LIGHTNING STRUCK THE TREE IN FRONT OF MY HOUSE.
THAT TREE SPLIT...
...RIGHT DOWN THE MIDDLE.
THOOM
SOME PEOPLE...
...REALLY DO WIN THE LOTTERY, HUH.
ALL RIGHT, HURRY UP AND EAT.
YEAH. LET'S EAT.
RHHM
RHHHHHM
FWAASH
EEK!
WAH!
GYAH!
KRAK
STAY CALM. IT'S ONLY A BLACKOUT.
IT'S PITCH-BLACK!
YEEEK
SHUK
OH.
GYAH!

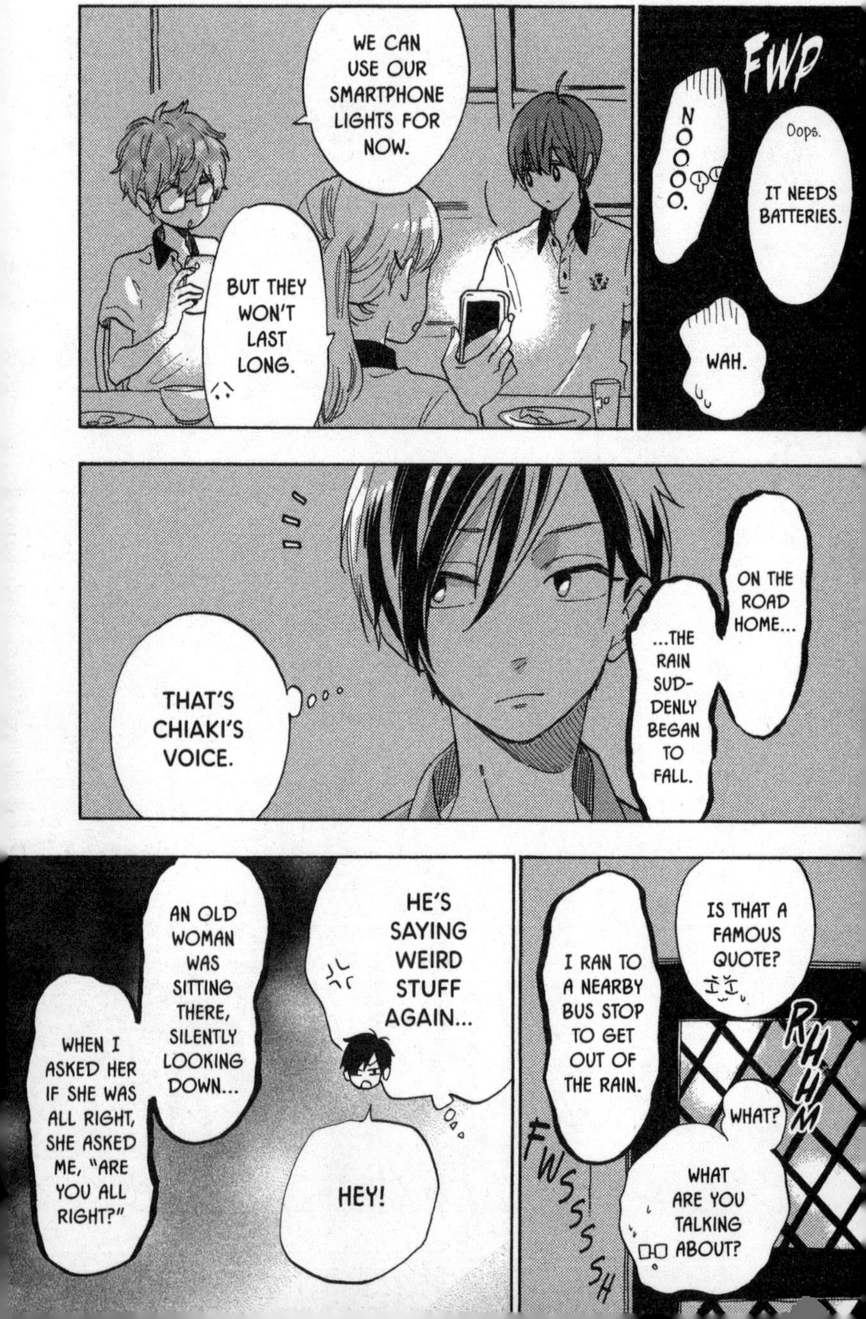
FWP
Oops.
IT NEEDS BATTERIES.
NOOOO.
WAH.
WE CAN USE OUR SMARTPHONE LIGHTS FOR NOW.
BUT THEY WON'T LAST LONG.
ON THE ROAD HOME...
...THE RAIN SUDDENLY BEGAN TO FALL.
THAT'S CHIAKI'S VOICE.
IS THAT A FAMOUS QUOTE?
I RAN TO A NEARBY BUS STOP TO GET OUT OF THE RAIN.
RHHM
WHAT?
WHAT ARE YOU TALKING ABOUT?
FWSSSSH
HE'S SAYING WEIRD STUFF AGAIN...
AN OLD WOMAN WAS SITTING THERE, SILENTLY LOOKING DOWN...
HEY!
WHEN I ASKED HER IF SHE WAS ALL RIGHT, SHE ASKED ME, "ARE YOU ALL RIGHT?"

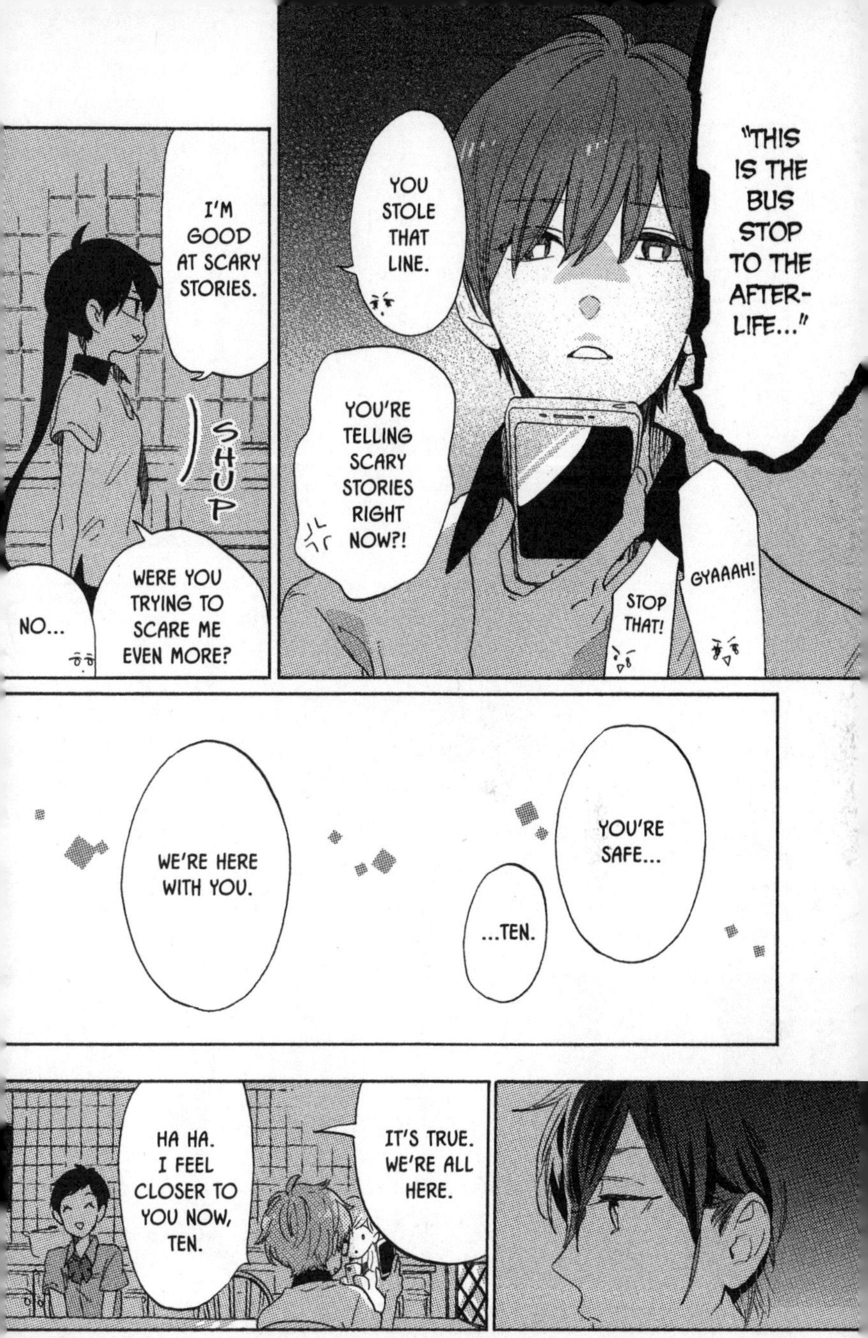
"THIS IS THE BUS STOP TO THE AFTER-LIFE..."
YOU STOLE THAT LINE.
YOU'RE TELLING SCARY STORIES RIGHT NOW?!
GYAAAH!
STOP THAT!
I'M GOOD AT SCARY STORIES.
SHUP
WERE YOU TRYING TO SCARE ME EVEN MORE?
NO...
YOU'RE SAFE...
...TEN.
WE'RE HERE WITH YOU.
IT'S TRUE. WE'RE ALL HERE.
HA HA. I FEEL CLOSER TO YOU NOW, TEN.

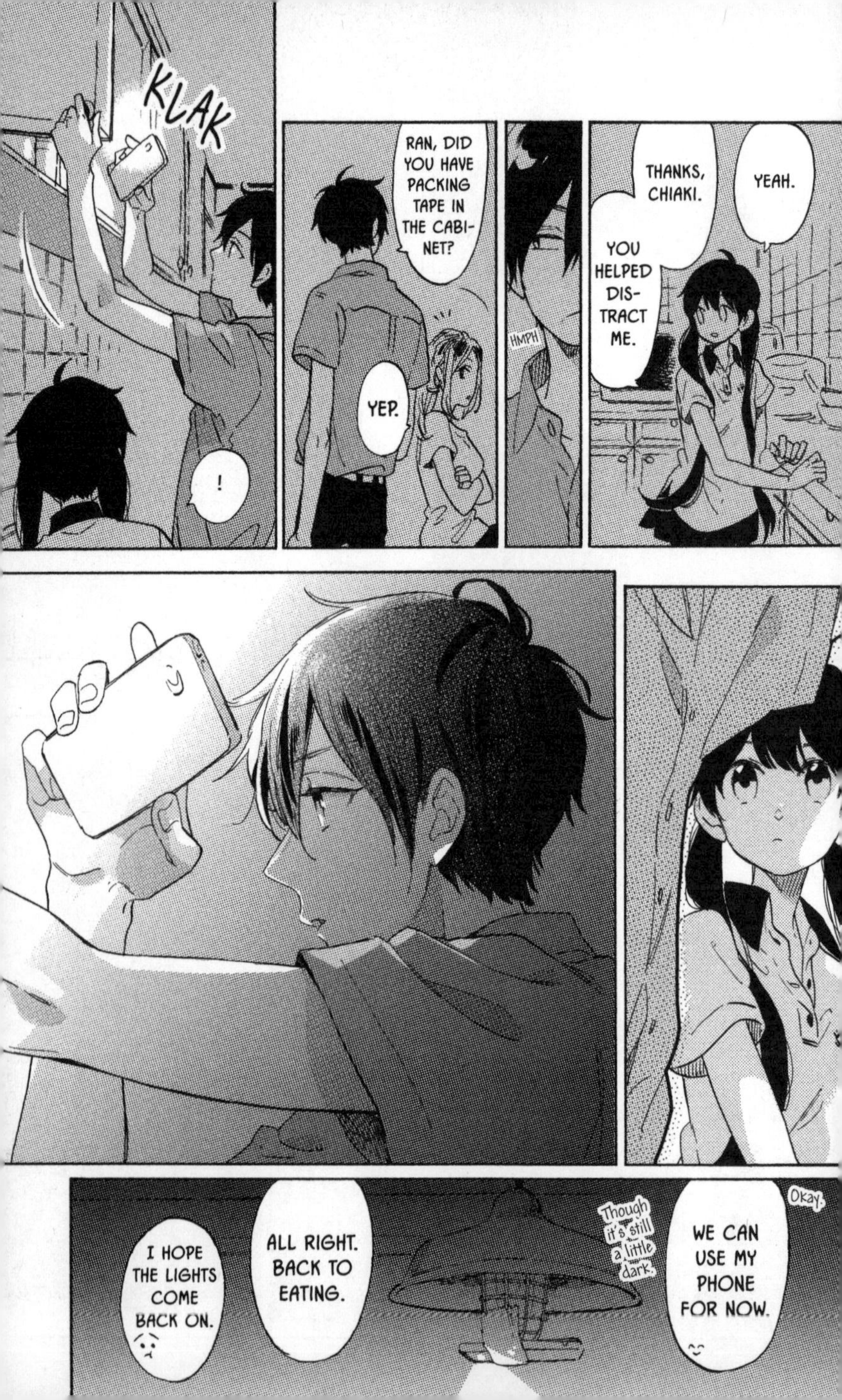
YEAH.
THANKS, CHIAKI.
YOU HELPED DIS-TRACT ME.
HMPH
RAN, DID YOU HAVE PACKING TAPE IN THE CABI-NET?
YEP.
KLAK
!
Okay.
WE CAN USE MY PHONE FOR NOW.
Though it's still a little dark.
ALL RIGHT. BACK TO EATING.
I HOPE THE LIGHTS COME BACK ON.

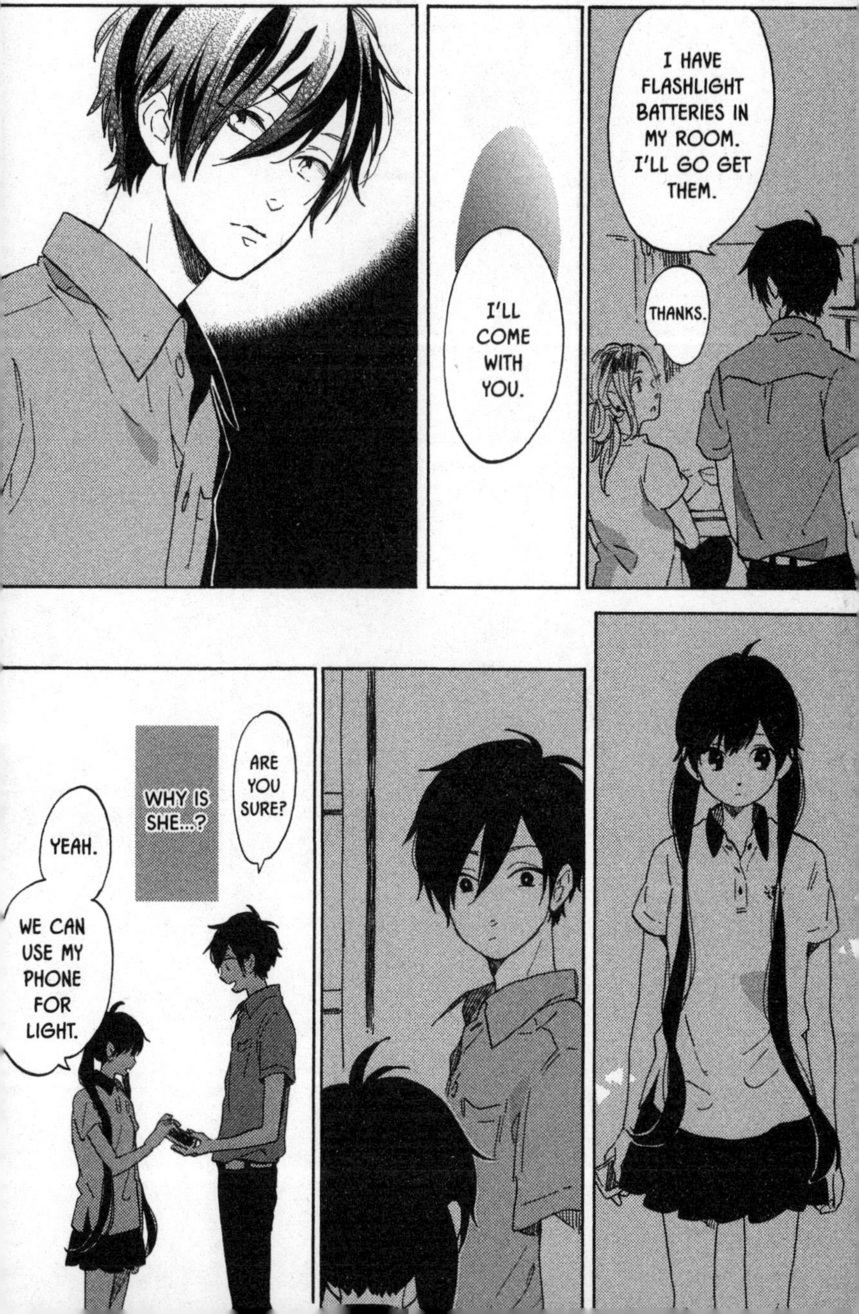
I HAVE FLASHLIGHT BATTERIES IN MY ROOM. I'LL GO GET THEM.
THANKS.
I'LL COME WITH YOU.
ARE YOU SURE?
WHY IS SHE...?
YEAH.
WE CAN USE MY PHONE FOR LIGHT.

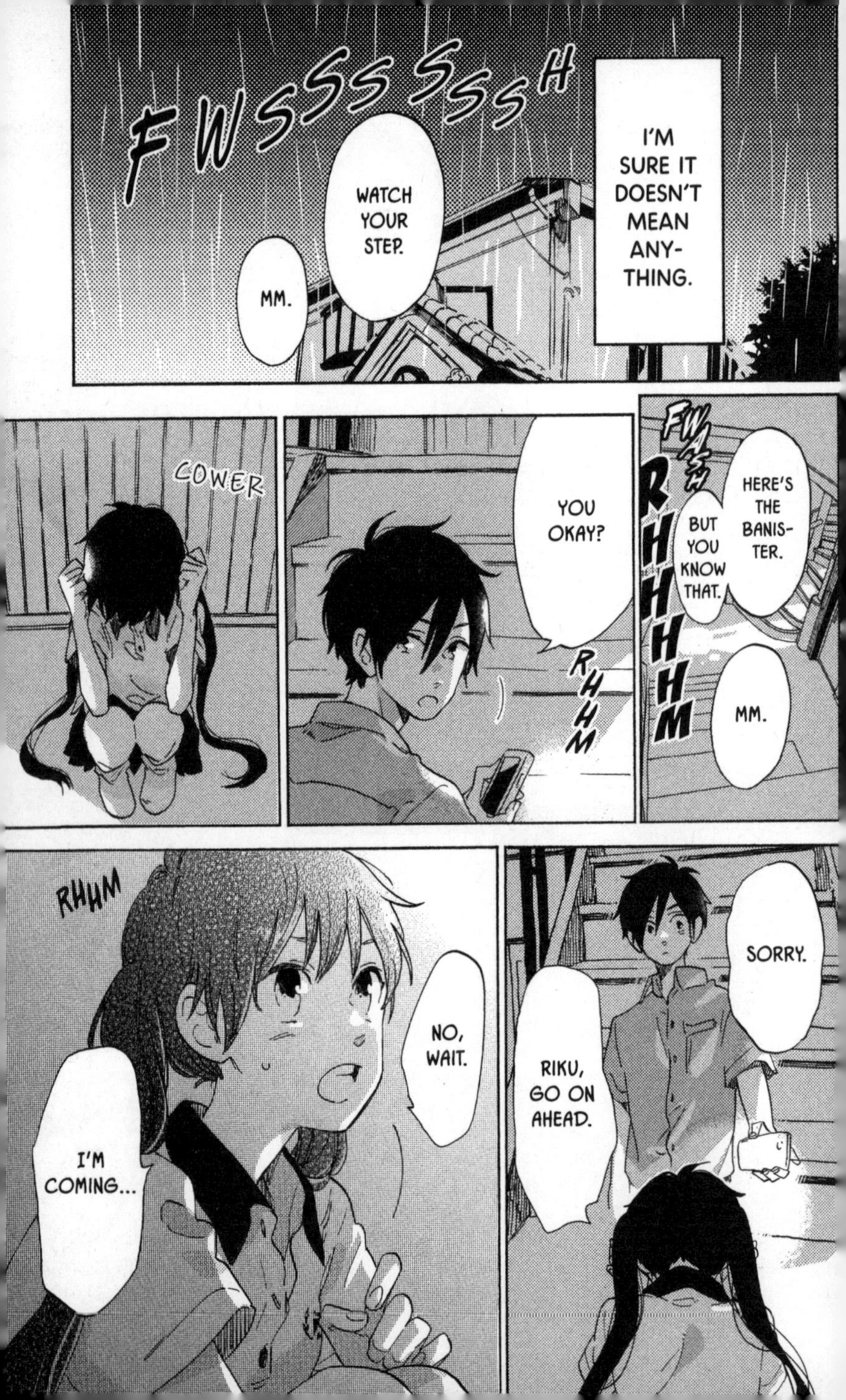
I'M SURE IT DOESN'T MEAN ANY-THING.
FWSSSSSSSH
WATCH YOUR STEP.
MM.
HERE'S THE BANIS-TER.
FWASH
RHHHHHM
BUT YOU KNOW THAT.
MM.
YOU OKAY?
RHHM
COWER
SORRY.
RIKU, GO ON AHEAD.
RHHM
NO, WAIT.
I'M COMING...

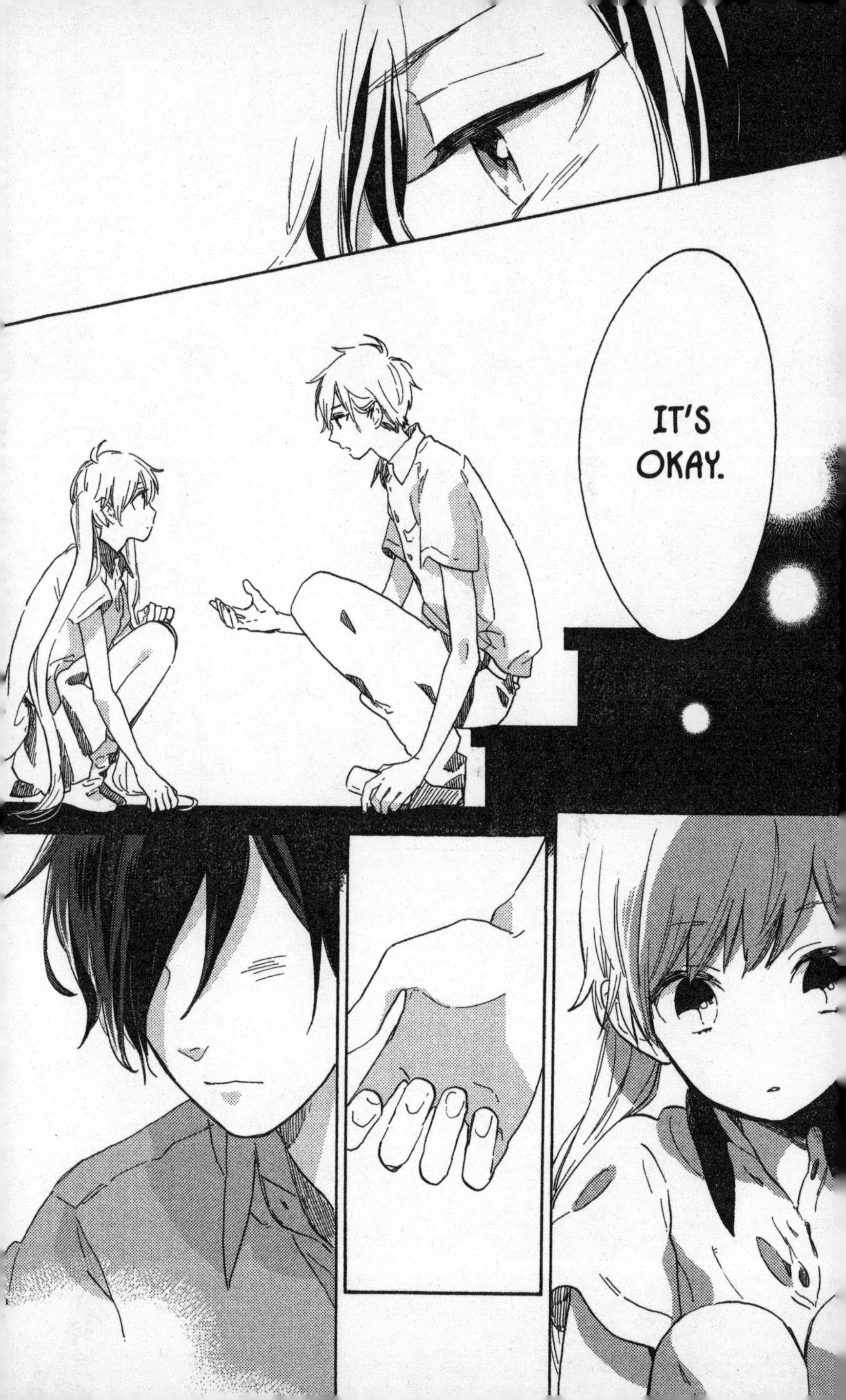
IT'S OKAY.

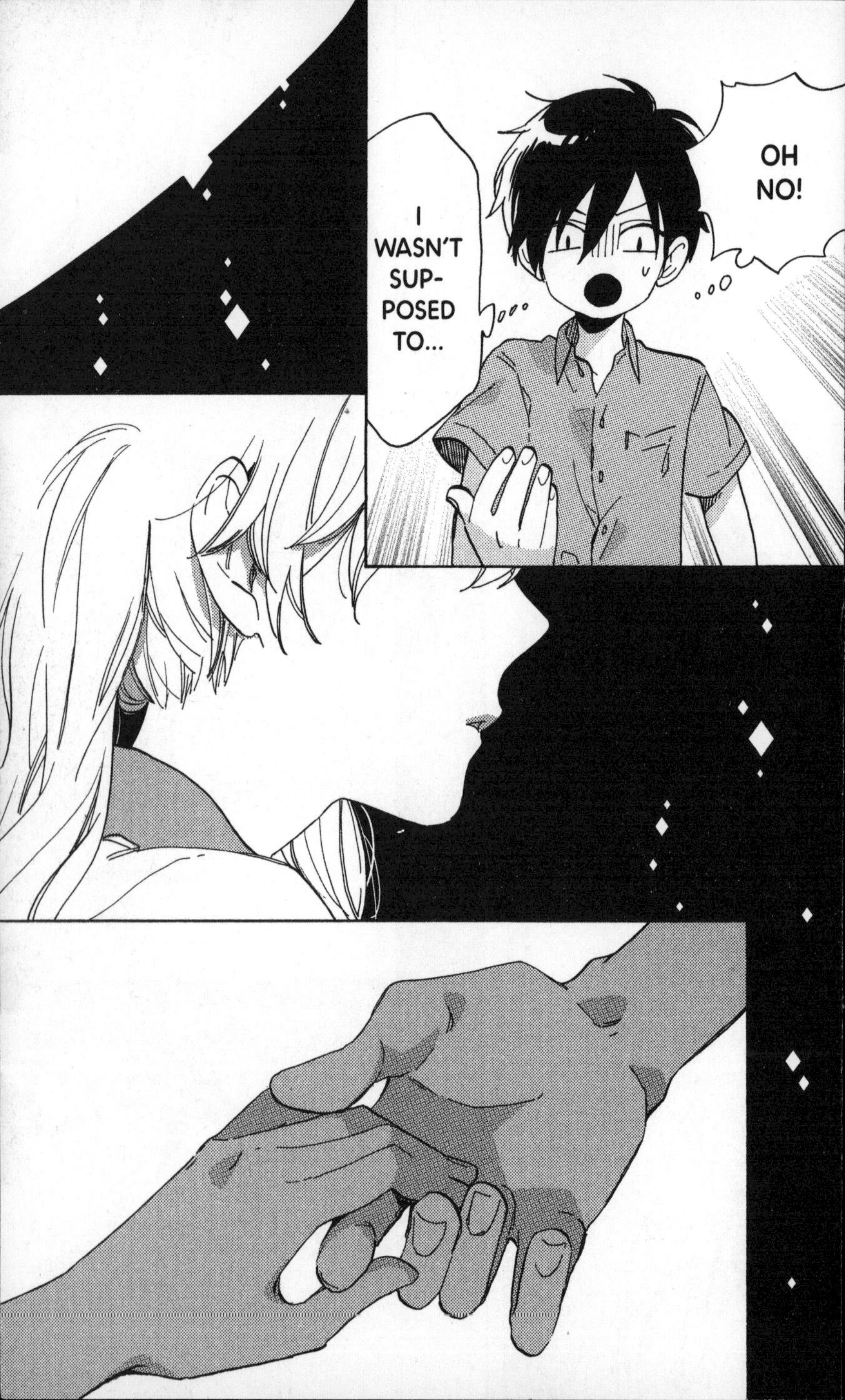
OH NO!
I WASN'T SUP-POSED TO...

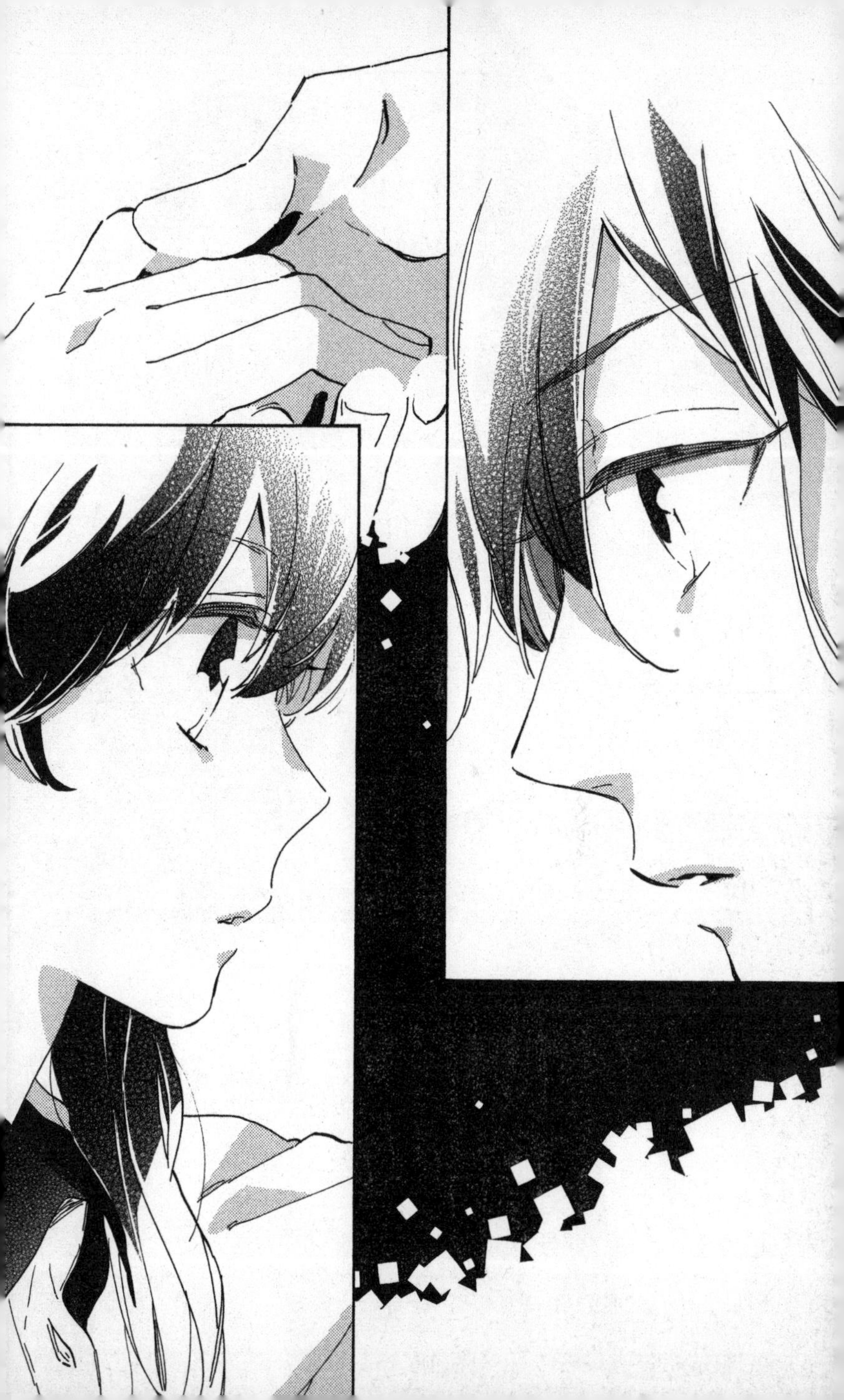

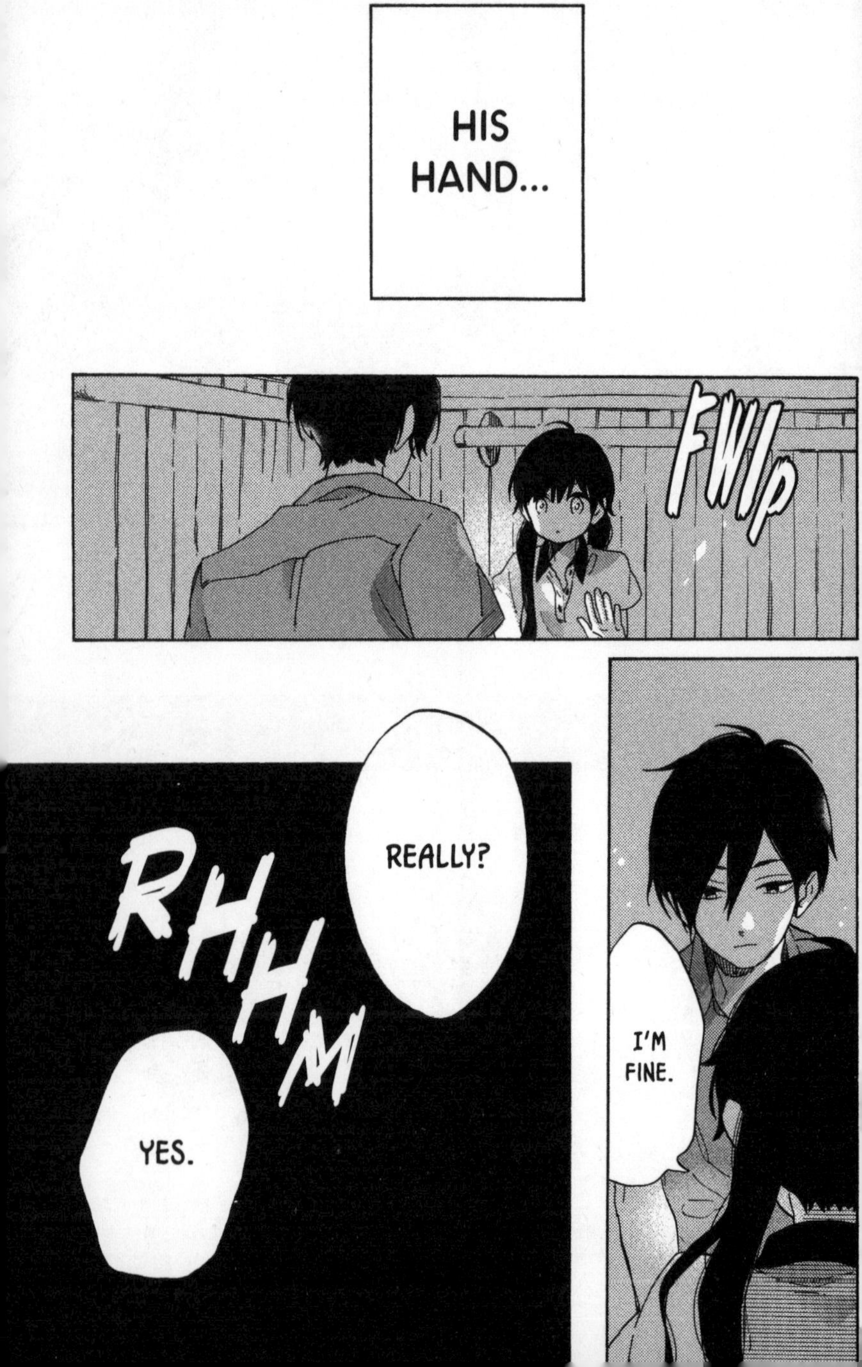
HIS HAND...
FWIP
I'M FINE.
REALLY?
RHHM
YES.

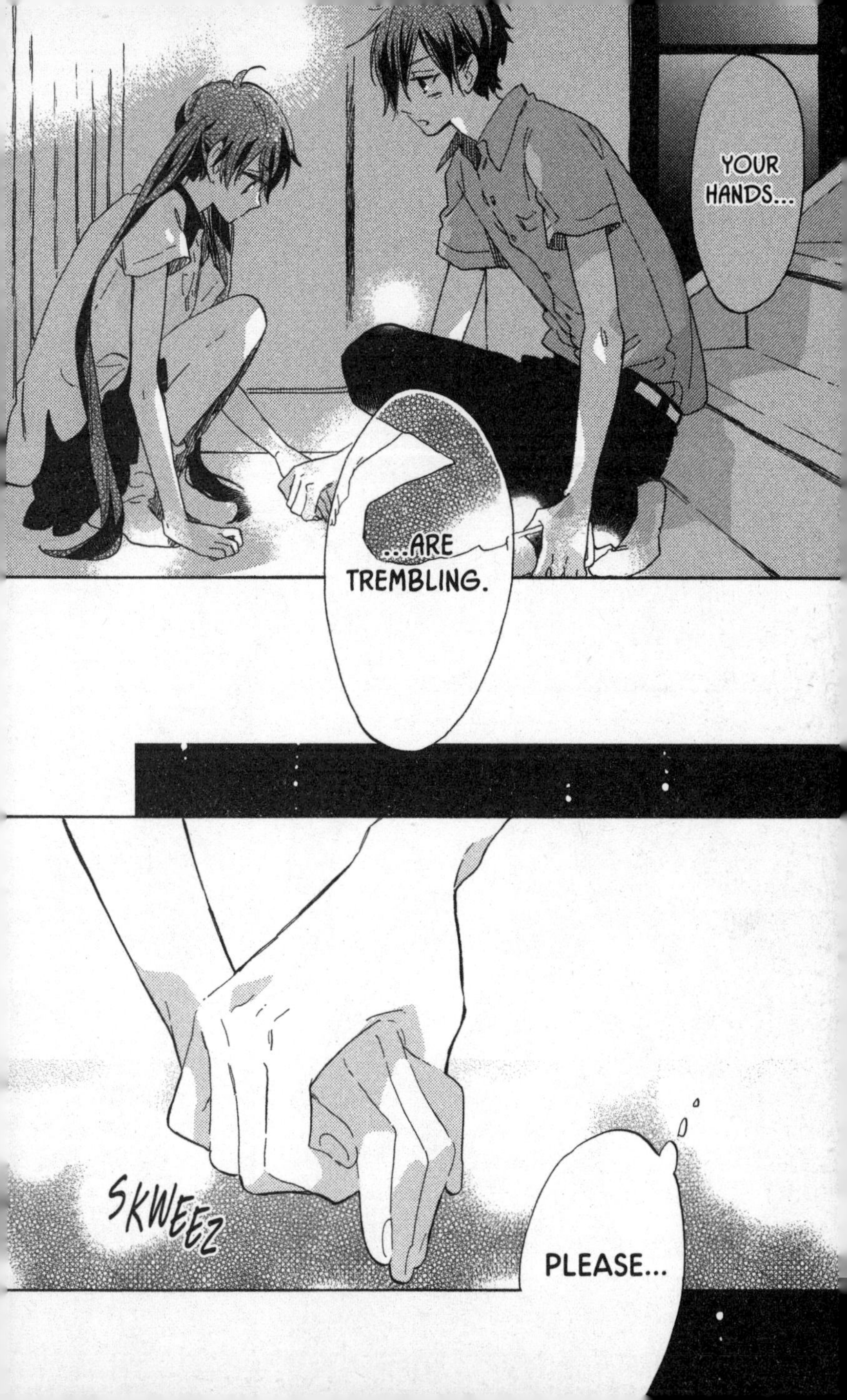
YOUR HANDS...
...ARE TREMBLING.
PLEASE...
SKWEEZ

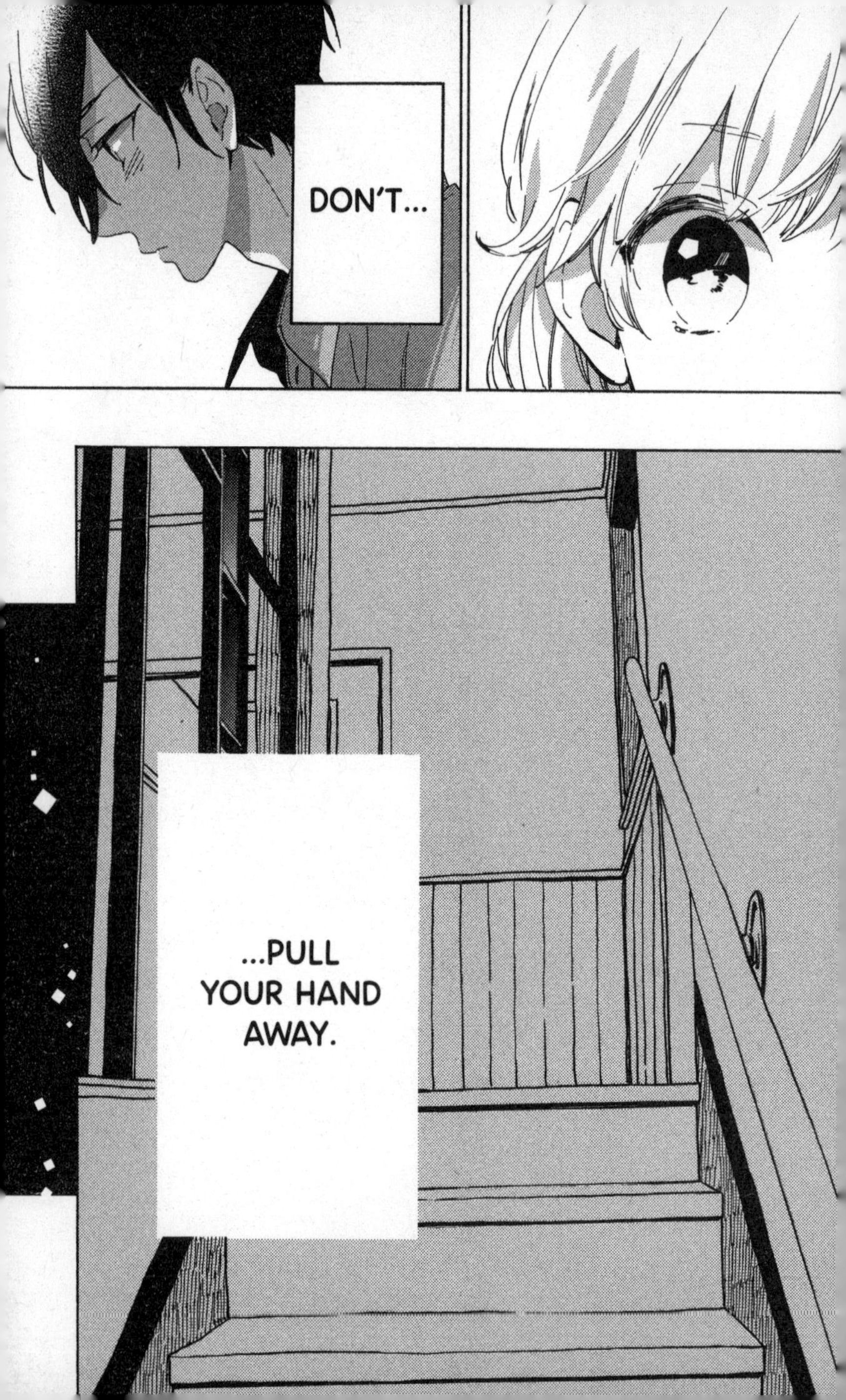
DON'T...
...PULL YOUR HAND AWAY.

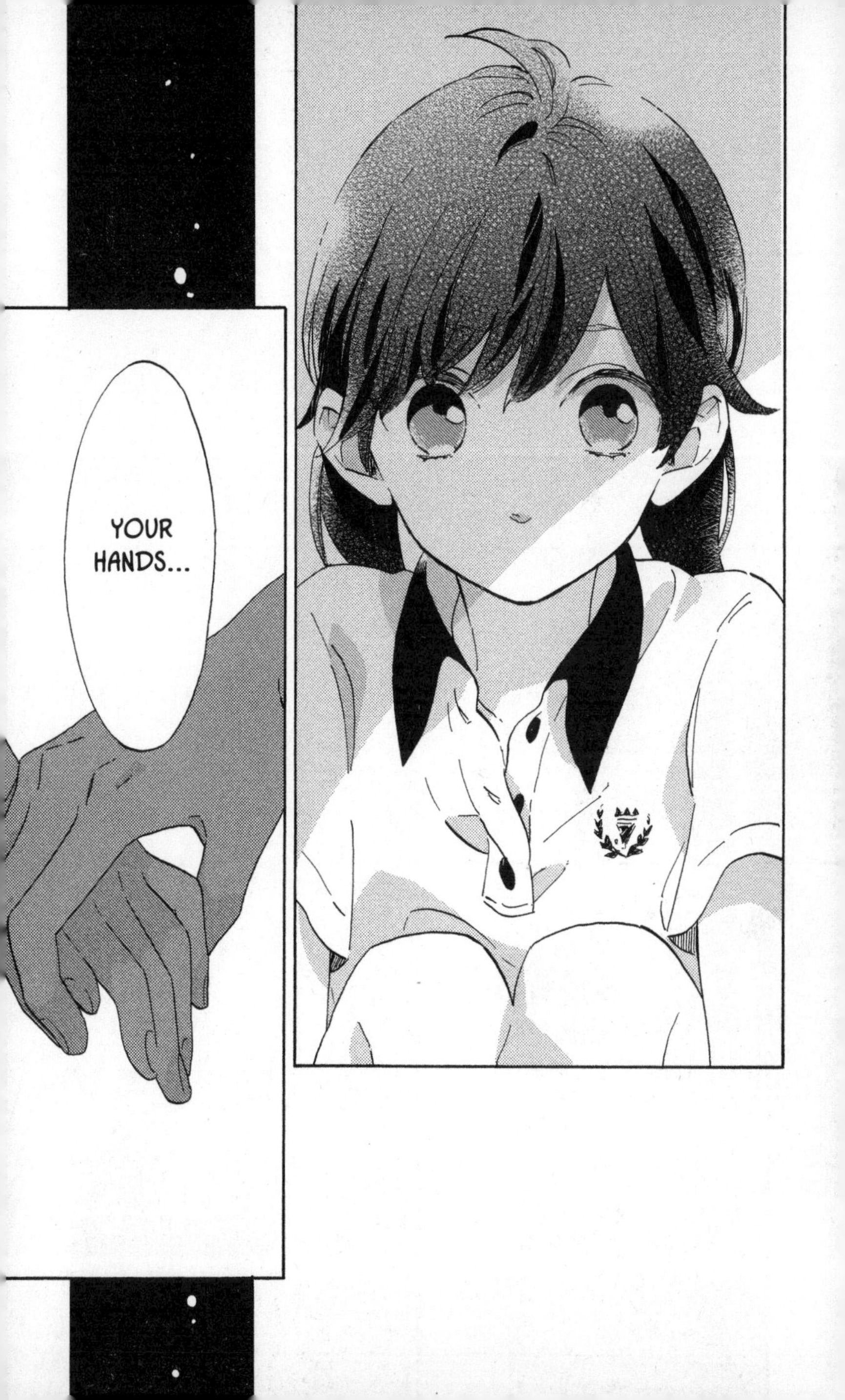
YOUR HANDS...

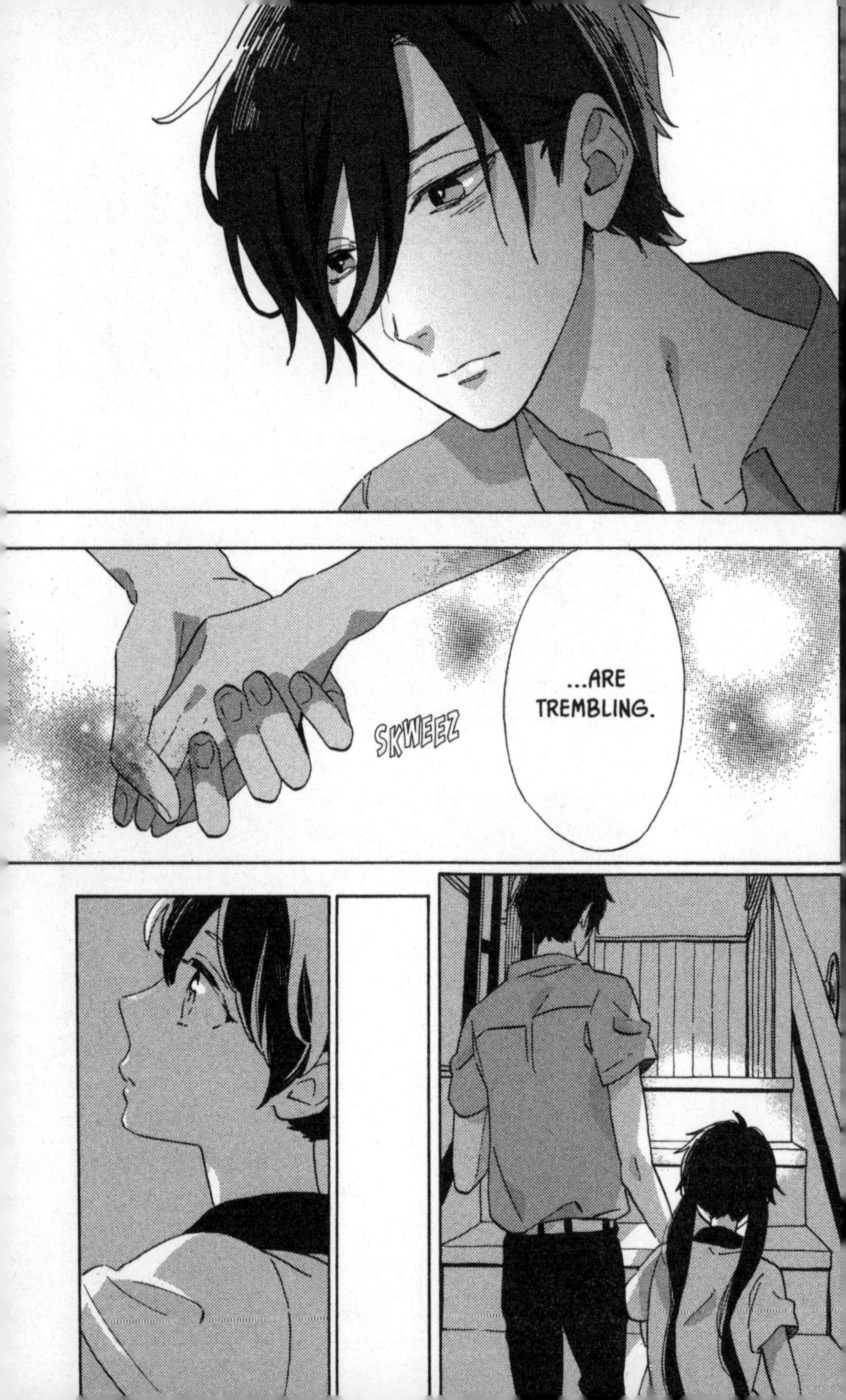
...ARE TREMBLING.
SKWEEZ

WHY...

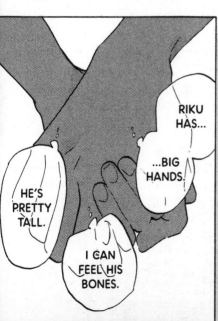

RIKU HAS...

...BIG HANDS.

HE'S PRETTY TALL.

I CAN FEEL HIS BONES.

*RHHM*

...IS RIKU...

...SO NICE?

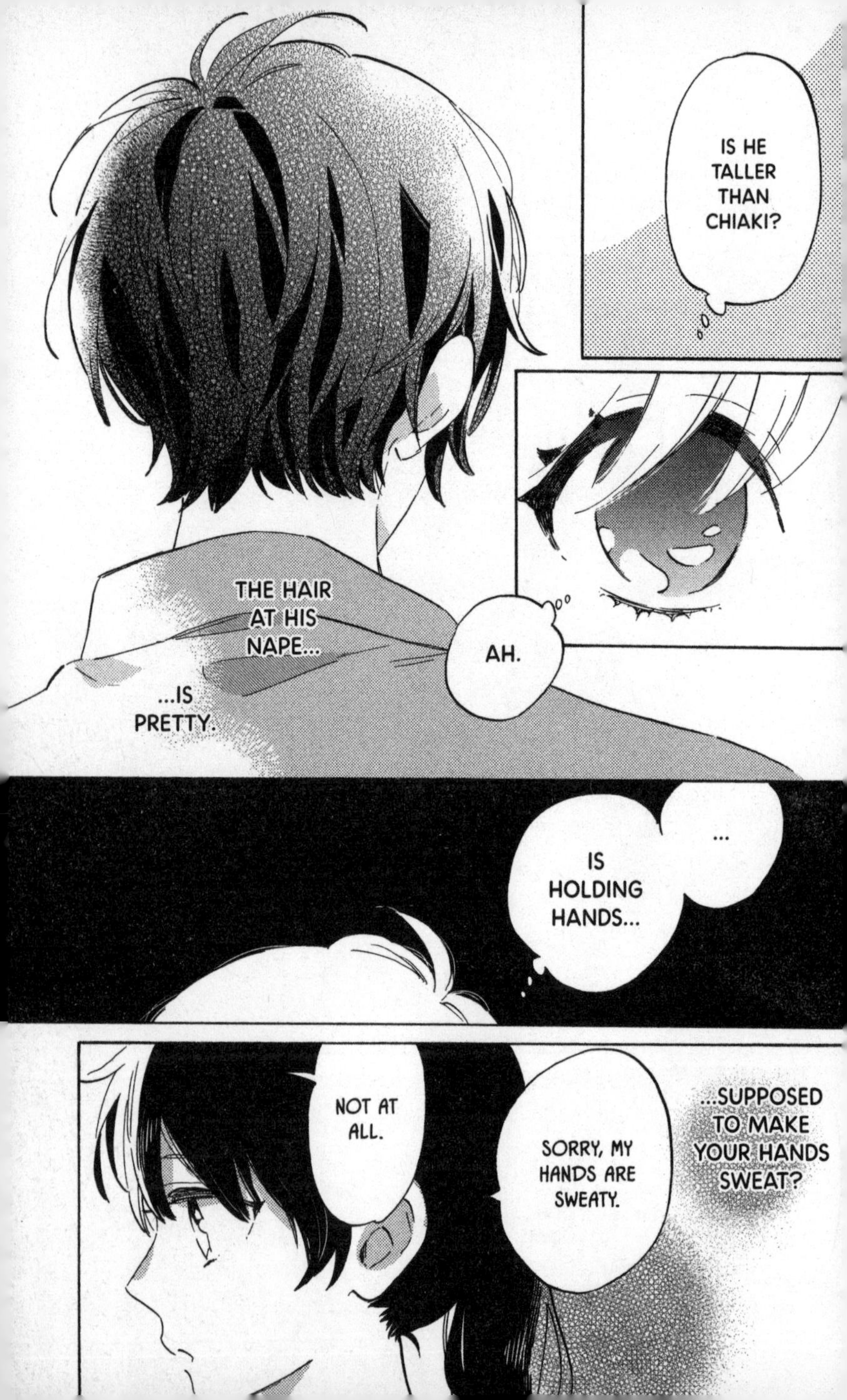
IS HE TALLER THAN CHIAKI?
AH.
THE HAIR AT HIS NAPE...
...IS PRETTY.
...
IS HOLDING HANDS...
...SUPPOSED TO MAKE YOUR HANDS SWEAT?
SORRY, MY HANDS ARE SWEATY.
NOT AT ALL.

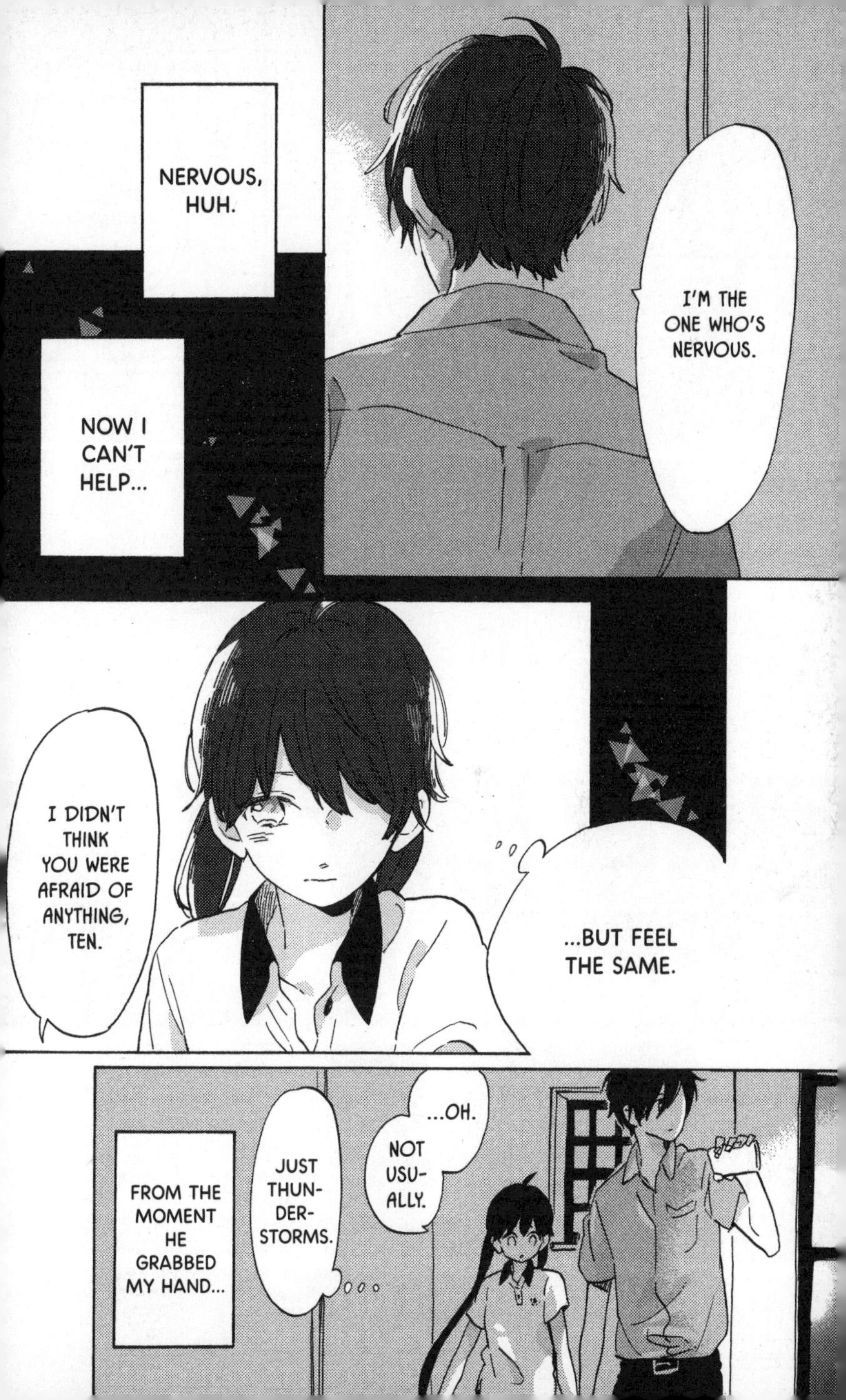
I'M THE ONE WHO'S NERVOUS.
NERVOUS, HUH.
NOW I CAN'T HELP...
...BUT FEEL THE SAME.
I DIDN'T THINK YOU WERE AFRAID OF ANYTHING, TEN.
...OH.
NOT USU-ALLY.
JUST THUN-DER-STORMS.
FROM THE MOMENT HE GRABBED MY HAND...

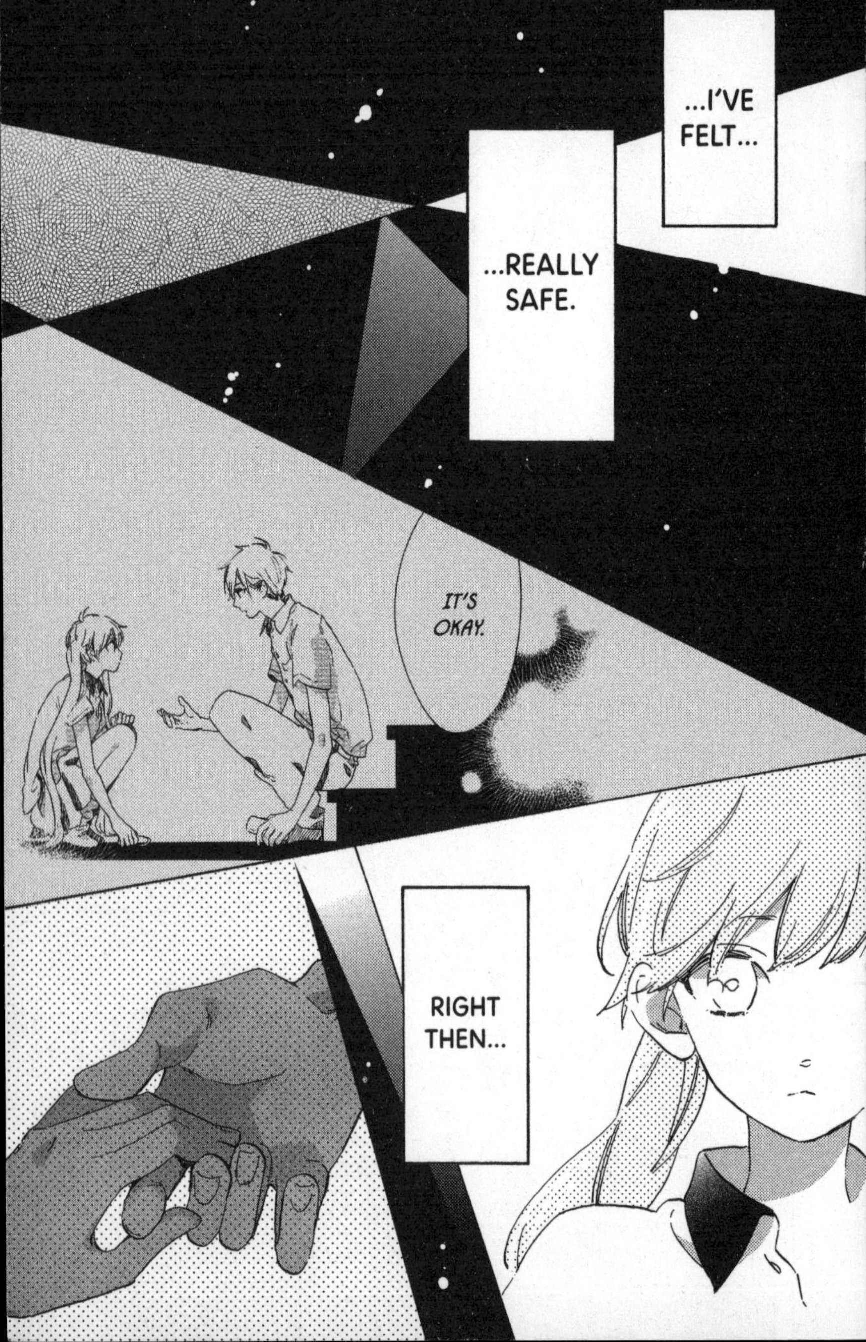
...I'VE FELT...
...REALLY SAFE.
IT'S OKAY.
RIGHT THEN...

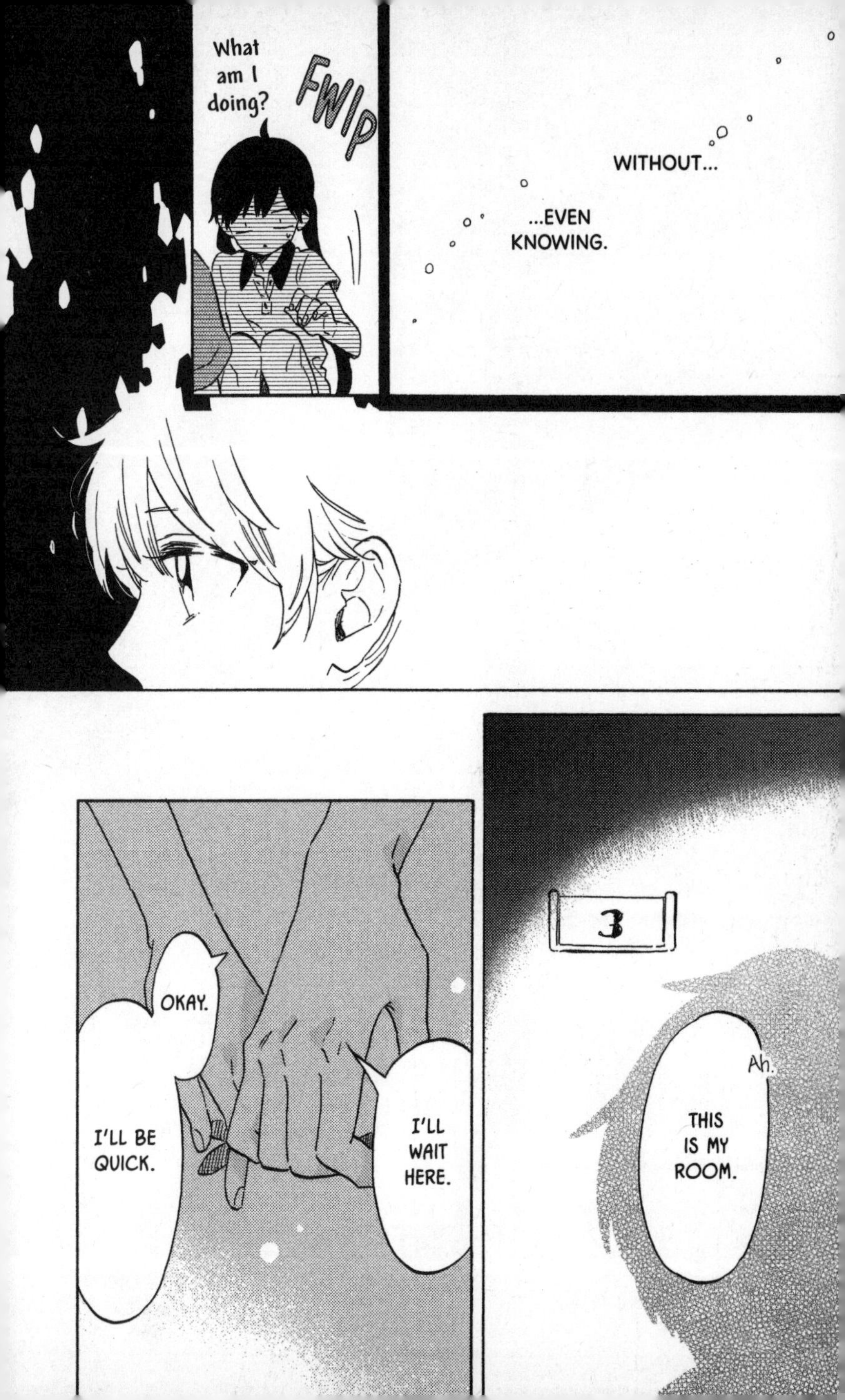
WITHOUT...
...EVEN KNOWING.
What am I doing?
FWIP
3
Ah.
THIS IS MY ROOM.
I'LL WAIT HERE.
OKAY.
I'LL BE QUICK.

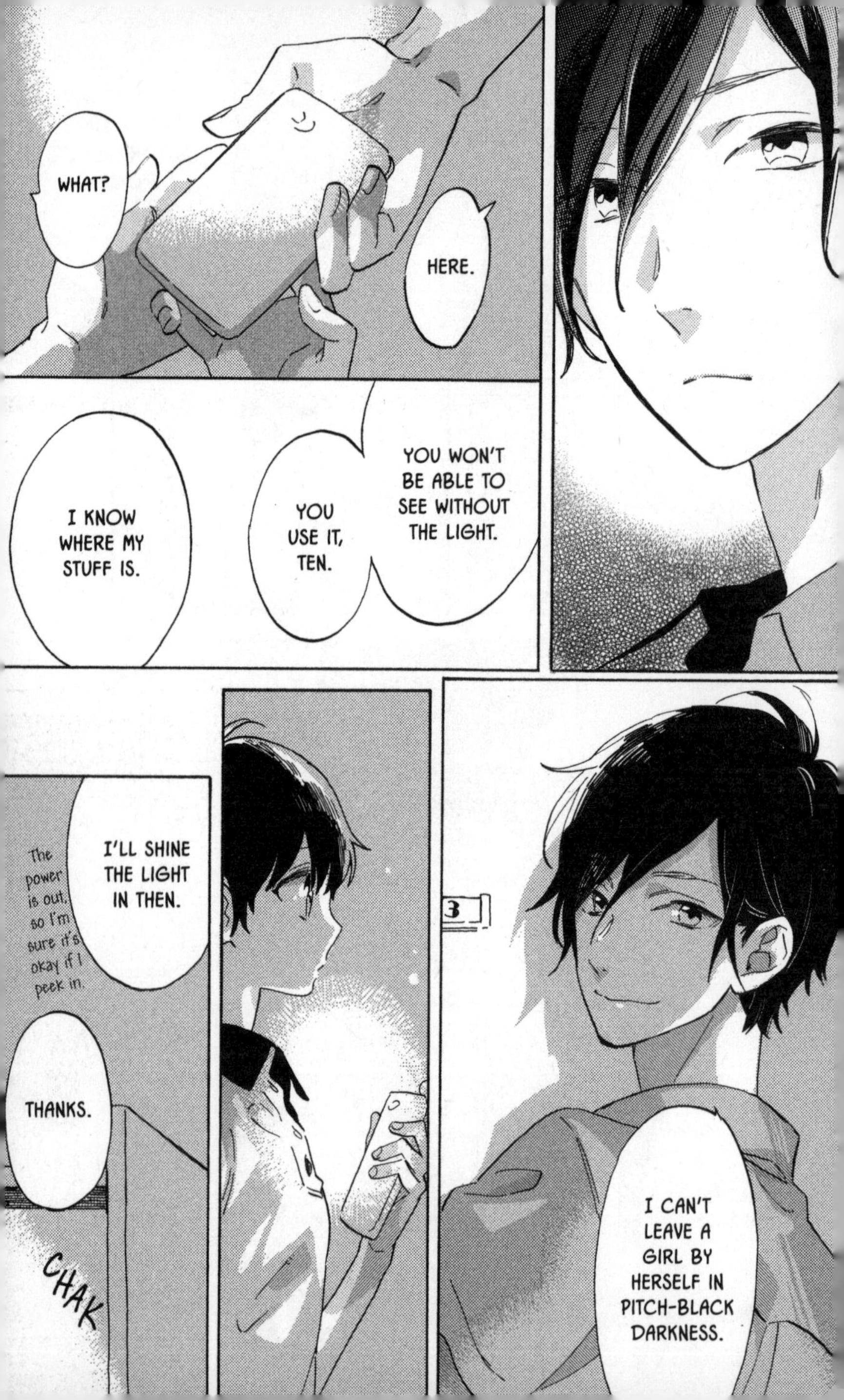
HERE.
WHAT?
YOU WON'T BE ABLE TO SEE WITHOUT THE LIGHT.
YOU USE IT, TEN.
I KNOW WHERE MY STUFF IS.
I CAN'T LEAVE A GIRL BY HERSELF IN PITCH-BLACK DARKNESS.
3
I'LL SHINE THE LIGHT IN THEN.
The power is out, so I'm sure it's okay if I peek in.
THANKS.
CHAK

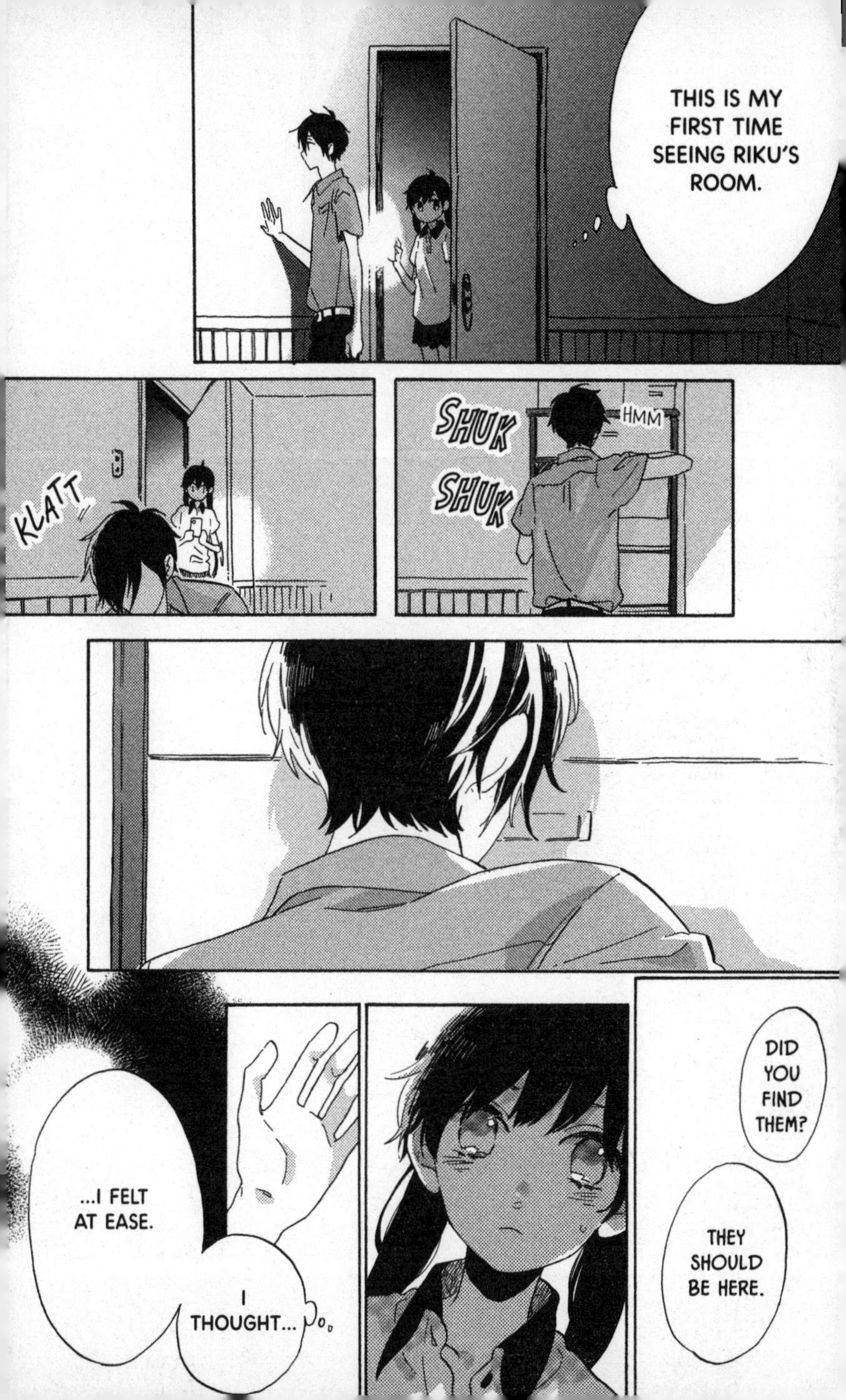

THIS IS MY FIRST TIME SEEING RIKU'S ROOM.
HMM
SHUK
SHUK
KLATT
DID YOU FIND THEM?
THEY SHOULD BE HERE.
I THOUGHT...
...I FELT AT EASE.

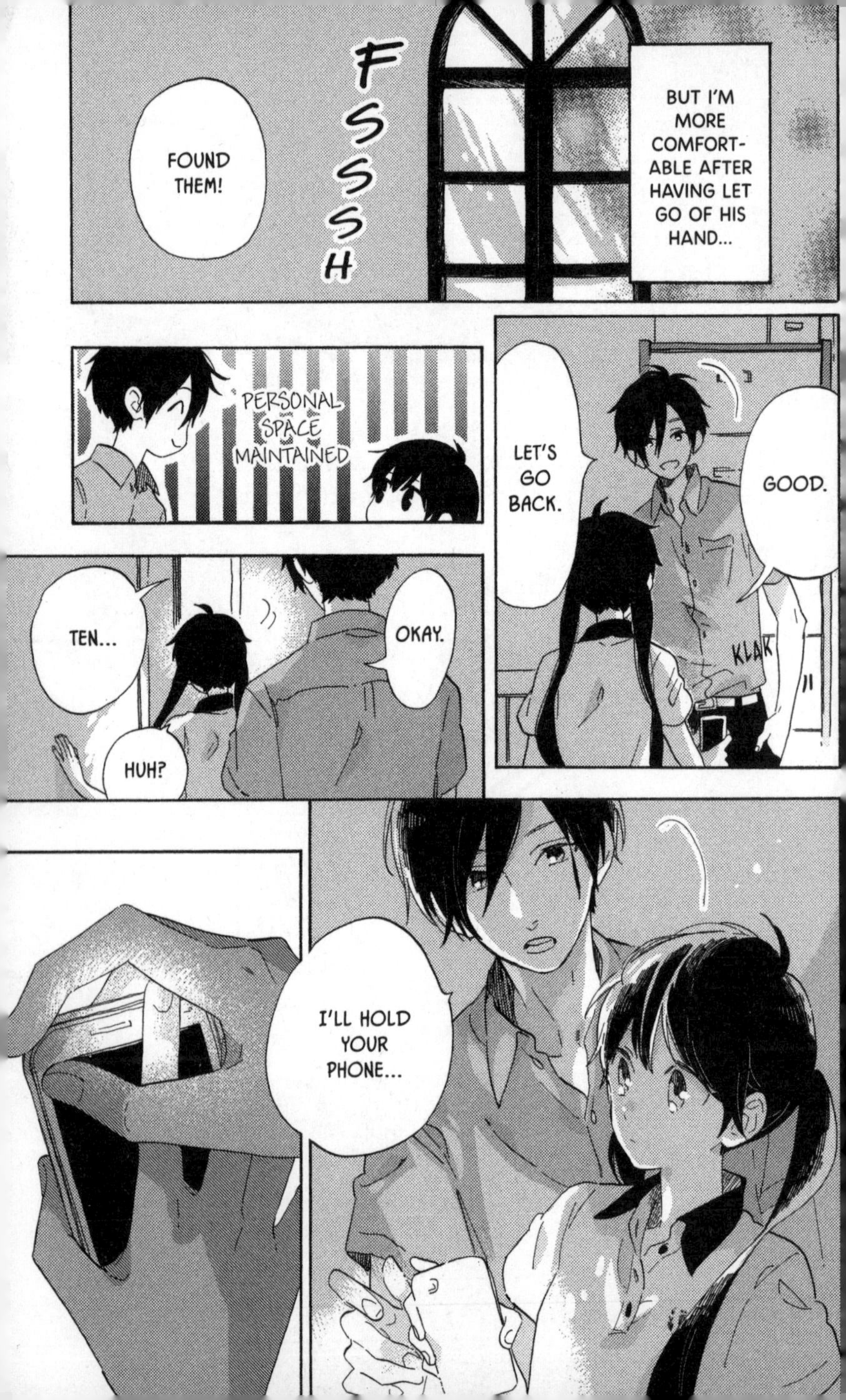
BUT I'M MORE COMFORT-ABLE AFTER HAVING LET GO OF HIS HAND...
FSSSH
FOUND THEM!
GOOD.
KLAK
LET'S GO BACK.
PERSONAL SPACE MAINTAINED
OKAY.
TEN...
HUH?
I'LL HOLD YOUR PHONE...

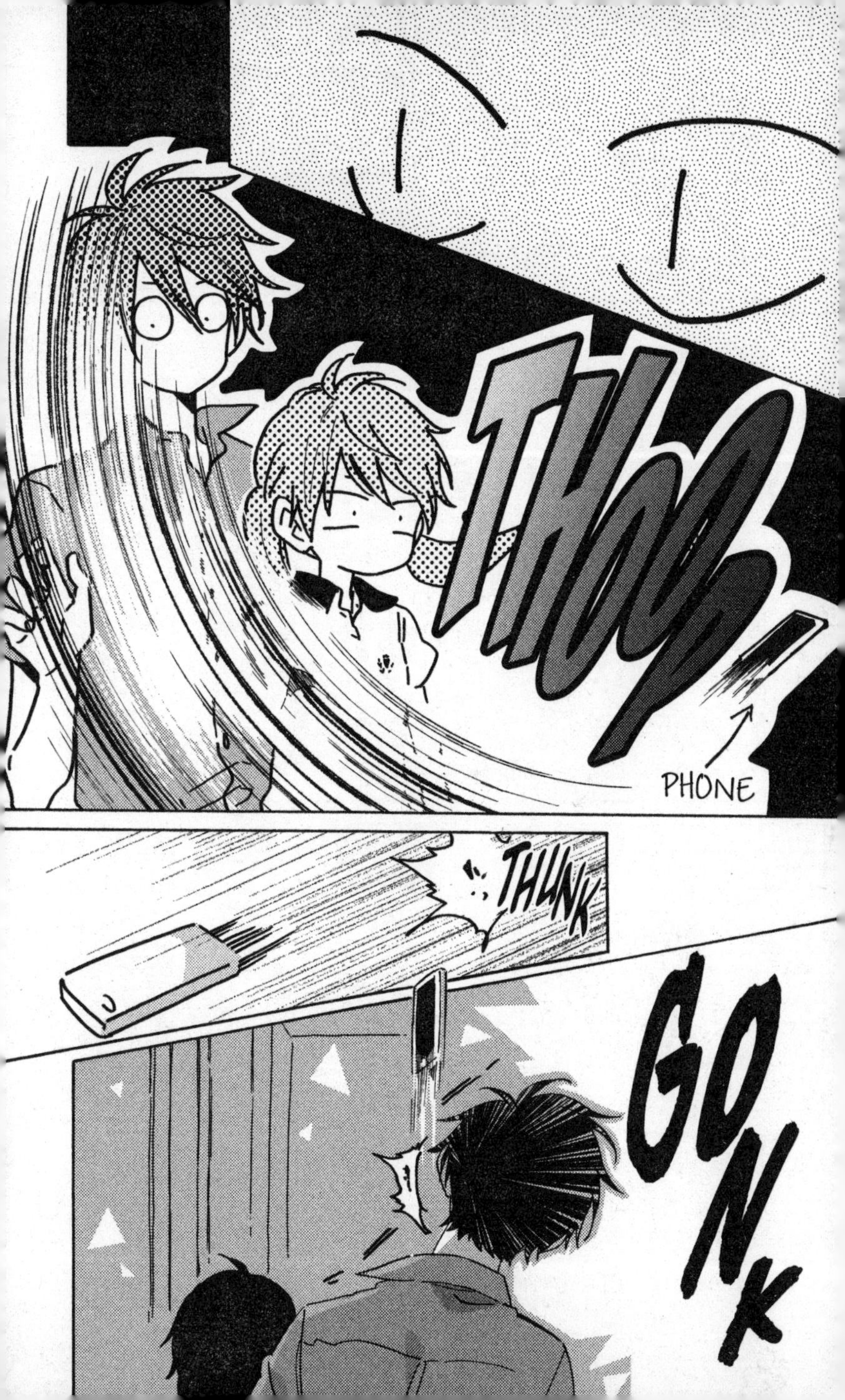
THUD
PHONE
THUNK
GONK

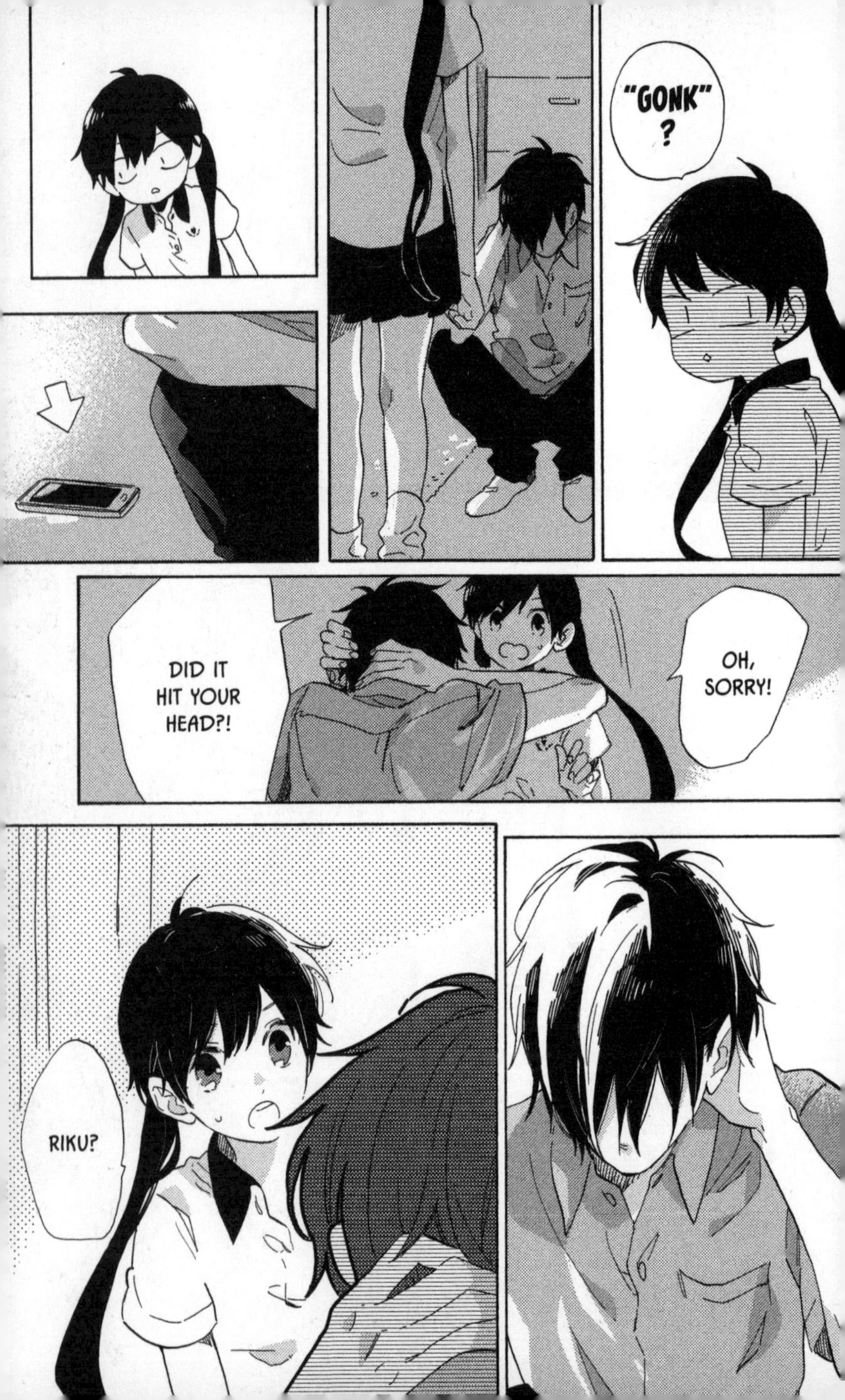
"GONK"
?
OH, SORRY!
DID IT HIT YOUR HEAD?!
RIKU?

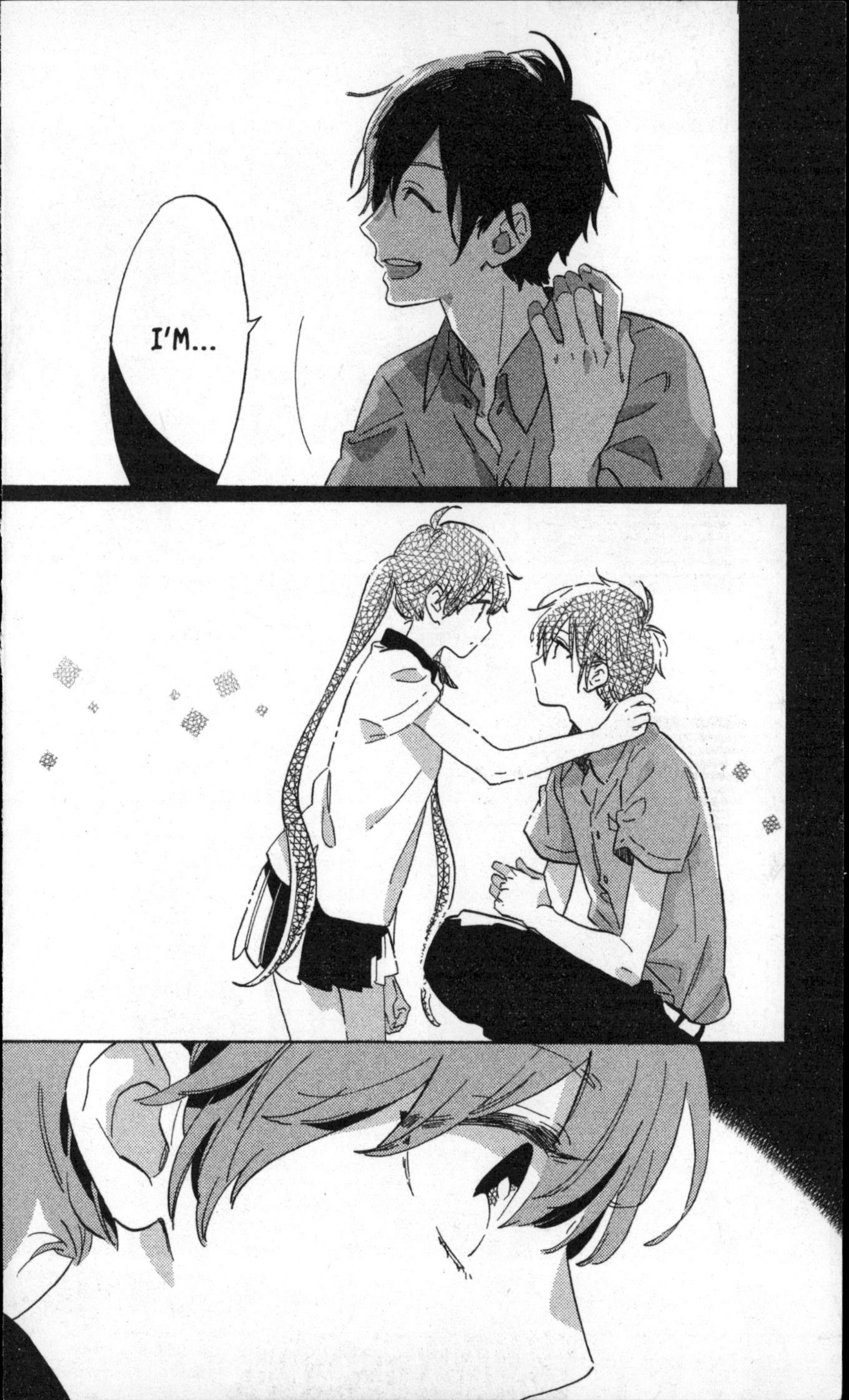
I'M...

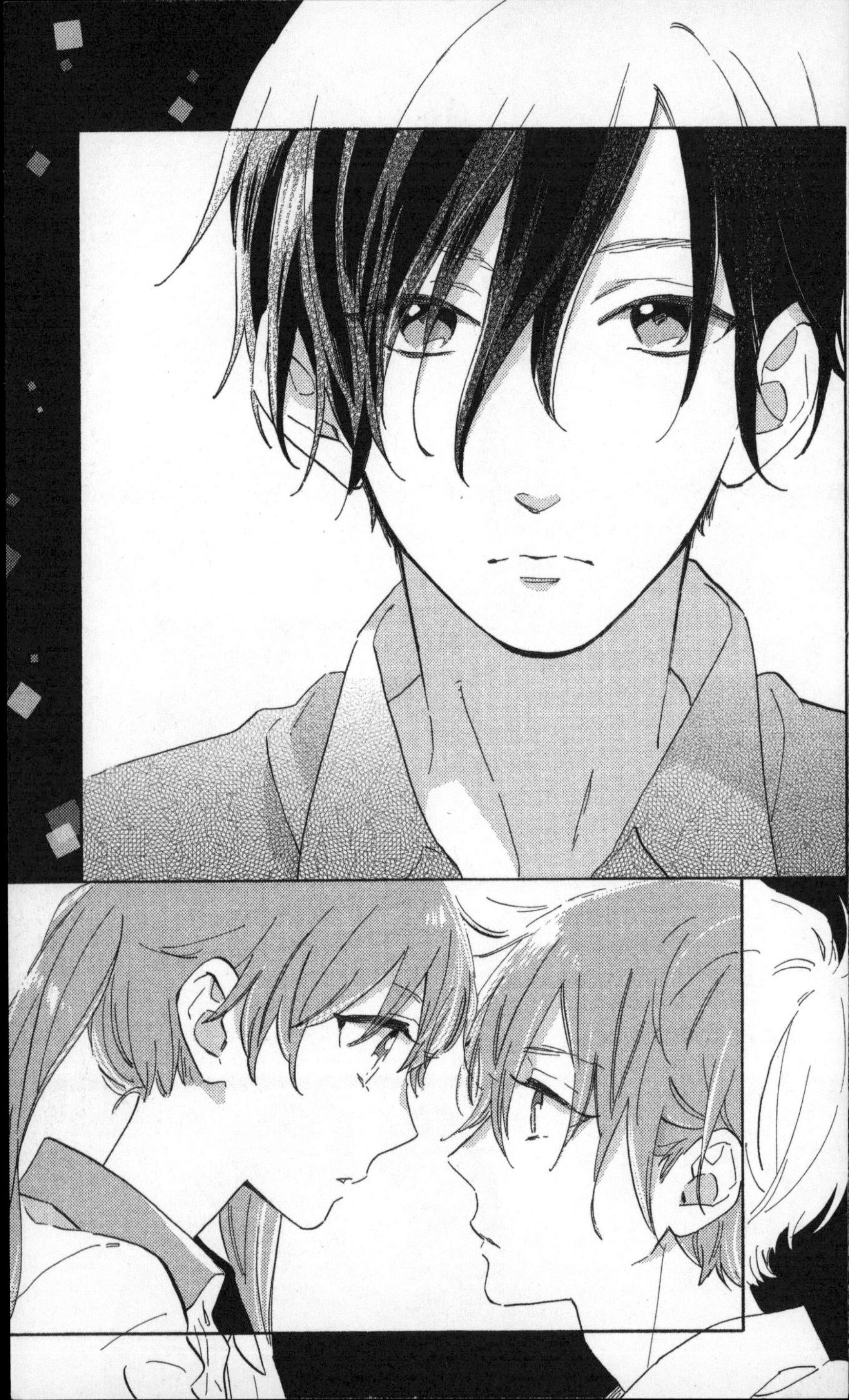

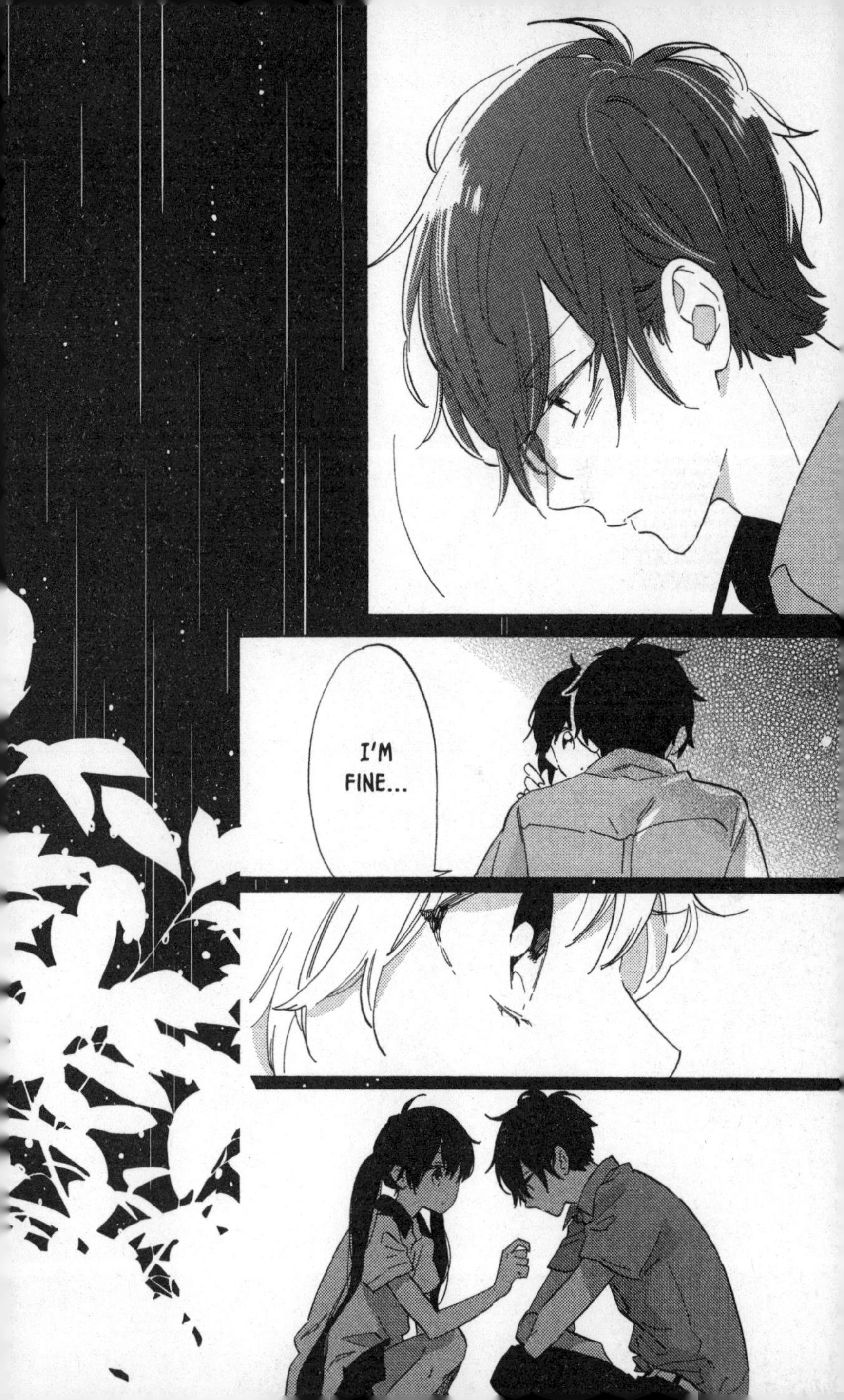
I'M FINE...

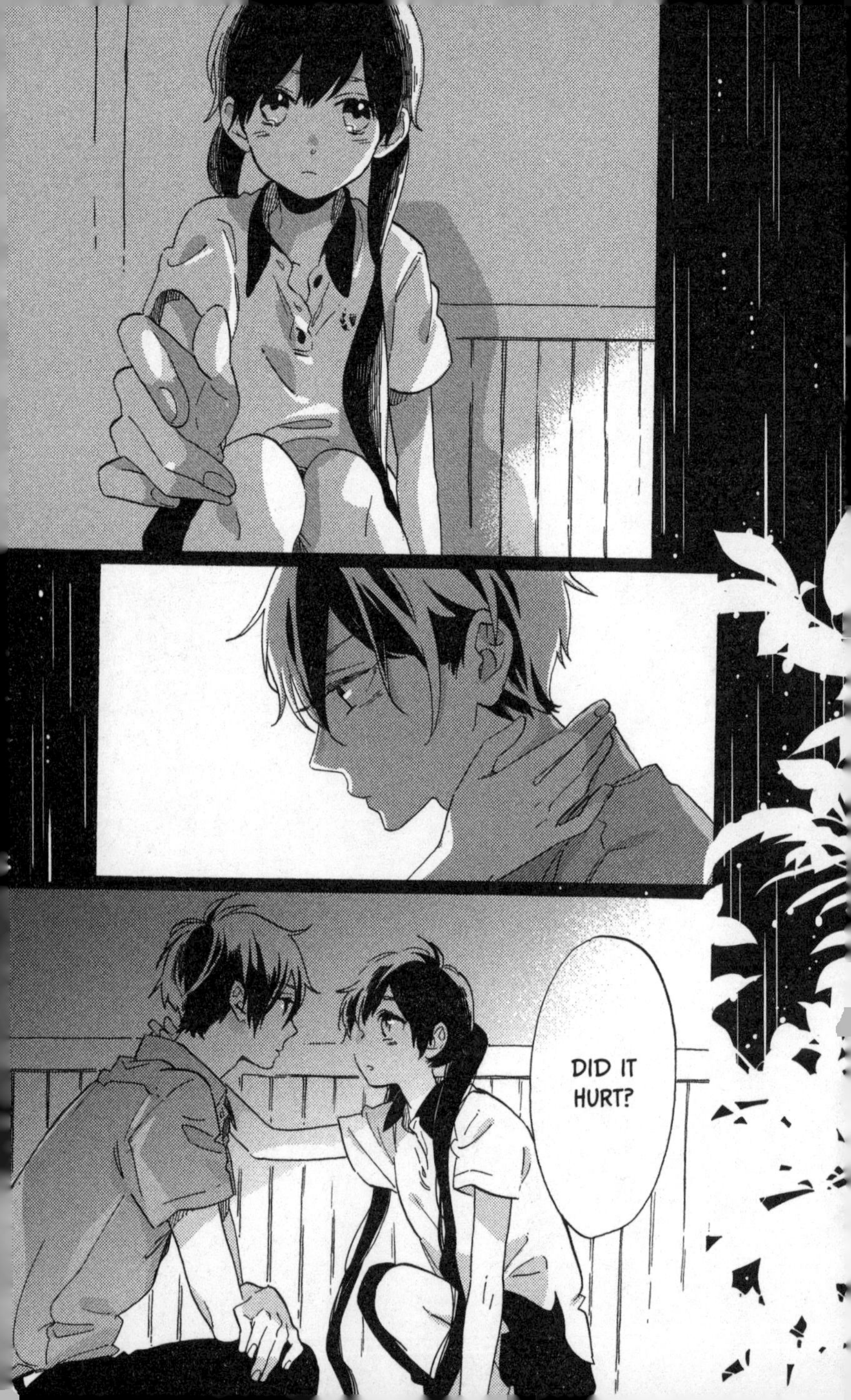
DID IT HURT?

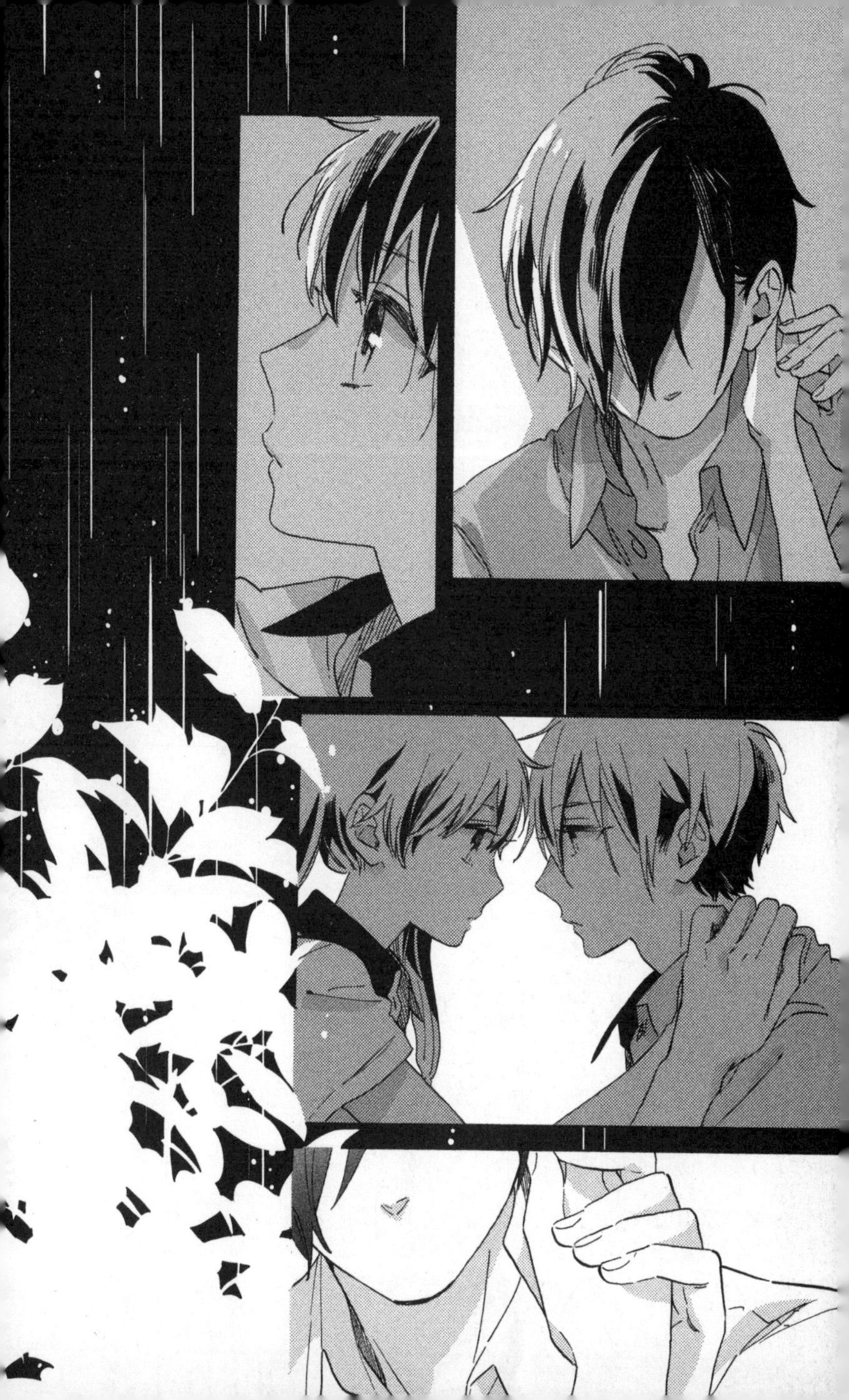

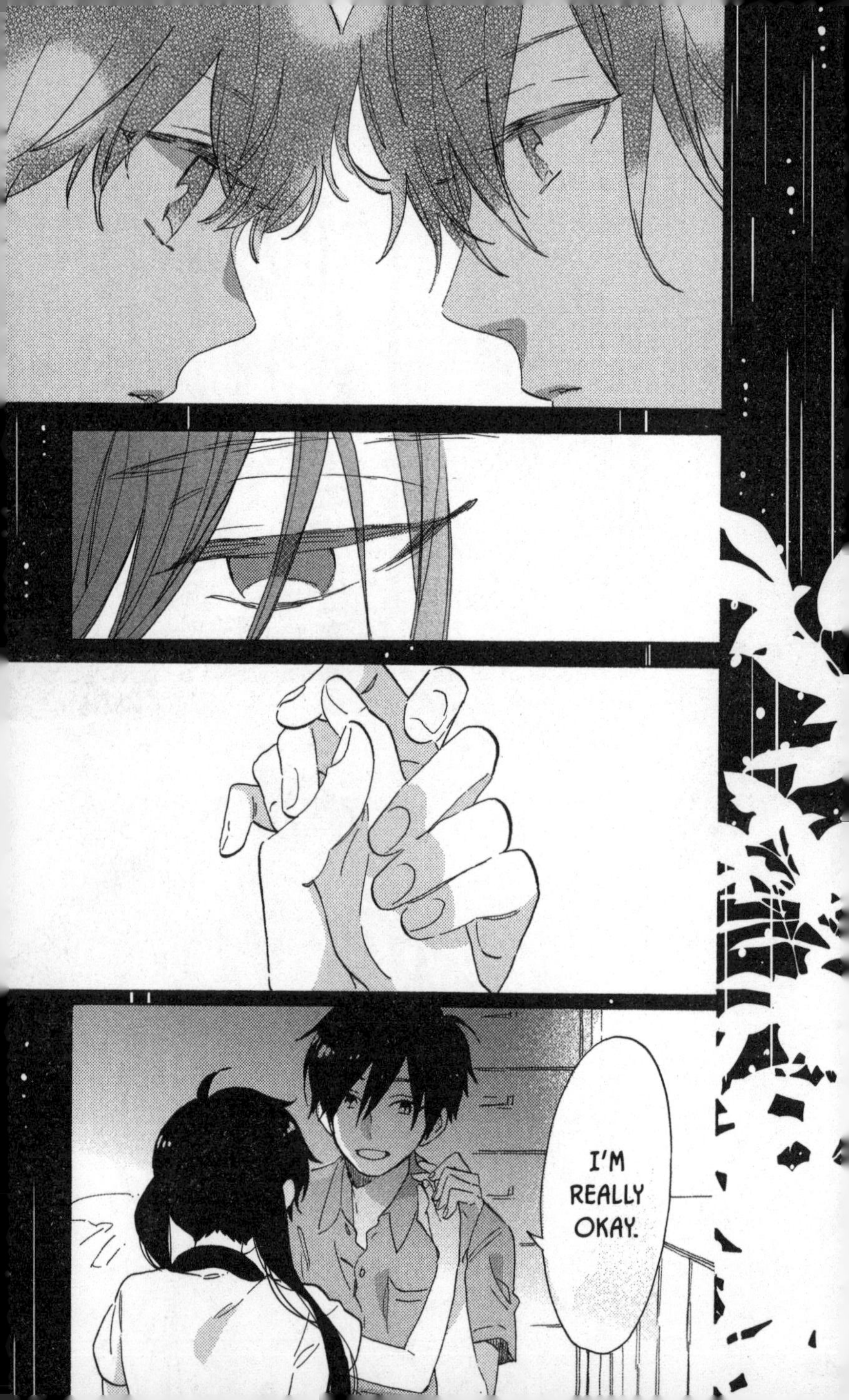
I'M REALLY OKAY.

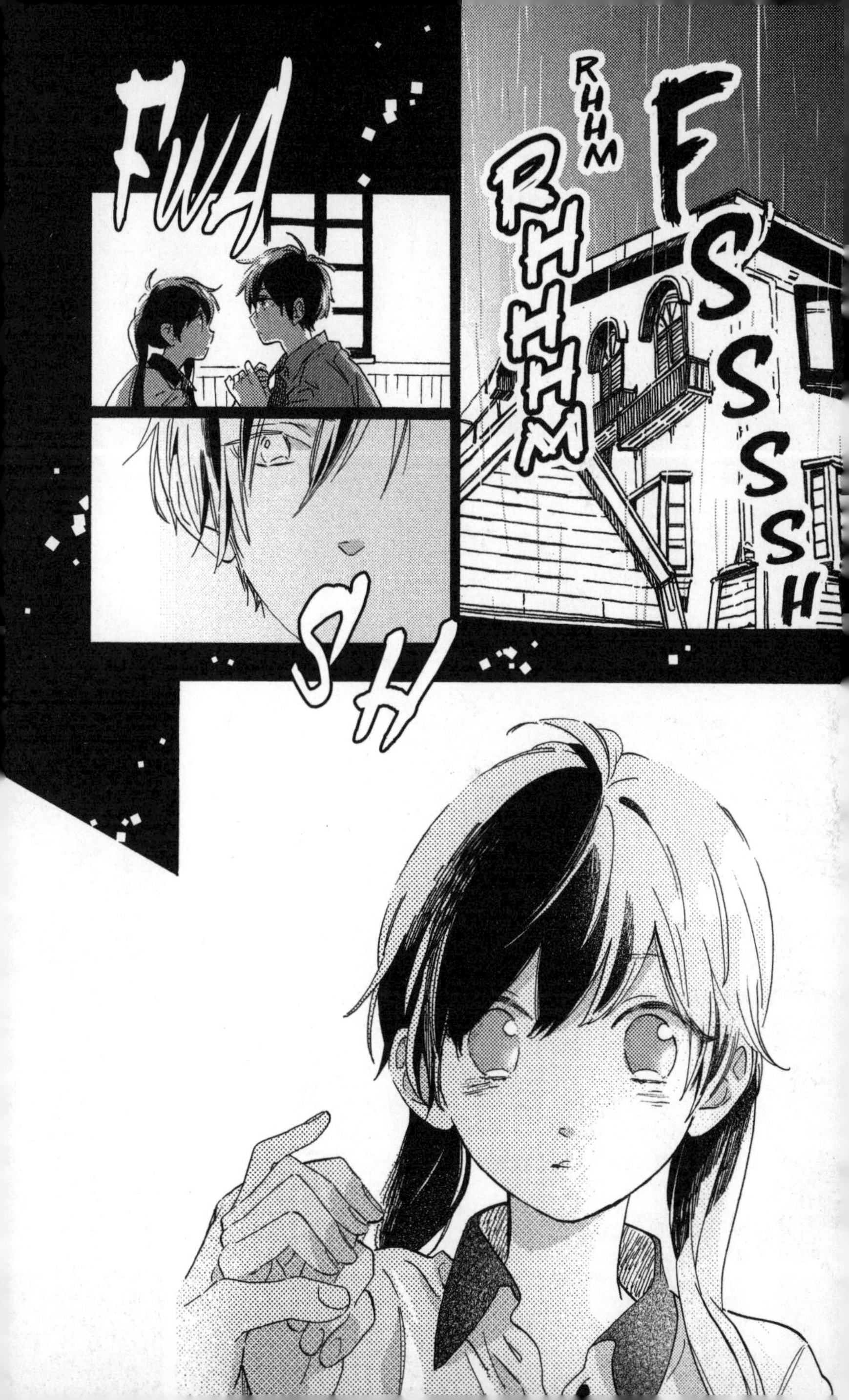
FSSSSH
RHHM
RHHHHM
FWA
SH

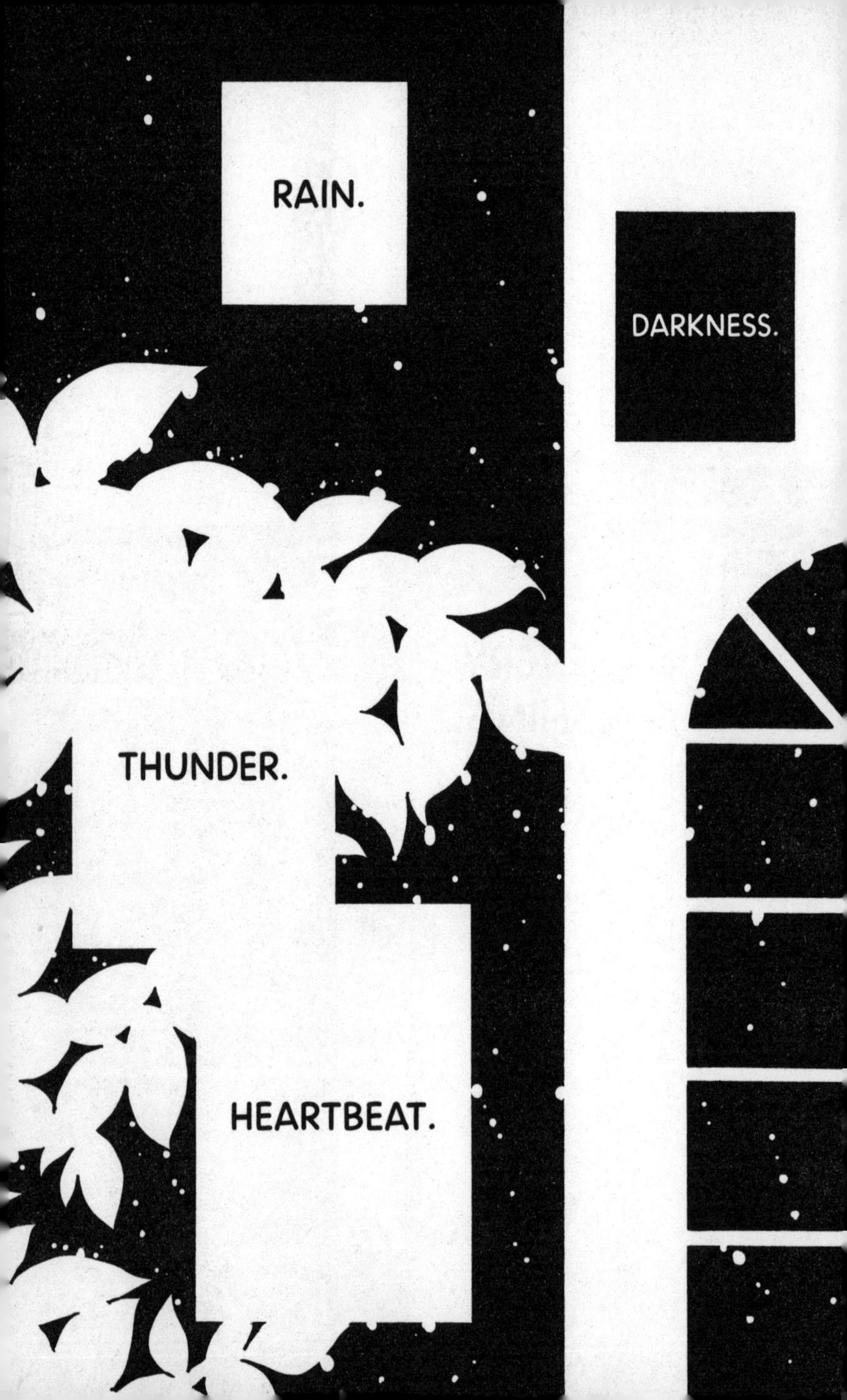
DARKNESS.
RAIN.
THUNDER.
HEARTBEAT.

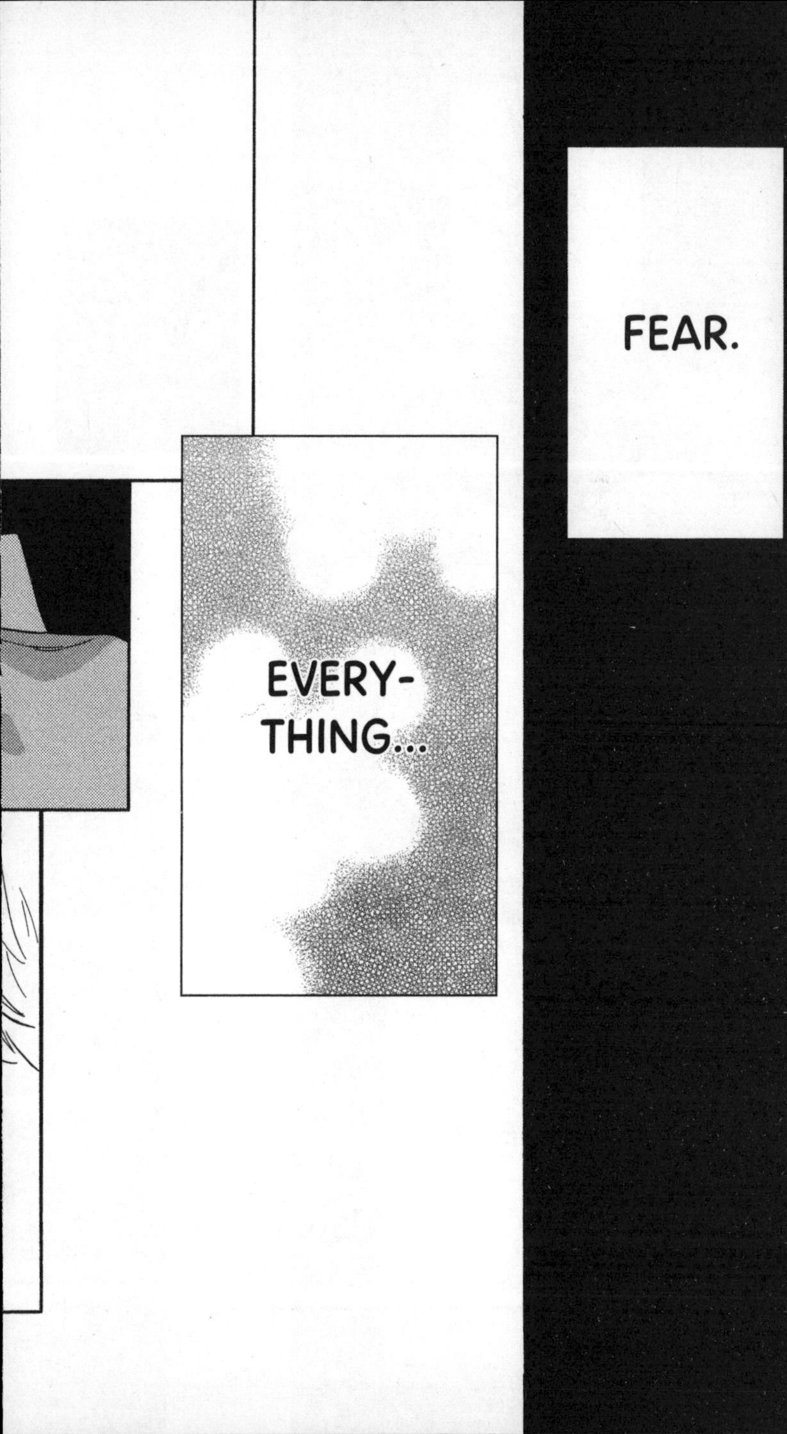
FEAR.
EVERY-THING...

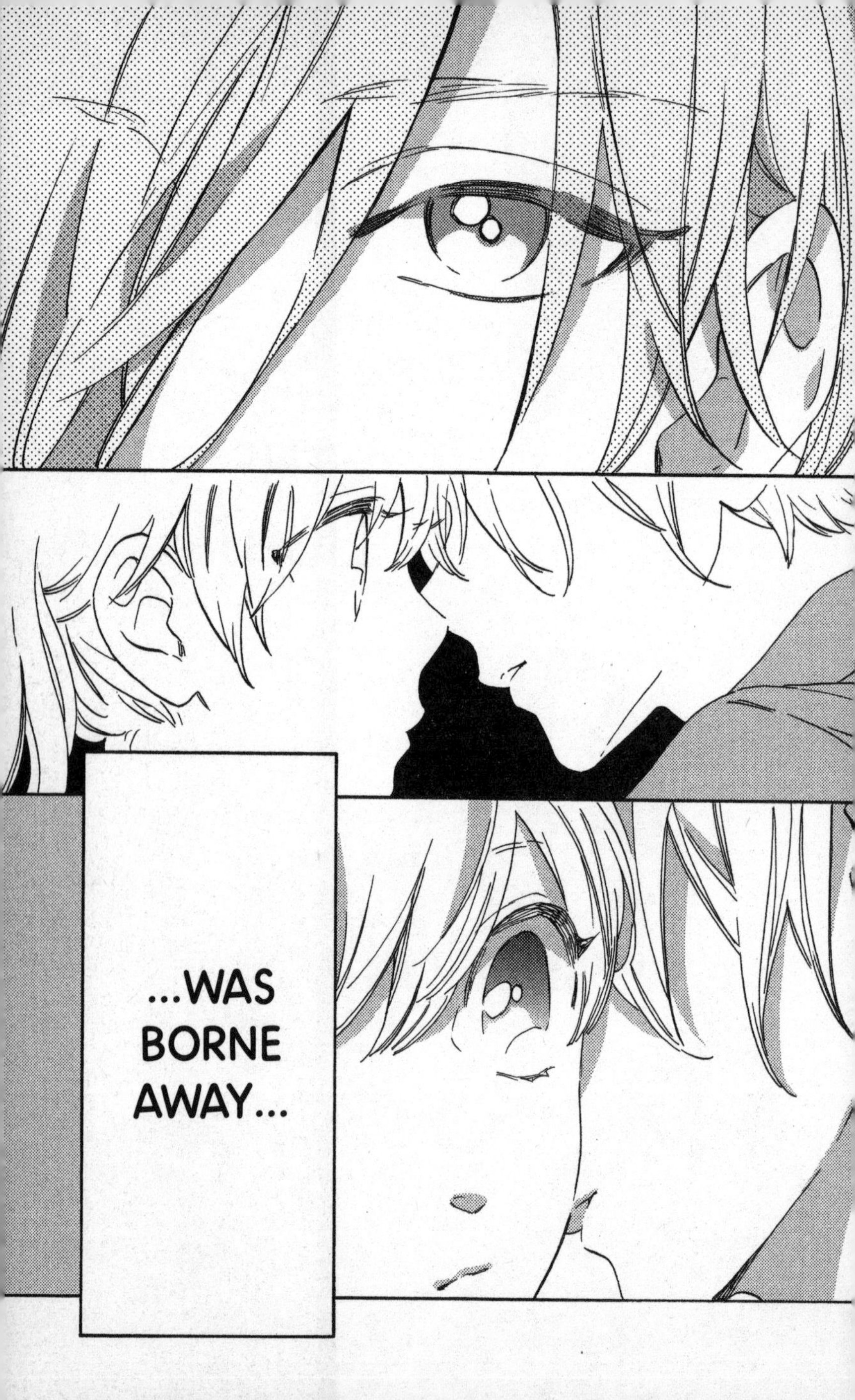
...WAS BORNE AWAY...

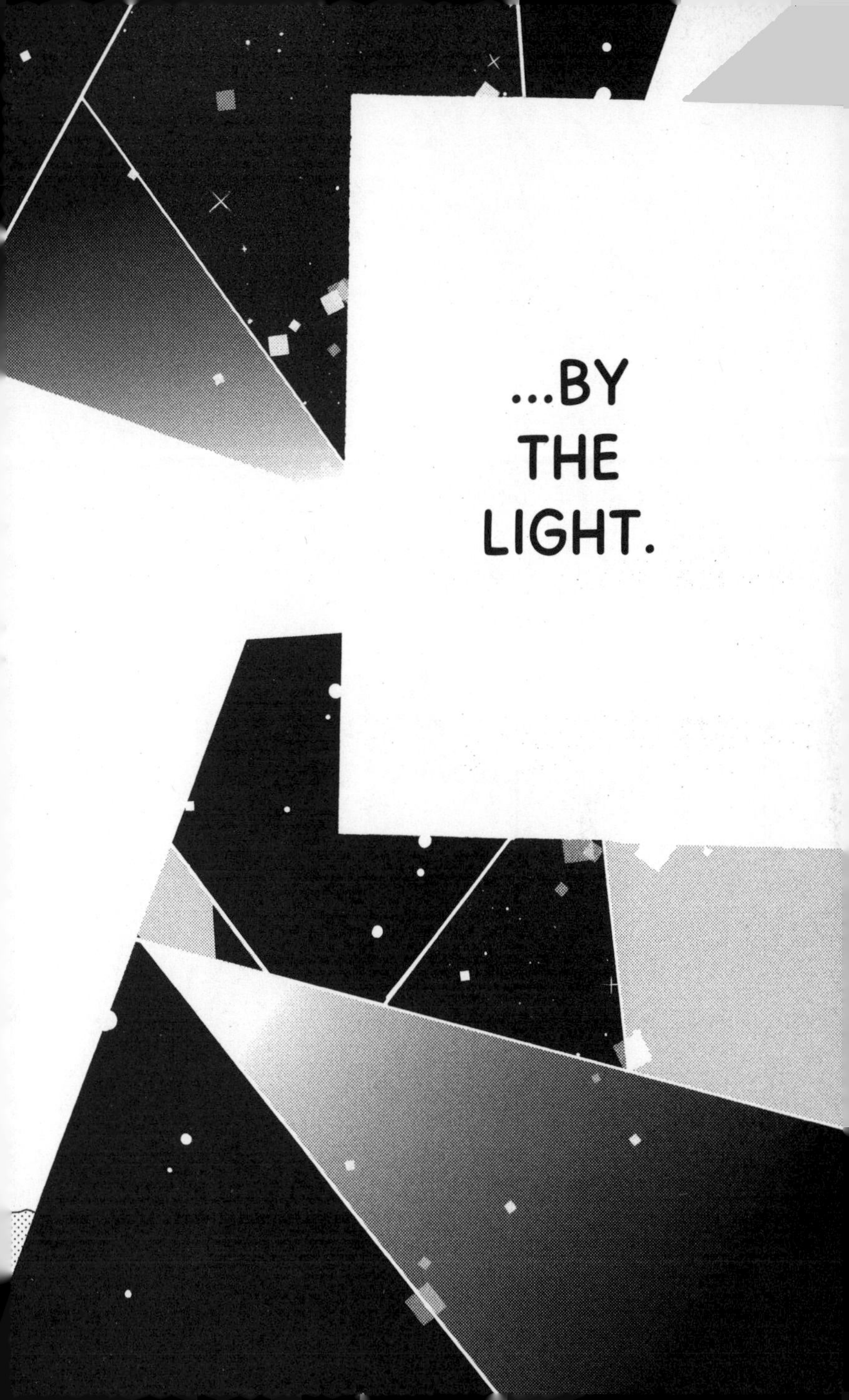
...BY THE LIGHT.

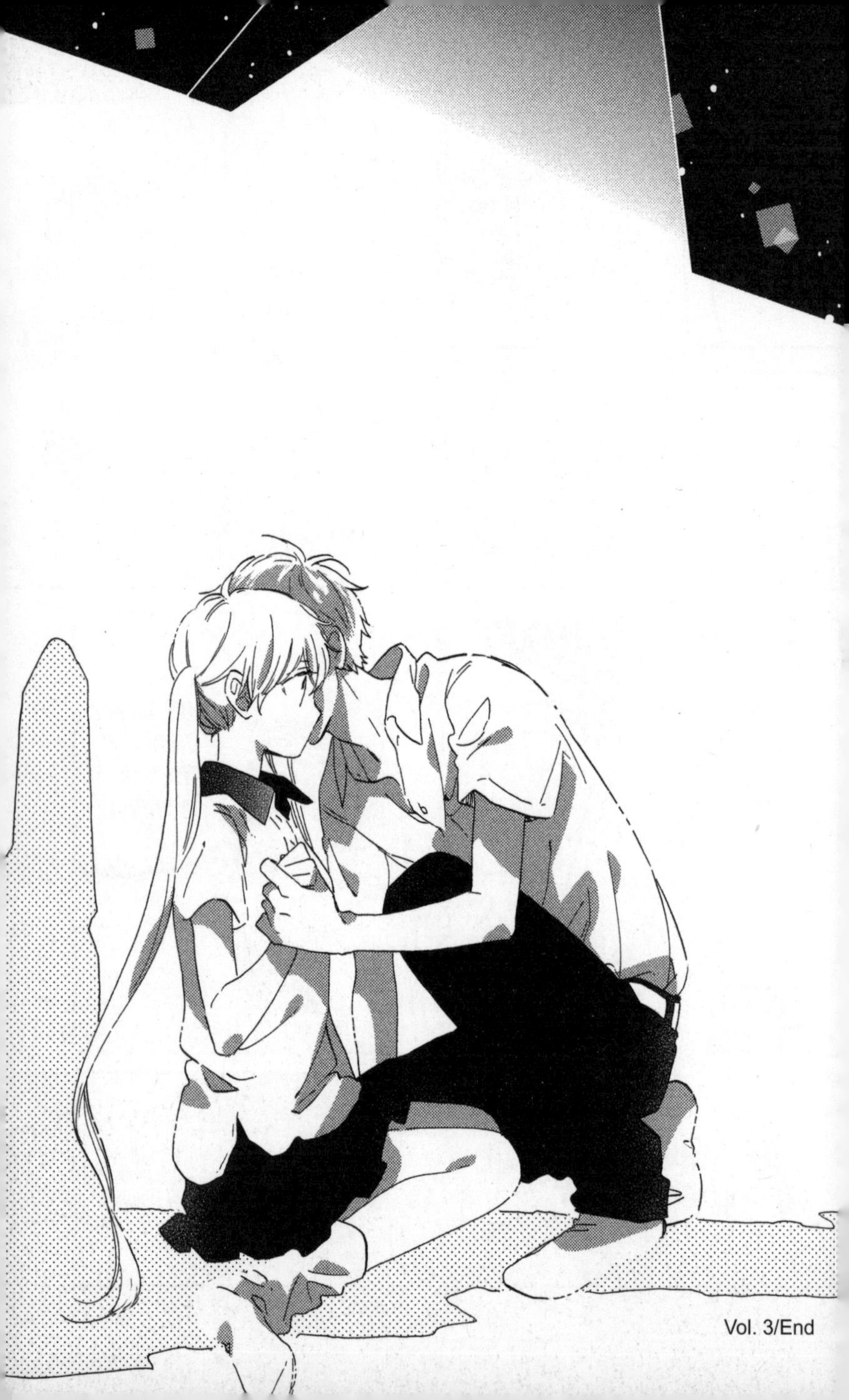
Vol. 3/End

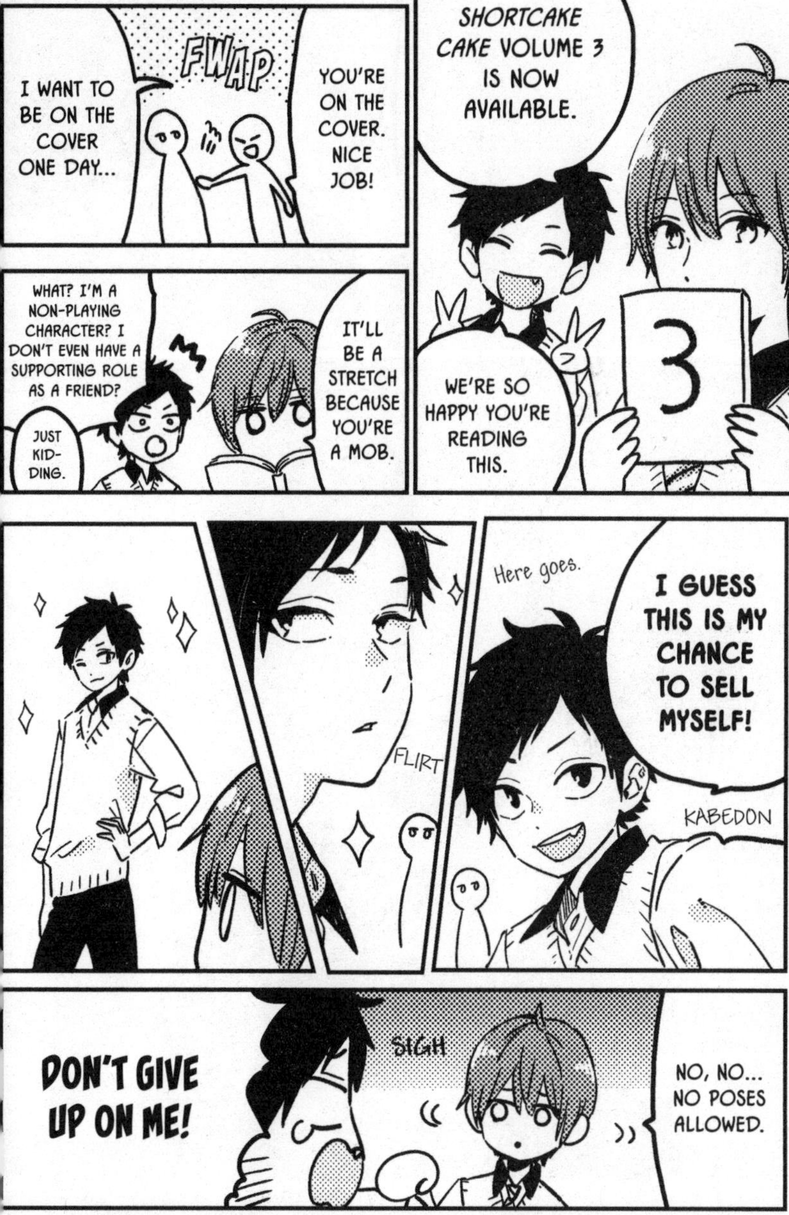
SHORTCAKE CAKE VOLUME 3 IS NOW AVAILABLE.
3
WE'RE SO HAPPY YOU'RE READING THIS.
YOU'RE ON THE COVER. NICE JOB!
FWAP
I WANT TO BE ON THE COVER ONE DAY...
IT'LL BE A STRETCH BECAUSE YOU'RE A MOB.
WHAT? I'M A NON-PLAYING CHARACTER? I DON'T EVEN HAVE A SUPPORTING ROLE AS A FRIEND?
JUST KID-DING.
I GUESS THIS IS MY CHANCE TO SELL MYSELF!
Here goes.
KABEDON
FLIRT
NO, NO... NO POSES ALLOWED.
SIGH
DON'T GIVE UP ON ME!

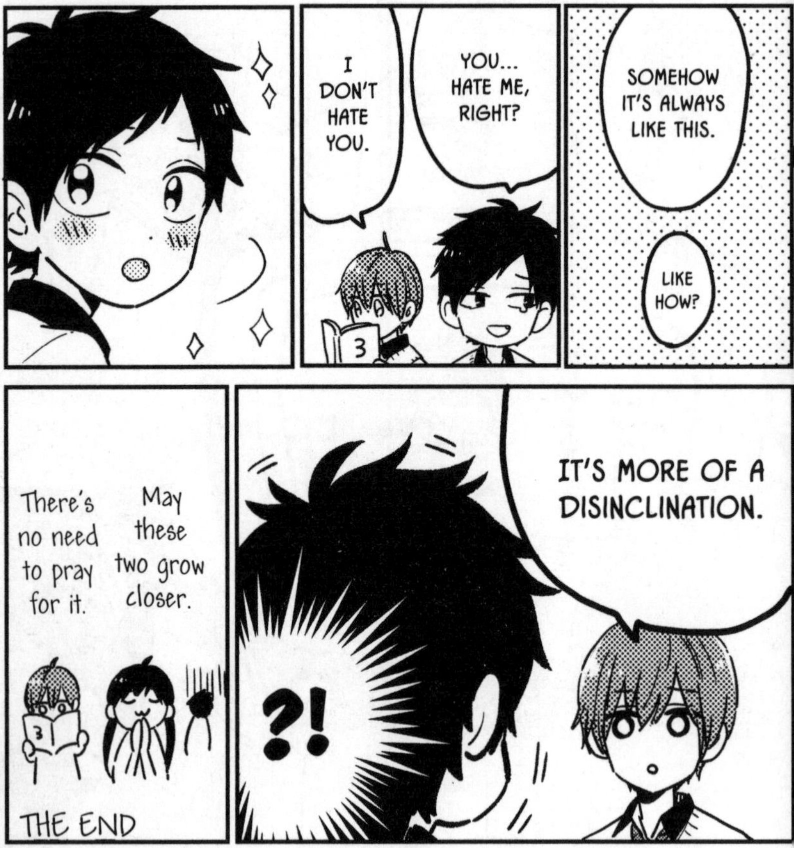
SOMEHOW IT'S ALWAYS LIKE THIS.
LIKE HOW?
YOU... HATE ME, RIGHT?
I DON'T HATE YOU.
IT'S MORE OF A DISINCLINATION.
?!
May these two grow closer.
There's no need to pray for it.
THE END

## Special thanks to:

- Nyakacchi
- the *Margaret* editorial department
- our designer, Yasuhisa Kawatani-sama
- our assistant, Nao Hamaguchi-chan
- our assistant's helper, Kame-chan

And all of our readers

Thank sooou!!!

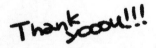

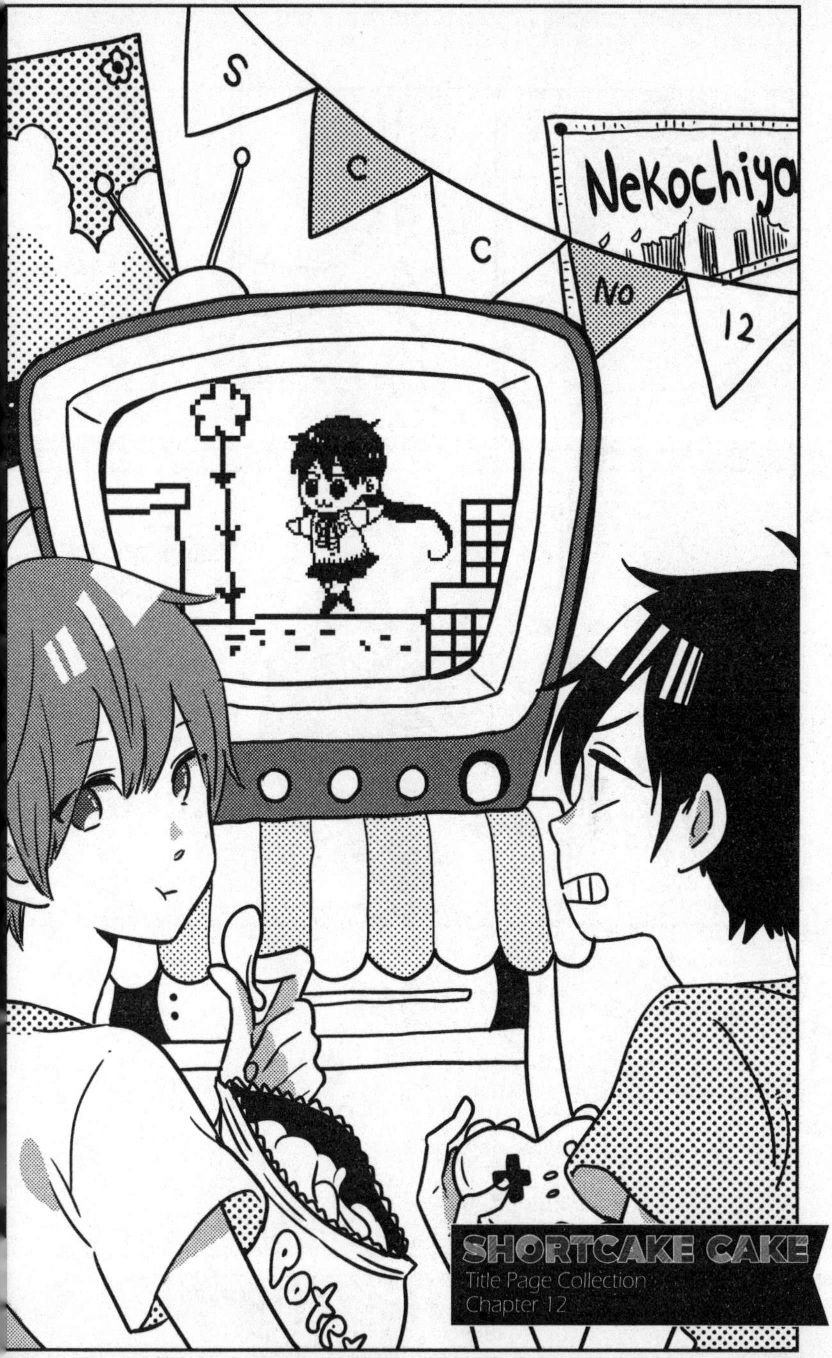
Nekochiya
S
C
C
No
12
SHORTCAKE CAKE
Title Page Collection
Chapter 12

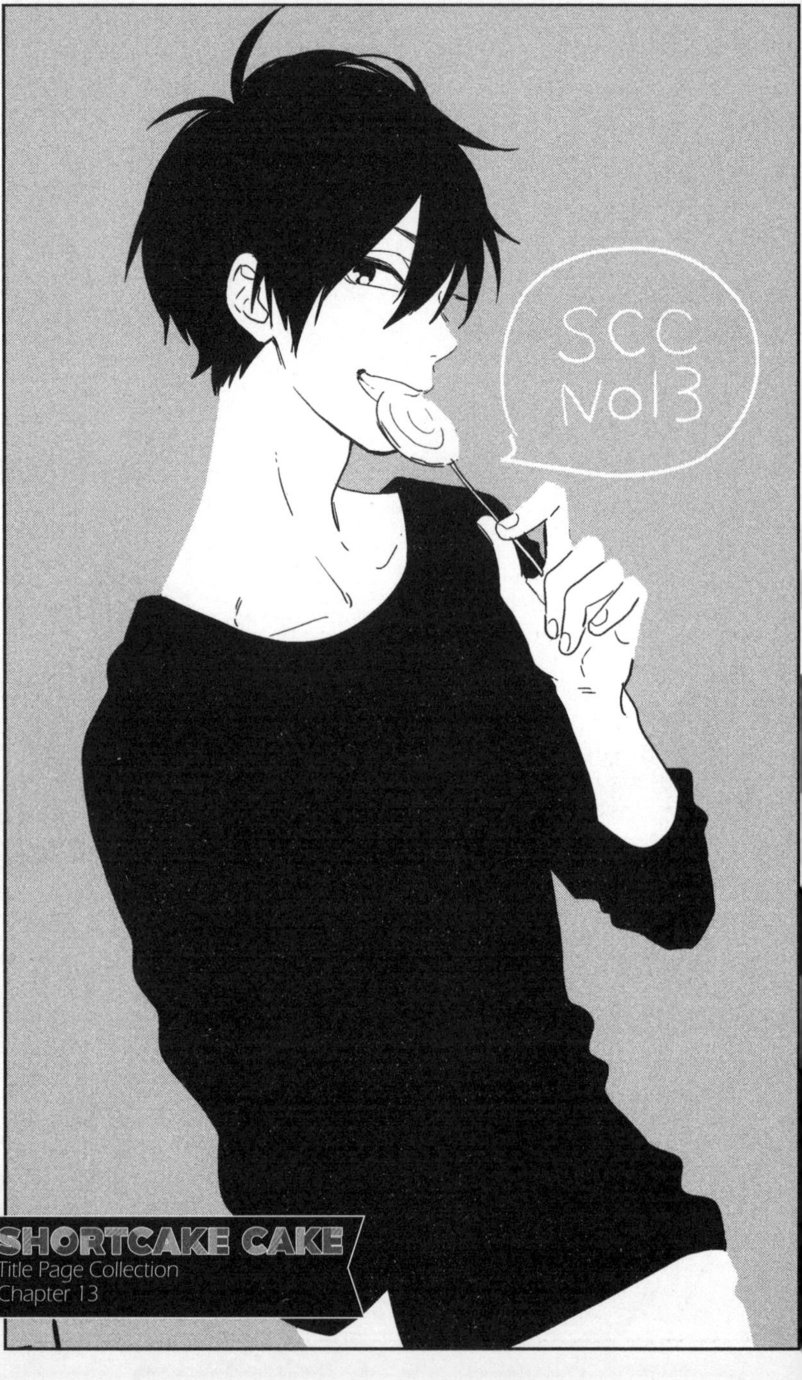
SCC
No13
SHORTCAKE CAKE
Title Page Collection
Chapter 13

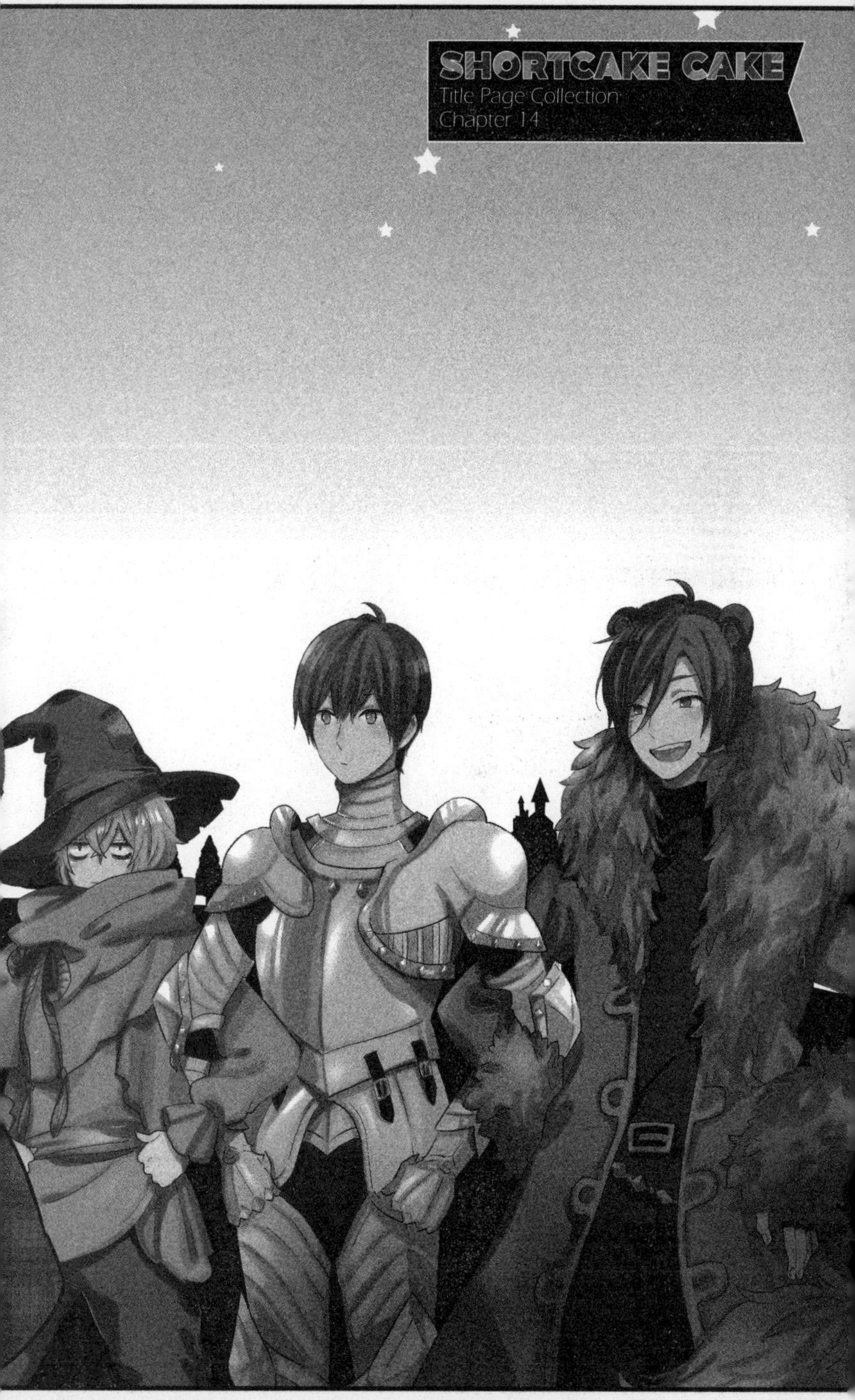
SHORTCAKE CAKE
Title Page Collection:
Chapter 14

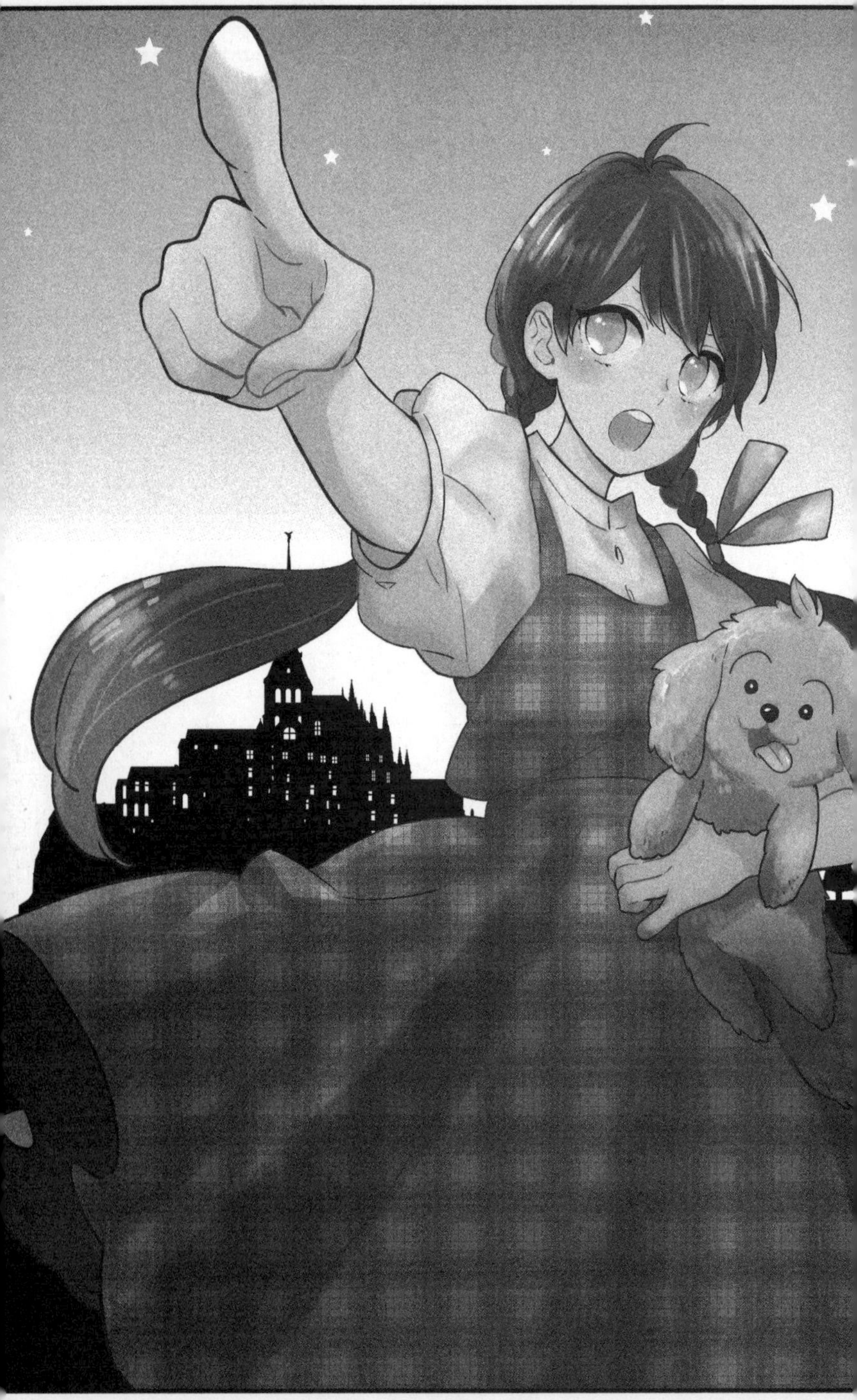

## SHORTCAKE CAKE
Title Page Collection
Issue 13 Magazine Cover

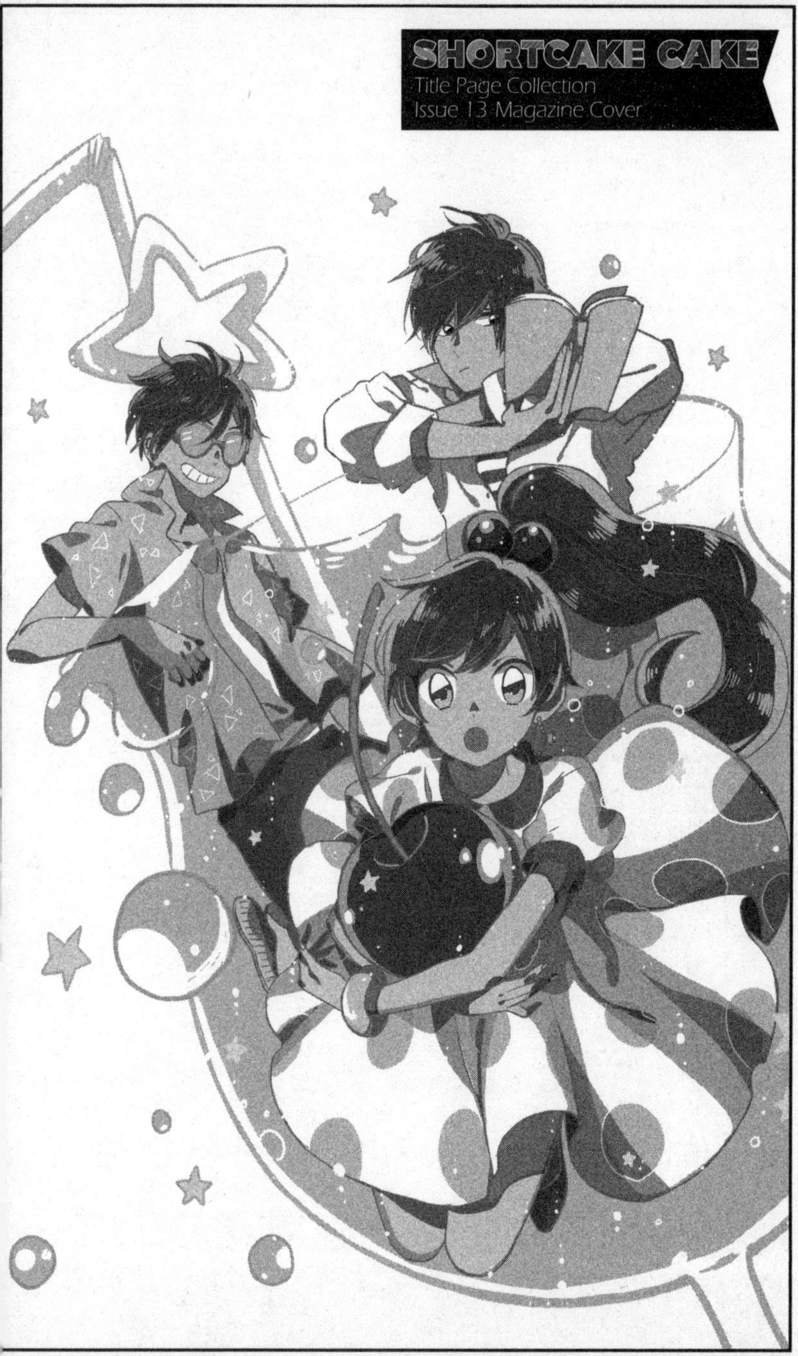

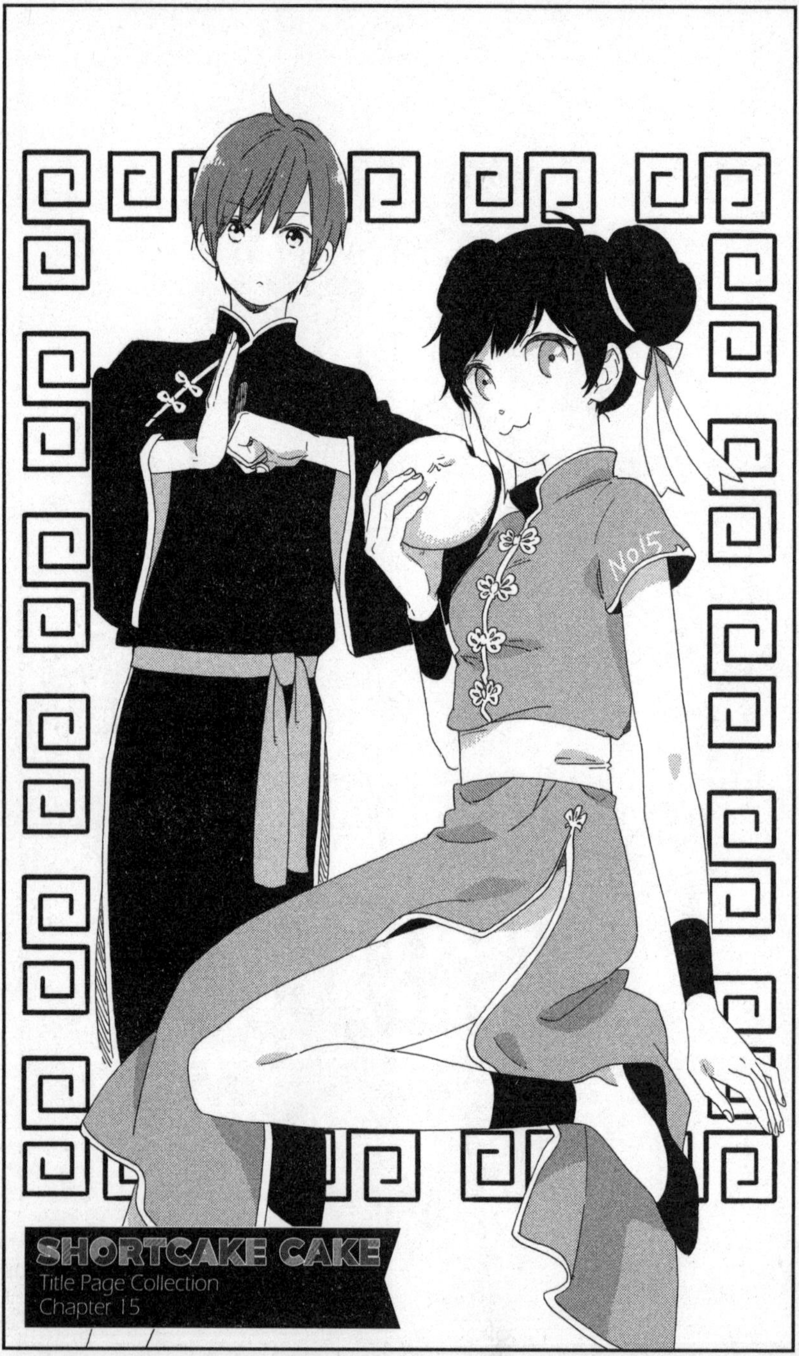
No15
SHORTCAKE CAKE
Title Page Collection
Chapter 15

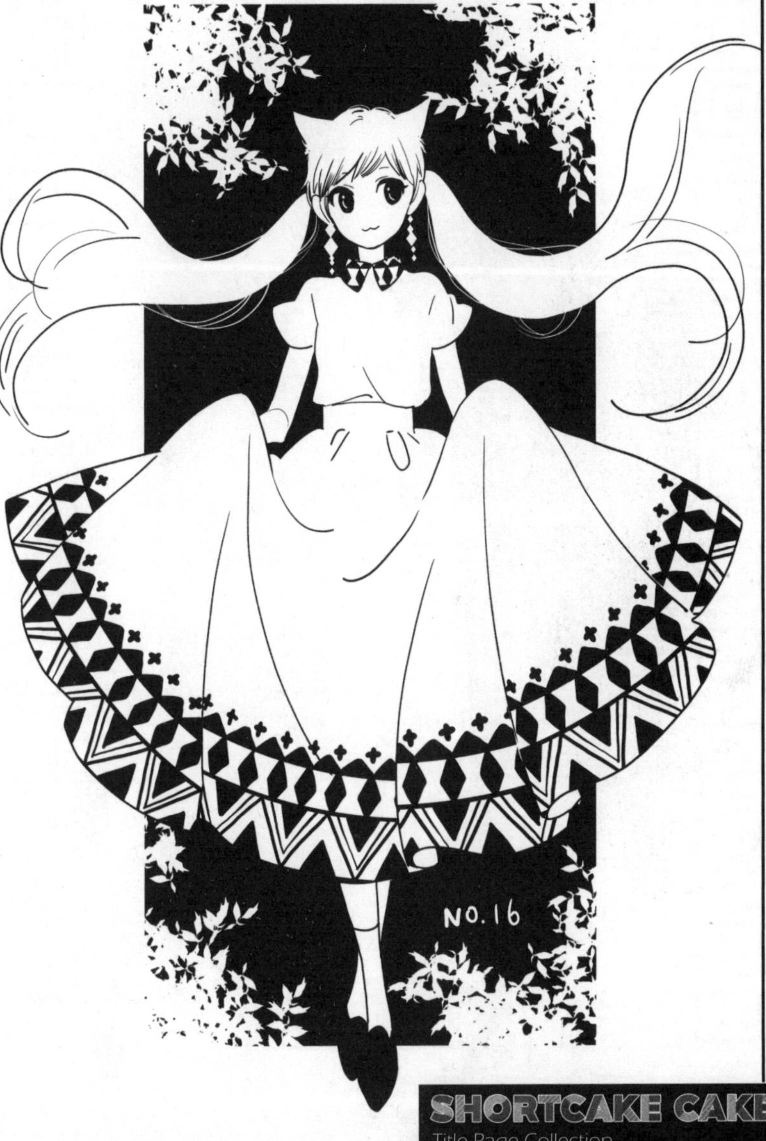
NO.16

**SHORTCAKE CAKE**
Title Page Collection
Chapter 16

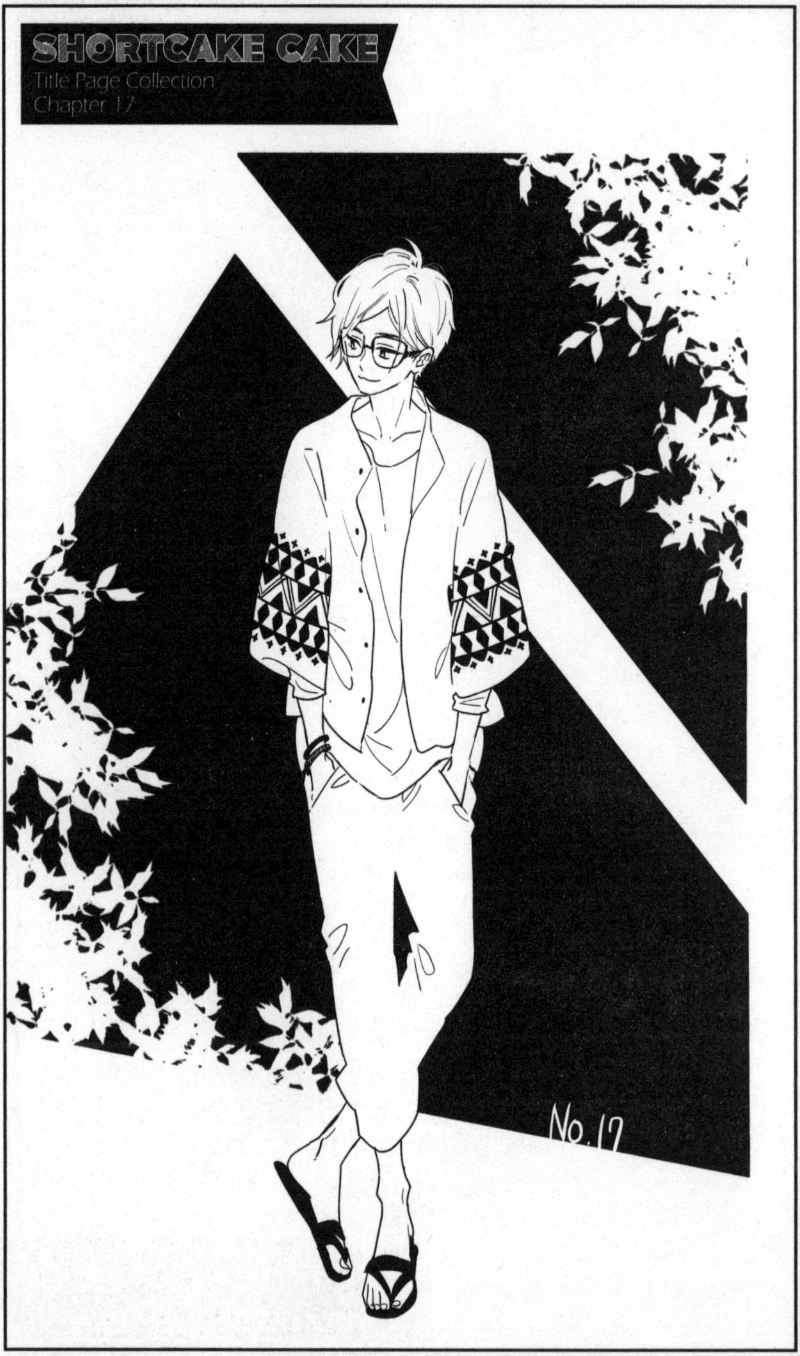
SHORTCAKE CAKE
Title Page Collection
Chapter 17
No. 17

Volume 3 already? It goes so fast.
Rei's drink, Yoghurppe, is a household name
in southern Kyushu. It's really good.

**—suu Morishita**

suu Morishita is a creator duo.
The story is by Makiro, and the art is by
Nachiyan. In 2010 they debuted with the
one-shot "Anote Konote." Their works include
*Hibi Chouchou* and *Shortcake Cake*.

**VOLUME 3**
**SHOJO BEAT EDITION**

STORY + ART BY **suu Morishita**

TRANSLATION **Emi Louie-Nishikawa**
TOUCH-UP ART + LETTERING **Inori Fukuda Trant**
DESIGN **Shawn Carrico**
EDITOR **Nancy Thistlethwaite**

SHORTCAKE CAKE © 2015 by Suu Morishita
All rights reserved.
First published in Japan in 2015 by SHUEISHA Inc., Tokyo.
English translation rights arranged by SHUEISHA Inc.

The stories, characters and incidents mentioned
in this publication are entirely fictional.

Printed in the U.S.A.

Published by VIZ Media, LLC
P.O. Box 77010
San Francisco, CA 94107

10 9 8 7 6 5 4 3 2 1
First printing, February 2019

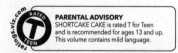

viz.com          shojobeat.com

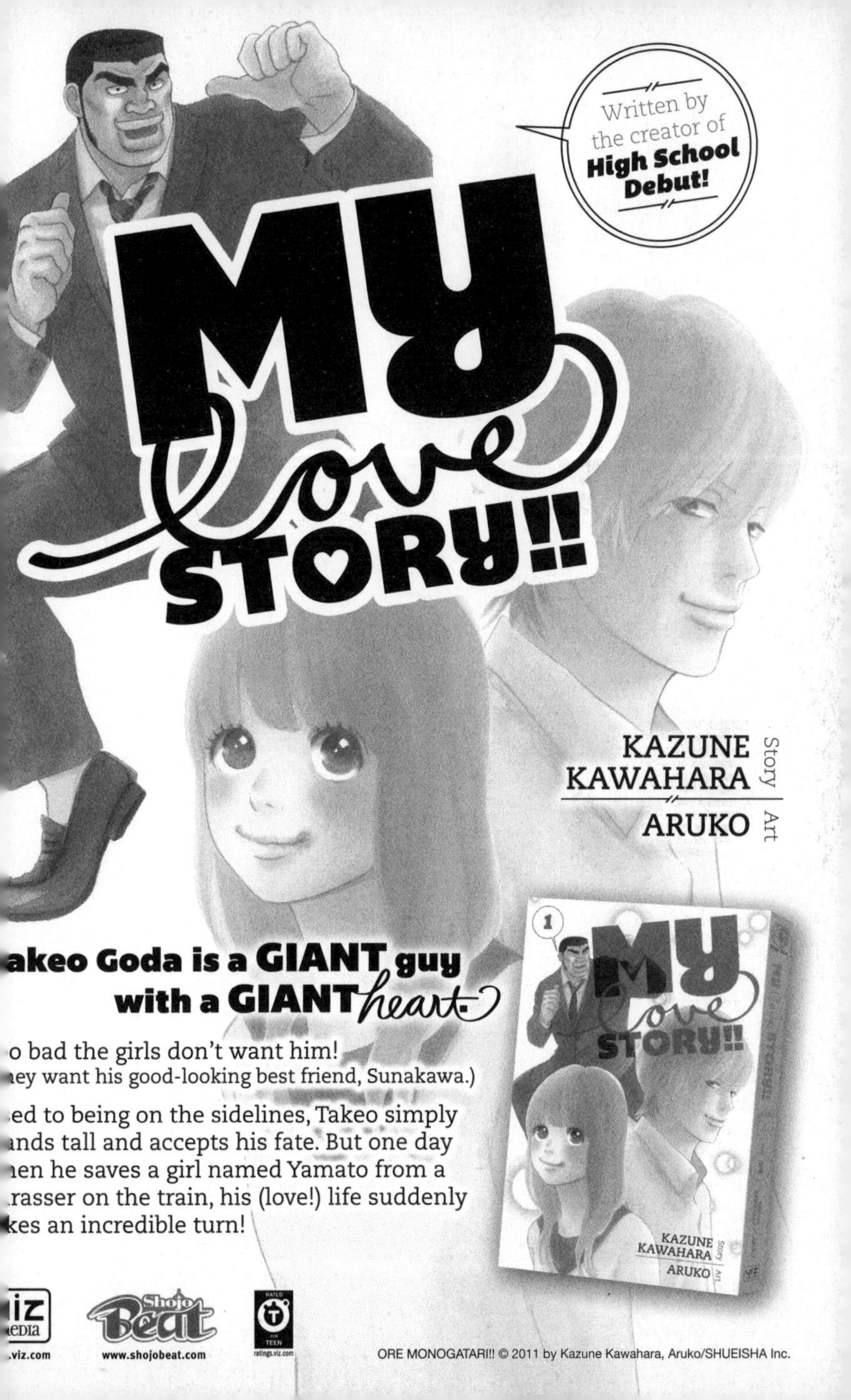
Written by the creator of High School Debut!
MY love STORY!!
KAZUNE KAWAHARA Story
ARUKO Art
akeo Goda is a GIANT guy
with a GIANT heart
o bad the girls don't want him!
ey want his good-looking best friend, Sunakawa.)
ed to being on the sidelines, Takeo simply
ands tall and accepts his fate. But one day
en he saves a girl named Yamato from a
rasser on the train, his (love!) life suddenly
kes an incredible turn!
iz
EDIA
.viz.com
Shojo Beat
www.shojobeat.com
RATED T FOR TEEN
ratings.viz.com
ORE MONOGATARI!! © 2011 by Kazune Kawahara, Aruko/SHUEISHA Inc.

# Honey So Sweet

Story and Art by Amu Meguro

Little did Nao Kogure realize back in middle school that when she left an umbrella and a box of bandages in the rain for injured delinquent Taiga Onise that she would meet him again in high school. Nao wants nothing to do with the gruff and frightening Taiga, but he suddenly presents her with a huge bouquet of flowers and asks her to date him—with marriage in mind! Is Taiga really so scary, or is he a sweetheart in disguise?

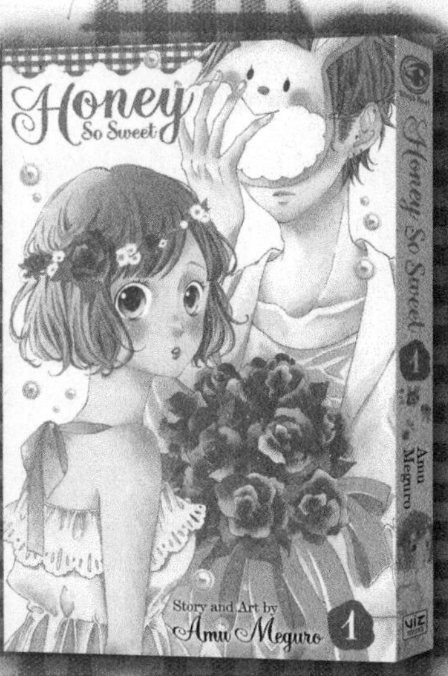

Honey So Sweet
Honey So Sweet
1
Amu Meguro
Story and Art by
Amu Meguro
1


Shojo Beat

RATED T FOR TEEN
ratings.viz.com

VIZ MEDIA
viz.com

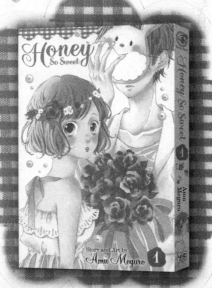

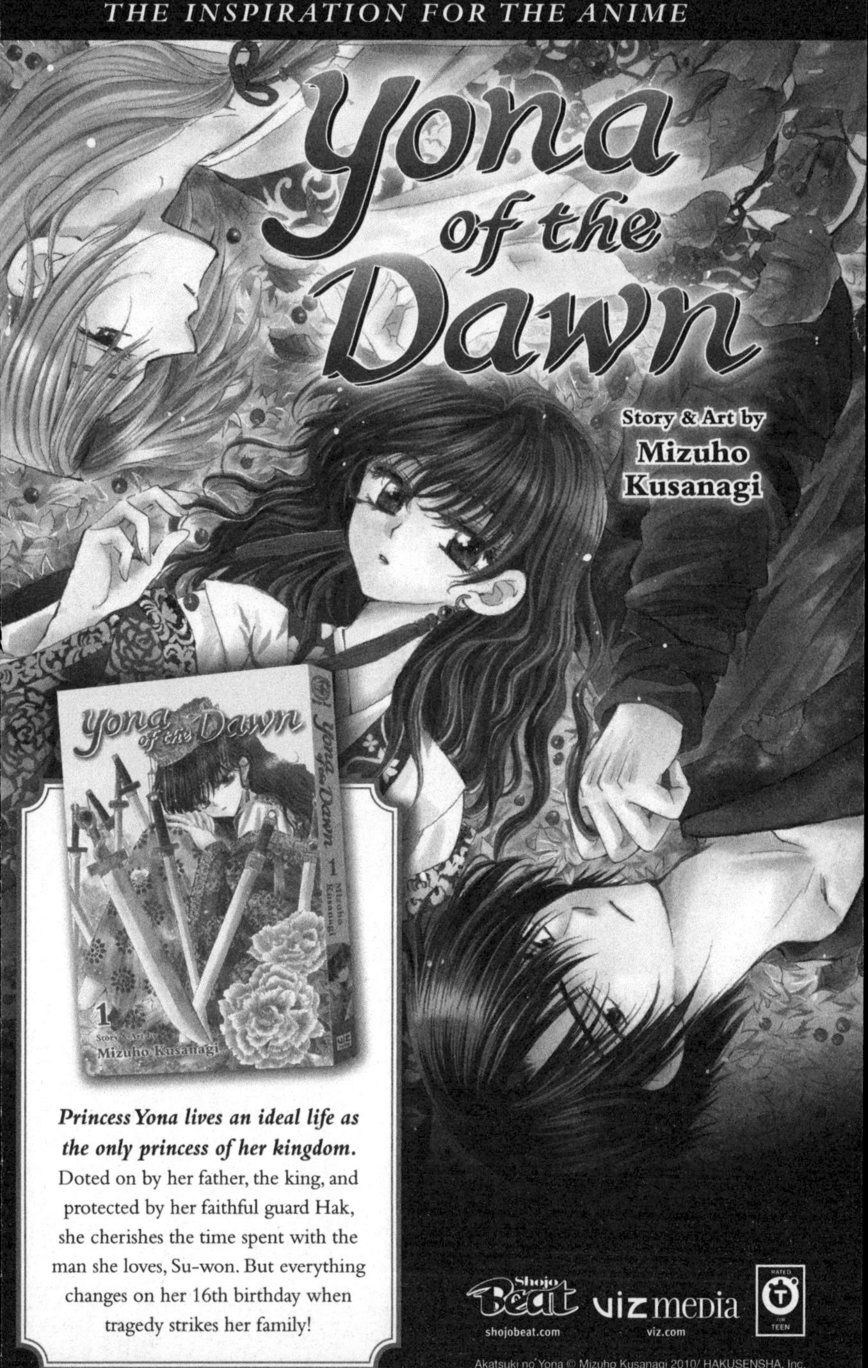
THE INSPIRATION FOR THE ANIME
Yona of the Dawn
Story & Art by
Mizuho Kusanagi
Yona of the Dawn
Yona of the Dawn 1
Story & Art by
Mizuho Kusanagi
Princess Yona lives an ideal life as the only princess of her kingdom.
Doted on by her father, the king, and protected by her faithful guard Hak, she cherishes the time spent with the man she loves, Su-won. But everything changes on her 16th birthday when tragedy strikes her family!
Shojo Beat
shojobeat.com
viz media
viz.com
RATED T FOR TEEN
Akatsuki no Yona © Mizuho Kusanagi 2010/ HAKUSENSHA, Inc.

# THE YOUNG MASTER'S REVENGE

When Leo was a young boy, he had his pride torn to shreds by Tenma, a girl from a wealthy background who was always getting him into trouble. Now, years after his father's successful clothing business has made him the heir to a fortune, he searches out Tenma to enact a dastardly plan—he'll get his revenge by making her fall in love with him!

viz.com

# Queen's Quality

**Story & Art by**
**Kyousuke Motomi**

Fumi Nishioka lives with Kyutaro Horikita and his family of "Sweepers," people who specialize in cleaning the minds of those overcome by negative energy and harmful spirits. Fumi has always displayed mysterious abilities, but will those powers be used for evil when she begins to truly awaken as a Queen?

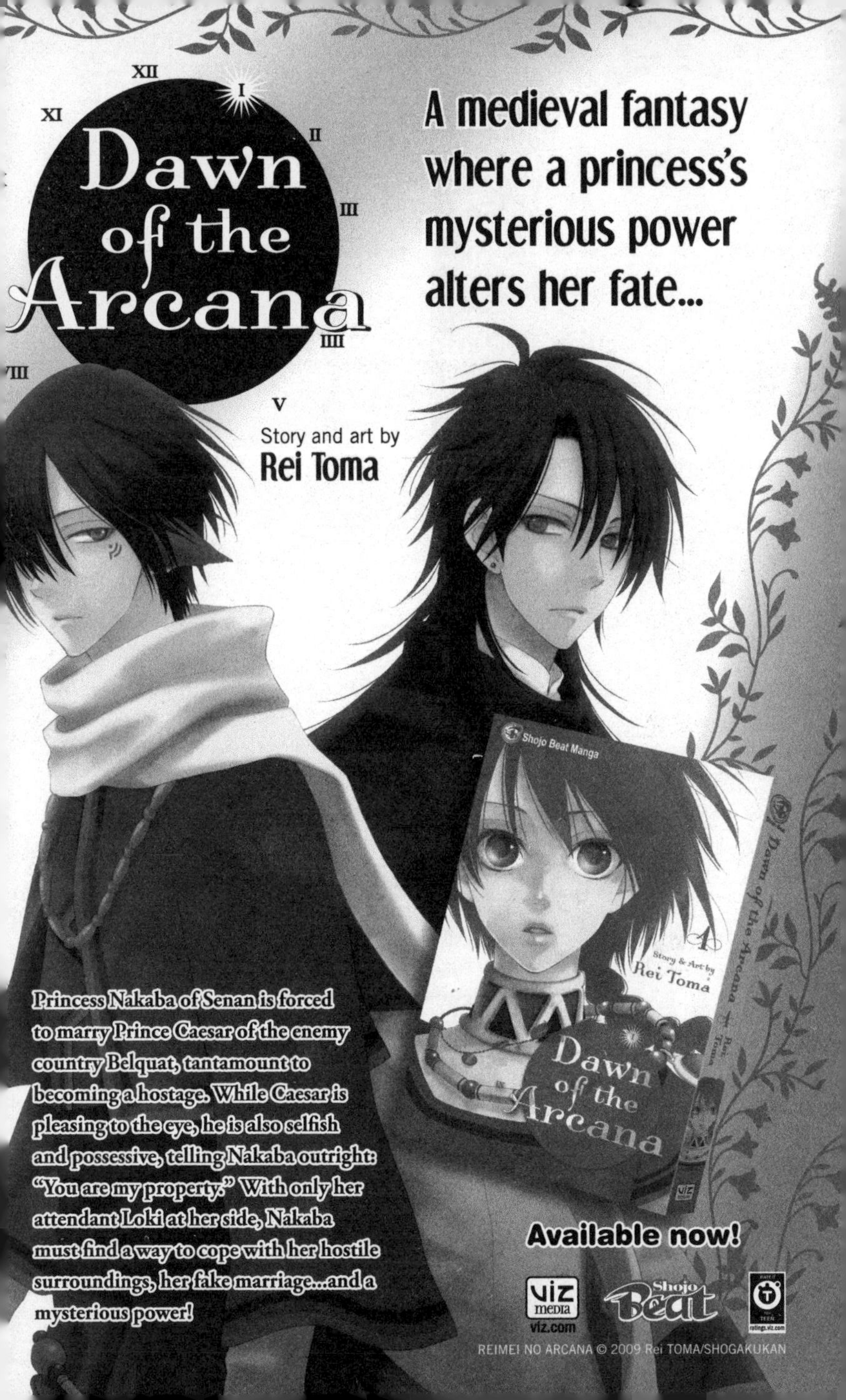
Dawn of the Arcana
A medieval fantasy where a princess's mysterious power alters her fate...
Story and art by
Rei Toma
Shojo Beat Manga
Dawn of the Arcana
1
Story & Art by Rei Toma
Princess Nakaba of Senan is forced to marry Prince Caesar of the enemy country Belquat, tantamount to becoming a hostage. While Caesar is pleasing to the eye, he is also selfish and possessive, telling Nakaba outright: "You are my property." With only her attendant Loki at her side, Nakaba must find a way to cope with her hostile surroundings, her fake marriage...and a mysterious power!
Available now!
VIZ media
viz.com
Shojo Beat
TEEN
ratings.viz.com
REIMEI NO ARCANA © 2009 Rei TOMA/SHOGAKUKAN

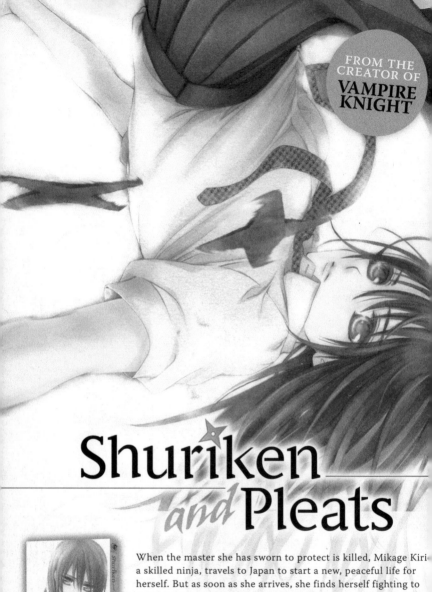

# Shuriken *and* Pleats

When the master she has sworn to protect is killed, Mikage Kiri, a skilled ninja, travels to Japan to start a new, peaceful life for herself. But as soon as she arrives, she finds herself fighting to protect the life of Mahito Wakashimatsu, a man who is under attack by a band of ninja. From that time on, Mikage is drawn deeper into the machinations of his powerful family.

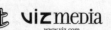
www.viz.com

RATED FOR TEEN
ratings.viz.com

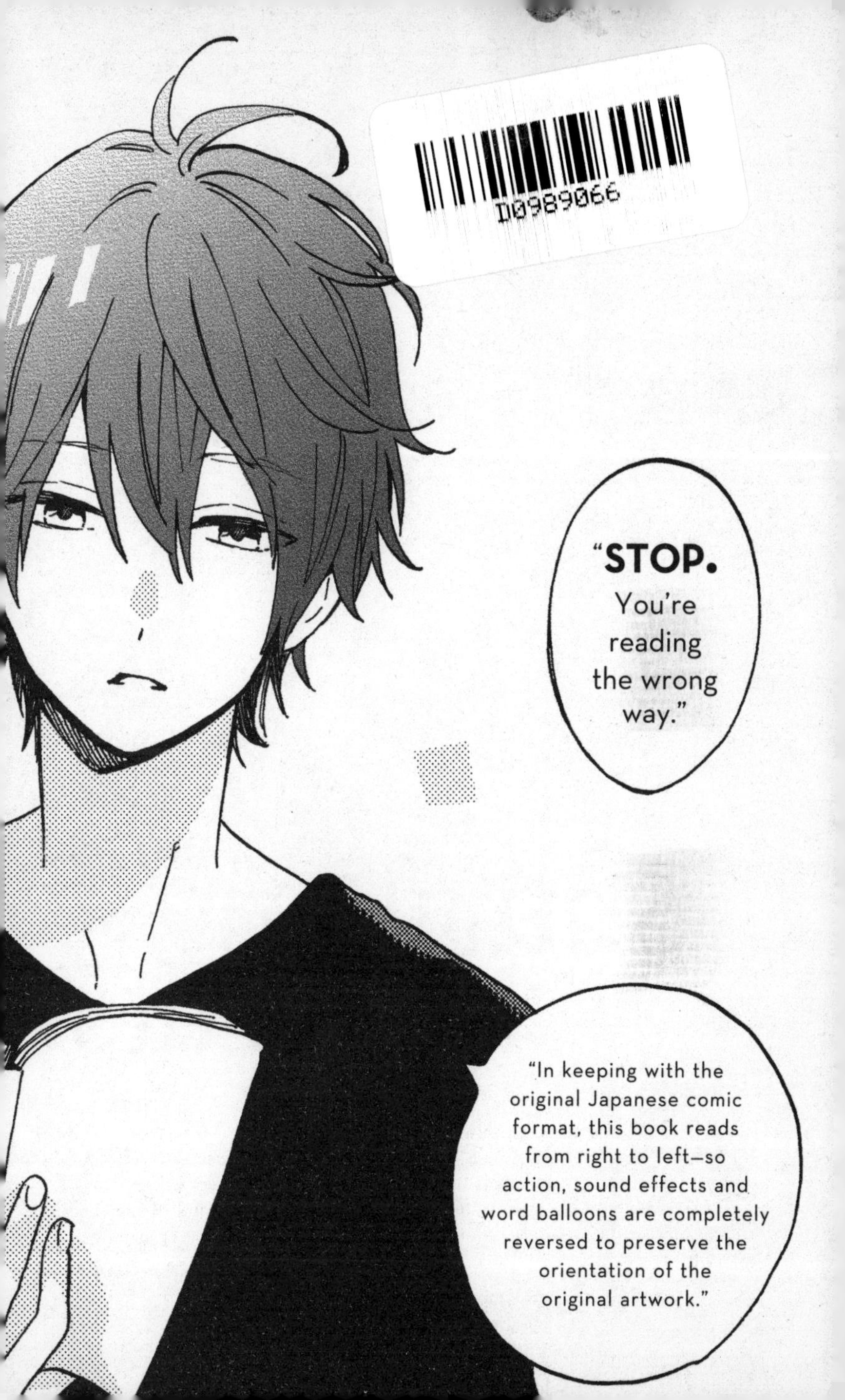
"STOP. You're reading the wrong way."
"In keeping with the original Japanese comic format, this book reads from right to left—so action, sound effects and word balloons are completely reversed to preserve the orientation of the original artwork."